THE PARABLES OF JESUS

THE PARABLES OF JESUS

LUISE SCHOTTROFF
Translated by Linda M. Maloney

FORTRESS PRESS
MINNEAPOLIS

THE PARABLES OF JESUS

Scripture quotations are from the author's translations, with reference also to the New Revised Standard Version Bible, copyright © 1989 by the Division of Christian Education of the National Council of the Churches of Christ in the USA and used by permission.

Cover art: *The Clever Bridesmaids* by He Qi (China). For more information and art by He Qi, please visit www.heqiarts.com.
Author photo: Scott Braley
Cover design: Zan Ceeley
Interior design: Ann Delgehausen

Library of Congress Cataloging-in-Publication Data
Schottroff, Luise.
     [Gleichnisse Jesu. English]
     The parables of Jesus / Luise Schottroff ; translated by Linda M. Maloney.
        p. cm.
     Includes bibliographical references (p.   ) and indexes.
     ISBN 0-8006-3699-6 (pbk. : alk. paper)
    1. Jesus Christ—Parables. I. Title.
     BT375.3.S3513 2005
     226.8'06—dc22

                                         2005024276

The paper used in this publication meets the minimum requirements of American National Standard for Information Sciences—Permanence of Paper for Printed Library Materials, ANSI Z329.48-1984.

Manufactured in the U.S.A.
10   09   08   07   06   1   2   3   4   5   6   7   8   9   10

Contents

PART 3

JESUS THE PARABLE-TELLER:
THE PARABLES
IN THE LITERARY CONTEXT
OF THE GOSPELS

Acknowledgments

This book has a long prehistory. Over many years my husband, Willy Schottroff, Professor of Old Testament in Frankfurt, and I planned a social-historical commentary on Jesus' parables. After Willy's death in 1997 I lost the will to write it. But later I tried to take up our shared project, and in the fall of 2002 I taught a seminar on the parables of Jesus.

So the book came into being during my time as Visiting Professor of New Testament at the Pacific School of Religion and the Graduate Theological Union in Berkeley, California, from 2001 to 2004. I owe much gratitude to these institutions, their students, and my colleagues there. That time was a gift to me. In particular I want to thank Delwin Brown, Professor of Systematic Theology and Dean of the Pacific School of Religion. He supported and encouraged me most graciously. My heartfelt thanks go also to Andrea Bieler, Professor of Liturgics at the Pacific School of Religion, for her friendship and constant, almost daily, participation in this project. Every parable I sought to understand became a surprise for me, and I always had to tell her about it right away. I thank Sean Burke, New Testament doctoral student at the Graduate Theological Union. We taught courses together, in particular one on Jesus' parables, which we offered twice. Without him the book would not have come about. His theological clarity enriched me and enabled me to break through the barrier of allegorizing interpretation of the parables. I write my texts by hand; I simply cannot work any other way. My friend Ute Ochtendung in Kassel then made an intelligible book out of my scratched-over and crossed-out pages. I owe her immense gratitude because her work was far more than mere technical support to an old-fashioned writer; she brought to the task her judiciousness, reliability, and a constant ability to follow my train of thought, all of which gave me new strength along the way.

I thank Claudia Janssen, Privatdozentin for New Testament in Marburg, for ongoing theological conversations. They are an enrichment and a challenge to me. For many years I have been supported by the "Paulines," including Claudia Janssen, Marlene Crüsemann of Bielefeld, and Beate Wehn of Kassel, as well as the Heidelberger Arbeitskreis. Social-historical interpretation of the Bible that reflects on the hermeneutical questions presented to our violent world by Christian theology is our common project. As representative of many from the Heidelberger Arbeitskreis, let me mention Frank Crüsemann, Professor of Old Testament in Bielefeld, and Rainer Kessler, Professor of Old Testament in Marburg. Our work together in Germany was not interrupted by my going to Berkeley, for which I am deeply grateful.

Many feminist exegetes at the Graduate Theological Union worked with me during my time in Berkeley. Let me mention especially Avaren Ipsen, New Testament doctoral student, and Professors of New Testament Antoinette Wire and Mary Ann Tolbert, because they gave me the feeling of being at home, both theologically and as a human being. I thank Annemarie Oesterle for her patient and selfless work in correcting the manuscript. Diedrich Steen, editor at Gütersloh, read the manuscript thoroughly and with professional acumen, which was an important support to me as the book came into being. For the careful English translation I thank my fellow New Testament scholar Linda Maloney.

It is an experience beyond price to be sustained by a network of friendships. I thank all those who form that network for me, even though I cannot mention all of them here.

Introduction

The parables of Jesus—those important narrative clues to the meaning of Jesus' proclamation and the life he envisioned—have been massively influential but widely and tragically misunderstood. This volume is intended to offer a new perspective on the parables, their original context, and their meaning for today. The social-historical method used in this book is hermeneutically indebted to a new paradigm in theology that has developed, since about 1970, out of Christian liberation and peace movements, feminist movements, and Jewish-Christian and other interreligious dialogues. All these movements regard their theology as contextual. That is, they consciously reflect on the social contexts in which theology arises, and the perspectives from which theological content and biblical tradition are viewed.

This new paradigm of theology is associated with a praxis of Christian life under conditions of growing militarism and intensifying economic imperialism in the dominant Western world. In this sense, theology and Christian praxis of life are as different as their different contexts, and yet they are closely related to one another. This relationship comes out of what Miguel de la Torre calls the "hermeneutical privilege of the poor." It demands of me, as a beneficiary of Western wealth, that I practice the repentance of the rich, an important theme in biblical texts. The search for a Christian praxis of life in the present brings to the fore the historical question of the Christian praxis of life in past times, including biblical times. Thus in this book the text of the New Testament is located not only in terms of its intellectual history but also and above all in its *social history,* and is questioned with regard to the praxis of life that is bound up with it.

In biblical exegesis, contextual theologies are, as a rule, interested also in the original, historical context; that is, they pose social-historical questions. The historical and text-analytical *methods*—I am using the plural deliberately—with which I will be working stem from research developments in historical criticism and various versions of textual analysis; their results must always be analyzed hermeneutically. Whenever possible I will build on the results of literary criticism and its variants, because I regard the parables also as a component of their literary context—the several Gospels. Nevertheless, I consider the death knell of historical criticism that is frequently sounded in North America to be a deceptive note. Historical criticism still yields methods and exegeses, even within the framework of text-analytical methods. These are often regarded as the obvious and correct readings, but they should be subjected to conscious criticism in terms of hermeneutical questions.

Many exegetical works, including books on the parables, suffer from a surfeit of explanation of their methods. Therefore I prefer not to place the explication of my methods at the beginning of the book; instead, readers will find it in the middle, after they have been introduced to these methods and my hermeneutic, step-by-step, in the course of a few interpretations. In this way the explanation of the methods will not require an excessive amount of space, and the theory can simply grow out of the interpretations of the texts.

The *eschatology* of the Gospels in their final textual form—as they have been handed down to us—is often interpreted as resulting from early Christianity's wrestling with the so-called delay of the parousia. According to this notion the eschatology of the Gospels arose out of the attempt to resolve the problem of the immediate return of Christ not having taken place. I consider this model—which constructs this problem out of a so-called immediate expectation on the part of the first Christian generations in order to furnish a foundation for the eschatology of the New Testament—to be an invention of biblical scholarship that is urgently in need of hermeneutical critique. It is based on linear conceptions of time and on a religious dualism that contrasts "the time of this world" with "the kingdom of that world/of God" *(basileia tou theou)*. But that was not the source of the Christian praxis of life in the early communities. The early Christians' relationship was to a God who was already near, whose kingdom had come close, to use the language of the Synoptic Gospels. Therefore—then as now—speaking of God means speaking eschatologically. Hence each interpretation in this book is from the perspective of eschatological hope for the coming of God ("the nearness of God") and of the justice that will put an end to all injustice and all violence.

This book develops a new, *non-dualistic* parable theory for the interpretation of parables in the Jesus tradition. I call "dualistic" those parable theories in which the content of the parable narrative, often called "image" in contrast to "substance," has no properly theological relevance; where the narrative, the "image," is thus regarded as merely an aid to clarifying the real "substance." But, in fact, the parables really talk about people's lives in the time of the Roman empire, and these depictions contain their own immediate message that needs to be heard. In addition, they contain links—bridges to an explanation of each parable that is part of this whole, one that speaks of the relationship between the people of God and God—for example, when they compare the content of the parable narrative to the kingdom of God. The New Testament Gospels contain references to oral responses that were to be expected from the listening community while they were being read aloud. I interpret the parables out of their individual literary contexts, their respective Gospels. The parables are part of a process of communication that contains both *oral and written material,* even if the oral dialogue can only be surmised.

In part 1, I will examine six parables and the so-called parable theory in Mark 4. The parable of the Pharisee and the toll collector (Luke 18:9-14) seems especially appropriate for laying out and resolving the fundamental problems involved in an "ecclesiological" reading of parables. In each of my subsequent expositions of the parables I will present the "ecclesiological" interpretive tradition and an alternative, eschatological interpretation.

Next, I will discuss the parable of the vinegrowers in Mark 12:1-12, the parable of the foolish and wise young women in Matt 25:1-13, and the parable of the great feast in Matt 22:1-14. In the dominant tradition of interpretation God is represented in these texts by the owner of the vineyard who destroys the murderous tenants, the bridegroom who excludes the "foolish" young women from bliss, and the king who kills his guests. This tradition of interpretation compels the interpreters to read a horror story as Gospel. Is God really to be compared with a king who executes his own guests?

I include the parallel to the parable of the great feast in Luke (Luke 14:12-24) because it appears to make an insulted host the representative of God, which is an example of one of the principal problems in parable reading: Should narratives about the capriciousness and brutality of the powerful be read as parables of God?

Fundamental to a renewed understanding of Jesus' parables is understanding their relationship to Torah. To clarify this relationship I have selected Luke 13:1-9, the parable of the barren fig tree, and the "parable theory" in Mark 4:1-20.

On the basis of these interpretations of the text, I will explain in part 2 my theoretical concept of a social-historical interpretation of the Bible and the explication of parables. The historical context in which Jesus' parables belong is postbiblical Jewish parable culture. This should be the primary source for learning how to understand the parables of Jesus.

I have prepared a short appendix in which I briefly summarize my methods for reading the parables of Jesus. Also, at the close of each section I offer a few "for further reading" references to the literature suited to deepen certain aspects of what has just been presented. A full bibliography is given at the end of the book.

The impulse to write this book came from students at the Pacific School of Religion and the Graduate Theological Union in Berkeley, California. They had experience with and expectations regarding preaching. They had discovered how difficult it is to preach on parables that talk about greedy, rich landowners, slaveowners, and brutal kings—all of whom are then supposed to be seen as representing God. It became clear to me: No! The king in Matt 22:2 "is" not

God, and does not represent God in the parable, even though a long and powerful tradition of interpretation has understood the parable that way. The students therefore took a keen interest in the writing of this book, and I am grateful to them for that.

PART 1

LEARNING TO SEE

1

The Pharisee and the Toll Collector

Luke 18:9-14

TRANSLATION

9   But then he also spoke to people who were convinced that they were righteous, and who despised others, with this parable:

10 Two people went up to the Temple to pray; the one was a Pharisee, and the other was a toll collector.

11 The Pharisee stood apart and prayed: God, I thank you that I am not like other people who steal, do wrong, commit adultery—or even like this toll collector.

12 I fast twice a week, and I tithe from my whole income.

13 The toll collector stood at the side and would not even lift his eyes to heaven. He beat his breast and said: God, be reconciled with me, a sinner.

14 I tell you, this one went home justified, and the other did not. For all who exalt themselves will be humbled, and those who do not try to rule over others will be exalted.

SOCIAL-HISTORICAL ANALYSIS

Before the destruction of the Second Temple in Jerusalem in 70 c.e. the Pharisaic mode of life was practiced by a relatively modest group of men and women. It had no political power. It was favored by the people because it took Jewish tradition and the Torah seriously and tried to interpret and live them in ways that touched daily life. They were the ones who taught the people to regard the gathering around the household dinner table as a community of worship. For Pharisees, both men and women, the handling of food and dishes, and women's work for the care and sustaining of life, were religious activities. After the destruction of the Temple, in a time when all the institutions of Jewish life were more or less disrupted by Roman violence, the Pharisaic tradition of teaching and living was a force that enabled the survival of the people. But the teachers of the Torah in this tradition did not call themselves Pharisees any longer. Most of the anti-Pharisaic texts of the Gospels probably stem from this period. In the Gospels two time periods are projected on top of one another: the time when Jesus lived and the time when the texts, in their final form, were told and written down. Jesus' attacks on the Pharisees tend to reflect this later time, since these attacks presume that the Pharisees have power over the people. One example is Matt 23:2. Here Pharisees have teaching authority among the people, but they are accused of not following their own interpretation of the Scriptures. The picture of the Pharisees in the Gospels is quite thoroughly differentiated and should not be read in a generalizing way that conceptualizes them as Jesus' "opponents."

In the history of Christian interpretation and application of Luke 18:9-14, the Pharisee is taken as proof of an exclusive Pharisaism that accused all Jewish people who did not live as Pharisees of not keeping the Torah. That is how the Pharisee's prayer is understood. The introductory verse (9) has been seen as Jesus' attack on Pharisaic exclusivism. This notion of a self-satisfied Pharisaism is in contradiction with the sources outside the New Testament,[1] but it is also contrary to the parable itself.

The parable is very carefully constructed in parallels: It reports how the Pharisee stands alone, thus visible, and the toll collector stands somewhat apart, perhaps at the margins of the praying assembly in the Temple, and strikes himself on the breast. Parallel to this gesture of sorrow and repentance, it may suggest a gesture of contempt on the part of the Pharisee toward the toll collector, implicitly expressed in the words "even like this toll collector." The self-confidence in the Pharisaic prayer of thanksgiving contrasts with the despair of the toll collector, who will not even lift up his eyes to God and utters only a brief confession of sin and a plea for God's mercy. The toll collector behaves like a woman who knows that nothing more is due her than a place at the margins. This parallelism in the literary structure has consequences for interpretation. If the Pharisee is seen as a typical representative of Pharisaism, the toll collector will also have to be seen as a representative of those in the customs service. But, correctly, that is not supposed. Thus the parable is not a story intended to show by its example: This is how all Pharisees are. The parallelism between the Pharisee and the toll collector leads to a different interpretation. Both behave in a way that is typically not expected of them. The listeners would have expected the Pharisee to be a careful observer of the Law, and would not expect the toll collector to go to the Temple at all, since, after all, he is a notorious violator of the Law. The implicit expectation directed at the Pharisee presumes a high regard for the Pharisaic movement. It *even* can happen that a Pharisee can pray in such a self-righteous way and violate the commandment of loving one's neighbor. Verse 9 does not criticize Pharisaism as such, but people who regard themselves as righteous and despise others. In Luke 16:15, another reproach directed at Pharisees, the subject is not exclusivity but secret greed, which Luke certainly does not attach to all Pharisees (see below on this passage). The Pharisee in Luke 18:10-14 thus embodies self-righteousness, something that can even happen to a Pharisee. So the Luke 18:9-14 text is by no means a sweeping documentation of Pharisaic exclusivism; in harmony with the extrabiblical sources, it represents a positive evaluation of Pharisaism.

The Pharisee's prayer, as it is presented, exaggerates his self-righteousness. This Pharisee despises all other people as unfaithful to the Law and in his prayer displays open discrimination against the toll collector. This kind of exaggeration in a parable is meant to make the meaning of self-righteousness unmistakably clear. It is intended to draw the hearers' critical attention to themselves. Where has such self-righteousness befallen me, and us, as we make other people "the others," worth less before God and human beings than "we" are? The parable criticizes the condescending dualism of "I/we" and "the others." The parable (as interpreted) tells a fictional story with narrative emphases. The condescending dualism of "we, the good" in contrast to the "others, the bad," is a basic feature of religious and political thought. It justifies violence against nations and individuals. Christianity has contributed to this kind of violent dualism by its interpretation of New Testament parables even though that very pattern of dualistic thought is criticized in this parable.

The toll collector was one of the customs officials, a group of people who were extraordinarily unpopular because they were present everywhere for the purpose of collecting money for market stalls, fishing licenses, the right to sojourn in a city, and the like from travelers, small merchants, people who sold goods in the markets and on the streets, fisherfolk. Often these employees of the customs businesses were escaped slaves and other homeless persons[2] who could be happy if they found such work, which might even offer them the opportunity to sequester some money illegally for themselves. In the Lukan context there is also mention of a "chief toll collector" who employed such people and profited from them, legally and illegally (19:1-11). Toll collectors, both male and female,[3] were regarded as notorious breakers of the Law (see only Matt 5:45, 46 *par.*), to be equated with sinners, both Gentile and Jew. The Luke 18:9-14 text also presumes that the toll collector was unfaithful to the Law and could only make right his relationship to God through acts of repentance. The active praxis that is part of repentance is not mentioned here (unlike in Luke 19:8), but in a Jewish context it can be presupposed as a matter of course.

ECCLESIOLOGICAL INTERPRETATION

The tradition of interpretation that regards the Pharisee's prayer as representative of a general critique of Pharisaism has had profound effects on Christian notions of Pharisaism and Judaism. Even in the common language of a post-Christian world the word *pharisaic* survives as a description for dishonesty and self-righteousness. In Christian exegesis since 1945, slowly, some caution toward this tradition of interpretation has appeared. I would like to discuss two examples of this and, in dialogue with these interpretations, pose a fundamental question to Christian parable interpretation.

François Bovon explicitly criticizes an "anti-Semitic reading" of the text (209).[4] His interpretation is that the text offers a polemical caricature of the opponent that could certainly be imagined as coming from the lips of Jesus (210). The text, he says, is an attack that, "on the basis of accurate elements (the comforting knowledge of election and the protection of God, pride in having adhered to moral values), tips the text into an unfriendly, even wounding comparison" (209). The toll collector is said to be justified, not the Pharisee (v. 14a). The toll collector, without doing any good works, has done exactly what God hoped from him (215). Bovon thus regards the text as a caricature that, however, strikes the polemical point: knowledge of election and pride in having adhered to moral values. Critically contrasted to the Pharisaic knowledge is the justification of the sinner—without good works. So, after all, this is about the religious errors of Pharisaism in general. Bovon is a captive of the traditional anti-Pharisaic/anti-Jewish interpretation even though he does not want to be. It is clear to him that the Pharisaic way does not lead to salvation before God. What I would criticize in this interpretation is not the supposition that the depiction of the Pharisee is a caricature, but only the evaluation of this caricature as an appropriate characterization of Pharisaism.

R. Alan Culpepper understands v. 9 as being directed at believers, disciples, and the Pharisees; they are all in danger of pride and self-righteousness.[5] Especially v. 14 forbids the readers to apply the parable to a single group. They have to picture the Pharisaic attitude in their own hearts (341). Then he reads vv. 10-13 without the framing verses. The parable itself forces the hearers to the decision that v. 14a makes explicit. He comments on the Pharisee's prayer within the overall framework of the Pharisaic movement, saying that this is a parable about a relationship to God founded on works and thus despising others (343). By generalizing self-righteousness to all Christians, Culpepper seeks to avoid identifying only Pharisaism with self-righteousness, but in the end he retains the notion of Pharisaism as a religious attitude founded on works and despising others.

Why is the anti-Pharisaic interpretation so tenacious and apparently insurmountable? The reason seems to be that the contrast between Pharisee and toll collector is read as a contrast between two mutually contradictory theological concepts: works righteousness versus *sola gratia,* the grace of God that cannot and need not be achieved through human works. These two theological concepts are implicitly or explicitly assigned to Christianity or Judaism/Pharisaism. The avoidance strategy (that the parable is a polemic but accurate caricature [Bovon], or that it refers to the Pharisee in all of us [Culpepper]) does not prevent the parable from being read with the implicit applications of "we" versus "the others"; "grace" versus "Jewish works-righteousness." Thus expressed, the dominant concept—a dualism of Christianity/church versus Judaism/Pharisaism—is not subjected to fundamental critique. But this must be deliberately and critically undertaken. I call this tradition of interpretation, which still largely shapes Christian reading of the New Testament, "ecclesiological" because its central reference is a Christian dogmatics in the sense of a teaching of the church as it now is. I put the word *ecclesiological* in quotation marks because I am not fundamentally criticizing the church as a reference point for Bible reading, but rather rejecting a triumphalistic understanding of church in the sense of a dominant "we" set over and against "the others," as primarily embodied in Pharisaism and Judaism.

The ecclesiological reading of parables has not only legitimized church dominance but, by its contrast of good and evil and the equation of the good with the "we," has achieved political significance. It contributes to the legitimation of violence in today's Western world. I consider overcoming this tradition of interpretation to be a necessity.

ESCHATOLOGICAL INTERPRETATION

If I am going to attempt to overcome readings of a parable that regard it as church dogmatics clothed in pictures, I need a different fundamental approach to the parables in the Jesus tradition. Thus I read this parable as part of a dialogical process between Jesus (whether the historical Jesus or the Jesus of Luke; I will return to this point) and the community of the faithful who are listening to him. This listening community of the faithful—implicitly presumed in all the gospel texts—is not to be understood as an audience being challenged to make an intellectual judgment (as they are for Culpepper when they are supposed to judge themselves in the sense given in v. 14). The listening community sees itself in relationship to God, the coming God who will judge and create justice. God's judgment and God's reign are the future the hearers hope for. The hour of their hearing is the hour of the great "now." Now is the time to listen and understand, which means to turn back, to repent, and to build God's reign.

This parable confronts the listening community with the power of sin. The Pharisee, who is so concerned for the Torah, violates the commandment of loving one's neighbor without knowing or willing it. The toll collector, whom everyone knows to be a notorious violator of the Torah because of his profession, at this hour becomes the teacher of the Pharisee in the framework of the parable story, and teacher of the listening community as well. Thus the listeners are encouraged to follow a teacher who is, in fact, regarded as a notorious shyster and robber. The parable expects an answer. The answer, in this case, can take up and carry forward the prayer of the toll collector: "Have mercy on me, O God, according to your steadfast love; according to your abundant mercy blot out my transgressions. Wash me thoroughly from my iniquity, and cleanse me from my sin. . . . Restore to me the joy of your salvation, and sustain in me a willing spirit" (Ps 51:3-4, 12).

There has been much reflection on how this parable relates to Paul's theology. The analysis of sin as a power against which no one can be secure is in fact the same as Paul's: "But if you call yourself a Jew and rely on the Torah and boast of your relation to God and know God's will . . . and if you are sure that you are a guide to the blind, a light to those who are in darkness . . . you, then, that teach others, will you not teach yourself? While you preach against stealing, do you steal? . . . You dishonor God by breaking the Torah" (Rom 2:17-24). Paul, too, should be read not ecclesiologically, but eschatologically. An ecclesiological reading here would speak of the false Jewish teaching of works-righteousness and the right Christian teaching of grace. An eschatological reading of Paul understands the listening community by its relationship to the coming of God, who alone will judge what is "right" and what is "false." The listening community's answer is: "Now is the hour to recognize our entanglement in death, and it is the hour to thank God for our liberation through Jesus Messiah." For Paul, liberation means to have the Torah as a guide in the midst of death, to want and be able to live by it. The listening community answers with a prayer to God and a life according to the Torah.

An eschatological reading of the parables makes use of a different language. Instead of describing theological propositions in statements like, "God does not desire the death of the sinner," the language of the listeners is that of relationship to God: "O God, you do not desire that we die the death that sin brings upon us. You desire that we live and do your will. Be gracious to us." The language of prayer means that the decision about truth and falsehood belongs to God alone. Praying and hearing create an open situation, and the next step for those who hear and those who pray is clear: doing the Torah.

The parable in Luke 18:9-14 is read as a contrast between works-righteousness and *sola gratia,* justification through faith without works. And indeed, the toll collector says nothing about his acts of repentance. But Luke 19:8, on the deeds of repentance by the chief toll collector Zacchaeus, should call us to pose the question of whether deeds of repentance are not mentioned in 18:9-14 because they are a matter of course. The confession, "God, be merciful to me, a sinner," cannot exist without consequences. God's acquittal, praised by the prayer of the listening community, unbinds human strengths so that they may refashion their lives with one another and not live according to the laws of sin.

How should the framing verses be read in combination with an eschatological interpretation of this parable? Jesus (the Lukan, the historical—I leave that outside the discussion for now) speaks as the prophetic voice of God: "I say to you, he went down to his house justified, and the other did not" (v. 14). He could also have said: "Today salvation has come to this house" (Luke 19:11). Jesus, as the voice of God, pronounces the healing that God desires, and makes it real. When this is read eschatologically, the response can only be: "I thank you, O God; help me on my way," and not: "Now I have no more worries, and I am fine." "Those who exalt themselves will be humbled, and those who humble themselves will be exalted" (v. 14b) is a statement of eschatological law, not moral coping skills. In the context of the Gospels, eschatological law means that the rule of human beings over other human beings (self-exaltation) is injustice in the eyes of God. The way of righteousness is opened when structures of domination are broken down. That happens where believers share, in solidarity, in the life of the lowly. And as to who the lowly are—Jesus speaks of that in every one of his sayings in the Gospels.

And v. 9? It indicates the direction the parable means to show us: avoiding the triumphalism that occurs when people regard it as a matter of course that they are in the right before God and despise other people. Or, to put it another way, v. 9 says that the parable intends to tell us to live in relationship to the God who is coming. The parable is an invitation to those who trust in themselves alone to turn about and follow the path of life.

The Pharisee's prayer stands within the tradition of Jewish and Christian catalogues of vice that list the sins of the non-Jewish world: See, for example, Paul's list in Rom 1:28-32.[6] But those catalogues of vices are not intended to position those who proclaim them in the place of God. Paul says this clearly: "For what have I to do with judging those outside? Is it not those who are inside that you are to judge? God will judge those outside. Drive out the wicked from among you" (1 Cor 5:12-13). God's eschatological judgment is not the community members' business; their task is rather to build up the communion of saints within their community. Concretely, this means not copying the way of life of "the world," of those "outside." In the rabbinic parallels, those who pray thank God that they are permitted to sit in the house of study and not in the theatres and circuses and among the inhabitants of the great cities, where theft, immorality, and other destructive forces reign.[7] These texts are concerned with shaping the individual lives of those who are to follow Torah and not the laws of the "world," as Paul calls it. The Pharisee in the parable uses this tradition ecclesiologically, or triumphalistically, to apply the terms we are using here, whereas Paul and the rabbinic parallels understand it eschatologically. The Pharisee's prayer is, in fact, a deliberate caricature of this tradition that makes its *misuse* obvious.

The old-fashioned word *sin* has been burdened by a great many misunderstandings. One of these is the notion that the New Testament primarily regards sexuality as sin. Individualizing and internalizing the idea of sin is another misunderstanding. Thus the forgiveness of sins appears to be healing a burden that is felt within and individually—independent of the question of human actions, their possibilities, and their limitations. The sin of the perpetrator and the suffering of the victim are obscured in this theological tradition, something that has been pointed out especially by Krister Stendahl and Elsa Tamez. The old-fashioned word *sin* is indispensable. In this parable, as especially in Paul, sin appears as the master of manipulation. It easily transforms even a Pharisee true to the Torah into someone who despises other people. Its power to wrest the tradition of the Torah, the tradition of loving one's neighbor, from anyone is insidious and, according to Paul, seeks to rule all humanity and destroy human community, even by the application of religious tradition. The parable speaks of this deliberately, and the anti-Jewish ecclesiological tradition of interpretation does so unwittingly. It falls into the trap the parable tries to warn us against: I thank you, O God, that I am not like this Pharisee.

FOR FURTHER READING

Anthony J. Saldarini, *Pharisees, Scribes, and Sadducees in Palestinian Society*
E. P. Sanders, *Jewish Law from Jesus to the Mishnah* and *Judaism*
Luise Schottroff, "Die Erzählung vom Pharisäer und Zöllner als Beispiel für die theologische Kunst des Überredens"
Krister Stendahl, *Paul among Jews and Gentiles, and Other Essays*
Elsa Tamez, *The Amnesty of Grace*

2

The Vinegrowers and Violence

Mark 12:1-12

TRANSLATION

1 And he began to speak to them in parables: A man planted a vineyard, built a fence around it, dug a winepress, built a tower, and gave it into the care of tenants and went away.

2 At the appointed time he sent a slave to the tenants, that he might receive a portion of the fruits of the vineyard.

3 And they seized him, beat him, and sent him away empty-handed.

4 Again he sent a slave—a different one—and they hit him on the head and dishonored him.

5 And he sent another, and they killed him—and many others, some they beat and some they killed.

6 He also had a beloved son. Him he sent last of all, because he said: They will not dare to assault my son.

7 Those tenants said to each other: This is the heir. Come, let us kill him, and the inheritance will be ours.

8 They seized him, killed him, and threw him out of the vineyard.

9 What will the owner of the vineyard do? He will come and kill those tenants and give the vineyard to others.

10 Do you not know the scripture: The stone the builders rejected has become the cornerstone.

11 This is God's doing, and it is wonderful in our eyes?

12 And they wanted to arrest him, but they feared the people. For they knew that he had told the parable against them. And they left him and went away.

SOCIAL-HISTORICAL ANALYSIS

The parable speaks of a violent conflict between a wealthy landowner and the tenants in his vineyard. Social-historical research has shown that this parable, in all its details, matches the reality of agriculture in Palestine.[1] It is thus not appropriate to adduce literary motifs or allegorically significant foreign elements for the explanation of the parable. Although they are present, nonetheless, we can look first to social-historical investigation.

The wealthy landowner has, through the work of his slaves, created a new vineyard—with a fence, a winepress, and a (watch)tower. The text concerning the layout of the vineyard has extensive connections to Isa 5:2 (LXX), but is nevertheless true to reality. The landowner can expect a larger return from letting a fully developed vineyard to tenants than from leasing fields for farming. We may suppose that the new vineyard is composed of lands that previously were cultivated in smaller parcels by subsistence farmers. Impoverishment through debt is common, especially among small farmers. It is also possible that the new tenants of the land are the previous owners, whom the new master was happy to put under contract. In any case, the land had already been cultivated, because we cannot suppose that there was any fertile land not under cultivation during that period in Palestine. The owner thus leases the new vineyard to knowledgeable vintners and goes abroad. Major landowners tended to prefer living in accordance with their status in the larger cities rather than dwelling on the land. Columella, a Roman author of the period, in his handbook for owners of large landholdings advises them that, if owners did not want to live on their lands, they should under no circumstances allow the property to be managed by slaves and a family of overseers. He recommends, as happens here, that the land be leased.[2] The parable says nothing about the contract between the owner and the tenants, but it appears from what follows that they had agreed on a specific share of the crop going to the owner.

When the time comes for the first grape harvest in the new vineyard, that is, probably at the end of five years,[3] the owner sends a number of slaves, one after another, to collect the owner's share and probably to sell it, on the owner's behalf, at the most advantageous price. We hear of three individual slaves, and then of several more who are not listed individually (v. 5). The tenants react with increasing violence. The first slave is beaten and sent away without the agreed-upon share. The second slave is hit over the head and "dishonored," probably raped. The third slave is killed. The killing or beating of the remaining slaves is only stated in general. Finally, as a last resort, the owner sends his only son. Here the owner's words are quoted: "They will respect him," not daring to beat or kill him. This part of the narrative also makes sense in the social situation here described. The son, unlike the slaves, is "in the sense of private law the fully competent representative of his father, and in certain circumstances would also be in a situation to validate his father's claim to the property in the procedural channels of the local courts."[4] The violence increases still further. The tenants kill the son and violate his corpse, not burying it but throwing it out of the vineyard into the open field, that is, abandoning it to be devoured by wild beasts and birds. In that period, not burying a corpse signified the extreme of violence and inhumanity and was the utmost degradation. The tenants promise themselves that, as a result of the murder of the son and heir, there will be no one left to drive them from the land. They hope that thereby *de facto,* if not *de jure,* they will come into possession of the land. Columella apparently knows of comparable cases: "For men who purchase lands at a distance, not to mention estates across the seas, are making over their inheritances to their slaves, as to their heirs and, worse yet, while they themselves are still alive."[5] But in the end the owner of the vineyard himself comes. The narrative heightens the horror of the event by its question to the listeners: "What will the master of the vineyard do?" "He will come and destroy those tenants and give the vineyard to other tenants" (v. 9).

The heightening of physical violence, in which ultimately even the owner participates, is in the foreground of the narrative. A horrifying bloodbath has occurred. Why the tenants did not hand over the share contracted is not said. Conflicts between landowners and tenants were pre-programmed and familiar.[6] Either the contracted shares were so substantial that the tenants were unable to deliver them, or they had bad yields and consumed the whole harvest for their own survival and for that of the women and children who worked the land with them. That debtors were often unable to pay their debts is an enduring theme in the Synoptic Gospels; it was *the* burning social conflict of the time. The violence of the tenants reflects the economic hopelessness of the increasingly poor agrarian population and their hatred for their new masters. We hear nothing here of forgiving interest and cancelling debts, both of which are important Jewish traditions in the Torah. Nothing is said about whether the new owner is a Jew or not. In any case, it appears that the Torah plays no part in his considerations. In the Jesus tradition the full forgiveness of debts is emphatically demanded (Matt 5:42; Matt 6:12 *par.*; Luke 6:35). God is compared to a creditor who forgives debts (Matt 6:12 *par.*; Luke 7:41-43). In this parable we hear how indebtedness turns those burdened with it into violent people filled with hatred. There is no reason to interpret the sending of the slaves allegorically (sending of prophets by God) or the son christologically. Even that he is the father's "beloved" son can be explained within the imagery of the story: he is the only son and heir. The reference to Isaiah 5 in v. 1, however, suggests an interpretation of the vineyard as Israel. Nevertheless, the matter-of-fact interpretation of the vineyard owner as God, which rules in the interpretive tradition with only a few exceptions, must be fundamentally called into question if we take the social-historical analysis of the text seriously. The owner of the vineyard acts like an opponent of God; he does the opposite of what the God of the Torah and the Lord's Prayer desires and does.

Thus we have before us a fictional narrative, yet one that is pointed toward reality and applied to Israel as God's vineyard through v. 1 (the quotation from Isaiah). Since the traditional exegesis originated with an allegorical interpretation of the individual persons and events, the fact that the parable, from a social-historical point of view, tells of an exaggerated exemplary situation in the life of the Jewish people of the period stands in opposition to such a process of allegorization, which does not take the social situation seriously.

The closing frame of this parable (vv. 10-12), however, offers a different approach to its interpretation. First of all, I would like to bring the parallel traditions in Matthew and Luke into the interpretation. In their closing, framing interpretation they are related to the text of Mark but clearly present independent variants, especially in the conclusion. An examination of the closing frame of the parable can give us some insight into the horizon within which the interpretation moves—in Mark as well.

Here is Matthew's version (21:33-46):

33   Hear another parable: There was a man, a landowner, who planted a vineyard and placed a wall around it, dug a winepress in it, and built a tower—and gave it to tenants and went away.

34   When the time for fruiting came near he sent his slaves to the tenants to receive his fruits.

35   And the tenants seized his slaves; some they beat, others they killed, and others they stoned.

36   Again he sent other slaves, more than before, and they did the same to them.

37   Later he sent his son to them because he thought: They will not dare to abuse my son.

38   But the tenants, when they saw the son, said to themselves: He is the heir. Come, let us kill him and take his inheritance.

39   And they seized him, threw him out of the vineyard, and killed him.

40   Now, when the owner of the vineyard comes, what will he do with those tenants?

41   They said to him: He will destroy those evil ones in an evil way, and the vineyard will be given to other tenants who will give him its fruits at the proper time.

42   Jesus said to them: Have you never read in the scriptures: "The stone the builders had rejected has become the cornerstone. This is God's doing, and it is wonderful in our eyes"?

43   Therefore I say to you: The kingdom of God will be taken away from you and given to a people who do the fruits of the kingdom.

44   And whoever falls on this stone will be crushed, and the one on whom it falls will be shattered.

45   And when the high priests and Pharisees heard his parables they understood that he was talking about them.

46   And they wanted to arrest him, but they feared the crowds of the people, for they thought him a prophet.

The parallel versions of the vintner parable in Matthew and Luke (20:9-19, not translated here) remain within the framework of the social-historical situation described in Mark. In Luke's shorter version it is noticeable that the tenants wound the slaves but do not kill them. They murder the son. But here, too, the story tells of an intensification of violence. In Matthew the son is killed outside the vineyard. Especially important in Matthew's version are the deviations from Mark at the end of the parable.

The question of the narrator, Jesus—"what will the owner do with those farmers?"—is answered by the listeners (v. 41), people from the crowd. It is true that in v. 45 the high priests and Pharisees are named as listeners (see 21:23, the high priests and elders of the people), but the situation described is one in which Jesus is teaching a crowd of people in the Temple (21:23). In Matthew, a crowd of people is also the audience for the parable discourse (13:34-35). The hostile leadership of the people understands Jesus' parable discourse as a critique of their actions, but they fear the crowd (v. 46). In v. 43 the leading individuals are addressed directly: "The kingdom of God will be taken away from you. . . ." That is: "You have handed the people over to violence within and without. God will turn away from you. Keeping the Torah alone decides who belongs to the reign of God." The fruits of the kingdom are "done," says v. 43. This "doing" (*poiein*) shifts the level of discourse. Verse 41 spoke of delivering the fruits within the frame of the parable narrative; v. 43 mixes the language of daily life in the narrated story with the way one speaks about the Torah, which is to be "done." "The people," Jewish and Gentile, are those who keep the Torah (28:16-20). God's judgment will decide who those will have been (25:31-46). Thus Matt 21:43 can be read eschatologically.[7] All the listeners now face the task of doing the Torah, including the high priests and the Pharisees. Verse 43 has been read for centuries as a solemn rejection of Israel and a transfer of the promise to the Gentile church. That is an ecclesiological reading. But only an eschatological reading of this verse is adequate to Matthew's gospel and its idea of God. In v. 44 the narrator, Jesus, adds another logion using the metaphor of a stone with two distinct biblical references. Verse 44a appears to play on the stone of stumbling in Isa 8:14-15 (Hebrew text: Godself is the stone of stumbling for the people; LXX is different). Verse 44b is meant to play on the stone that—according to Dan 2:34, 44-45—falls on the feet of the metal idol that embodies the mighty world empires: "Then the iron, the clay, the bronze, the silver, and the gold were all broken in pieces and became like the chaff of the summer threshing floors; and the wind carried them away so that not a trace of them could be found" (2:35). The Greek verb in v. 44b also refers to "dicing." By its allusion to Daniel 2, this verse says that the mighty Roman empire will be shattered and the wind will scatter its ruins so that not a trace of them remains. For Rome embodies the *imperium* of that period, the time of Jesus and also the time of the communities that originated Matthew's gospel. This political prophecy in v. 44, the promise of a people that does the Torah (v. 43), suggests that the "stone the builders have rejected" is to be read as a metaphor for the suffering of the people, represented in the brutal events that happen in God's vineyard (vv. 33-42). Thus vv. 33-45 would apply to the fate of Israel in the political present and in God's future.

It is true that in Luke, as also presumably in Mark, Jesus (the narrator) answers the question about the reaction of the owner of the vineyard: "He will come and destroy those tenants and give the vineyard to others." But after the answer the listeners protest: "That must not be!" (Luke 20:17). The protest of the people Jesus is addressing (v. 16b; see also v. 9) makes it clear that Luke wants to see the parable as applying to this people's situation. It is they who are threatened by the violence of the landowner (v. 16a), and the promise is for them (v. 17). These variants in Matthew and Luke show how much a matter of course it was to understand this parable as part of a dialogue (I will return to this in my interpretation). A glance at the closing frame of the parable in the Gospels of Matthew and Luke shows that the christological allegorization of the son in the parable, and the stone in the frame, must be called into question, just as a social-historical analysis makes the identification of this violent vineyard owner with God problematic—to say the least.

William R. Herzog's book *Parables as Subversive Speech* can be seen against this background as a breakthrough in a long and fateful tradition of parable interpretation. Herzog breaks up the identification of the rich slaveowner, the proprietor of the vineyard, with God. For him the rich vineyard owner, who leaves the country, is not an image for God, but part of the parable imagery. Herzog understands the parable imagery in terms of the concept of Paulo Freire's "pedagogy of the oppressed" as a set of "codifications." By this Freire means, for example, an image or a photograph that transforms words into an image that the oppressed themselves can use to express their view of the world. These "codifications" are then deciphered by the poor, as "teacher-learners," in a process that moves from "social description" to "social analysis."[8] For the interpretation of Mark 12:1-12 this means the codification/deciphering of a class conflict. In his social-historical analysis Herzog emphasizes the dispossession of the real heirs of the land, who have become dependent tenants. For him the parable ends with the open question in v. 9: "What will the owner of the vineyard do?" It is clear to the listeners that this revolt is futile. The parable calls into question the claims of the new rulers to the heritage and property. When we understand the futility of the tenants' violence, we are faced with the question: Are there other ways to make our demands effective?

Herzog's proposal—that we not understand the vineyard owner in this parable and other comparable figures in the parables as images for God—is invaluable for parable interpretation. But I would criticize his work on two points: (1) His interpretation is based on reconstructed parables of Jesus, which are intended to be freed from later, allegorizing elements applied by the evangelists—much as Joachim Jeremias did in 1965. In contrast, I see it as necessary to read the existing texts in their literary context, without proposing any textual reconstructions. (2) In his parable interpretation Herzog distinguishes between the codification (parable image) and the deciphering and social analysis that follow. I read the parables as transparent, fictive narratives about real life that teach the listeners to "see" in the full sense of the word: to recognize the God of Israel and God's action in this distorted world. (See part 2 below, on parable theory.)

The end of the parable (Mark 12:9) should be related to the war and threat of war in the context of Israel's history in the first century c.e. As a result of the severe economic exploitation of the population by Rome and Jewish attempts at resistance, the Jewish land during this period existed either in a state of anxiety under the threat of war or in a condition of suffering from actual war and its consequences. This was true both of Jesus' lifetime and the period of the messianic groups of his disciples after his death. Matthew 22:7 relates, in a parable about a banquet, "The king was enraged. He sent his troops, destroyed those murderers, and burned their city." We cannot say when this statement was made or when it was written down. It may be a prediction after the fact of something that had already happened (*vaticinia ex eventu,* "prophecy from the event"), or a prediction of a feared and approaching war. It made sense both in Jesus' lifetime and in the period when Matthew's gospel was composed. Something similar can be said of the experience of war reflected in Mark 13:7, 8, 14-20 and the parallels in Matthew and Luke. The political dread is also expressed by the High Priest in John 11:48: "the Romans will come and destroy both this place and our existence as a nation." The parable in Mark 12:1-12 *parr.* speaks of the hatred that arose from economic exploitation at the hands of foreign property owners, of the counterviolence of the victims, and of Roman dominance. These themes are as present in the work of Josephus concerning the period before the war of 66–70 c.e. as they are here. The victims of economic violence become murderers; their actions lack all perspective. They are at the center of the narrative. In particular, they mistreat and murder slaves who are themselves already the victims of economic and physical violence. The parable speaks in a distilled form of multilayered experiences of violence.

ECCLESIOLOGICAL INTERPRETATION

As a conversation partner representing the ecclesiological tradition, I have chosen Joachim Jeremias's interpretation in his *The Parables of Jesus.*[9] It was the most influential exegesis in the second half of the twentieth century, and its influence continues today. Jeremias distinguishes an allegorical version of the parable, as found in the Gospels, from an original Jesus parable. The allegorical interpretation relates the tenants to Israel's regents and leaders, the messengers to the prophets, the son to Christ; the punishment of the tenants is God's rejection of Israel, and the "others," to whom the vineyard now belongs, are the

Gentile church (70). The original Jesus parable is said to have contained vv. 1-8, but without the reference to Isaiah in v. 1 and without v. 5b. This Jesus parable, according to Jeremias, was faithful to reality in every detail, including the sending of the son. It reflects "the revolutionary attitude of the Galilean peasants towards the foreign landlords, an attitude which had been aroused by the Zealot movement which had its headquarters in Galilee" (74). But what is the original meaning of the parable? "Like so many other parables of Jesus, it vindicates the offer of the gospel to the poor. You, it says, you tenants of the vineyard, you leaders of the people! You have opposed, have multiplied rebellion against God. Your cup is full! Therefore shall the vineyard of God be given to 'others' (Mark 12:9). Since neither Mark nor Luke give[s] any further indication who the 'others' may be, we must, following the analogy of the related parables . . . interpret them as the *ptōchoi*" (76). Jeremias thinks he is not interpreting the Jesus parable as an allegory, but he is doing just that. The last messenger from God is Jesus. The "rebellion" of the "leaders" of Israel against God is not explained by Jeremias, but it is linked to the rejection of messengers from God. For him it is a matter of course that God is the owner of the vineyard. Jeremias does not consider Mark 12:9 part of the ancient Jesus parable (74), and yet it appears here. The only difference in content for the allegorical interpretation, which Jeremias declared to be post-Jesus, is that the "others" are not the Gentile church, but the poor. According to Jeremias the poor are "sinners" who do penance (124–25; see also 132 and elsewhere). But for Jeremias the addressees of the parables are the pious people who "[have] too good an opinion of themselves" (140 n. 38). Jesus justifies his good news to them and accuses them. Jeremias's language continually reveals a sharply emotional tone when he speaks of Jesus' complaint against Israel or groups in Israel; his book was written in 1947. Tania Oldenhage shows convincingly to what a degree this complaint by "Jesus" against the Jewish people or Jewish groups contains implicit accusations against European Judaism at the beginning of the Third Reich, which did not react appropriately against the threatened catastrophe. We must say as well that Jeremias rejects an ecclesiological and allegorical interpretation for the ancient Jesus parable, but that is exactly what he presents. The poor and sinners compose "the humble appearance of the Messianic community" (146). The good news to the poor is at the same time an accusation against the Jewish people or Jewish leadership and implicitly a triumphalistic presentation of the church in the form of the gospel for sinners. He interprets the parable in terms of the rejection of Jesus (the son) and God (the owner of the vineyard).

The persistence of this tradition of interpretation can be illustrated by an essay by Edward H. Horne published in 1998.[10] He regards the Moses tradition of social justice as central to Jesus' conflict with the leadership of the Jerusalem Temple. The Temple "authorities" claim to be the legitimate interpreters of Moses. Jesus disputes that. He speaks to them and in the parable identifies them with the tenants, although these "authorities," as rich landowners, would prefer to identify themselves with the rich landowner in the parable. They are forced to understand this ironic turn in Jesus' parable as an attack on the legitimacy of their leadership. "Jesus has accused them of having failed . . . and of being rebellious against God in their desire to murder God's son" (113). All the elements of the ecclesiological-allegorical interpretation are maintained: the tenants as Jewish leaders, the son as the son of God whom they want to murder; it is true that the church does not appear explicitly as the heir to the vineyard, but the legitimate interpretation of the Torah of Moses is in Jesus' hand. Thus the reference to the church is implicitly present.

ESCHATOLOGICAL INTERPRETATION

In Mark 2:10-11 Jesus adds a Scripture quotation from Psalm 118: "The stone the builders rejected has become the cornerstone." In Acts 4:11 and 1 Pet 2:4, 7, this psalm verse is christologically interpreted in reference to the condemnation and resurrection of Jesus, and is at the same time applied to the salvation of the people (Acts 4:12; 1 Pet 2:9, 10). This psalm verse already had a history, before the origins of the New Testament, as a text of hope for the suffering Jewish people, comparable to the songs about the suffering servant in Deutero-Isaiah. An anti-Jewish reading of this psalm verse denies to the Jewish people the salvation associated with this scriptural tradition. But the New Testament texts, in describing Jesus' resurrection with these images, have in mind the salvation for the people of Israel and for the world that the praying community hopes for. The "salvation" (Acts 4:12) that is "in no other" than Jesus, the Messiah, is the salvation desired for the people (see only Luke 1:68-79). In Mark's gospel, too, it is this suffering people *(ochlos)* that surrounds Jesus and on whom he has compassion (Mark 6:34; 8:2). This people will experience salvation when God alone is king. The quotation from Ps 118 in Mark 12:10-12 should not be read with an exclusive, anti-Jewish Christology but in light of its Jewish history of interpretation. In the Targum, David is the stone that the builders left behind and who would become king. "'This is YHWH's doing,' the builders said. 'It is wonderful in our eyes,' the sons of Isaiah said. 'This is the day YHWH has made,' the builders said."[11] David is the embodiment of the fate of the humiliated people that will be raised up and liberated by God. The messianic reading of Psalm 118, if we want to call it that, is not meant to separate the event of salvation from the fate of the people, either in the Targum or in the New Testament. Since the Targum reads the psalm in different voices, which are indeed grounded in the psalm (see Ps 118:2-4), we should consider with regard to Mark 12:10-12 whether v. 11 is spoken by the people *(ochlos),* who are considered to be present: "This has been done by Adonai." "It is a miracle in our eyes." The transformation of the suffering people is to be seen with the eyes of hope, in the midst of the humiliation of the people through indebtedness and violence—violence endured and violence committed.

An eschatological reading of Mark 12:1-12 sees the listening community, the people and Jesus' followers, as opposite the God who is coming. God's judgment will show who are the "living stones,"[12] the holy people of God. It will be the people of God that has done God's will. In connection with the parable, this means that it will be the people that does not respond to Rome's exploitation with hatred and violence, but that works together and nonviolently for the future. The tradition of nonviolent resistance among the Jewish people is the unspoken but clear counternotion to the violence of the tenants. Josephus tells us a good deal about the nonviolent resistance of the Jewish people in the period before the war of 60–70 C.E.[13] This parable in Mark and Matthew addresses Jewish leadership groups. They are accused of political failure (Matt 21:45; Mark 11:27; 12:12; see also Luke 20:19). The critique of the political and religious leadership of the Jewish people is sustained by the whole parable. The accusation is not singularly that the son is murdered, but rather that the people live "like sheep without a shepherd" (Mark 6:34 and frequently elsewhere; the quotation is from Num 27:17). The leadership groups have not prevented the indebtedness of the agrarian population from accelerating to this catastrophic extent. These elites are not reflected in the tenants. The allegorical interpretation of the tenants as the addressees—in Mark they are the high priests, the scribes, and the elders (11:27; 12:12)—is a bastion of anti-Judaism in the history of Christian interpretation. It also contains the difficulty that why those with political power should, of all people, see themselves mirrored in the indebted and murderous tenants seems questionable. In a 1991 essay, I myself adopted the traditional identification of the tenants with leading persons, though with misgivings. But this tradition of interpretation can be overcome. It is not given in the text, but arises out of the Christian charge that the Jewish people or the leaders of the people were guilty of the murder of Christ. The people are present. In Luke's version they have an explicitly active role. Here Jesus addresses the parable to the people (20:9). They say "this must not be," that the vineyard is given to others (20:16). And Jesus looks at the people when he is quoting the promise from Psalm 118 (20:17).

In all three versions found in the Gospels, the parable interprets the present: It is the hour of repentance for the political leadership and for those among the people who react with hatred and violence against their own powerlessness. The Scripture can lend a voice to the responding community. Through the people's sin the land has become impure; "therefore keep my ordinances" (Lev 18:24-30). God's vineyard, laid waste in Isaiah 5, "is the house of Israel. . . . He expected justice, but saw the breaking of the Law" (Isa 5:7). The people's collective sin, which defiles and endangers the land,[14] must now be brought to an end so that God can again dwell in the midst of the people. The holy vineyard has been defiled, its holiness destroyed, but God's faithfulness will come to the people's aid.

Mark 12:1-9, regarded from the point of view of parable theory, is a narrative from life. That it is about the life of the people of Israel is clear from the beginning because of the reference to Isaiah 5 in v. 1. But the "vineyard" itself is not a metaphor that can be understood apart from the history of the fields and vineyards of the land. In this one vineyard, within the narrative, is concentrated the history of the people. The interpretation of the fictional narrative in 12:1-9 is given by the text itself through the reference to Isa 5:1, 2, in Mark 12:1, and by Mark 12:10-12. This is about Israel and its liberation (vv. 10, 11) from its suffering—violence endured and violence perpetrated, so pointedly portrayed in the narrative.

Reading: Tania Oldenhage on Mark 12:1-12

Tania Oldenhage presupposes a critique of Christian anti-Judaism, something already carried out by the generation of her exegetical teachers. Her dialogue with Aaron Milavec's work typifies this concern in her book. In his essay "A Fresh Analysis of the Parable of the Wicked Husbandmen in the Light of Jewish-Catholic Dialogue," Milavec developed an analysis of anti-Judaism in the traditional interpretation of Mark 12:1-12 and proposed a new location of the parable within the Jewish tradition.

For Oldenhage the ecclesiological reading is already overcome insofar as the critique of the anti-Jewish tradition of interpretation is taken for granted. But she does not believe that this in itself achieves the goal she aims at—a post-holocaust hermeneutic. She criticizes Milavec's essay because his critique of anti-Judaism in the interpretation of Mark 12:1-12 remains within the framework of historical-critical thought. For him the anti-Judaism of Jeremias is structurally equivalent to that of the fourth-century church father John Chrysostom. According to Oldenhage, the Holocaust is only a "temporal marker" for Milavec.[15] He hopes to find in Mark 12:1-12 an innocent Jewish text within the New Testament, which may be useful for recognizing Christian anti-Judaism, but it remains inadequate, for example, for the recognition of Jeremias's inability to experience sorrow.[16] Jeremias titles the chapter in which he treats Mark 12:1-12 "The Imminence of Catastrophe." With this he refers to Jesus' preaching as an urgent warning to the Jewish people, who are running blindly toward catastrophe. According to Oldenhage, Jeremias intended to speak of Judaism in the time of Jesus, but in fact he was speaking, in 1947, of Jewish people in Germany before 1938: "Why did you not recognize the crisis that was threatening you?" Jeremias' language, which he places on the lips of Jesus, is the language of inability to sorrow in postwar Germany. While I agree with Oldenhage's analysis of Jeremias, I want to return once again to her critique of Milavec.

Oldenhage's own interpretation of Mark 12:1-12 deliberately excludes the literary context. She reads the parable narrative itself poetically. In the violence of the tenants she sees the violence of the Nazi thugs who heap terror upon terror as they perpetrate the incomparable crime of the mass murder of Jewish people in Europe. Oldenhage's own interpretation begins with an experience: In 1992 she read the gospel text of Mark 12:1-12 in a worship service in southern Germany. Not only did she find the anti-Jewish associations unpleasant; her discomfort was much deeper, and could not be analyzed with the methods of historical criticism.[17] But a method that grasps the poetic power of the text provided the key: literary criticism—that of Paul Ricoeur, for example—in combination with a post-Holocaust hermeneutic.

Ricoeur reads parables as metaphorical narratives that are capable of opening for their hearers a new insight into the world: "the trait which invites us to transgress the narrative structures . . . is . . . the element of extravagance which makes the 'oddness' of the narrative, by mixing the 'extraordinary' with the 'ordinary'."[18] For Ricoeur the "extravagance" lies in Mark 12:6. No rational landowner would be so foolish as to expose his own son to such violent tenants. Oldenhage sees the unusual feature of the parable in a different place: "The realism of the story . . . breaks down and gives way to surprising developments long before the landlord decides to send his only son." The violence of the tenants is an unusual feature from the start. "The tenants do not just refuse to comply with the collector, they grab him and beat him up!"[19] According to Oldenhage, we encounter the familiar world of "business" at the beginning of the parable, and the eruption of the tenants' violence puts an end to it. The parable reminds Oldenhage of the Holocaust because it is poetic—much more powerful than descriptive language.[20] Two levels of meaning are intertwined: that of anti-Judaism and that of the poetic making-present of violence in the violent actions of the tenants—in Oldenhage's context, the violence of the Holocaust.

I regard Oldenhage's book as fundamental to a further development of exegetical scholarship. Two crucial new steps lead her beyond previous critiques of anti-Judaism: (1) The contextualizing of scholarly exegesis with the aid of Holocaust research: Those who write about the interpretation of the Bible speak not only of Judaism, for example, at the time of Jesus, but also about Jewish people since the Holocaust. (2) A critique of anti-Judaism in Christian biblical interpretation and the reconstruction of a non-anti-Jewish historical biblical text exculpate the Christian Bible of guilt. Its centuries of murderous misuse cannot be made not to have happened by means of historical reconstruction. This history of violence, which remains associated with the text, must again and again be publicly named in order that the text may become anew a source of Christian faith.

I have no desire, by criticism, to diminish these fundamental insights in Oldenhage's *Parables for Our Time*. And yet I think—differently from Oldenhage—that overcoming anti-Judaism through a new historical and theological interpretation of the biblical text is both possible and necessary.

Oldenhage's critique of an exegesis that, while it criticizes anti-Judaism, nevertheless attempts to reconstruct a New Testament that is not yet anti-Jewish, is quite correct. But her rejection of such historical work is not persuasive. Such historical work on the texts of the New Testament remains necessary, even though it ought to reflect more clearly than is the case in Milavec's work how a Christian use of New Testament texts in the wake of their misuse might look.

I would also like to offer a social-historical and methodological critique of Oldenhage's interpretation of the text. Whether a particular aspect of a parable is an "extravagance," in Ricoeur's and Oldenhage's sense, is a social-historical decision. It is true, of course, that neither Ricoeur nor Oldenhage undertakes a social-historical examination of the texts. Oldenhage considers the starting point of Mark 12:1 to be the "familiar world of business," the normal and ordinary in contrast to the abnormal, in this case the violence of the tenants. Thus the equally violent injustice of the owner of the vineyard and those like him—without Oldenhage's intending it—becomes a peaceful normality. The tenants remain the guilty ones, either as embodiments of the Jewish people or of the Nazi thugs. It is certainly true that the parable does not present them as innocent, but rather as the victims of economic violence who strike back with futile and extremely bloody violence and attempt to defend themselves by using the wrong means and "out of all proportion."[21]

However, this social-historical background cannot be seen as one possible way of reading a poetic text among others. For me, historical work is an act of solidarity with other people, even over a span of centuries. I share with Oldenhage, and most of the initiatives of liberation theology and feminist theology, a stake in the contextualizing of theology and theological scholarship. But I think that there must be a connection between the content in the first context (the time of Jesus or of the Gospels) and the second context (the present time of the interpreters). That the text is poetic cannot mean that we hear in the same language both the fatal Christian accusation against the Jews and the tread of the Nazi thugs who torture and murder Jewish people. Nor can it mean that we overlook an injustice that is clearly described in the text. In doing that we would make the suffering of the agrarian population of the first century invisible, without expressly being willing to do so.

How, then, would a post-Holocaust hermeneutics of this text look? In my interpretation I must speak of the suffering of the agrarian population, their rage, and the false expressions of that rage. I must speak about the history of the anti-Jewish interpretation of this text, and about how the surrender of the tenants to violence awakens layered associations in the present context: associations with the violence of the Nazis and Christian complicity because of anti-Judaism; with the exploitation of the agrarian populations of many countries through the concentration of the land in great estates; with the indebtedness of the lands of the southern hemisphere that is suffocating them. In this, a hierarchy of catastrophes (which is the most important?) can only get in the way. The Holocaust was an incomparable crime. The enrichment of the Western world at the expense of the lands of the southern hemisphere is a catastrophe that stands within the tradition of exploitation Mark 12:1-12 speaks about. A sermon on this text must attempt to work through the anti-Judaism that is still anchored in Christian consciousness, and thus to take a stance toward the Holocaust from our own perspective. But at the same time it can certainly focus on the question of debt and enrichment at the expense of others: the catastrophe the text speaks about, which is assuming greater and greater proportions as globalization is further and further perfected.

In light of the methods of historical criticism and of the literary criticism that is Oldenhage's starting point, I consider the setting up of an alternative—either the mistakes of historical criticism or a further development of literary criticism—to be reductionist. It is true that historical criticism as practiced especially in Germany has emphatically obstructed contextualization. It is considered proper scholarly practice to set aside the present (see, for example, the accurate analyses in *Parables for Our Time*). It is true that literary criticism is exposed to the same error, despite its intention to give voice to the text in and for the present. But the necessary contextualization can be accomplished through a further development of historical scholarship, literary criticism, or both at the same time. The methods thus described are of secondary value in face of the hermeneutical decisions to be made: whether I read a biblical text in today's historical context, and which analysis I apply to the present and the historical contexts.

FOR FURTHER READING

Martin Hengel, "Das Gleichnis von den Weingärtnern"
William R. Herzog, *Parables as Subversive Speech*
Tania Oldenhage, *Parables for Our Time*
Luise Schottroff, "Gewalt von oben und Gottes Zorn"
Willy Schottroff, *Gerechtigkeit lernen*

The Closed Door

TRANSLATION

1   Then the kingdom of heaven will be compared to reality in the following story about ten young women: They took their lamps and went out to meet the bridegroom.

2   Five of them were naïve and five were clever.

3   For the naïve took their lamps, but no oil with them.

4   But the clever took oil in their jugs together with their lamps.

5   When the bridegroom delayed, they were all weary and fell asleep.

6   In the middle of the night a cry was heard: Here is the bridegroom. Go out to meet him.

7   Then these young women all woke up and trimmed their lamps.

8   The naïve said to the clever: Give us of your oil, because our lamps are going out.

9   The clever answered: Then there will surely not be enough for us and for you. You should instead go to the merchants and buy some for yourselves.

10   While they went out to buy it the bridegroom came, and those who were prepared went with him to the marriage feast, and the door was closed.

11   Later the other young women came and said: Lord, Lord, open to us.

12   But he said: This I say to you: I do not know you.

13   Keep awake, for you know neither the day nor the hour!

SOCIAL-HISTORICAL ANALYSIS

The ten women are called "virgins" (parthenoi) in the text. This refers to young women, usually twelve to twelve-and-a-half years old, who are regarded as marriageable. The word designates their status in patriarchal society: They are available on the marriage market, which, as a rule, was regulated by the girls' fathers and their potential husbands. It is the duty of the young women to present themselves as good future wives. And that is what this story is about.

The word virgin (parthenos) was used differently in the church's later development. It became the designation for an unmarried woman. In addition, the word acquired the sense of virginity as a rejection of sexuality. This Christian history of the word has influenced the later interpretation of the parable in the same way that later ideas about the virgin birth have influenced the word *virgin*. But in the New Testament the word, both here and in the story of Mary, the mother of Jesus (Matt 1:23; Luke 1:27), is used as a designation for a young woman ready for marriage and without previous sexual experience.[1]

The Mishnah tells us: "Rabban Simeon b. Gamaliel said: There were no happier days for Israel than the 15th of Ab and the Day of Atonement, for on them the daughters of Jerusalem used to go forth in white raiments; and these were borrowed, that none should be abashed which had them not; [hence] all the raiments required immersion. And the daughters of Jerusalem went forth to dance in the vineyards. And what did they say? 'Young man, lift up thine eyes and see what thou wouldest choose for thyself: set not thine eyes on beauty, but set thine eyes on family; for *Favour is deceitful and beauty is vain, but a woman that feareth the Lord she shall be praised;* moreover it saith, *Give her of the fruit of her hands and let her works praise her in the gates.*'" (*m. Ta'an.* 4:8). The words of the daughters of Jerusalem are partly taken from Prov 31:30, 31. In the Babylonian Talmud their beseeching words are changed: "The beautiful among them said: Look only to beauty, for beauty is the chief thing in a woman. The patricians among them said: Look only to family, for a woman exists only for children. The ugly among them said: Accept your purchase for the sake of heaven, that you may crown us with gold pieces." The Talmud also adds: "Whoever had no wife went there" (*b. Ta'an.* 31b). In Matt 25:1-13 the occasion for the young women to offer themselves in the marriage market is a wedding, not a festival in the vineyards. Nevertheless, the women's[2] self-presentation is comparable. In Matt 25:1-13 the issue is that they show their skill by the way they handle their lamps. The Wisdom tradition of the capable woman and praise of the diligent echoes here as well: "A slack hand causes poverty, but the hand of the diligent makes rich. A child who gathers in summer is prudent" (Prov 10:4-5). "She perceives that her merchandise is profitable. Her lamp does not go out at night" (Prov 31:18). "A sensible *(phronimē)* daughter obtains a husband of her own, but one who acts shamefully is a grief to her father" (Sir 22:4). The contrast between "sensible" *(phronimoi)* and "naïve/stupid" *(mōrai)* young women also relies on this Wisdom tradition.[3] In Matt 25:1-13 the clever are separated from the naïve by their prudence, and perhaps also their diligence. The naïve were careless and inadequately prepared. The fact that they are opposed to one another in a competitive situation is made clear by the extended dialogue between the two groups. The competitive situation also plays a role in the version presented by the Babylonian Talmud: The beautiful point to their beauty, the women from good families to their origins. The contrast between the good and bad woman is an instrument of education and also of oppression, found not only in the Bible but also in many patriarchal societies.

The bridegroom in Matt 25:1-13 has the duty to speak the social judgment on the naïve women: "I do not know you." For the naïve women, the door is closed. It seems very likely that the marriage celebration is a testing situation for girls. We should not be surprised that the bride is unimportant in this story. It is about the young women. The details of the narrative are very clear when it is about them. They seem to be waiting in the bridegroom's house for the moment when the bridegroom, surrounded by friends and guests, will bring the bride to his house in a festive procession, and there the celebration will take place. A good deal of work has been done on the details of the lamps and marriage customs,[4] but almost nothing has been said about the actual social situation of young women as reflected here.[5]

From which perspective is the parable narrated? Verse 1, in a kind of super-scription,[6] gives the patriarchal perspective: the separation of good future wives from bad ones on the occasion of a marriage. This perspective is maintained throughout. The refusal of the clever women to share their oil is not criticized. They are meant to demonstrate their capability. But the unspoken critique is also audible: Where is their neighborly solidarity? There is no need even to bring the commandment of love of neighbor into play to show that, measured against the biblical tradition of the shaping of human relationships, the clever women are behaving in an unsolidary manner and are subjecting themselves to the socially expected condition of competition. The final scene, which in terms of a marriage feast is exaggerated, nevertheless shows that something dreadful has happened here. The future is closed—at any rate the future that, in the opinion of almost everyone in patriarchal societies, is the sole future for a young girl: finding a suitable husband. In the history of interpretation we often encounter the puzzled reflection that it would scarcely ever happen, at a village wedding, that guests who arrived late would be so severely treated. That is certainly correct. The final scene reveals the ugly face, the hard reality of a society that defines women in terms of their accommodation, subjection, and marriage. Within the narrative itself, the dialogue of the women and the final scene are presented in such a way that they must necessarily arouse critical questions: Why are the clever women so unsolidary? Why is a comparatively small mistake on the part of the naïve women, namely that they have no oil with them, so consequential? Why is the door closed? Why does the bridegroom's speech sound like a death sentence?[7] The narrative sets before our eyes the situation of girls on the marriage market, and in such a way that critical questions must necessarily arise.

ECCLESIOLOGICAL INTERPRETATION

The ecclesiological interpretation prevails. In this interpretation, right and wrong behavior are explicitly or implicitly attributed to particular groups, and the judgment on the naïve women has already been given: The door is closed.

As an example I will choose an interpretation that remains within this framework, yet is uncomfortable with it: that of Ulrich Luz.[8] He believes there was an original parable going back to the historical Jesus, almost entirely without allegorical elements, but in the form it exhibits in Matt 25:1-13 it is laden with allegories: The bridegroom is the returning Christ; the marriage is the time of God's salvation. In v. 10 "Christian metaphors pile up" (476). The closed door represents the eschatological judgment. The fault of the naïve women on the level of the community's interpretation, or that of "Matthew," is that they have no oil, no good works (477). In the parable that may go back to Jesus, the bridegroom represents God. "The one who is not prepared may also miss this *kairos* of joy!" (473). "Participation in the saving moment of Jesus' presence" has been frittered away by the naïve women (473). Luz directs a critical question to the Matthean version: "One would have to ask this Jesus whether in his story God's love still has the last word" (492). But he relativizes the question once again: The naïve women have not taken the saving God seriously (492). Luz, with visible discomfort, succumbs to the ecclesiological tradition of interpretation. But even in interpreting the reconstructed Jesus parable Luz does not break out of the framework of this tradition of interpretation. The bridegroom/God condemns the naïve women because they have had the wrong attitude toward Jesus.

Vicky Balabanski[9] presents the critical question more unrelentingly. She rightly sees the refusal of the clever women as complicity in patriarchy/kyriarchy (73). And feminist readers should, in fact, reply to the bridegroom: "I do not know you" (78). She sees the ethics of the parable as rooted in a binary contrast dependent on Wisdom traditions, and distinguishes between a relational *sophia*-ethics and the *phronimos*-ethics of the parable, which, from the perspective of a liberating ethics, must be rejected (82). She regards the women as guests at the wedding and as virgins in the sense described above ("nubility," "sexual availability," 84). From a patriarchal/ancient perspective the parable would at first have been heard as a joke at the expense of both groups of women. Ultimately even the naïve women will have achieved their goal, though somewhat later. But v. 12, the bridegroom's rejection, puts a sudden end to the fun. The male hearers would have identified with the bridegroom, but now they ask themselves: Could that really happen? What befell the naïve women? Is God that unpredictable? Women who heard the story at that time would have taken note of the pressure to belong to the group of "clever" women. Perhaps a few would have identified with the naïve ones. In both cases they would not have heard Jesus' message of liberation but instead oppression and degradation. Although we may perceive these perspectives as possible for an ancient audience, they are impossible for hearers today.

> The bridegroom cannot symbolize for us Jesus Christ, the liberator. . . . If we allow the closed door to be the final word, we have accepted the *two*

way paradigm which sees the world as a series of binary distinctions. . . .
However, in Matthew's gospel, the word "door" *(thyra)* is to occur again
at 27:60, where it refers to the door of the tomb of Jesus. . . . As we search
for a symbol of Christ in this story, we can invoke the one who said "I am
the door" (Jn 11.9) . . . to open the door to the marginalized, to those who
are, like so many of us, the "foolish." . . . If [the door] remains shut, then
Christ's presence is hidden among those on the outside.[10]

Here, from a feminist perspective, a parable narrative is ethically questioned and
critiqued with a consistency similar to that shown by William R. Herzog (see
chap. 2 above on Mark 12:1-12). I cannot go beyond this question. The traditional allegorical interpretation of this parable makes the representative of social
injustice, the bridegroom, a divine figure and thus corrupts the Gospel. However,
my critique is directed at the idea of eschatology presupposed by Balabanski. She
sees the parable as a prescriptive text that divides the world into good and evil,
insiders and outsiders. The insiders are the clever ones, and so Christ can only
be with the naïve ones, the outsiders, who remain excluded—that is, unless the
door is opened. This presumes that a message of God's universal love, which
is available and present, demands nothing and sets no boundaries. This is the
Western Gospel, the love-message of a church that desires to exclude no one.
The door of salvation is open, and all are inside, without needing to ask whether
their salvation rests on injustice and may be only the religious expression of
their Western wealth. This interpretation is a variant of the ecclesiological interpretation that, while it puts an end to a division between inside and outside,
does not take seriously how many people in the world stand before closed doors
because they suffer from poverty and violence. Or, to say it without imagery:
This general message of Jesus' love cannot reach those who suffer from violence
and injustice, the majority of people in today's world. It is no help to them when
God's undistinguishing love is preached. It remains grace for those who are already sitting at the table, at the wedding feast, who have access to nourishment,
medical care, and education. The message of judgment and of God's justice,
which is able to distinguish between the perpetrators and the victims, is fundamental to the Jesus tradition.

ESCHATOLOGICAL INTERPRETATION

No allegorical reading can elevate the text of this parable to the condition of
innocence: It is a story that speaks of social oppression, indeed, of violence. It
may be that in social reality people laughed at ugly or naïve girls, but in fact that
laughter was something like a social death sentence. That tradition of interpretation has made the clever girls a metaphor for right behavior before God, at
the expense of the naïve girls, and found this to be the Good News. For me, as
for Balabanski, this is a path that can no longer be followed. The story told as a

parable is heard as a message about women, even when the interpreters use it only as an "image," as a quarry for material to be transferred to a different level. When interpreting the application of the parable, the message of the "imagery" must not be neglected.

Matt 25:1-13 as Part of Jesus' Eschatological Discourse (Matthew 24–25)

Then where, if at all, is the Good News? The parable concludes so harshly that we may well ask if it is intended to evoke protest. Jesus, the narrator, adds a challenge that clearly moves outside the picture: "Keep awake therefore, for you know neither the day nor the hour!" (v. 13)—that is, wait for God's coming and God's royal reign (see Matt 24:42; 25:1). This challenge fits a picture in which the bridegroom is coming at a time that cannot be predicted. But it does not fit the picture here, because in the narrative the clever women also fall asleep; therefore sleeping cannot be the mistake made by the naïve women. The challenge to "keep awake" is repeated several times, appropriately, in Jesus' eschatological discourse in Matt 24:1—25:46: at 24:42 and 44 (see also 24:36, 50), within the parable imagery. The individual parts of Jesus' eschatological discourse are linked by their content, and not only through the repeated call to remain awake. At the beginning of the parable of the closed door there is a statement of time: ". . . then the kingdom of God will be compared to ten young women" (Matt 25:1). This time statement links the parable to the whole discourse, where we encounter *tote,* "then," seventeen times (Matt 24:9, 10, 14, 16, 21, 23, 30[bis], 40; 25:1, 7, 31, 34, 37, 41, 44, 45). Uses of the word occasioned by the requirements of the narrative (25:7, 34, 37, 41, 44, 45) can be distinguished from those that indicate an eschatologically qualified statement of time. In any case, this repeated time statement is significant for the understanding of this parable and the eschatology of the discourse. I consider the eschatology of the discourse relevant also to an understanding of the eschatology of Jesus/the historical Jesus. This is a topic that will require further reflection in the course of this book.

In Matthew 24 and 25 distinctions are drawn between times: the time of the end (*telos,* 24:6, 13, 14) and the time of the beginning of the birthpangs (24:8). In 24:3 the disciples ask Jesus: "Tell us, when will this [the destruction of the Temple in Jerusalem; see 24:2] be, and what will be the sign of your coming (*parousia*) and of the end of the age (*aiōn*)?" Here again, two times are distinguished: the time of the destruction of the Temple and the time of Jesus' coming as Son of Man for judgment (see 24:30, 31, 39, 42, 44; 25:31-46). This is the last act before the "end" of the age. The "end" is the kingdom of God, when God will be all in all (1 Cor 15:28). The destruction of the Temple is one of the events that constitute the "beginning of the birthpangs" of the end—like the false messengers of salvation (24:5, 11, 24-28), war (24:6, 7, 16-21, 40, 41), famines and earthquakes (24:9), and the internal destruction of the Christian community

(24:10, 12) through the cooling of love, lawlessness, and betrayal to the officials. But the events before the end also include the worldwide proclamation of the Gospel (24:14). The whole human race will hear the message and beat their breasts in sorrow (over their own deeds, 24:30) when they see the Son of Man coming. The Son of Man will gather the elect from all the ends of the earth (24:31) and then will exercise judgment over the righteous and the unrighteous (25:31-46). The time of the beginning of the birthpangs is also interpreted as the time of Noah's generation, the time of the generation before the great Flood (24:37-39). The "end" is longed for, not feared. Then God alone will be king (24:14; 25:1, 34). Before this, in God's judgment, all injustice done to the least of Jesus' siblings will be punished, and the righteous will receive everlasting life (25:46). The perspective of these two times, the beginning of the birthpangs and the end as the beginning of worldwide righteousness, is determinative for the present of the addressees. They ask longingly about the end; they are enduring persecution, war, and all the other horrors that precede the end (24:13). They are consoled by Jesus that God will prevent a universal destruction (24:22), and they hear the promise that the end of this era, the end of suffering, is soon to come (24:34)—in their generation. The coming God is already close, at the door (24:33). The signs of hope are visible (24:32-34), like the new leaves of the fig tree and the sap in its branches in springtime. The time when the doors of the reign of God will open is at hand. The dreadful events that belong to the "beginning of the birthpangs" are already present in part, and in part lie in the near future. The text deliberately leaves a good deal vague in this regard. The hearers will know how to interpret the events when they occur. Jesus has already predicted them (24:25). The believers know that they are necessary (24:6) but that God is more powerful than these horrors. The eschatological time indications (*tote*, "then") refer to the coming of the Son of Man (24:14, 30) but also to the events at the beginning of the birthpangs (e.g., 24:9, 10, 16).

The idea of time in this eschatology is not intended to present a coherent scenario for the end-time but to help the listeners to understand their own present in relation to the coming of God. These listeners are to be strengthened to maintain their hope that injustice will have an end and justice alone will rule on earth. This is an open present in which all the tribes of the earth have time for repentance. It is not yet determined who will be the elect and who will be the unrighteous. The Son of Man and God the Father will be the judges—no one else. The addressees are therefore by no means identical with those who have eternal life promised to them. The present is the time of longing, of standing fast in resistance, and of testing.

The eschatological interpretation of time is misunderstood if we interpret it in terms of the linear notion of time that is current now. Here the future is God's nearness, God's universal kingship in righteousness, not a time that goes on and on in hours, days, and years. Here nothing goes on as before.[11] Catastrophes and injustice will come to an end. This eschatology interprets the present of the listeners in terms of their relationship to God. "Nearness" is a relationship word, not a word that can be deciphered in terms of the notions of linear time.

"Then the kingdom of God will be compared to ten young women" (25:1). This is not the "then" of the end, but the "then" of the beginning of the birth-pangs. The event that is told in the parable interprets the present as the time of the imminent end—like the "then" in 24:40, 41, or the other instances listed above on page 34.

The Parable "Image" and the Terrors of This Age

In a concentrated form the parable tells of another aspect of the horrors of the present. But it is a parable, not a prophecy of catastrophe such as a prophecy of war would be. In order to understand the parable as parable I would like to bring together the interpretation of the people of the present as the generation of the Flood (24:37-39) with the interpretation of the present in the parable of the Closed Door (25:1-13). In 25:1 it is pointed out that the issue is the comparison of the story in the parable with the kingdom of God. Thus the parable has two levels that must be appreciated, seen, and heard, and that should lead to an alteration in the lives of the addressees. The parable narrative moves on the same level as the condensed description of the generation of the Flood. In the one case the present is interpreted with the aid of the human history in the Bible. You are, like the generation of the Flood, blind and unwilling to listen. You go on living blissfully, eating and marrying, as if the world would always continue just the same.[12] Then, in the parable, another social reality is described as injustice. But here a second level is brought into play: the kingdom of God. If the hearers understand, if they really see and hear the parable (see the so-called parable theory in Matt 13:13-17), they will recognize God's dealings. The parable, with its condensations and sharpenings, makes the present age transparent for God's righteousness. Within the parable narrative there is not a sign of hope—to the bitter end. Just so, in the behavior of the generation of the Flood there is no sign of hope. God will put an end to this injustice, says Matt 24:39. The injustice itself is a sign of the end, a sign of the nearness of the kingdom of God. The parables in Matt 24:45-52; 25:1-13; and 25:14-30, within the framework of the eschatological discourse in Matthew 24–25, are intended to locate present experiences in history within God's time. They make the catastrophes of the present transparent to God's righteousness, which will make the last to be first. The "comparison" that is spoken of in Matt 25:1 refers to learning, understanding, hearing with new ears, and seeing with new eyes. These condensed stories from life, the parables, are meant to make it easy to understand God, so that all can hear, learn, and "compare." The "comparing" is itself an eschatological event, not a formal, intellectual process. It takes place at the hour of repentance. The closed door characterizes this age, which is coming to an end. The listening community perceives the signs of the times.

The parable speaks of the time now, before God's coming. It does not compare an event with the kingdom of God as a condition, but rather it tells, in parable form, about the people of the time in which God is coming to become king. It is an ancient exegetical tradition that such an introduction to a parable does not mean that the kingdom of God is to be compared to ten young women.[13] That "the kingdom of God" does not represent a condition is likewise exegetical tradition.[14] God's coming for liberation, God's kingdom, is a hoped-for event that causes the human world to be made visible in all its misery. The hearers are to compare their world with God's kingdom and derive hope that God will renew the world. Those who can hear and see will be transformed; they awaken; they remain awake; they recognize Jesus in their suffering brothers and sisters (Matt 25:31-46).

Parables expect a response. That is what Jesus urges at the end of the parable: "Keep awake. . . ." The last scene in the parable image leaves the hearers behind in a gloomy situation. The door is closed to the young girls: "I do not know you." The response of the hearers can only be: But we know you, and we will receive you. This door is not closed. We still have time to put an end to violence.

It is entirely possible that in the application of the parable to the current situation of the hearers there is also a reflection on the closed or open door in the sense of a metaphorical discourse about God's judgment.[15] Revelation 3:7-13 contains such a metaphor: "These are the words of the holy one, the true one, who has the key of David. [God] opens and no one can shut. [God] shuts and no one can open. I know your works. Look, I have set before you an open door, which no one is able to shut. I know that you have but little power, and yet you have kept my word and have not denied my name." The listening community is encouraged to live according to Torah. But it is faced with tasks in which it may fail. The possibility that God will close the door is part of the Gospel.

The parable does not end with the description of a condition, but with a challenge (v. 13). The hearers can also hear God's promise in it. The listening community knows what it has to do. It can keep awake and recognize that now there is still time to act according to God's will. This eschatology does not speculate about who, at the judgment, will stand before closed doors or who will be saved. It opens up the present and transforms it into a time of hearing and acting.

FOR FURTHER READING

Vicky Balabanski, "Opening the Closed Door"
Ulrich Luz, *Das Evangelium nach Matthäus,* especially vol. 3

4

Politics with Carrot and Stick

Matthew 22:1-14

TRANSLATION

1   And Jesus continued and spoke to them again in parables.

2   The kingdom of God is to be compared to the reality in the following story of a human king who made a wedding supper for his son.

3   And he sent his slaves to call those invited to the wedding supper, but they would not come.

4   Then he again sent other slaves and said: Say to those invited: Listen! I have prepared my supper, my oxen and my fatted calves have been slaughtered, and everything is ready. Come to the wedding feast.

5   But they made light of it and went away, one to his farm, another to his business.

6   The rest of those invited seized the king's slaves, mistreated them, and killed them.

7   Then the king was enraged. He sent his troops, destroyed those murderers, and burned their city.

8   Then he said to his slaves: The wedding supper is prepared, but those invited were not worthy.

9   Go to the places where the streets leave the city and invite everyone you find to the wedding supper.

10 And those slaves went out into the streets and gathered all whom they found, both bad and good; so the wedding hall was filled with people reclining at table.

11 The king came in to see those reclining at table, and saw there a man who was not wearing a wedding robe.

12 And he said to him: My friend, how did you come in here without a festive garment? But he was speechless.

13 Then the king said to the attendants: Bind him hand and foot and cast him out into a place of absolute darkness. There he will weep and gnash his teeth for fear of death.

14 God calls all peoples, but the weakest he loves above all.

SOCIAL-HISTORICAL ANALYSIS

A king throws a huge feast on the occasion of his son's marriage. Whether we are to think of a Roman emperor or one of his representatives in the territories ruled by Rome is an open question. Feasts put on by ruling elites were an instrument of imperial politics.[1] The Gospels mention a feast hosted by Herod Antipas at which John the Baptizer was executed (Matt 14:3-12 *parr.*). The rabbinic parables speak critically and with much detail about the feasts of the "king."[2] The allegorical tradition of interpretation must not obscure our clear view of the story that is being told here.

This ruler commands absolute power. He alone dictates what happens. Some of the guests invited to the feast are only briefly described: "The one went to his farm, the other to his business" (v. 5). I am deliberately analyzing the version in the Gospel of Matthew separately from its parallel in Luke, and so here I will not be considering the reasons given in Luke for the refusal of those first invited. The characterization of those first invited in Matthew makes us think of established subordinates of the king, rather important people who are charged with implementing his policies in their spheres of influence. At the crucial moment they refuse the invitation, which had already been conveyed to them previously.[3] The king's slaves who summon them to the feast hear their refusal. The king sends a second group of slaves to fetch the guests, with the polite message: "I have prepared my meal, my oxen and fatted calves are slaughtered, and everything is ready. Come to the wedding" (v. 4). This second invitation is formulated in very personal style: my meal, I have prepared, my oxen. Everyone knows that he himself didn't have to do the work; the slave men and women have prepared the gigantic feast for perhaps a hundred people. But the personal style and the fact of a second invitation show that the king is making it clear to those refusing that their refusal is insulting the ruler. His second call sounds both invitational and threatening. Some of those invited still refuse and go about their business. But a larger group of the invitees curse and kill the king's slaves. That is political rebellion. The invited guests' refusal of the invitation calls the king's lordship into question. The king reacts with military means: The rebels' city is burned, and the "murderers" (v. 7) are destroyed. In traditional interpretation there is discussion about whether there is a reference here to the destruction of Jerusalem in 70 C.E. That is possible. But we should also remember that imperial Rome did not make war on a city just that one time. That political experience is alluded to as well.

Now the king invites other guests: "Go to the places where the streets leave the city[4] and invite everyone you find." The guests from the streets are then described: "bad and good." These are now no longer the men of the city elite, but politically insignificant people, just anyone. It is not really important whether the "streets" are thought of as the places where beggars and the homeless gather. Does the second invitation have any political significance from the king's point of view? It does not seem obvious that he wants to shame and exclude those first invited. Most of them, after all, have already been killed. Roman emperors and other imperial representatives very frequently threw feasts for the impoverished underclass of the city. Ignaz Ziegler's collection of relevant rabbinic parables[5] rightly bears the title: "*Panem et circenses,*" "Bread and circuses" (311). Often the whole population of the city was invited to such feasts.[6] Emperors invited clients to dinner:[7] "The fruit of powerful friendship is—a meal. Account it to your 'king.' . . . When it occurs to him after two moons to invite his forgotten client to a meal because otherwise there would be an empty place down the table, he says: 'Let's have a meal together.' O goal of all desires! What more can one wish for?" (5, 10ff.). Then the poor receive only cheap food, while the host is served delicacies. The slaves serving at table look down on the poor guests (60ff.). "That one is right to deal with you so," says Juvenal. "Add to it that you are acting like an idiot when you offer your bare head to have your ears boxed and to receive heavy blows: then you deserve both the meal and the host!" (170ff.). The feasts were observed by the emperor's spies, who were to note any who talked politics openly and critically.[8]

I would like to describe the atmosphere of such banquets, as Matt 22:1-14 envisions them, by using one of Seneca's stories. It helps us to understand the plausibility of Matt 22:1-13, including the final scene. Caligula had executed the son of a man from the equestrian class at the very instant when the father was begging for his son's life

> but so as not to act with utter inhumanity toward the father, he then invited him to dinner on the same day. Pastor came, his face revealing no reproach. The emperor caused a half-liter to be poured for him and placed someone next to him to watch him: the poor man endured it no differently than if he had been drinking his son's blood. [Gaius] sent ointment and wreaths and ordered that it be observed whether he took them; he did. On the very day on which he buried his son, or rather, on which he had not buried him, he reclined at table as the hundredth guest and tossed down the drinks, scarcely appropriate to his children's birthdays, this arthritic old man, and without shedding a tear, without allowing the pain to emerge through a single sign: he ate as though his plea for his son had succeeded. You ask why? He had a second son.[9]

The parable does not say where the guest was supposed to have obtained a "wedding garment," that is, a clean festal robe. It is presumed that even people who were brought in from the streets should have been appropriately dressed, either because they had been given time to prepare their clothes or because the king had distributed proper garments. Rabbinic parables tell of both cases.[10] The king controls the guests as Caligula controlled the wretched father. He sees the fact that one guest is not festively garbed as deliberate disdain for the banquet. He has this guest locked in a dungeon to die in the darkness, presumably without water or food. In Matt 8:12 the "utter darkness" in which "there will be weeping and gnashing of teeth" is used as an image for the "eternal punishment" (Matt 25:46) that, through God's judgment, falls on those who have lived unrighteously and unlovingly (Matt 25:31-46), even if they are from the people of God, Israel (Matt 8:12). But the place of pain and darkness is an image of the dungeons of the palaces, where horrible punishments were inflicted. Emperors carried out dreadful punishments even on their own sons.[11]

In 1912 Ziegler published a collection of rabbinic parables about kings, placing those parables in the historical context of the Roman empire.[12] These rabbinic parables permit us to reconstruct a detailed and critical history of many aspects of the Roman imperial age. Samuel Krauss also regarded the history of the Roman emperors as reflected in rabbinic sources, including many parables, as an important subject of research.[13] Neither, however, was interested in the significance of these rabbinic parables for Jewish interpretation of Torah or the Jewish idea of God. Nevertheless, I want to point out the relevance of their source collections for a social-historical analysis of the parables of Jesus and an understanding of the kingdom of God. I will take Ziegler's brief observations on the notion of God as a starting point for the question of how the kingship of God is related to the story of the emperors, or rulers, described in the royal parables. He sees the rabbinic parables as "the favored form, both for preaching and for homiletic discussion" (xxi). "But no matter how natural and ordinary the use of parable in discourse was, the choice to speak to the people in royal parables was both original and clever" (xxii). He sees this cleverness of the "Haggadists" in the fact that they "set divine power over that of the emperor" (xxiii). Up to 135 c.e. there were only scattered royal parables, but after that, "the more the Principate developed into a despotism, the greater the unfolding of its power, the more numerous were the parables" (xxiii). For Ziegler the popular nature of the parables was in their application to "reality" (xxiii). "An indispensable precondition for the effectiveness of a parable is the hearer's cooperation, as he or she must for the moment be able to internalize and expand the given picture within his or her own spirit" (xxiii–xxiv). He asks where the "Haggadists" obtained such an intimate knowledge of the details of the imperial history, but especially how the mass of the Jewish people could have had such precise knowledge. His answer: The Roman rulers in Caesarea and other powerful people must have imitated the imperial court. "The learned depicted the life and activities within the circles of the highest Roman worthies, but replaced the various titles of the officials with that of the 'king'" (xxvi; in the original the sentence is in boldface).

The royal parables bring together the scriptural traditions of the First Testament, which know God as king, and the critical perspective of the preacher and the people on Roman rule. The royal parables, as well as others of Jesus' parables about power, are thus early testimony to this Jewish discourse about God and Roman rule in parable form. Whenever the concept of the "kingdom of God" appears, or whenever a parable about a powerful man is told, the contents of the Scripture that speaks of God as king, father, and ruler are present to the speakers and the hearers. It is, of course, clear and a simple matter of course that God's kingship is mightier than and different from that of the rulers depicted in the parables. The different quality of God's power is occasionally mentioned, but it is always presumed. The distinction between a "human king" and the divine king (*anthrōpos basileus,* Matt 18:23; 22:2; cf. 20:1) points to this distance. Regarding this distinction between a human king and God as king, Paul Billerbeck notes the rabbinic reflections on the difference between a king "of flesh and blood" (1:797) and God: God's eternity, God's eternal wrath is different from the mortality and therefore limited wrath of a king of flesh and blood.[14] Kings desire to be praised first, and only then do their deeds of kindness ensue; with God it is the other way around.[15] For the interpretation of parables this implicit or explicit distinction means that it must be considered in each individual case where the difference from God is to be found in the depiction of a human king or powerful person. The same is true for rabbinic parables that link their homiletic application to God to a detail in the parable with "so." An equation of the behavior of the king with God's attitude is contradictory to the Jewish idea of God and the long history in Judaism of criticizing power. Apart from parables also, the word *king* is used for God in the awareness that this is the application of a word from the human world, and that God is by no means to be equated with a "king."

The concept of *basileia tou theou* (kingdom/reign of God) is always to be understood, against the background of the Jewish designation of God as king, as political discourse about God that is critical of power. "God is already of course King of Israel. But he does not exercise his sovereignty to its full extent; it is rather that he has surrendered his people temporarily to Gentile powers to chastise them for their sins. But in the glorious kingdom of the future he will take back its government into his own hands. For this reason it will be called, in contrast to the Gentile kingdoms, the kingdom of God. . . . It is a kingdom that will be governed not by earthly powers, but by heaven."[16] This older interpretation of the concept of *basileia tou theou* by Emil Schürer is still widely current, even though the phrase *empire of the future* must be called into question, according to my understanding of this eschatology (see chap. 3 above on Matt 25:1-13).

I would like to illustrate this further with a rabbinic parable that at first glance appears to contradict this understanding of the kingdom of God—the parable of the wicked guests (the king's enemies).

The parable plays on five verses of scripture: "Remember what Amalek did to you" (Deut 25:17). Another verse says: "You shall not abhor the Edomite, for he is your brother. You shall not abhor the Egyptian" (Deut 23:8). "Egypt shall become a desolation and Edom a desolate wilderness" (Joel 4:19). The sense of the parable is that because of Joel 4:19, Deut 23:8 has lost its obligatory character for Israel. The parable narrator gives the salvation-historical reason for this. The parable occurs in two versions, represented here in columns:[17]

Pesiq. Rab. Kah. 3b (MbI 36)	Shir. R. 8,12, on Deut 8:14 (II 82b)
Rabbi Levi said: With what is this to be compared? It is like a king, who gave a banquet. He had two enemies;	So you find: After all the wickedness of Egypt and Edom against Israel
he invited them and said to those seated at table: Receive these, my enemies, with respect.	God commanded: "You shall not abhor the Edomite, for he is your brother. You shall not abhor the Egyptian" (Deut 23:8).
And so they did. After the meal	The (Egyptians and Edomites then began
they took iron axes and in the palace of the king they chopped everything to pieces.	to lay his house in ruins.
	For it says: "Remember, Eternal One, against the Edomites" (Ps 137:7). And it is also written: "Egypt made a pact" (Lam 5:6).
Then the king said to them: Have I not done enough for you, when I commanded that you be honored? But you are chopping everything in my palace to pieces. And you do not value the honor I have shown you.	
	Then the Israelites said: Lord of the universe, see what they have done to us, they of whom it is written: "You shall not abhor the Edomite, for he is your brother"!?

| | The Holy One, blessed be he, said: |
| He had them taken out and hanged facing each other. | Facing each other let him hang them! For it says: "Egypt shall become a desolation and Edom a desolate wilderness" (Joel 4:19). Therefore it says: "Remember" (Deut 25:17). |

It seems obvious that we should read this parable, in most details, allegorically: King = God; two enemies = Egypt and Edom; people at table = Israel, and so on. The editors resolve it this way (1:125); however, they distinguish between analogies using comparisons and metaphors on the one hand and allegories on the other (1:24, 25). Nevertheless, they draw analogies between individual elements in the body of the parable and the application (*Hidduş*, "something new," a novelty that is taught by means of the parable). Thus they understand such parables as theological metaphoric compositions and express this in their ordering of the text, reproduced here. When the parable is read this way, the historical content of the "body" becomes incidental, as the king is understood as "an actor for God" (1:29). But what is said of this king? He invites two enemies to a banquet and causes them to be honored by the group at table. Nothing is said about his motives. After the banquet, the enemies chop up the furnishings of the palace. It appears from the king's closing speech that he had attempted to win over his enemies by honoring them. He interprets the behavior of these enemies as a rejection also of his honoring them: "You do not appreciate the honor I have shown you." He has both enemies executed; the manner of execution is perhaps to be understood as especially brutal and a demonstration of their accursedness ("facing each other"). In the added interpretation (here set in parallel) God's history with Israel is narrated. God commands Israel: "You shall not abhor the Edomite, for he is your brother" (quoted twice in the application). The people Israel complains before God because Egypt and Edom have attempted to destroy Israel, God's house. Then God lifts his order to treat the enemies as brothers by repeating the order for execution given by the king in the body of the parable, thus explicating Joel 4:19. Thus the destruction of Edom and Egypt will be a consequence of God's wrath. Thoma and Lauer see only a "very small discrepancy between the image and the intended meaning" (1:124) because the enemies in the application are also enemies of Israel, not only enemies of the king, as in the "image."

I want to counter this interpretation. The "image" is drawn from the history of Roman rule, and the application from the history of God with Israel. The two sides of the parable tell completely different stories, linked together by a few bridges. The divine history primarily explains God's wrath and prophecy of destruction on Edom and Egypt. The parable narrative attempts to explain that prophecy of destruction. There is a bridge between the narrative (the king's wrath) and the divine history (God's wrath on Edom and Egypt, despite Deut 23:8). But the story about God is concerned with God's people, and this has no parallel in the story of the king. God acts on behalf of his people; the king, on the other hand, acts in the interest of his own rule. The hearers are acquainted with both these contexts within their own experience. To equate the king in the parable narrative with God would be to misunderstand God. It is sensible and necessary to decipher the parable "imagery" historically, as Ziegler did.[18] This is the only basis on which royal parables can be interpreted. The word *king* for God must above all be read against the background of the history of God's *kingdom,* as it appears in Scripture, and placed within the contemporary historical-political context of the particular text.

ECCLESIOLOGICAL INTERPRETATION

John Chrysostom left us an extensive homily on Matt 22:1-14 containing all the elements of the ecclesiological tradition of interpretation.[19] He reads the parable allegorically. It is so obvious to him that the king is to be equated with God that he offers no further commentary on that equation. Equally obviously, those first invited are "the Jews," those later invited "the Gentiles." He reads the parable as the Lord Jesus' prophecy of the history of salvation and non-salvation. For Chrysostom it refers to the time after Jesus' death, since the preceding parable of the vinedressers (Matt 21:33-44) already presupposed Jesus' death (21:39). The emphasis in his homily is on depicting the guilt of the Jewish people: "They had deserved the harshest punishment, and yet he still invites them to the wedding and gives them special honor. . . . Can there be a more detestable ingratitude than that they refuse to come to the wedding to which they are invited?" (3:381–82). "Because they refused to come and even killed the messengers, the Lord sets their cities on fire and sends his troops to destroy them. In these words Christ prophesies what in fact later happened under Vespasian . . . therefore it is also he [= God] himself who applies their punishment. Therefore the siege does not happen immediately, but forty years later. . . . God thus revealed his patience" (3:384). Chrysostom's contrast between the reality and the intention of the individual elements is so radical that he even speculates that the bride is wife to the Son and to the Father at the same time. In terms of his salvation-historical projection he must obviously equate the bride with the church—and thus, properly, she would be identified with those invited later. But he breaks off this speculation. His primary interest is in the Jews' guilt and then, in light of Matt 22:11-13, in the instruction of "those who already believe toward an orderly way of life" (3:387). Those who really wear the wedding garment are, for him, the Christian monks. "Listen, you women; listen, you men. It is not gold-embroidered garments to make you beautiful on the outside that you need, but garments that adorn you within" (3:388). His interpretation shows that this parable, along with many others, has been made into a powerful instrument for the theological destruction of the Jewish people. Crucial for this exegesis is the equation of the king with God: God personally sent the Roman troops as God's own army against the Jewish cities.

The parable theory presupposed by Chrysostom, and his interpretation in terms of a history of salvation and non-salvation, has shaped biblical interpretation to the present day—independently of the scholarly methods with which the New Testament and the parables are read.

ESCHATOLOGICAL INTERPRETATION

The parable of the king's banquet is to be compared to the kingdom of God, the introduction to the parable says. The parable ends with a Jesus saying: "For many are called, but few are chosen"—thus the traditional translation. The traditional interpretation of this Jesus saying applies its content to the allegorical interpretation of the preceding parable: "Both for Israel and for the Gentile church" it is true "that all are invited, but only some will be saved."[20] This interpretation is suspicious because to be called but not chosen would have a negative significance here: Most of those called by God would be those who were *not* saved. This does not fit the New Testament usage of the word *kalein*, "call," which is rather to be equated with being chosen, and in any case permits no contrast between the two ways of God's saving action (see Rev 17:14 and the Pauline usage of *klētos* and *eklektos*). Moreover, this interpretation does not fit within the history of thought about election and call in the First Testament.[21]

The Jesus logion in Matt 22:14 does not fit the parable itself, just as Matt 25:13 does not fit with Matt 25:1-12 (see p. 34 above). It ignores the sequence of the two invitations, and in the parable itself there is no point of contact for the notion of a group of "few."

The First Testament and the literature of postbiblical and rabbinic Judaism reflect repeatedly on the peoples of the world and the elect people of Israel.

> For you are a people holy to Adonai, your God; Adonai, your God, has chosen you out of all the peoples on earth to be his people, his treasured possession.
>
> It was not because you were more numerous than any other people that Adonai set his heart on you and chose you—for you were the fewest of all peoples. It was because Adonai loved you and kept the oath that he swore to your ancestors, that Adonai has brought you out with a mighty

hand, and redeemed you from the house of slavery, from the hand of Pharaoh. . . . (Deut 7:6-8)

From all the birds that have been created you have named for yourself one dove, and from all the flocks that have been made you have provided for yourself one sheep, and from all the multitude of peoples you have taken for yourself one people; and to this people, whom you have loved, you have given the law that is approved by all. And now, O Lord, why have you handed the one over to the many . . . and scattered your only one among the many? (2 Esdr 5:26-28)

Here the prophet bewails the election of the people Israel, which is not evident in the real-life situation of the people: It lives scattered throughout the Roman empire, given over to the power of Roman rule. The book of 2 Esdras (4 Ezra) comes from the same period as the Gospel of Matthew, the time after the destruction of the Temple in Jerusalem (70 c.e.). In the Eighteen Benedictions for feast days we read: "You have chosen us from all the peoples, loved us, shown us your graciousness, and elevated us above all the nations. You have made us holy through your commandments. You, our King, have led us into your service and called us by your great and holy Name."[22] In the First Testament and post-biblical Judaism there is a strong tradition of universalism,[23] that is, hope for the salvation of all people, all the nations among whom tiny Israel lives. That all peoples are called by God to choose life—like Israel—is also contained in Matt 22:14.

A midrash on the Song of Songs reflects that Israel's election does not mean that God has rejected the nations; instead, God has said to the peoples of the world "that they should do penance, and that he will [then] bring them close beneath his wings."[24] Matthew 22:14 fits exactly within this Jewish tradition: God calls all peoples, "the many," and loves the weakest among the peoples. God's love to the one little people, the "few" in relation to the rest of the world, does not exclude the other peoples from salvation. Election means for Israel that it must prove itself holy by keeping the Torah for God. The translation of this logion should eliminate the misunderstanding, so frequently encountered, that Matt 22:14 means salvation for a small, elite group and rejection of the rest of the world. Therefore I translate: "God calls all peoples, but God loves the weakest most." Matthew 22:14 has traditionally been read ecclesiologically but should be read eschatologically.

In the context of Matt 22:1-14 this logion calls us to compare the human king's banquet with God's. God, as king, calls all peoples to the banquet and loves the weakest among them. The response of the listening community could be the address to God quoted above from the Eighteen Benedictions: "You, our King, have led us into your service. . . ." And all peoples are equally faced with the task of working in God's service for justice in the world. The prayer praises God for choosing the weakest nation but places those praying it in an open situation: God's judgment is coming; now is the hour of the Torah. The genre of Matt 22:14 is not the judge's pronouncement of salvation for the few and non-salvation for the many; it is praise of God who has called and chosen, and thus has given a task to both the many and the few. The human king's banquet also refers to "calling," inviting, *kalein*. But the invitation serves imperial purposes and ends in murder, war, and darkness. "But God does not act this way"—as it says at the end of a rabbinic parable.[25] The parable in Matt 22:1-14 describes the imperial politics of meal-hosting and imperial power. Reflecting on God's history with Israel and the nations reveals the contrast in its utmost harshness. Matthew 22:1-14, like Matt 25:1-13, speaks of God not by analogy, but by contrast. God's action cannot be interchanged with imperial politics and power, especially when it is a matter of a contrast between kingdoms.

This interpretation fits well within the literary context of Matt 22:1-14. Jesus is speaking publicly, in the Temple, with repeated critical references to the High Priests, the Pharisees, and the Elders (21:23), or the High Priests and the Pharisees (21:45). The people are present, and the High Priests and Elders do not dare to publicly deny that the Baptizer (21:25-27) and Jesus (21:45) are prophets, or to have Jesus arrested. They are accused of not doing the Torah (21:28-32) and of permitting the people, in their poverty, to use violence and to be threatened by a more powerful and violent force (21:33-45; on this, see pp. 19–20 above). The increasing violence of political conflict, by which the Roman power is succeeding in its aim of domination, is the theme of Matt 22:1-14. The parallel is unmistakable between the parable of the vineyard and that of the king's wedding banquet in their telling of violence that is answered by violence. Some of the invitees who refuse the "king's" invitation kill the king's slaves. He responds with military power and kills the murders and "their city." The ensuing narrative about the "king's" violent act against an individual guest, because of its gruesome character, feels like a further intensification of the brutality of this king.

This people is victim of that social and political violence, a victim with bloody hands. Jesus contrasts God's promise for this people and for all peoples with this violence: The stone becomes the cornerstone; the miracle of salvation is near. The nations and the nation are "called" by God (v. 14). The fact that after this parables discourse the Pharisees, who apparently are also present, immediately ask (or have someone ask) Jesus the political question about paying taxes to Rome fits well with the highly political parable in Matt 22:1-14.

FOR FURTHER READING

Ignaz Ziegler, *Die Königsgleichnisse des Midrasch beleuchtet durch die römische Kaiserzeit*

5

The Snubbed Host

TRANSLATION

12   He said to the one who had invited him: When you give a breakfast or a dinner, do not invite your friends or your immediate family or your relatives, and do not call on your rich neighbors, lest they invite you in turn, so that you receive a reward.

13   Rather, when you prepare a festive meal, call together the poor, the handicapped, the lame, and the blind.

14   And you will be happy, because they have nothing to offer you in return. Instead you will receive your reward at the resurrection of the righteous.

15   One of the guests heard this and said to him: Happy is the one who eats bread in the kingdom of God.

16   But he answered: A man prepared a great supper and invited many.

17   And at the hour of the meal he sent his slave to urge the guests he had invited: Come, everything is ready.

18   And at once they all began to make excuses. The first said: I have bought a farm and must go out and view it. I pray you, hold me excused.

19   The next one said: I have bought five yoke of oxen and am on my way to try them. I pray you, hold me excused.

20   And another said: I have married a wife, and therefore I cannot come.

21   The slave came and gave these messages to his master. Then the householder was angry and said to his slave: Go out immediately into the broad streets and the lanes of the city and bring in the poor, the handicapped, the blind, and the lame.

22   The slave then said: Master, it has been done as you said. But there is still room.

23   Then the master said to the slave: Go out into the roads and to the walls and compel them to come in, so that my house may be filled.

24   I tell you, none of those men who were invited will taste my supper.

SOCIAL-HISTORICAL ANALYSIS

The crucial social-historical question is whether the second invitation to the poor and the sick is to be regarded differently from the invitation to the people of the streets in Matt 22:8-10. There the invitation is not intended as support for the poor. The text says nothing about that. Thus the invitation must be placed within the social-historical context of the public dinners given by representatives of Rome (see pp. 39–41 above). These were not meant to be a support for the poor.[1] Hendrik Bolkestein, in his comprehensive study of philanthropy and care for the poor in pre-Christian antiquity, drew a sharp line between Roman and Greek culture on the one hand and Jewish and Egyptian culture on the other. Thus against this background we need to ask whether the action of the *oikodespotēs*, "householder," in Luke 14:21 belongs within the context of the Jewish tradition of loving deeds and is therefore to be distinguished fundamentally from Matt 22:8-10. The thesis that the issue here is the rights of the poor in the sense of Israel's Torah is supported by Luke 14:12-14 and the parallel listing of the guests in Luke 14:21. A certain skepticism, however, is aroused by vv. 23-24 and the anger of the host in v. 21.[2] For here the invitation to the poor appears as an invitation to substitute guests, who are to demonstrate to those first invited that the banquet can happen without them. This depiction of the attitude of the host also creates a tension with 14:12-14. That passage very clearly represents a policy of hospitality that—in place of the class-determined policies that were a matter of course among the upper classes throughout the Mediterranean world, including Israel[3]—regards banquets for the poor as a support for them and a consequence of the rights of the poor according to Torah.[4] In spite of the difficulty presented by the figure of the "man" and "householder" in the parable, the immediate context of Luke 14:12-14 and the overall context of the Gospel of Luke make it clear that within this framework the intended reference is to this right of the poor. The parable narrative is clearly interpreted within the literary context, even though the parable in itself is not unmistakably clear.

The Gospel of Luke proposes a radical social politics for Israel and for the Christianity drawn from among the nations. People who are in a position to forgive debts should forgive debts and thus be prepared not only—as the Torah demands—to renounce interest, but even to renounce the payment of the principal (Luke 6:34, 35).[5] The gulf between rich and poor is described in the Gospel of Luke as a catastrophe for the rich, who are referred to the Torah for guidance (Luke 16:31). Jesus, the Messiah, proclaims God's year of release when he interprets the Scriptures in Nazareth (Luke 4:16-21).[6] I am mentioning here only a few aspects of the Gospel of the Poor according to Luke that are fundamental to the interpretation of Luke 14:12-14. According to "Luke" the banquets of the homeless, the beggars, and the handicapped that are supposed to take place in the houses of the well-to-do, instead of the usual feasts with people of the same class, continue Jesus' meal practices. In Luke 15:1-3 there is reference to another aspect of Jesus' meal practices, and Jesus tells three parables about it (Luke 15:4-32). The meals with sinners celebrate messianic community (see pp. 138–51 below on Luke 15:11-32). Jesus' feasts with sinners and the poor, the new meal practices of well-to-do people who follow Jesus, and the meal practices of the Christian communities (Acts 2:42-45; 4:32-35), including the Eucharist, signify the feeding of the hungry, the realization of solidarity within the people of God, and an experience of the kingdom of God. This is the horizon of interpretation for the parable of the banquet, made unmistakably clear by Jesus' speech about the new form of meal practice that is placed ahead of it. But the parable itself remains subject to misinterpretation as regards the figure of the host. It makes no sense that his interest in filling the banquet hall and excluding those first invited is a fulfillment of Jesus' admonition to invite the poor. In this respect the parable is related to the story of the toll collector's son in the Talmud:

There were two pious men in Askalon; they ate together, drank together, and together they studied Torah. One of them died, and the [final] service of love was not paid him [no one accompanied his body to the grave]. The son of the toll collector Ma'jan died, and the whole city took a holiday [from work] in order to pay him the [final] service of love. Then the [surviving] pious man began to grumble; he said: Woe to those who hate Israel [= the wicked Israelites]; this one [the pious man who had died] committed one sin, and he escaped it thus [through his lonely burial his guilt was expiated]; and that one did a single good work, and he escaped it thus [through his solemn burial he was rewarded for it]. What sin did that pious man commit? Far be it, that he ever committed a [serious] sin in all his life; but once he set the head tefillin earlier than the hand tefillin. And what good work did the son of the toll collector Ma'jan do? Far be it, that he ever did a [truly] good work in all his life; but once he gave a morning meal for the ruling men [of his city], and they did not come to eat of it. Then he said: Let the poor eat it, that nothing be lost [thus according to *p. Sanh.* 6.23c]. But some said: He was crossing the marketplace, and in doing so he lost a loaf of bread; a poor man saw it and took it, and he said nothing to him about it, so as not to bring shame upon his head. A few days later this pious man saw [in a dream] the other pious man, his companion, walking about in gardens, under groves of trees, and by springs of water. And he saw the son of the toll collector Ma'jan stretching his tongue toward the bank of a river; he was trying to reach the water, but he could not.[7]

Here the insulted host is not regarded as a hero, as is the case with Luke 14:15-24, as long as the host is interpreted as representing God.

The solemn exclusion by the host of those first invited, reported at the end of the Lukan parable (Luke 14:24) and addressed to all those present ("I tell you . . ."), remains within the framework of the story as narrated, a story about the disappointment of a well-to-do host. Luke 14:24 should not be read as a Jesus logion. The hearers or readers learn Jesus' intention in Luke 14:13. The unknown guest (Luke 14:15) who calls the guests in God's kingdom happy speaks the truth, but not completely: He ought to have pointed to the necessity that the rich, in order to live according to Torah, must make the poor the center of their lives.

The parable narrative describes the poor as homeless people, to be found in all the streets, both narrow and broad (Luke 14:21). In the second invitation of substitute guests, also, people are brought from the "streets and walls," the latter enclosing the houses of the well-to-do. There is abundant social-historical material about the poverty of the people who live in the streets of the cities.[8] The Jewish tradition of generosity, better called "the practice of the rights of the poor," also includes inviting the poor to meals in the houses of all those who have houses, not only the rich:[9] "Let your house be wide open, and let the poor be the companions of your house" (*m. 'Abot* 1:5). The Jewish sources also speak of how some hosts treat the poor shabbily. That Jewish hospitality to the poor explodes any practice of almsgiving that leaves homeowners unchanged is also clear from the fact that we read of women who invited poor people to their tables against the will of their husbands.[10]

The first invitation, to guests from the same class (14:12, 18-20), is commented in the parable through their refusals. These are insulting to the host—a frequent theme in ancient literature on banqueting.[11] The contents of the refusals show the guests first invited to be well-to-do householders, like in rank to the host: They have their own land or their own cattle. Their refusals characterize them as householders who head large, patriarchal houses.

There is a literary tradition in the New Testament that describes such patriarchal households. The Lukan version (17:27-28) of Jesus' eschatological logion about the generation of the catastrophe reads: "They ate and drank, they married and were given in marriage" (the generation of Noah); "they ate and drank, they bought and sold, they planted and built" (the generation of Lot). In Matthew's version it is said of Noah's generation: "They ate and drank, they married and gave in marriage" (24:38). In this context also belongs the distancing from patriarchal structures in 1 Cor 7:29-31: "Those who have wives should live as if they had none; those who mourn as if not mourning; those who rejoice as if not rejoicing; and those who buy as having nothing; and those who use the world as though they had no need of it; for the state of this world is coming to an end." These are the structures of the patriarchal household, as they also appear in the so-called household codes. The historical Paul calls them the structures of this world, which will come to an end. In the Christian communities of his time, and beyond them, an attempt was made to alter these structures, which were regarded as humanly oppressive.[12] An orientation to the preservation and increase of possessions and to patriarchal marriage with its instrumentalization of women and slaves gave people's life together a direction that distanced it from God. In the post-Pauline letters of the New Testament, then, we can see how the patriarchal household had again succeeded in dominating the life-orientation of many Christian communities. In the Gospel of Luke, as in Paul, the structure of the patriarchal household is clearly criticized as "care for the things of daily life" (Luke 21:34; see also 8:14).

As the social-historical analysis shows, the parable of the great supper in the Gospel of Luke is a story, plausible in itself, of a well-to-do Jewish householder who invites people like himself to a meal. The refusals of those invited are insulting to him. Their own tasks in their own houses are more important to them. Out of anger he invites the poor people from the streets. The narrative contains emphases and exaggerations, as usual in such parable narratives, but they make it clear what the story is meant to tell about: the deep wound inflicted by the refusal of *all* the guests and the rage of the householder, who fills his house to the very last place with poor people and finally declares: I will never again invite people from my circle of business acquaintances, neighbors, and relatives! Unlike the version of the parable of the supper in Matthew's gospel, this story moves within a Jewish milieu and the tradition of Jewish care for the poor, without any idealizing. The prelude in Jesus' speech in 14:12-14 nevertheless evaluates this story as a clarification of what he insists upon as a new meal practice. The well-to-do are not to invite those like themselves, but the poor. Both this demand and the critical view of the actual praxis of the rights of the poor stand within the Jewish tradition. The host is not to be regarded as a metaphorical depiction of God. In other respects as well the story is not meant to be read as a sequence of metaphors, but as a story drawn from life, fictional and close to reality at the same time.

Both versions of the parable (Matt 22:1-10; Luke 14:16-24) use a similar framework for the narrative. They take place in different milieux, that of the representatives of Roman rule in Matthew and that of a well-to-do Jewish man in Luke. How the parable was told in the tradition available to the Gospels (Q and the historical Jesus) is something we can no longer reconstruct.[13]

ECCLESIOLOGICAL INTERPRETATION

The previous analyses of parables have made the structure of the ecclesiological tradition of interpretation so clear that here I will only summarize briefly the contents and, following that, the methodological and hermeneutical bases. I will take as an example the interpretation by François Bovon.[14]

Bovon reads Luke 14:16-24 as a parable, a narrative similitude that moves on two levels. Verse 24 is said to be the speech of the householder and at the same time of the Lukan Christ, who is talking about "his banquet," the reign of God (2:503). He regards the traditional exegetical alternatives of reading the parable in terms of salvation history or ethically as inappropriate: "In reality the two readings complement one another: The text criticizes Israel and its leaders, those first invited, but afterward it opens itself to the lost sheep of the house of Israel, that is, the poor and those injured by life" (2:512–13). The second invitation to people from the "paths and hedgerows" of the land is to be understood as an invitation to the nations (2:507, 513). The people of God now includes "—what an unexpectedly new thing—people from Israel and from the nations" (2:514). But v. 24 speaks of a definitive exclusion. Bovon asks: "Is [Luke] really speaking in favor of an ultimate rejection of the resistant part of Israel? I hope it is not so" (2:515). But Israel or its leaders are not explicitly mentioned. "Still more, the parable is not a statement, but a painting. It leads to reflection, 'compels' to dialogue. 'What shall I do?' ask the Jewish or Gentile readers." Bovon calls the parable a "parabolic fresco, partly allegorical" (2:515). He prefers to understand the implacable judgment in v. 24 as a call to repentance (2:516).

Bovon's interpretation is, on the one hand, a prisoner of the salvation-historical ecclesiological reading, but on the other hand it develops an interpretation that could overcome it. Despite the condemnation he finds in v. 24, he sets the parable within the context of a gospel that does not desire "'the death of the sinner,'" but rather "repentance and life" (2:516). He thus frees himself from the allegorical reading of v. 24 and places the parable within an open situation of dialogue. He sees that Israel and its leaders are nowhere explicitly named, but he does not draw the consequence by abandoning the allegorical interpretation of the first-invited in terms of Israel and its leadership.

Methodologically, this internal contradiction makes it clear that a parable theory that reads parables as sequences of metaphors (banquet = reign of God; invitation = invitation into the reign of God; truly I tell you . . . = Christ's judgment) is tied firmly, in its content, to the salvation-historical, or, as I call it, the "ecclesiological," interpretation and its anti-Judaism. I myself, for a long time, shared the supposition that parables, when they contain individual metaphors, are in part to be read as ambiguous. It was only by reading many rabbinic parables and applying a social-historical analysis to parable narratives that I understood that this metaphorical reading does not do justice to the parables. The householder in this parable is not an implicit portrayal of God, the banquet is not an implicit depiction of the reign of God, and v. 24 remains within the framework of the narrative. It is not spoken by Christ, but by a fictional host who is enraged. God's banquet is a major theme in Jewish tradition (e.g., Isa 25:6-8),[15] one that is also continually present in the Synoptic Gospels, and thus implicitly here as well. God's banquet is different from this meal offered by an insulted host. It is the task of the hearers or readers to express the difference. Luke 14:24 cannot be reconciled with the Lukan vision of the reign of God. The

Gospel of Luke fights for the repentance of those who reject Jesus' message and praxis (see chaps. 3 and 6).

ESCHATOLOGICAL INTERPRETATION

Verse 15 makes it clear that the parable is meant to be applied to the reign of God. But the happy exclamation of the nameless guest in the house of a Pharisee in a position of authority (14:1) is corrected by the parable. It remains an open question how the listeners may have reacted. The opening words (14:12-14) have already referred them to the Torah and its vision of the rights of the poor. The banquets to which the poor and disabled are invited are not meant to be metaphorical. The Gospel of Luke intends to point Christian communities to a radical interpretation of the Torah and the rights it gives to the poor. That banquets are to be made a locus of solidarity means that hunger among the people requires the opening of the houses of those who have enough to eat. In this way the hosts become siblings of the poor. Because the experience of being the people of God together with the poor is made possible through eating together, such a festive meal was understood as the beginning of the reign of God. In case the hearers were to ask, in spite of vv. 12-14, "what are we to do?" the parable gives a broad hint: Your feasts should certainly look different from that of the insulted host in the Matthean version of the parable. In the Lukan work there are continual references to the experiences of communities with regard to common meals. Those gathered for a meal recognize the risen Christ when he blesses and breaks bread (Luke 24:30-31). "Day by day . . . they broke bread at home and ate their food with glad and generous hearts, praising God" (Acts 2:46-47). This is meant to characterize the fundamental significance of common meals for the life of the earliest communities. The cries of joy are an expression, effected by the Holy Spirit, of the bliss that the reign of God will mean and already means for earth and heaven. The experience of sharing food—and economic resources—with the poor evokes this happiness, just as does the nearness of God that is celebrated in these meals.

Joy in the closeness of the coming God of Israel unites Jewish and "Gentile" people, or, better said, people from the nations. That God also calls people who are not Jewish in their origins is not something that needs to be allegorically read out of the parable. The second invitation to the place-fillers from the roads and walls is frequently interpreted as an invitation to the Gentile church. But that God calls all nations is Torah tradition (see pp. 46–48 above on Matt 22:14), and is clear in the Gospel of Luke also, from the outset (see Luke 2:32). But the place-fillers in the parable have nothing to do with the nations. They are poor people who are used as place-fillers by an arrogant host.

The eschatological interpretation the parable acquires through 14:12-15, which is intensified by the literary context of the two-volume Lukan work, permits us to read the parable not as a narrative with allegorical features (as Bovon does) or as a sequence of metaphors, but as a story from real life. The insulted householder practices the Torah's rights of the poor, but only halfheartedly. The parable criticizes him and those like him. The refusals of the first-invited guests show how inconsiderate people had become as a result of the structures of the patriarchal household. This idea also has its analogies in the New Testament. The parable as a whole, as a tale of real life, requires the hearers to take care in constituting their own meal practice and the rights of the poor. Because it tells a fictional story, no one is accused or confronted with reproaches. It opens the way to a meal community of well-to-do and poor in which the latter are not place-fillers but have a right to share in the joys of creation, food, and health (see 14:2-6).

FOR FURTHER READING

Hendrik Bolkestein, *Wohltätigkeit und Armenpflege im vorchristlichen Altertum*
Marlene Crüsemann and Frank Crüsemann, "Das Jahr das Gott gefällt"
Luise Schottroff, "Das Gleichnis vom großen Gastmahl in der Logienquelle"

6

The Barren Fig Tree

Luke 13:1-9

TRANSLATION

1   At that hour people came to him and told him about some Galileans whose blood Pilate had mingled with the blood of their [animal] sacrifices.

2   And Jesus answered and said to them: Do you suppose that these Galileans were more sinful than all others in Galilee, that they had to suffer this?

3   No, I tell you, if you do not repent, you will all perish in like manner.

4   Or those eighteen on whom the tower of Siloam fell and killed them—do you suppose they were more guilty than all the people who dwell in Jerusalem?

5   No, I tell you, if you do not repent, you will all perish in like manner.

6   And he told them this parable: Someone had a fig tree planted in his vineyard. And he came and sought fruit on it and found none.

7   Then he said to the vinedresser: For three years now I have been coming to look for fruit on this fig tree and have found none. Dig it up. Why should it occupy the ground?

8   But the (vinedresser) answered him: Master, leave it for one more year, and let me dig around it and fertilize it.

9   If in future it yields fruit—; but if not, you can dig it up.

SOCIAL-HISTORICAL ANALYSIS

The parable of the barren fig tree is closely linked to the preceding narrative and the Jesus saying in 13:1-5, which in turn refers to the preceding speech of Jesus to the crowd (12:54-59), in which Jesus is concerned that the people recognize the time, the *kairos,* and what is now to be done (v. 56), what is right (v. 57). In 13:1 we read, "At that time (*kairos*)" people came to him. In my translation of Luke 13:1 I have translated the word *kairos* with "hour," which seems to me more adequate because it refers to a time that is designated as *kairos;* it is the hour to know what is to be done because the present is truly appreciated for what it is. From the events that have taken place in Jerusalem the people should recognize the time, the hour in which they find themselves, and understand the consequences. The parable itself is thus the end of a speech of Jesus to the people, during which some people bring him the latest news about a murder in the Temple (13:1). A social-historical analysis must take into account not only the parable narrative, but also the political situation to which the parable is closely related.

Pilate, the new arrivals announce, has had a group of Galileans murdered within the precincts of the Temple, so that their blood mingled with that of the sacrificial animals. A great many brutal and oppressive acts are reported of Pilate, the Roman prefect in Judea from 26 to 36 c.e.[1] Even if none of them exactly fits this event, the report is not simply a rumor plucked from thin air about a Roman authority.[2] The murder by Roman soldiers of Galileans offering sacrifice in the Temple precincts indicates that a group of people were being killed who, like Jesus himself, were regarded by the Roman authorities as politically dangerous. At the same time the place and time of the murder were a deliberate religious provocation to the whole Jewish people. Josephus also reports such provocations by Pilate: He provoked the population by marching troops into Jerusalem with the emperor's image on their standards and by using money from the Temple treasury to build an aqueduct.[3] The outrage over these provocations is expressed in the assertion that Pilate had mingled the blood of the murder victims with that of their sacrificial animals.[4]

Jesus himself adds to this news of a fresh experience of oppression the recollection of an accident that probably had taken place some considerable time in the past: Eighteen people had been killed by the falling of a tower at the pool of Siloam. There are no sources regarding the accident outside this text, but it is entirely possible that the tower was connected with the aqueduct that Pilate had built.

There are discrepancies in the evaluation of Jesus' perspective on these two instances of violence. Frequently in the history of interpretation, emphasis has been placed on Jesus' apolitical point of view. It is said that he did not react to the news of Pilate's bloody deed with a condemnation of Rome, as those present would have expected. In addition, he paralleled it with an accident, in fact, a natural event.[5]

Jesus criticizes a possible personalizing of the events as the fault of those affected by them (vv. 2, 4). He regards the murder and the accident as consequences of the guilt of the whole people to whom he belongs (vv. 3, 5). He does not quote the Torah explicitly here, but in the content of what he says he places himself within the Torah tradition. God punishes the whole people Israel, the people of God, which has made itself guilty: "Do not defile yourselves in any of these ways. . . . Thus the land became defiled; and I punished it for its iniquity, and the land vomited out its inhabitants" (Lev 18:24-25).[6] Above all, "idol worship," that is, the practice of other cults, sexual sins in the sense of Leviticus 18, and shedding blood are regarded as this kind of pollution of the people as a whole.[7]

When enemies are in a position to bring shame upon the people, it is the hour of repentance. Jesus' goal in this section is again, as in 12:54-59, to bring the crowd to an awareness of the "signs of the times" (Matt 16:2, in parallel to Luke 12:56), of the *kairos*. These experiences of violence should be recognized as God's visitation for the guilt of the *whole* people, a sign of the threatened catastrophe. A consequence should be drawn: repentance. All ought to repent, all are in danger, the people Israel is in danger. The word *all* appears four times in vv. 1-5.

The danger for the people in vv. 3 and 5 is often interpreted in Christian exegesis as the threatened end-time *judgment of God* on Israel: if Israel does not repent or, still more generally, if people do not repent because they are not pure before God. But these theological generalizations are not appropriate. "You will all perish in like manner." This statement in the first century, before the Jewish-Roman War, was an expression of the fear that the war with Rome was coming. Jesus feared it (see only Mark 13:2 *parr.*), and other Jewish teachers also saw the signs of the coming destruction of the Temple even forty years before the war.[8] Josephus repeatedly testifies to this fear.[9] Since the Gospels achieved their present form after this war, as is frequently supposed, Jesus' words about a threatened war are said to be *vaticinium ex eventu,* a back-dated prophecy of the war. Certainly the experience of the war entered into the tradition after 70 C.E. Nevertheless, we should take seriously the fact that a whole generation before the war the Jewish people felt itself threatened by the brutal military attacks of Roman troops. This threat was expressed clearly enough by Rome's own representatives.[10] In Luke 13:1-5 Jesus speaks of the impending war, which he interprets within the tradition of the Torah as God's punishment for the sins of the people. David Flusser has expressed very clearly the reference of Luke 13:1-9 to the war: "If you do not do penance you will all perish in the same way. That is neither a generalized theological saying nor an eschatological dictum. The great Hugo Grotius himself recognized that 'here Jesus speaks of the imminent catastrophe at the hands of Rome that will fall upon all the people, and that is almost unavoidable.'"[11]

For Christian interpreters these Jesus traditions are inextricably tied to their anti-Jewish misuse: the positing of the righteous punishment of God that is supposed to have led Israel into catastrophe. Tania Oldenhage has rightly pointed to the implicit justification of the Holocaust when Christians have spoken since 1945 about the threatened catastrophe of Israel.[12] This Christian tradition of interpretation has disregarded both the threat to the Jewish people in the real history of the first century and their long suffering from the consequences of that war.

A social-historical analysis of Luke 13:1-5 thus yields as a conclusion that this text refers to Rome's impending war against the Jewish people. The history of Christian interpretation has often set aside this reference and referred the text to the approaching judgment of God. In this way Israel's guilt, from a Christian perspective, has been emphasized from outside and the anchoring of this idea in the Torah goes unmentioned.

A social-historical view of the parable of the fig tree in Luke 13:6-9 itself shows that the owner of the vineyard, like the one in Mark 12:1-9 *parr.*, has leased his vineyard, including the fig tree, and, as v. 7 shows, comes every year to receive the fruits. He wants to have the tree cut down because he is interested in the yield. The leaseholder in the little fictional narrative is a marginal figure to begin with; it is his task to carry out the owner's orders. But in v. 8 he becomes a key figure of hope in the midst of the crisis of the approaching war, since in the parable he counters the threatened destruction by delaying it. The fact that in that time of economic hardship barren trees had to be cut down was obvious to most of the people. All the more astonishing is the leaseholder's action. From the point of view of the owner of the vineyard it is an issue of profit, his profit, because he is certainly not one of those who have to make use of every bit of earth in order to avoid starvation. This brief social-historical analysis of the parable narrative must suffice at this point.

ECCLESIOLOGICAL INTERPRETATION

Paul Billerbeck's commentary has all but cemented one Christian tradition of interpretation within the subsequent generations: Jesus is opposing a Jewish teaching and an opinion that was widespread among the Jewish people of his time, "as if a particular accident that befell a person should be regarded as proof of the existence of a particular sinfulness."[13] Jesus' alternative to this remains unexpressed in Billerbeck's work, but it does appear in exegeses that rely on it: Jesus, in contrast to such Jewish teaching, proclaims the universality of sin. All people are sinful and need penance and the grace of God. I call this Christian tradition of interpretation "ecclesiological" because it ties Christian self-understanding to a "better" theological doctrine of sin. Thus in the figure of Jesus a superior theological doctrine is contrasted to a less valuable one.[14] A Christian dogma of the universality of sin and the corresponding universality of penance and grace are sketched in this tradition of interpretation. But in the process words of Jesus that apply to a concrete situation are dehistoricized and made into a generally applicable theological doctrine.

For the sake of clarity I will contrast my interpretation of these verses with an ecclesiological interpretation. Jesus criticizes an understanding of these horrible events—one possibly supported by some of the people in the crowd—as a consequence of the special guilt of some individuals. In doing so, he does not criticize the connection between sin and punishment in the sense of the Torah, but rather the application of the Torah tradition to this situation in order to individualize and play down the situation as a whole. For him, too, the connection between guilt and God's punishment is clear, but in this situation he draws different conclusions from his reading of the Torah: The life of the whole people is in danger, and not merely the lives of some especially guilty individuals. It is a matter of recognizing the hour, the present moment. The threat is vitiated if it is thus personalized. Jesus understands these events as "signs of the times." The exonerating interpretation of the horrors of the present as the misfortune of "the others" hinders a recognition of the danger of the impending war, which will be dreadful and will bring down the nation. The Torah, which Jesus has received and which he hands on, refuses to look away from such a situation but instead seeks to bring the whole people to act, for the "repentance" Jesus intends takes place not in the hearts of individuals but in community and in public.

The ecclesiological tradition of interpretation sees Jesus as the teacher of a timeless theology, even at this point where the issue is the recognition of the *kairos,* the time before the impending war. There is a fundamental difference between teaching the universality of sin as the nature of human existence and, in a concrete situation, prophetically naming the peril of the people and their rescue through the repentance of all.

ESCHATOLOGICAL INTERPRETATION

Now is the hour to repent, Jesus says in his admonitions in 13:1-5 and in the parable of the barren fig tree. Now is the hour in which the leaseholder of the vineyard is imploring a delay on behalf of the barren tree. Does not such an admonition to repentance addressed to an endangered people represent "blaming the victim"? Rome has a modern army, armed to the teeth, against which Jerusalem will not be able to defend itself for long. Jesus has learned from Torah that in such a situation there is only one way to act: to keep God's commandments and live according to Torah. Like the prophet Jeremiah, he sees the cause of the danger in his own people's violation of the Law. That does not mean that he denies the imperialistic interests of Rome, which will lead to such a war (see Luke 22:25). Rescue from danger can only come from repentance on the part of his own Jewish people. But is not this people the victim of a dominant power, from which there is no hope of rescue?

The impressive prophet Jesus ben Ananias, of whom Josephus writes,[15] is part of the same tradition. He begins his prophetic proclamation of the fall of Jerusalem four years before the war. He repeats his horrifying message again and again, undeterred even when he is beaten. He says nothing about repentance, and yet that is the sense and purpose of his desperate cries. He says nothing, either, about a final deadline. And yet his shouts and his suffering offer a clear message: You can still make a change, and avert the imminent war.

In the passage that precedes Luke 13:1, Jesus uses a parable to make clear how pitiless is the political situation: "And why do you not judge for yourselves what is right? It is as if you were going with your accuser before the magistrate. On the way make an effort to settle the case, so that he will not drag you before the judge, and the judge hand you over to the officer, and the officer throw you in prison. I tell you, you will never get out until you have paid the very last penny" (Luke 12:57-59). This is the merciless situation in which debtors find themselves when they are unable to pay their creditors, the nightmare of many people at that time.[16] It is a situation in which the debtors must seek to achieve some compromise with the creditor; otherwise they will find themselves in debtors' prison until their family has been bled dry. This is the hour that has struck. That is how extreme and pitiless the danger is. But there is still a chance to act: to recognize what is just (12:57), to turn and repent (13:1-9). With Jesus ben Ananias and in the words and parables of Jesus in Luke 12:57-59 and 13:1-9, we find a political analysis of the situation of the Jewish people before the Jewish-Roman War. Rome has the power to make war and to win it, but the people has a chance to act, a final deadline.

What would such action look like? Jesus gives no details, at least not at this point. Since Jeremiah it has been clear that in this situation repentance means following God's Torah, what is just (12:57). The gigantic war machine of the Roman military threatens the land, and especially Jerusalem—and these prophets see a way out, one that must appear to twenty-first-century people as truly odd: The people should live according to Torah, and the enemies will have no hold over them. What takes place in repentance, in *metanoia* (Greek), *teshubah* (Hebrew)? The poor share their bread, they heal the sick among the people, they do everything that Jesus and other Torah teachers have taught them. They transform themselves from threatened victims into acting subjects. They work for righteousness and law as intended by Torah.

The man in Luke 13:8, who has leased the vineyard, opposes the owner, who wants to have the fig tree cut down, just as Moses once countered God, when God in wrath intended to hand over the rebellious people (Exod 32:11-14).[17] The parable is not to be allegorically interpreted by asking whether Jesus is now the petitioner, like Moses before, or whether the owner of the vineyard represents God. These questions are inappropriate. The logic of the vineyard owner is determined by considerations of profit. The parable narrative should not be read as a quarry for metaphors, but as a fictional and concentrated reflection of social experiences.

The parable gives an eschatological determination to time, to now. Now is the hour in which the door is once again opened, the door that is already closed. It is the hour of action and of repentance. In the Jewish world a great many parables were told involving fig trees. And yet each is different. This one interprets "the time" in the language of hope, which the leaseholder of the vineyard has surprisingly discovered: "Let the tree alone this one more year." The violence of an imperial war power is here countered by the hope for a people that has the strength for justice, for turning back to Torah. The strength for justice is attributed to the downtrodden, and they are promised the ability to act. The crowd's answer to Jesus' words, not contained in the text but hoped for, can nevertheless be imagined: "There is still time—now—for us to repent together and to do everything God has appointed for us in the Torah."

And after the Jewish-Roman War? How were such parables of encouragement read when the destruction of Jerusalem had already happened and the people's suffering still continued? Truthfully, there was no longer any basis for hope. But we know from the history of Israel after 70 C.E. that the survivors did not give up. When the Lukan gospel became a written text, the war had already occurred. How was it redacted in the communities that followed the Messiah Jesus? Traditionally it is supposed by Christian exegetes that early Christianity saw the destruction of Jerusalem as God's punishment on Israel because of Israel's rejection of Jesus. It is also supposed that Christian texts placed prophecies of the destruction of Jerusalem on the lips of Jesus after the fact (*vaticinia ex eventu*). But these prophecies may indeed be genuine. C. H. Dodd has shown that all the prophecies of the destruction of Jerusalem in the Gospel of Luke rest on the language of the Septuagint about the destruction in 587 B.C.E., and therefore could most certainly have been spoken before the war.[18] There is a fundamental difference between talking about the people Israel's suffering from the perspective of an outsider and an insider. I mean to say that when Christian people who no longer live in solidary community with the Jewish people talk about the destruction of Jerusalem as God's punishment, they intend thereby to demonstrate God's final rejection of Israel. But as long as the Jesus movement, even after Jesus' death, understood itself to be part of Israel, even though many of the people in it were no longer of Jewish origin, just so long was the language of hope for Israel to be found within it. I see nowhere in the Gospel of Luke, or in the other canonical Gospels, an alteration—from the perspective of a Christianity that had established itself as the heir of Israel—of the scriptural traditions about the sin of Israel and Israel's repentance so as to establish that Israel has been finally rejected. The repentance in Luke 13:1-9 is a repentance that preserves the people Israel as the people of God, and not a reference to a conversion to Christianity as a religion separated from Judaism. Luke 13:1-9 was still read after 70 C.E. in solidarity with Israel.

I want to set alongside Luke 13:1-9 a text from Tertullian that makes clear the difference between speaking about Israel in solidarity and asserting the rejection of Israel. The destruction of Jerusalem is now understood as a final divine judgment, and the possibility of the people Israel's repentance is disputed: "They failed to understand that the time that intervened between Tiberius and Vespasian was [a time for] repentance. So their land was made desolate, their cities burnt with fire, their country, strangers devour it in their presence . . . since the time, in fact, when Israel knew not the Lord, and the people would not understand him, but forsook him, and provoked the Holy One of Israel to indignation . . . proved that it was Christ whom they refused to hear, and therefore perished."[19]

Thus the eschatological interpretation of the parable of the fig tree centers on hope for the threatened people. Even after the destruction of Jerusalem in two Jewish-Roman wars in 66–70 C.E. and 132–135 C.E. the voice of hope was not extinguished. I would like to set a rabbinic parable alongside the one in Luke 13:6-9, one that—though using other parable material—speaks of this hope and within the parable, or better the *mashal*, makes that voice audible. The interpretation of this parable was unlocked for me by David Stern.[20] It is attributed to Rabbi Eleazar ben Pedat (ca. fourth century):

> Psalm 79:1 says: "Song of Asaph. O God, the nations are entering into your inheritance." This psalm should not have the superscription . . . Song of Asaph, but . . . Wailing of Asaph, or . . . Weeping of Asaph, or . . . Lamentation of Asaph. Why is it called . . . Song of Asaph? It is as with a king who made the bridal chamber ready for his son, having it painted and beautifully adorned. But when his son angered him, the king went into the bridal chamber, tore down the curtains, and broke the poles. But the prince's pedagogue cut a pipe and played upon it. They said to him: The king has torn down the bridal chamber of his son, and you are sitting there playing? He answered: I am playing because the king has torn down the bridal chamber of his son and has not poured out his wrath upon his son. So also Asaph was asked: God has destroyed the sanctuary and the Temple, and you are sitting there singing? I am singing, he answered, because he has poured out his wrath on wood and stone and not on Israel. Thus does it say: "A fire goes forth in Zion and consumes its foundations."[21]

This *mashal* is part of the answer to a question touching Ps 79:1: Why is it called "A Song of Asaph" and not "Asaph's Weeping," when in fact the psalm is about the destruction of the Temple? The answer is found in Lam 4:11: "[The LORD] . . . kindled a fire in Zion that consumed its foundations." Asaph sings for joy because God has only destroyed the Temple, *only* the foundations, but *not* Zion itself.[22] The pedagogue in the parable sings in the face of the destruction of the king's son's bridal chamber because the king has destroyed only the bridal chamber, but not his son. Stern sees the occasion for this unusual exegesis on two levels. First, the text is meant to defend the people against Christian interpretations of the destruction of the Temple and the hard fate of the Jewish people. We are not destroyed; Zion has not been laid low. But the text also speaks to Jewish people who might read Lam 4:11 as a prophecy of the continuing wrath of God that threatens to destroy the people. Thus Lam 4:11 ought to be read as a source of hope, "to counter the awesome despair Jews themselves felt after the Destruction."[23] The fictional narrative in the *mashal* "provides a model for the activity of interpretation. Just as the pedagogue explains his paradoxical behavior, so the equally paradoxical logic of the interpretation itself—first of

Asaph's singing in Ps. 79:1; then, of the exegesis of Lam. 4:11—is also explained and thereby justified."[24] Thus the *mashal* offers a model for how Scripture can be a source of hope.

The image of the pedagogue who sits in the ruins and sings, or plays the flute, adds a strong and clear image to the praxis of this exegesis of hope. It would not be appropriate simply to allegorize the *mashal*: The king is God, and so on. Its message is not intended to present God in the figure of a violent king who strikes when his son annoys him. Here again a response to the *mashal* is expected from the readers or hearers: that they should transform themselves into people who trust their God so unconditionally that even in the ruins they can begin to sing of their hope for God's salvation.

FOR FURTHER READING

Josef Blinzler, "Die Niedermetzelung von Galiläern durch Pilatus"
David Flusser, *Die rabbinischen Gleichnisse und der Gleichniserzähler Jesu*
Jonathan Klawans, *Impurity and Sin in Ancient Judaism*
David Stern, *Parables in Midrash* and "Rhetoric and Midrash"

7

Hearing and Doing the Torah

Mark 4:1-20

TRANSLATION

1   And again he began to teach by the sea. And a great crowd of people came to him, so that he had to get into a boat that was on the sea. He sat down. And all the people were on the land, on the seashore.

2   And he taught them many things in parables and said to them in his teaching:

3   Listen! See, someone went out to sow.

4   And it happened during the sowing that one fell on the path; and the birds came and devoured it.

5   And another fell on rock, where there was not much earth, and it sprouted at once, because it did not have deep ground under it.

6   And when the sun rose it was scorched and, because it had no roots, it withered.

7   And another fell among thorns. And the thorns grew up and choked it. And it yielded no fruit.

8   And others fell on good ground and yielded fruit; they sprouted and grew and bore thirtyfold, sixtyfold, and a hundredfold.

9   And he said: Anyone with ears to hear, listen.

10   And when he was alone those who were with him, with the Twelve, asked him about the parables.

11   And he said to them: To you has been revealed the mystery of the kingdom of God! But to those who remain outside, everything is said in parables,

12   so that they may see with their eyes and yet not recognize it, and hear with their ears and yet not understand, lest they repent and be forgiven.

13   And he said to them: You do not understand this parable; how will you all comprehend all the parables?

14   The sower sows the word.

15   These are those on the path: The word is sown among them and as soon as they hear it the Satan comes immediately and takes away the word that has been sown in them.

16 And these are they that are sown on the rock: When they hear the word they receive it immediately and with joy.

17 But they have no roots in themselves; they are superficial. Then when they come under pressure or are persecuted because of the word, they are tripped up immediately.

18 And there are others who are sown among thorns: These are they who have heard the word,

19 and the cares of the world and the weight of riches and the desire for all other things push their way in and choke the word, and it bears no fruit.

20 And these are they who are sown on good ground: They hear the word, receive it, and bear fruit, thirtyfold, sixtyfold, and a hundredfold.

21 And he said to them: Is light made in order to be put under a bushel or under the bed? No, but so that it may be put on the lampstand!

22 Nothing is concealed that will not be revealed; and nothing is hidden that will not be made known.

23 Anyone with ears to hear should listen.

24 And he said to them: Pay attention to what you hear. By the measure with which you measure it will be measured to you, and more than this.

25 Whoever has, will be richly rewarded, and who has nothing will lose everything.

. . .

33 And in many such parables he spoke the word to them, as they were able to hear it.

34 Without parables he did not speak to them; when they were alone, he explained everything to his disciples.

I understand Mark 4:1-34 to be a literary unit that must be read within its context. Only for the sake of clarity do I devote a special chapter to the two parables of the seed sown and the mustard seed (Mark 4:26-29; 4:30-32), but I am reading them in the context of Mark 4:1-34.

SOCIAL-HISTORICAL ANALYSIS

A social-historical analysis is necessary here, both for the imagery in the parable and for the basic theme of this discourse of Jesus: hearing the word. The text takes as its subject a failed hearing and a successful hearing. Failed hearing is first addressed in the parable (4:3-7) and afterward in a Jesus saying with a scriptural quotation, this latter addressed only to the disciples (4:11b-12). The explanation of the parable (4:14-19) and a closing image also refer to failed hearing (4:25b). Successful hearing is also present in every part of this discourse of Jesus: in 4:8, 11a, 20, 24, 25a, 34. As a whole the discourse is to be read as an appeal for hearing, for that appeal extends throughout the speech: vv. 3, 9, 23, 24. The disciples' understanding is not yet a successful hearing; they ask about the meaning of the parables (4:10) and receive additional explanations (4:13-20, 34). The appeal for hearing is thus directed to the crowd that is addressed, to the circle of Jesus' followers, and to the readers of the text, or rather to those who hear Jesus' speech from the lips of later preachers. In what follows I will not always refer to the distinction between Jesus' situation as depicted in the text and that of the addressees of the text, but I will always presuppose it. The addressees are challenged at both levels to hear the word.

A Successful Hearing of the Word

The word (*logos* appears eight times in 4:14-20) that is to be heard is Jesus' word (4:33) in which the kingdom of God is revealed by Godself (4:11, 21-22). I read the passive *dedotai* in 4:11 as a *passivum divinum,* a circumlocution for God's action. Jesus is the teacher of the word of God (4:2), and his parables are revelations of the word of God. Birger Gerhardsson wrote an important essay on this text in which he shows that the *Shemaʿ Israel,* "Hear, O Israel," the daily prayer of Jewish men (and women?), represents the basis of Jesus' teaching about "hearing."[1]

I will quote this prayer here in the shortened version[2] in Mark 12:29, 30: "Hear, O Israel; Adonai, our God, is one. And you shall love Adonai, your God, with your whole heart and your whole life and your whole mind and your whole strength" (Deut 6:4-5). I see references to the *Shemaʿ Israel* both in the appeals for hearing and indirectly in the verses that speak of failure to hear (4:14-19). We may conclude from this that successful hearing is the kind of hearing intended by the *Shemaʿ Israel*: a hearing that includes the commitment of the entire person, a successful life in relationship to God. In social-historical terms, then, we should ask what such a hearing is in the sense intended in the Gospel of Mark. In Mark 4 itself successful hearing is only depicted in images: in the abundant fruit of the seeds that fall on good ground (4:8, 20). But the depiction of the failure in 4:14-19 permits us to draw the contrary conclusion: Successful hearing is resisting the Satan (4:14), not going astray when pressure and persecution threaten one's life and existence (4:17), and not allowing one's way of life to be determined by "this world," the chasing after wealth and other objects of greed (4:19). The gospel as a whole develops this content of successful hearing, successful living before God. In the sense of the text the word that is to be listened to is God's Torah. Jesus is the teacher of the word of God; he instructs people about how Torah is to be heard today, in the present situation. For the rich man in Mark 10:17-22 this means not only living according to the Decalogue, but also selling all his possessions and giving the proceeds to the poor (10:21). Mark 4:19 and Mark 10:17-22 both rest on a critical analysis of the money economy, whose lordship over people and whose character as the cause of *pleonexia,* "greed," is subjected to a fundamental critique in postbiblical Jewish and early Christian tradition.[3] The communities whose experiences are given expression in the Gospel of Mark suffer under the destructive power of *pleonexia,* which prevents people from living with the word of God.

Mark 4:17 relates to the pressure of persecution that is thematized throughout Mark's gospel. Peter goes astray because of the fear of persecution he experiences during Jesus' trial (14:67-72). But it is clear to those who hear and read the Gospel of Mark that the disciples who, for fear of death, have fled before Roman persecution (Mark 14:50-52) have nevertheless become fathers and mothers of faith.

The Disciples' Hearing and Understanding

In Mark 8:14-20 the struggle of the disciples over hearing the word in their situation is again developed at length. They have eyes to see that five loaves were enough for five thousand people, and yet they do not see; they have ears to hear, and yet they do not hear. "Are your hearts hardened?" asks Jesus (8:17). There is no immediate answer to his critical questions (see also 8:20). To the very end of the gospel (16:8) we read of the disciples' fear and failure. And yet these are the ones with whom the readers and hearers are to identify. That is the unique quality of this gospel, not to be found in Matthew and Luke. Jesus' critical question in 4:13, "How will you all understand all the parables?" is absent in Matthew and Luke. This critical question by Jesus is not about doubting his disciples' comprehension, but their ability to hear, to understand, to shape their lives entirely according to God's will. The Gospel of Mark lets us glimpse one situation of Christian communities after 70 c.e., when disciples of Jesus are feeling themselves extremely threatened.[4] Their lifestyle brings on them hatred and persecution. Even members of their families (13:9-13) are handing them over to the Roman authorities.

In Mark 4:10-13 Jesus addresses the broadest circle of his disciples: "To you the mystery of the kingdom of God has been revealed." Julius Kögel has called this statement a "shout of jubilation."[5] It can be compared, for example, to Matt 13:16 (and Luke 10:23): "Happy your eyes, because they see, and your ears, because they hear!" But in Mark 4:13 this is followed by the critical question whether they will see and hear anything at all. This tension is not a self-contradiction in the text, but rather reality in the lives of the people discernible in Mark's gospel. God's kingdom has been revealed to them, but they have to fight hard to hear and do the word of God.

Failed Hearing

Who, then, are "those outside" (4:11)? Their fate is sealed. A great deal of exegetical effort has been expended on lightening the severity of Mark 4:12 and Isa 6:9-10. But both the Hebrew text of Isaiah and Mark 4:12 are clear in their language: The people (Isaiah) or those "outside" (Mark) hear the word, but they are not willing to accept it, to live by it. They are hardened, unrepentant.[6] Their hardening is by divine purpose (*hina* and *mēpote* are to be read as indicating purpose).[7] Repentance and divine forgiveness are impossible for them. I will here discuss this idea only with regard to Mark (and not Isaiah). In the context of the Gospel of Mark those "outside" are those on whom the final sentence will be pronounced at the last divine judgment. The disciples, whose hearts could be hardened (4:13; 8:17) are called by Jesus to repentance. Mark 4:1-34 is this preaching of repentance by Jesus the teacher of Torah and Jesus the prophet, who cries out that now is the time for repentance. "The time is fulfilled and the kingdom of God is at hand; repent and believe the Gospel," as the Gospel of Mark summarizes the message of Jesus at the very beginning (Mark 1:14-15). It is addressed to the people, to the disciples, to people from among the nations like the Syrophoenician woman (Mark 7:24-30), to the Roman centurion who heads the execution squad (Mark 15:39). Now is the hour (*kairos*) for repentance. No one is denied hearing; God's call is public (4:21, 22). The light is on the lampstand, not under the bed. But the call to hear is combined with a clear announcement that life before God can also go completely astray. God's judgment will speak a final sentence on those who have acted wickedly (7:23). From a social-historical point of view Mark 4:11-12 is an expression of what has been experienced in people who refuse to follow the *Shemaʿ Israel* and who likewise reject Jesus' call to repentance. This experience with people who, with full knowledge, reject the word of God is interpreted here: It is God's will that such a thing should happen; it is not the end of the Gospel, the good news of God. The perspective on those "outside" is that of the God who is at work.[8] God will pass judgment, and no one else. Jesus, those who are his, the people, the nations—for them it is the time of teaching, calling, and hearing, the time of repentance. The "outsiders" are here an eschatological concept. The experience of people who reject the message is present. But the judgment on them is God's business and God's alone. Thus Mark 4:11-12 does not permit anyone to judge or condemn another human being or group of human beings as the "outsiders."

Successful and failed hearing—both can only be evaluated by God at the judgment. Now is the *kairos,* the hour of repentance and of struggle for true life according to God's will under the conditions imposed by Roman persecution, the money economy, and the other difficulties of life for subject peoples in the Roman empire. The disciples' situation is no different from that of the crowd to which Jesus preaches.[9] The mystery of the kingdom of God has been revealed also to the crowd, and the cry of jubilation is for them, too.

Why does Jesus then give his own an additional explanation of his teaching (*epelyen*, 4:34)? This additional explanation furnishes them with no special revelation, no privileges in their relationship to God. It offers them a further instruction from Jesus, the teacher of Torah, as is shown, for example, by the teaching to the disciples in 10:10-12. Moreover, this *epilysis* is not a resolution of the parable imagery in an allegorical or nonillustrative interpretation, as is too often supposed.

In the preceding social-historical analysis of Mark 4:1-34 I have made a number of exegetical decisions that I want to list in detail, because most exegetes of this text take a different tack.

Mark 4:10-12 is almost without exception regarded as a parable "theory," according to which the parables are veiled speech, obscure discourse requiring additional explanation. Against this tradition of interpretation, to this point Julius Kögel[10] and Brad H. Young[11] alone, and without much success, have pointed to the clear text of Isa 6:9-10 and Mark 4:12. The parables enable hearing and seeing, but they are rejected by hearing ears and seeing eyes. According to Mark 4:11 and 4:33, in this view, parables are Jesus' method of teaching precisely because they are easy to understand.[12]

Another exegetical decision touches on the relationship between Mark 4:3-8, the parable of the sower, and the interpretation of that parable in 4:14-20. Since the end of the nineteenth century the parable has quite often been seen as a "genuine" Jesus parable and the interpretation as subsequent and inappropriately allegorical. I consider it necessary to read Mark 4:(13), 14-20 as a homogeneous component of the account of the discourse in Mark 4:1-34 not only for reasons of literary method, but also in light of the history of Jewish parable culture, whether oral or written. It does not follow a parable theory that distinguishes between parable and allegory. The *meshalim* of Jewish tradition, besides fictional narratives from the lives of kings, other people, and living beings, can also make use of linguistic symbols or metaphors. David Stern calls the distinction between allegory and parable in the Jesus tradition and the other *meshalim* of the Jewish tradition into question and criticizes the presuppositions associated with this distinction as inappropriate: "The terms allegory and parable, as they have figured in past scholarship, are simply not relevant to understanding the mashal and its tradition."[13] Scholars like Gerhardsson[14] or Young,[15] influenced by the history of Jewish *meshalim,* had already, and correctly, criticized Jülicher's parable theory and its consequences for the relationship between 4:3-8 and 4:14-20. Mark 4:14-20 follows no parable theory of any kind. The meaning of the images shifts back and forth within a single sentence. If human beings are the seed, is the fate of the plants the fate of human beings—or is the word the seed, so that people are the ground and the fate of the plants is the fate of the word among humans? Still, despite this "disorder" (measured by some theory or other) the meaning of the content is quite clear. The fate of the plants is the fate of the word among human beings, and thereby also the human fate. It does not make sense to speak of an allegory here. I understand Mark 4:14-20 as the application of the parable in 4:3-8 to the contemporary situation, using part of the imagery of the parable. In light of rabbinic parable culture, Mark 4:14-20 can be compared to the *nimshal,* the "explanation or solution, usually beginning with the conjunction *kakh,* 'similarly,' that accompanies virtually every mashal recorded in midrashic literature.... The mashal is to some extent allegorical. But the mashal is allegorical—or as I would prefer to call it, referential—only to the extent that it must allude to the ad hoc situation which gives it a concrete meaning."[16] Mark 4:14-20 accomplishes this clarification of the concrete situation that Mark 4:3-8 applies to.

In the next sections I will further explain my decision not to identify two groups of people in 4:10-12 (disciples versus those "outside"), but instead to read the text eschatologically. The decision to find in the parable and its interpretation not four types of people but the contrast between failed and successful hearing is based not only on my understanding of these texts as eschatological texts of hope, but also on my observation of the literary structure of the narrative, which focuses on vv. 8 and 20 as a brilliant climax in contrast to the preceding speech about failed hearing.[17] The internal connection with the *Shema^c Israel* and its idea of successful hearing also speaks in favor of this interpretation. From a social-historical point of view vv. 3-7 and vv. 14-19 do not speak about different hearers of the word, but present different aspects of life reflected in the Gospel of Mark—persecution, pressure, and the power of mammon in the experience of Jewish, Jewish Christian, and Gentile Christian people, probably after the war of 66–70 C.E.

The Parable Imagery: Sowing and Yield

In New Testament research on the parable of the sower there is a general discussion about how the loss of seed that the sower takes into account is traceable to a highly uneconomical method of planting used in first-century Palestine, as in Arab agriculture of the nineteenth and twentieth centuries. People sowed unplowed ground and then plowed it, with the result that weeds and footpaths were plowed under as well. Against this theory—although it maintains itself persistently among theologians—one must object, with those knowledgeable about ancient farming methods, because such waste is unthinkable alongside the refined techniques of land improvement and methods for increasing the harvest yield that existed in ancient agricultural practice.[18] Furthermore, sowing on unplowed ground, observed among Arab farmers in the nineteenth and twentieth centuries, was misinterpreted by theologians like Gustaf Dalman[19] and Joachim Jeremias, who were influenced by the parable of the sower. There are more objective accounts of Arab agriculture on Lake Genesareth[20] that say that the fall sowing is done on unplowed ground if the field "had lain fallow as a summer pasture after the last spring rains" or had recently yielded a summer harvest—not at all an uneconomical method.

In addition, in the parable the loss of seed is by no means described as very great; this impression has arisen only because of the emphatic depiction of the negative fate of the seed. Given the shortage of good agricultural land in

Palestine, and indeed in the whole Mediterranean basin in antiquity, a certain loss of seed had to be accepted, even when the best planting techniques were used.[21] The parable of the sower hints at a minimal field size, since, as we may gather from the parable itself, with the swing of the sower's arm some kernels fell on the path at the edge of the field, which of course was not plowed with the rest. There are also archaeological findings of such miniature fields in first-century Palestine.[22] The thorns at the edge or as islands in the field (there is evidence of both) and the sowing of patches with a rocky base also point to the shortage of plowland. The parable thus documents not an uneconomical method of planting, but the critical economic situation of the people in Palestine at this time, who had to cultivate the tiniest bits of ground, even when they contained rocky areas. This observation, incidentally, is repeatedly confirmed in the nature parables and imagery of the Synoptic Gospels—that nature is observed from the perspective of people who wrest their food from it with an effort. Trees that bear no fruit are cut down and burned; even the sparrows are eaten, and there is scarcely any perception of nature that lacks an economic basis—with one important exception in Matt 6:25-33 *par.*

With regard to another aspect of the parable, we must also inquire about the relationship between the parable imagery and reality: the abundant yield. I will simply mention my conclusion here, without being able to pursue the discussion in detail. The parable thinks of fruitfulness per seed, a consideration that is also used in other texts to demonstrate great fertility, for example of a particular region. The stages (thirty-, sixty-, hundredfold) are occasioned by narrative technique. A hundredfold yield per seed grain is also cited elsewhere as attesting abundant, but not fantastic fertility. The parable thus keeps within the framework of imaginable reality, even though—as regards the rich yield—not within that of daily experience. Such a rich harvest is unusual, an exception that causes astonishment.

"Whoever Has . . ."

In Mark 4:25 a saying that describes the logic of the interest economy is applied to the hearing of the word. In Matt 25:29 it is placed on the lips of the rich man who forces his slaves to increase his wealth through profiteering. While uttering this saying, he takes back the money he had "entrusted" to the third slave, who had refused to cooperate. There are ancient parallels for the use of this saying to characterize the money economy.[23] In Mark 4:25 the saying is applied to an idea found in biblical and rabbinical wisdom: God gives wisdom only to those who possess wisdom: "Give to the wise, and they will become wiser still; teach the righteous and they will gain in learning" (Prov 9:9; cf. 1:5).[24] This tradition serves to encourage people to go on learning always. It contains nothing of the cynicism in the saying about the money economy that is fully evident in Mark 4:25.

Midrash Qoheleth 1:7 offers an interesting parallel to Mark 4:25 because it also uses an example from the money economy to clarify a Wisdom concept:

> A matron asked R. Jose b. Halaphta and said to him: "What does it mean: 'He gives wisdom to the wise and knowledge to the intelligent' (Deut 2:21)? Should not the scripture have said: 'He gives wisdom to those who are not wise and knowledge to those who are not intelligent?'" He answered: "A parable. If two people come to you to borrow money, one rich and the other poor, to which one will you lend, to the rich or to the poor?" She said: "To the rich one." He said: "And why?" She answered: "If the rich one loses my money, he has something from which to pay me; but if the poor one loses my money, wherewith will he pay me?" He said to her: "And will your ears not hear what you say with your mouth?" If God gave wisdom to the foolish, they would sit and speak of it in the toilets and theaters and bathhouses; God has given wisdom only to the wise, and they sit and speak of it in the synagogues and houses of learning."[25]

Wisdom is not to be made available for misuse by the foolish, by people who live according to the logic of the Roman empire; this is what is meant by characterizing them in terms of toilets, theaters, and bathhouses, the public institutions of the worldly empire.[26] There is a similar thought in Matt 7:6 (not throwing pearls before swine, etc.).

What does it mean that in Mark 4:25 (and the parallels in Luke 8:18 and Matt 13:12) and *Midr. Qoheleth* 1:7 the brutal logic of the money economy is used to explain God's acts in relation to human beings? The cynicism of the money economy is precisely *not* repeated in the situation of people who hear the word of God and go on hearing it and growing in their relationship to God (Mark 4:25). There thus arises, as with many parables (e.g., Matt 25:14-30) that describe the brutality of the money economy, a tension between the imagery and the situation to which the parable is applied. This tension leads to a twofold message: God gives more and more to those who listen—but how different is God's logic from that of the money economy! After all, it has just been clearly said that the audience is suffering from the money economy and its contradiction of God's word (Mark 4:19).

ECCLESIOLOGICAL INTERPRETATION

Two models of interpretation dominate in regard to the parable of the sower (Mark 4:3-8): one in terms of Jesus, the sower, and one in terms of "many types of ground," four types of people in relationship to the word. Both these models can be found in the titles placed over the parable in Bible translations ("The Parable of the Sower," "The Parable of the Soils").

In the interpretation in terms of Jesus, he is understood to be the primeval model of all preachers whose words ("seed") also fail to succeed. These interpretations in terms of speaking without good result or with success vary according to the evaluation of the lack of success. "The normal success of the word of God is not to succeed."[27] An example of an interpretation that considers lack of success a minor matter can be found in Hans Weder's work.[28] A little bit is lost, of course, but the description of this lack of success serves to underline the good outcome, "most of it, in fact, yields fruit."

A variant of this tradition of interpretation foregrounds christological content. The loss of seed in the parable is said to express the inevitable danger involved in the sending of Jesus: "The affirmation of the dangerous sending, however, rests on the knowledge that in the danger, and not only because of it, the meaning of the sending is accomplished."[29] On the basis of their literary-critical method, John Donahue and Daniel Harrington come to a similar result: "The manner in which the climactic verse (4:8) explodes, after the lull of the three previous verses, conveys the advent of the kingdom in Jesus' teaching and activity (1:14-15) as something that shatters the way by which life normally operates."[30] The Markan theology of the cross is "the mystery of the kingdom of God" (4:11), "the paradox of God's will manifest in the cross of Jesus." "Insiders" in the sense of 4:11 are those who accept this will of God, and "outsiders" are those who reject it; even "'disciples' may become 'outsiders.'"

The relevance of the theology of the cross for the Gospel of Mark is clear, but we must ask what function the theology of the cross serves in these christological interpretations of Mark 4:3-8 or 4:1-20. Here the affirmation of the theology of the cross becomes a criterion of true hearing. But in this way a dogmatic definition of the church is set at the center of the interpretation. For Donahue and Harrington the "context of Jewish rejection of Christian claims" is the implicit context of the discussion.[31] Thus this interpretation perpetuates an opposition between insiders and outsiders in ecclesiological terms and in regard to a theology of the cross, which already has a long Christian history. The blind synagogue is implicitly the counterimage to the insiders who accept the cross of Christ.

The interpretation in terms of Jesus, the sower, and the extent of the success, or lack of success, of his preaching has the same basic structures. It is not God who decides about people's listening or acting, but their yes or no to Jesus' (or Christian) preaching.

I will take Gerhardsson's interpretation in "The Parable of the Sower and Its Interpretation"[32] as an example of the reading of the parable in terms of four types of people and their hearing. Measured by the contemporary scholarly discussion, it was an especially early and outstanding attempt to overcome anti-Judaism and an ecclesiological reading. He understands the four fates of the seed to be representative of four timeless types of hearers (175, on Matt 13:18-23;

181, on Mark 4:13-20). The successful fate of the seed refers to "the true members of the covenant" (182; see also 178). "But they are not referred to as any particular historical group, as 'the church' over against 'the synagogue' . . . but as an existential category" (179). He understands the insiders and the outsiders as two groups within Israel (178), the blind crowd in contrast to those who hear and do (174, 179). Despite his admirable attempt to avoid anti-Judaism, he constructs an internal Jewish contrast between two groups modeled on the structure of the traditional ecclesiological interpretation.

The ecclesiological interpretation is independent of historical methods and is, even in the face of hermeneutical mistrust as shown by Gerhardsson, and also by Donahue and Harrington,[33] the scarlet thread that runs through and links these and other exegeses of Mark 4:3-8.

Something similar can be said of Mark 4:10-12. The traditional interpretation understood the statement "To you the mystery of the kingdom of God has been revealed" (4:11) as a shout of jubilation addressed to the male disciples— there was no thought of female disciples, of course. Implicitly or explicitly, the shout of jubilation for the disciples was understood to be a promise of salvation for the Christian church. In contrast, "those outside" became the Jewish people that God had hardened, the blind synagogue. As an example of such an interpretation let me point to Kögel: "The religious knowledge of Israel, what had previously been given to the people in divine revelation and as their religious treasure . . . is now definitively lost to them."[34]

In *Mark's Audience*,[35] Mary Ann Beavis carefully reflects on her methods. She combines "literary criticism" with a "sociological" method that investigates the "social setting" of Mark's gospel, in this case especially the (Jewish) Hellenistic background of education and "literary culture" (10). By observing how intricately 4:10-12 is interwoven with the whole Gospel of Mark and by inquiring about those who hear the gospel (the "audience"), she is able to interrupt the dualistic contrast between disciples/church and Israel/synagogue. "It is unlikely that a community . . . concerned to preach the gospel to all nations (13.10) . . . wished to hide its light under a bushel! The Marcan sect, which defined itself over and against society, had nevertheless to remain open to 'outsiders'" (170–71). She believes the elements of "mystery" and "enigmatic parables" to be propagandistic, skillful literary means for winning the audience to Jesus. "Like the other esoteric elements in Mark, the use of mystery terminology involves the reader in the story, encouraging him/her to see, hear, and understand the meaning of the life of Jesus" (172–73). But even for Beavis the hearers of the gospel appear as a religiously self-aware group that feels itself superior to the much-criticized disciples in the gospel (97) and that successfully resists Satan (151) "and of whom the son of man will not be ashamed on the last day" (98). She successfully terminates the anti-Judaism of the exegetical tradition,[36] but the triumphant, all-knowing church is replaced by a triumphant, all-knowing "audience," the hearers of the gospel.

Joel Marcus regards Mark 4:11-12 as a contrast between Israel, which had refused the Messiah, and the Markan community.[37] God has rejected Israel, says the community. But that is not the final word. In 4:21-22 the truth is again revealed, and blindness and condemnation do not have the last word. Thus the way to repentance is again open to Israel.

I will not discuss the exegetical plausibility of these interpretations in this book. My concern is to acknowledge the aftereffects of the ecclesiological tradition of interpretation. Except for the older interpretation by Kögel (1915), I have selected newer interpretations that reveal some hermeneutical discomfort with the traditional reading of 4:10-12. For Marcus, Mark 4:10-12 is exclusivistic and deterministic, but it is relativized by Mark 4:21-22. For Beavis the contrast between insiders and outsiders is only apparently exclusionary, but the Gospel of Mark is aimed at the audience that knows it is on the safe side at the divine judgment. Donahue and Harrington's conclusion was similar; they maintain an ecclesiological interpretation in spite of their unease with the exclusivism and determinism they see in Mark 4:10-12.

A reflection on the methods with which the texts have been investigated needs to be augmented by a hermeneutical reflection on the tradition of interpretation. Otherwise the internal connection between anti-Judaism and triumphalistic ecclesiology will not be overcome, not even when anti-Judaism is avoided. It has been shown to be necessary to discuss anti-Judaism explicitly and with all its ecclesiological consequences.

ESCHATOLOGICAL INTERPRETATION

Brad H. Young consistently locates Mark 4:1-20 within its Jewish context. He reads the parable of the sower and its interpretation as analogous to Jewish texts that characterize four types of Torah students. Still more important, like Gerhardsson, he emphasizes the connection between hearing and doing the Torah. Young does not reflect on how the right hearing and doing of the Torah in the sense of the text can be recognized. The followers of Jesus "hear the word and do it. They can understand the mystery because of their decision to obey. But for others the message is heard only in simple parables, so easy to understand but so difficult to put into practice."[38] (As mentioned above, Young understands the parables, according to 4:10-12, not as obscure discourse but as a way of speaking that is easy to understand.) The mysteries of God are understood through the doing of the Torah. "The kingdom of heaven means that people can acknowledge his reign and receive the power to dedicate their lives to God."[39] I would add only a few additional remarks: (1) The people also trust in God as their future and the righteous judge of human deeds. (2) The field that brings abundant fruit is an image of hope in the face of a reality that makes it hard to be disciples of Jesus, to do the Torah. (3) A social-historical analysis of the situation of the Markan community can explain the critical situation of followers of Jesus as seen by Mark. In this way it becomes clear why the struggle to hear and do the word is so severe.

How should we imagine the reaction of those listening? Hints of it are the repeated challenges to hear, to hear and to see. What is to be heard, and the idea that hearing and doing belong together—these are familiar to all concerned, including Gentile Christians, from Jewish tradition. But how hard it is to hear and to see in a situation as we behold it in Mark 13 or in the figure of Peter: That is what the parable and its interpretation tell. In this situation the promise of fruitfulness is a consolation and an encouragement. Mark 4:24-25 is, indeed, not the end of this discourse of Jesus according to Mark, but it is a shining promise: God will give to you far beyond the measure with which you yourselves have measured.

In the struggle of the disciples in Mark—who live in a world that makes it almost impossible for them to live according to Jesus' word, according to his teaching of the Torah—I see a narrative parallel to Paul's lament over the power of sin and his trust in the love of God. The internal relatedness—within which still other texts, for example 4 Ezra, should be included—rests not on a unified doctrine but on the comparable experiences of Jewish people and their Gentile Christian sisters and brothers, all of whom suffer from the fact that it is hard to live according to Torah under the conditions imposed by the Roman empire.

FOR FURTHER READING

Birger Gerhardsson, "The Parable of the Sower and Its Interpretation"
Julius Kögel, *Der Zweck der Gleichnisse Jesu im Rahmen seiner Verkündigung*
Luise Schottroff, "Verheißung und Erfüllung aus der Sicht einer Theologie nach Auschwitz," "Wir sind Samen und keine Steinchen," and "'We Are Seeds, Not Pebbles'"
Brad H. Young, *The Parables*

PART 2

IN SEARCH
OF A NON-DUALISTIC
PARABLE THEORY

8

Social-Historical Interpretation
of the Bible in the Framework
# of Contextual Theologies

Every interpretation of the Bible rests on hermeneutical presuppositions that are often not explicitly discussed, because for a long time there was neither a scholarly nor an ecclesial tradition of such discussion. It was first of all the liberation theologies that made a point of naming the social context of those who interpret texts. The methodological necessity of this reflection, however, has still been acknowledged only in marginal fields of scholarly interpretation. Besides, when it takes place it often possesses all the charm of an immigration form: white, female, middle-class, Western European, and so forth.

This contextualization of one's own interpretation is not thorough enough, as feminist and Jewish-Christian discourse in particular have shown. These approaches have brought to light presuppositions that, for the most part, have influenced Christian biblical interpretation for hundreds of years.

I see four fields of hermeneutical assumptions that require critical attention: (1) the ideology of Christian *superiority* over other religions, especially Judaism; (2) *dualisms* in various areas of theology; (3) assumptions that underlie Christian notions of *guilt and sin* and human suffering through violence; and (4) orientation toward a "Christian" duty *to maintain* the social status quo and its *structures of power.*

IDEOLOGY OF SUPERIORITY

The presupposition that the Christian religion is superior to all others—and combined with it the presupposition that "the church" receives a promise of divine salvation in the biblical texts—dominates biblical interpretation, as we have already seen above. Now perhaps, at the beginning of the third millennium of the Common Era, there are many Christian people who would no longer want to say that Christianity is superior to all other religions, but in biblical interpretation the idea persists that in Mark 4:11 Jesus is addressing his disciples and thus, indirectly, the church: "To you has been given the secret of the kingdom of God." Or, to take another example: The kingdom of God is taken away from Israel and given to the church, the people that yields fruit (that is, the kingdom of God) (Matt 21:43).

Even when such an "ecclesiological" interpretation of the biblical text is qualified by postmodern discomfort or presented in a diluted form, it continues to dominate the interpretation of the New Testament. The conclusion to be drawn is that any implicit claim to power, any assertion of superiority, must be reflected upon: white, female, middle-class, Western European, Christian, and the opinion that Christianity is superior to other religions—or not. This contextualization thus calls for an additional and *explicit* critique of hermeneutical models. At that point we have taken the first step in overcoming the notion of superiority. Applied to the examples cited above, this offers two possibilities: I can describe the biblical texts of Mark 4:11 and Matt 21:43 *themselves* as legitimating power structures, or I can say this of broad swaths of the *tradition of interpretation* of these texts. Thus the critical question: What power structures could the Gospels of Mark or Matthew wish to legitimate? Was there, in their time, already a Christian group that saw itself as the recipient of divine salvation, in contradistinction to other religions, especially Judaism? The ecclesiological tradition of interpretation, or its critique, when faulting the text itself as the expression of a triumphalistic religious self-consciousness, makes a historical presupposition: that Christianity had separated from Judaism at the time the texts originated. A variant of this presupposition is the understanding of Jesus' message itself as a proclamation of salvation already divorced from Judaism. Social-historical interpretation of the Bible, in light of the hermeneutical presupposition that underlies the ecclesiological tradition of interpretation, implies three things: (1) a critique of this hermeneutical presupposition; (2) the development of a hermeneutical alternative; and (3) the establishment of a historical hypothesis about the origins of the Jesus movement in Palestine and the Diaspora as a movement within Judaism and a hypothesis concerning the process by which Christianity and Judaism separated. The hermeneutical alternative with which I am working is the interpretation of New Testament texts as eschatological.[1] The separation from Judaism, in my view, only occurred after the end of the second Jewish-Roman war in 135 C.E. With the expulsion of the Jewish population from Jerusalem, the Jewish Christians of Jerusalem were also expelled, and as a result Jewish Christianity lost its significance within Gentile Christianity.[2] After that, Judaism was seen by Christians, for the most part, only from the outside.

Through Jewish-Christian, feminist, and liberation-theological discussions, further hermeneutical assumptions have come to light that rest essentially on the same level as the ecclesiological assumption. In the sketch that follows I am concerned to summarize these hermeneutical assumptions systematically in order that they may yield the questions that can be posed to Christian theologies, and so that alternatives within contextual theologies and social-historical biblical interpretation can be developed.

DUALISM AND ESCHATOLOGY

I use the concept of *dualism* to describe oppositions whose content is a set of relationships that are based on violence or domination and/or are associated with hierarchical values. Such dualisms, based on Western philosophical traditions and Christian theologies, are, for example, soul–body, culture–nature, spirit–matter, male–female, and *agapē–eros* (love-of-neighbor–erotic love). As a rule they are traced to Platonism and Hellenism, but they should more properly be associated with Descartes.[3]

Anthropological dualism has influenced biblical interpretation almost seamlessly in the exegesis of 1 Cor 15:44. The *sōma pneumatikon* is understood as a "spiritual body" (Luther's translation) in dualistic opposition to the *sōma psychikon*, and thus as a nonphysical "body."[4] This dualism evaluates mortality, transitoriness—and often even being born—as a consequence of human distance from God, and therefore as an evil condition.

Anthropological dualism is tied up with a dualism of temporal modes: before physical death and after physical death. Thus, in terms of this hermeneutical framework, resurrection cannot be an experience *during* a person's life (if at all). Anyone who asserted such a thing is disqualified as heretical: see the tradition of interpretation of 1 Corinthians 15 and 2 Tim 2:18. A further expansion of the dualism of temporal modes is the contrast between "this world" or "this eon" as the realm of evil and "eternity" as the realm of good, of salvation. Thus most interpretations of New Testament eschatology are constructed on a dualistic evaluation of present and future; in addition, they use the idea of *linear time* as their framework. So arose the model of imminent expectation of the end and delay of the parousia. I find that the dualistic interpretation of eschatology has been overcome, thus far, primarily in womanist theology.[5] I would also mention, as theological and philosophical teachers of a non-dualistic eschatology, Ernst Bloch, Johann Baptist Metz, Jürgen Ebach, and Rosemary Radford Ruether.[6] I regard the eschatology of the New Testament and early Christianity as a mythical way of expressing an interpretation of the present experience of believers in relationship to God. Speaking eschatologically means speaking about God in relationship. That the kingdom of God has come near is not to be interpreted as an expectation of the end of history, nor as an expectation that it will end in the near future (i.e., linear time). Jesus' statement in Mark 1:15, rather, is an expression of the basis of every relationship to God: God is near.

A difficulty for the further development of an eschatology in this sense is the fact that in Western Christianity two dominant models of perception of Christian eschatology stand as enormous stumbling blocks: the fundamentalist idea of eschatology and that of biblical scholarship since the end of the nineteenth century. Scholarly interpretation of New Testament eschatology since the end of the nineteenth century has been shaped by a linear notion of time that has been accepted as obvious: Jesus expected the reign of God in the foreseeable future. His expectation was disappointed. It proved to be in error. Later generations of his disciple communities that shaped the Gospels in the form we now have them were therefore faced with the necessity of living with the extension of time and of explaining the delay of the parousia. This model of interpretation is so dominant that even today it shapes the primary current of New Testament exegesis, even if the exegetes deliberately distance themselves from the methods of historical criticism.

The fundamentalist model of interpretation is employed, especially in the United States, by ultraconservative Christian groups to threaten outsiders with divine punishment and reinforce insiders' assurance of election. It is thus used ecclesiologically. It has also found entry into American political language, for example in President George W. Bush's 2002 expression "axis of evil." This model of interpretation is so powerful in the United States that it indirectly dominates the hermeneutics of liberal theology as well. The noneschatological Jesus—Jesus the Wisdom teacher and social prophet, the model presented especially by the Jesus Seminar but most prominently by Marcus Borg[7]—is an inversion of fundamentalism. Eschatology that could mean something different from what the fundamentalists assert is not even considered. Thus the interpretive superiority of the fundamentalists is indirectly affirmed when Jesus is understood as noneschatological.

The interpretive tradition with which I am connecting, in contrast, has a difficult stance precisely because these two dominant models are strongly rooted in both church and university. Nevertheless, I have not abandoned hope that the relevance of this alternative will ultimately be recognized and more broadly received.

Anthropological dualism is the basis for Christian *body politics* in all its phases: sexual ethics, understanding of the Lord's Supper (the Body of Christ as metaphor), and economics, to the extent that an economy of God is not deliberately considered as a possible alternative in this world. Anthropological and theological dualism result in *dualistic theories of religion, symbolism, and metaphor* in which the divine is assigned to a sphere separate from the real life of human bodies.

Metaphors play a double role in the overall fabric of dualism. First, the metaphorization of words that have real content absolves interpretations from the necessity of social and political consequences. Thus the Gospel of the Poor becomes a gospel of the metaphorically "poor," those who stand with empty hands before God. Second, together with such metaphorization, a dualistic parable theory or metaphor theory can declare the world of human life to be nonessential and can even legitimate power and violence. A good example of this is the third slave in the parable of the so-called talents (Matt 25:14-30): The sharpness of the slave's critique of a destructive economy of interest and money is seen as "impudent" because the story told in the parable is not taken seriously as a critique of the interest and money economy; these are just metaphors—we are only talking about illustrative material. The real meaning of the parable, according to this interpretation, lies in a statement about God's instructions to human beings, who have nothing to do with the illustration, the fictional story told as a parable. Thus God is represented by the slaveowner. The violence of the slaveowner portrayed in the parable is given implicit religious legitimation. In light of such dualistic assumptions a social-historical interpretation of the Bible means: (1) critiquing the dualism in hermeneutical assumptions that generally go unnamed; (2) developing a non-dualistic hermeneutical alternative—a body theology, an eschatology—that must be combined with a theory of religion and metaphor that does not construct a special sphere for religion and relationship to God alongside the human world; and (3) taking the fictional narratives of the parables seriously in their relationship to the world of real life, and giving a nonmetaphorical interpretation to central contents that are de-radicalized by metaphorization. These are, above all, the "Gospel of the Poor" and the "Body of Christ."

In this book, then, I am working with a non-dualistic eschatology, and I understand the parables to be discourse about the kingdom of God, which is already changing the lives of believers. I am following the tradition of a non-dualistic interpretation of eschatology, and I read the Jesus tradition as being closely connected with biblical and postbiblical Jewish apocalyptic.

The more successful the development of Jewish and early Christian eschatology/apocalyptic, the more this tradition is also seen as relevant for contemporary theology. An interpretation of this eschatology from the (supposed) detachment of religious studies remains on the level of mythological ideas and, because of its very basis, cannot attain to an empathetic appreciation of that mythology. The mythology is language about God, a language that even today is irreplaceable.

GUILT AND SUFFERING

The third field of hermeneutical assumptions appears in Christian ideas about guilt, or sin, and human suffering, especially the experience of violence. I see here two fundamental tendencies: the ontologizing of guilt (sin) and suffering and their individualization. Sin and suffering, supposedly part of the "human condition," are thus justified and declared unchangeable. Theological language that expresses itself in generalizing statements about "the human being" before God is incapable of differentiating among culpability, victimization, and complicity. This has led to a situation in which the promise of the forgiveness of sins absolved the Western European perpetrators of colonialism of their guilt without the victims' being heard. Thus the guilt was obscured, covered up.[8] But today theology can only speak responsibly about sin, guilt, and suffering if such discourse is combined with an analysis of the power relationships within society. In this way generalized theological language will give way to a contextualized theology without any claim to universal validity or timelessness. The individualizing of our relationship to God has prevented us from discovering the critical power of the tradition of the community that is the Body of Christ. In particular, the notion of sin has been ontologized and individualized, and thus misused to become an instrument of oppression toward sexuality and the power of resistance. Because we are all sinful we stand before God "with empty hands" and our own strength, in any case, "can do nothing."

In consequence of all this, faith has been confused with passivity and acceptance of injustice; moreover, a willingness to sacrifice that leaves action in the hands of the powerful is confused with the willingness to sacrifice that involves active intervention. Equating sexuality and sin has served for centuries, up to and including the current discussions of abortion, to oppress women's bodies and women's sexuality. At the same time it is a powerful instrument for the imposition of heterosexuality.

It is the duty of a social-historical biblical interpretation to (1) make visible the hidden hermeneutical assumptions; (2) develop a hermeneutical alternative—in this case the contextualization of theology in history and society; and (3) contextualize biblical texts in order to name their liberating or oppressive potential—in relation to concrete social relationships then and now.

Social analysis must encompass all the spheres in which power relationships affect and distort human lives: economics, relationships between the sexes, colonialism, the destruction of nature, the enslavement of human beings (racism), sexuality. Models of social analysis are to be critically reviewed in terms of their unspoken hermeneutical assumptions and applied only conditionally to other historical or present relationships; that is, they must be tested against concrete material. For example, it is a historical mistake to work with the concept of a middle class or middle layer of society when examining the Roman empire. Social-historical biblical interpretation is one version of a contextual theology—applied to biblical traditions. It encompasses all the fields of theological tradition and theological thought, and not only subfields. Its underlying hermeneutical assumptions are alternatives to Western dualism, alternatives that can be rethought and expressed especially in dialogue with the Bible and in the praxis of life.

OBEDIENCE TO AUTHORITY AND THE AVOIDANCE OF THE GOSPEL OF THE POOR

The fourth field of hermeneutical assumptions that, as a rule, is not discussed and that nevertheless influences the interpretation of Scripture consists of an orientation toward maintaining the political and social status quo and avoiding the Gospel of the Poor.

Phrases like "obedience to authority" are scarcely ever spoken positively any more in Western Christianity. The revision of Martin Luther's translation of Rom 13:1 still uses the word *authority,* but a note adds a relativizing explanation: "For Luther the word denotes the ruling authorities and officials of the state."[9] But when the texts containing this word are exegeted, as a rule, obedience to authority is neither explicitly criticized nor called into question by a corresponding interpretation. I will choose a representative example from an exegesis of Mark 12:13-17: "Jesus allows them to pay the tax . . . but goes on to challenge his audience to be as exact in serving God as they are in serving Caesar."[10] In this interpretation the spheres of power of the emperor and God stand equally alongside one another. Obedience to the state and to other authorities, including those of the church, appears as a duty of Christian faith. This model of scriptural interpretation is also found in the exegesis of the corresponding warnings in the New Testament, but also in other contexts, for example, the interpretation of the Roman empire, the representation of Pilate,[11] and the evaluation of the supposed representatives of church offices, especially Paul.[12] The relationship between Paul and "his" communities is interpreted, with very few exceptions, in terms of the model of command and obedience, something that affects even the translation of the biblical text: "But this I must command you . . ." (Revised Luther Version, translating *parakalein,* in 1 Cor 11:17; this is one example among many). In addition, the still broadly influential interpretation of the Lukan double work as apologetic on behalf of Rome, which goes back to Hans Conzelmann in 1954, is a consequence of the plausibility the thesis acquired in the context of the history of Christian theology, with its deference to authority. Obedience to authority as a hermeneutical given, something that is no longer even noticed, has had an enduring effect on the interpretation of parables. God is identified with powerful ruling figures, even those who are cruel, arbitrary, and extremely greedy for money: The king destroys a state because some of the members of its elite have murdered his messengers (Matt 22:7). The king orders a guest who lacks a wedding garment to be bound and cast into the outer darkness (Matt 22:11-13). The slaveowner punishes a slave who has refused to acquire 100 percent profit with the money entrusted to him (Matt 25:14-30). The examples can be multiplied. Not even the most refined metaphor theories have questioned that the "king" who acts, for example, as described in Matt 22:1-13 represents God. The words *homoioun* and *homoios* in parable introductions are understood as "equate," not as "compare"; in the latter case it is possible that *differences* may also play a role. It is often said that parables demand an active reaction and response from the hearers; but if the parable "equates," there is no longer room for reflection and creativity. I can, however, explain the fact that such hideous despots could be understood to represent God: namely, Christian obedience to authority has forced the interpreters to accept such equations. These parables come from the tradition of Jewish critique of imperialism, something that was lost in the ancient church and replaced by obedience to authority, as Chrysostom's interpretation of Matt 22:1-14 (see pp. 38–48 above) already shows.

Skepticism toward this tradition of parable interpretation is the exception: Bertolt Brecht in the *Threepenny Opera,* Nikos Kazantzakis in *The Last Temptation of Christ,* William R. Herzog, Norman K. Gottwald, Richard Rohrbaugh, Amy-Jill Levine, Vicki Balabanski[13]—and a few preachers who find it difficult to locate the Gospel, the Good News, in Matt 25:14-30 (for example).

The avoidance of the Gospel of the Poor is the obverse of obedience to authority. The content of the parables that tell of economic injustice and misuse of power is not connected in the traditional interpretations with the Gospel of the Poor and Jesus' critique of social injustice. Parables tell about agricultural day laborers, tenants, slaves. On the other side, texts appear again and again in the Synoptic Gospels that speak of the necessity of forgiving debts. Indebtedness caused the economically weak to lose their land and resulted in the heaping up of wealth on the other side. How can the Lord's Prayer—". . . as we forgive our debtors"—be prayed while at the same time the slaveowner who expects a 100 percent profit from his store of talents is regarded as a depiction of God? The theological instrument that makes possible this absurdity is a theory of metaphors or of parables that dualistically renders the parable imagery incidental, as I have already shown. In addition, there are other strategies for making the Gospel of the Poor invisible. As regards the parables, they can be studied in interpretations of Luke 12:16-21 and 16:19-31. Greed for money is regarded as an individual moral fault, not as an attitude that is structurally conditioned. But Luke 12:16-21 is not a discussion of a regrettable single instance. Another strategy for avoiding the Gospel of the Poor is the minimization or reinterpretation of traditions that tell of eschatological repentance: "The last will be first." In this way an appeal for almsgiving is read even out of Luke 16:19-31. But the parable speaks of the repentance of the rich who finally orient themselves to Torah.

Traditional Christian Strategies for Avoiding the Gospel of the Poor in the New Testament

These strategies for avoiding the Gospel of the Poor have shaped exegetical discussion in Western scholarship and in many of the churches' theological utterances.

Perceiving greed as an individual moral failure. Rich people are supposed to change their inner relationship toward their riches but are not required to question their complicity in economic structures. Such a strategy is evident in interpretations of Luke 12:13-21 (the "rich fool")—and yet the text describes economic structures that maximize profit.

Presuming the Gospel of the Poor means giving alms. The word *alms* has become old-fashioned, but the thing itself is present in circumlocutions such as "works of mercy." In this strategy the poor are seen as the objects, not the subjects of the Gospel. The implicit, or sometimes even explicit assumption is that the church of early Christianity consisted of people from a middle class for the most part. Sometimes "sharing" means nothing more than an alms that does not cost the giver very much.

Presuming Jesus' command to surrender possessions was intended only for a limited circle, that of the disciples. The construction of two ethics here, one for "normal" church members and one for special groups, for example monks and nuns, is not mentioned anywhere in the New Testament. It can be found, however, in many interpretations of Luke 12:33.

Spiritualizing the Gospel of the Poor. This is incorrectly located in Matt 5:3. The distinction between spiritual and economic poverty makes possible a generalizing of the blessing of the poor into a blessing of all those who are "poor" in any way at all.

Ignoring or reinterpreting the tradition of eschatological repentance in the New Testament. The question is: Shall the poor now sit on the thrones of the formerly powerful (Luke 1:52) and continue their injustice? Critique of liberation theologies as "ideological" and as not serious scholarship arises from this source.

9

Dualism in Parable Theories

In this section I want to question the hermeneutical presuppositions that govern the interpretation of parable narratives in some important contemporary parable theories. The following questions for examining parable theories arise out of my previous analysis of parables and my observations on hermeneutical dualisms:

- How is the relationship of the parable narrative to social reality assessed?
- How is the relationship of the world within the parable to God assessed?

For this investigation I will choose only systems for parable analysis that are helpful in advancing a non-dualistic parable theory, even if they are subject to criticism from this point of view. Older parable research, which also offers a valuable heritage, is nevertheless so thoroughly dualistic in its conception that it is scarcely worth examining from this point of view. Rudolf Bultmann gave a very appropriate assessment of Adolf Jülicher's legacy in the evaluation of parable imagery. Bultmann regarded the "images" in the parables as neutral matter: "In my view the difference between the nature of similitudes and parables on the one hand and allegory on the other is most clearly formulated by saying that the former involve the transference of a judgment (derived from some neutral field) from one sphere to another, which is under discussion."[1] The narratives from daily life (similitudes in the narrower sense) and the narratives of interesting particular cases[2] in the world of human beings and animals (parables) are not intended, according to Bultmann, to say anything about daily life and the world, but to present a judgment about the reign of God. The images in the parables are thus certainly of historical interest, but theologically they are neutral territory. The world of a woman baking bread is thus an aid in interpreting the reign of God. Nothing is said theologically about women who bake bread. God and the world of human life stand, as to content, unrelatedly alongside one another.

Joachim Jeremias also had no theological interest in those narratives, although he developed important social-historical material for many of the parable narratives. He called them "embellishment"[3] and continued working with Jülicher's theory of the *tertium comparationis*.[4] But in this way the "imagery" is only linked to the theological subject at a third level, and it has no theological significance of its own. Jeremias's interest was in recovering the biographical situation within the life of Jesus in which a parable was told. For Jeremias, the relationship between the parable narrative and the world of daily life is uncomplicated. "The hearers find themselves in a familiar scene where everything is so simple and clear . . . that those who hear can say 'Yes, that's how it is.'"[5]

Paul Ricoeur[6] developed a parable theory based on contemporary parable study (by Eberhard Jüngel, Dan O. Via, and others) and linguistic philosophy and working with a theory of metaphor that was fundamentally different from that of Adolf Jülicher: "For Jülicher the metaphor is the rhetorical method of allegory, which in turn is the method by which Mark and the primitive church interpret the parables, i.e., as a *dark* kind of comparative speech. Metaphor . . . is defined by Jülicher as the *replacement* of a word by another, similar one."[7] In contrast, Ricoeur understands parables as poetry, whose whole text is "the bearer of metaphors"; they are found in a bundle or net of many metaphors.[8] At a crucial point he cites Max Black:[9] "A memorable metaphor has the power to bring two separate domains into cognitive and emotional relation by using language directly appropriate to the one as a lens for seeing the other."[10] "It is . . . the task of poetic language to weaken the referential link at the first level of ordinary language in order to create an entrée for this referential link at a second and higher level."[11] In the narrative framework metaphorical quality belongs above all to "extravagance, paradox, hyperbole" (336). He then rejects the possible accusation of supranaturalism by interpreting paradox as *"the inbreaking of the outrageous"* (336), the expression of human experience. "To this extent we must say that the ultimate point of reference of parables, wisdom sayings, and eschatological sayings is not the reign of God, but the whole of human reality" (338). "Experiences of distress . . . experiences of high points in life"—these are the conditions of human existence (338–39).

Metaphorical language like that of the parables thus brings two spheres into relationship with one another: ordinary life and marginal human experiences outside the bounds of ordinary life. The ordinary life the parables tell about has no relevance of its own in this theory; it is the material that, through the extravagance of the narrative, becomes transparent, so that marginal experiences are revealed. Ricoeur ontologizes the marginal experiences themselves, understanding them as the conditions of human existence. He does not recognize the extravagance of parables through posing social-historical questions. Here again, Ricoeur apparently accepts that human life can be reduced to a common denominator. He is certain that the vineyard owner who sends his son (Mark 12:6) acts stupidly, and also that the boss in Matt 20:8-16 acts "extravagantly" by paying the workers hired at the eleventh hour the same wages as those who worked from early morning on. In fact, he makes social-historical judgments without reflecting on them historically. Ricoeur's interpretation of metaphors is important for overcoming the division in parables between image and subject that has

been rooted in biblical interpretation since Jülicher, even though Ricoeur himself does not overcome that division. His interpretation is exciting in its linking
of the parables to poetry, which helps to block the drawing of general moral
teachings from parables. But it draws a separation between ordinary life and
God, between ordinary life and marginal experience.

In my search for a non-dualistic parable theory I would like to enter into
dialogue with a variety of partners who are as different from one another as
possible. Thus I will not, at this point, question Eberhard Jüngel and Wolfgang
Harnisch, whose approaches are close to that of Ricoeur, regarding the dualism
of their hermeneutics. Instead, I will turn to an initiative stemming from a completely different context of experience: that of Kenneth E. Bailey. In two books,[12]
Bailey has developed the project of an "Oriental exegesis" (29ff.), "Recapturing
the Middle Eastern Culture that Informs the Parables" (xiv). He calls his project "literary-cultural." His sources for an oriental exegesis of the parables are:
(1) the culture of conservative rural villages in the Middle East, (2) parables in
Bible translations made by churchmen from the Middle East, and (3) ancient
literature akin to the New Testament. He uses these sources in conjunction with
a literary analysis of the texts. His books are full of stimulating details, to which
I can refer only in general terms here.

According to Bailey, every parable has three parts: (1) the parable narrative,
(2) the response of the listeners, and (3) the reflection on theological themes
that underlie this response. This approach to parables is a step toward overcoming the distinction between the image and the subject, so long as the response
and reflection need not be deduced from the implicit subject, but play themselves out in the life of the listeners. "Depending on the nature of the parable, the
response of the listener may be a decision to act in a particular way or to accept
a new understanding of the nature of God's way with men in the world" (40).
However, in his interpretation of the parable narrative he does not take seriously
its reference to the everyday world within the parable. For the parable of the lost
coin in Luke 15:8-10, the story of a woman's experience is relevant for him only
insofar as "the inferior woman" is thematized. In doing this, Jesus is said to reject
the Pharisees' attitude toward women (158). But the content of the narrative is
for him only a means for inducing a new understanding of repentance in the
hearers (155–58). The clarity with which Bailey makes "response" and "reflection" components of the parable is suggestive, but his allegorizing reading of
the parable narrative itself is not. Here he remains within the framework of the
dominant reading of the parables.

Another noteworthy contribution to a non-dualistic theory of parables is
found in the work of C. H. Dodd.[13] He emphasizes the realism of the parable
narratives and sees the reason for it in the connection *within the content* between
the parable narrative and the reign of God. "Since nature and super-nature are

one order, you can take any part of that order and find in it illumination for other parts" (10). God as creator is present in the falling of the rain and in the love of a father for his worthless son. But he does not pursue this insight in his interpretations. It is true that he refuses to read, for example, Mark 12:1-12 (or the underlying Jesus parable) as an allegory, but in the historical situation its "veiled allusions" (102) cause the listeners to recognize the crisis of Israel, which has rejected not only the prophets, but Jesus, who is more significant than the prophets. What Dodd does not consider is his own evaluation of the human world as presented in the parable narrative as the locus of divine action. The tenants in the vineyard are criminals to him (91). He says nothing about God's action in this human world. But as a result the material world of human history and human bodies once again becomes incidental. The light of the parable does not fall on God's history with believers and unbelievers, for their real-life world is only the stage.

Justin S. Ukpong[14] stands within the tradition of liberation-theological and "postcolonial" Bible reading. He calls his approach "Inculturation Biblical Hermeneutic." By this he means a reading of the Bible "that consciously and explicitly seeks to interpret the biblical text from socio-cultural perspectives of different people" (190). He wants to avoid the "classical," dominant approach to the text, which supposes that there is only *one* correct interpretation, that of the "dominant cultures" (191). He then shows, using the parable of the "unjust steward" in Luke 16:1-13 as an example, that the dominant interpretation identifies with the rich man and therefore brands the steward as unjust and criminal (194). In this interpretation the rich man represents God. A Bible reading "against the background of West African peasants" instead sees the "steward" as the hero of the story: he releases the farmers from debts that have been imposed on them unjustly and illegally (205). Thus the parable itself contrasts two concepts of justice: the exploitative concept of the rich man and that of a new system of justice, one that in today's world as well would mean release from debt for debtors in the Two-thirds World (207). The rich man in Luke 16:7 praises the steward for acting "wisely." Ukpong sees in this a turning of the rich man toward righteousness in the sense of the Torah (201) and of Jesus. The kingdom of God and God's salvation "begins on earth, but continues into eternity. It is a reality that is both present and eschatological, material and spiritual" (206). This article is absolutely clear and suggestive in its overcoming of a dualistic parable theory. It criticizes the Western tradition of interpretation that identifies God and oneself with the unrighteous wealth of the rich man and that also insists it offers the only correct interpretation. Instead, Ukpong takes it as given that there is no one correct interpretation (190). In fact, however, his interpretation demands the repentance of people in the Western world who exploit the Two-thirds World. He does not claim to offer a correct interpretation for all time, but he does offer the *one* that has a compelling force in the context of today's Western world. I wonder whether the "plurivalence" (191) of the biblical text is the right word for this. The word is much used in Western biblical interpretation, but in a different sense. It is meant to say that there is not just one correct interpretation, but different ones depending on the presuppositions that are brought to the text. But that precisely does not connect with the idea of an ethical obligation arising out of a reading of the Bible in a given community of interpretation.

Miguel A. De la Torre[15] addresses this question clearly: "If a biblical text can be read and interpreted in several different ways, which interpretation is correct? The challenge faced by those who read the Bible from the margins is that the dominant culture has the power to shape and legitimize the religious discourse. . . . Reading the Bible from the social location of oppression does not call for the treatment of all biblical interpretations as equals, where the interpretation from the margins is but one competing perspective. Rather, an affirmation and an option are made for the interpretations of the disenfranchised, taking priority over the interpretations of those who still benefit from societal structures of oppression" (27). He calls this the "hermeneutical privilege of the oppressed" (27). Jesus' first audience also consisted primarily of the outcasts of society (31). I acknowledge the hermeneutical privilege of the oppressed and see reasons for it in the biblical tradition itself and in an ethical decision within the current context: the biblical idea of justice, Jesus' Gospel of the Poor, and the option for justice in the world in which I live. I read the parables as an unwilling beneficiary of and accomplice in the Western culture of wealth derived from exploitation and violence. The biblical tradition places me face to face with the question of what the repentance of the rich would mean. *This* is the Gospel for the Western world that comes from the hermeneutical privilege of the oppressed. It means cooperating in the surrender of economic and political power over poor countries and people.

A postmodern initiative that disputes the assertion of a correct, or even objective, interpretation can be used in an ethically relativizing fashion. But it can also lead to making ethical reflection the subject of biblical interpretation, as is done in liberation theological, postcolonial, and some feminist initiatives (Elisabeth Schüssler Fiorenza, Mary Ann Tolbert).[16]

David Flusser's[17] work is important for parable scholarship because of the clarity with which it integrates the parables of the Jesus tradition within Jewish parable literature. His parable theory does not rest on a hierarchical dualism. His theory for the "subject portion" of the parables locates the demand he finds expressed in the parables in human life (20); it is a question of human deeds and people's turning back to God (33, 40). The parable "image" he regards as pseudorealistic (35). It is meant to induce the impression of taking place in everyday life, but in reality these images are an arrangement of motifs that bear a traditional allegorical meaning. "The interpretable motifs of the subject are the hooks on which the teaching of the parable hangs" (189). Thus the parable narratives are only artificial literary products out of which arises the religious teaching, the content that is the object of the parable. But this theory of parable narratives (the image portion) fails to recognize the fact that they always have reference to daily life, no matter how unusual they are. Thus the social message of the parable narrative remains unacknowledged, and with it the difficulty of seeing God or Christ as represented in the landowners and others in dominant roles. Nevertheless, Flusser's proposal is an important dialogue partner for the development of a non-dualistic parable theory, for the content of the subject portion remains, for Flusser, grounded in the earth where people suffer and act; it is not shifted into a "beyond" divorced from social life.

David Stern's contribution to a theory of Jesus' parables and the rabbinic *meshalim* advances Flusser's proposal.[18] For Stern, Jesus' parables are early examples of the rabbinic parable culture. Previous Christian attempts to prove the unique character of Jesus' parables pose the wrong question.[19] Therefore the later rabbinic parables can indeed contribute to our understanding of Jesus' parables. Stern uses Mark 12:1-12 as an example to illustrate this mode of analysis. He emphasizes that the basis for interpreting Jesus' parables must always be the text in its literary context in the Gospels—just as the *meshalim* must be read in the literary context of the rabbinic collections.[20] He regards his project as historical, in contrast to literary-critical readings that are deliberately *a*-historical. Stern distinguishes two stages in the history of Jewish parable culture. In a later stage there are "regularizations," and stereotypical narrative structures emerge.[21] Many parables were now told as royal parables: In the parables of the Tannaim[22] and those of Jesus these regularizations are not yet present. They represent an early stage of Jewish parable culture. According to Stern the parables in the Midrash consist of a narrative that has an "ulterior meaning," and the *nimshal* ("application"). The stories are fictional, "shaped through their form and rhetoric to impress a particular worldview on their audience."[23] "It does show how profoundly familiar the Rabbis were with the greater political and cultural world in which they lived, and with what little hesitation they transformed the *realia* of that world into subject matter for midrash."[24] But they may not be used uncritically as historical sources.[25] The *nimshal*[26] helps the hearers to interpret their concrete situation. "The task of understanding the parallels and their implications is, on the whole, left to the audience." The parallels between what the *mashal* tells and the concrete situation of the hearers are the "ulterior meaning" of the *mashal.*[27] However, Stern does not draw from his view of the *meshalim* the fundamental conclusion that the fictional tales are to be investigated from a social-historical point of view. Even though I share his evaluation of the narratives as fictional and constructive, I, unlike Stern, consider it necessary to take seriously the construction of reality in the *meshalim* as a statement about the present world of the narrators and to read them not simply as collections of motifs from which parallels should be drawn.

Stern's approach to Jewish parables is not dualistic, but, like Flusser's, it is not interested in the *realia* of the parable narrative and its social message. Stern's contribution to parable theory is basic to my understanding of Jesus' parables, even if I do not share his evaluation of the irrelevance of the *realia*. Stern reflects especially the stance of the "king" image for God. The use of this image in the rabbinic *meshalim* is said to be paradoxical. On the one hand the rabbis utterly reject the Roman imperial cult, but on the other hand they model the image of God as king after the figure of the emperor in Rome. The result of this paradox is that there are both antithetical royal parables and—as I will now call them—conforming royal parables. The antithetical royal parables demonstrate the dissimilarity between God and the emperor.[28] The conforming royal parables, in which the emperor is "a symbolic figure for God," require explanation. Stern finds the explanation in comparable material in Jewish and early Christian art that uncritically adopts elements of Greco-Roman iconography because they are no longer being used in conjunction with foreign cults. "The same logic . . . is at work in the royal parables and their use of imperial images."[29] But on closer examination of their content I do not regard this explanation of the conforming royal parables as convincing. The king in the parables is almost always represented as a ruler who acts arbitrarily and violently. I doubt, therefore, that these parables are adopting imperial imagery uncritically. The relationship between the parable imagery and its application, and whether and how the king is a representative of God, must be examined from one case to the next. I have presented such an examination of Luke 13:1-9 (chap. 6 above) in opposition to Stern.

Stern explains as anthropomorphism the peculiar characterizations of God in royal *meshalim* that, according to Stern, are not antithetical: "The king in the parable tends to use his power in extreme, often apparently incomprehensible ways. He is either a tyrant or a victim of circumstances. When he expresses his feelings, it is often in the most intense and impulsive form. When he is angry, he sometimes reacts violently and recklessly; when he loves he can be desperate, obsessed, almost madly jealous."[30] Thus he is the only figure in the parables who has personality. Stern discusses this anthropomorphism using an example that I will quote here in order to give a basis for my doubt about Stern's view of the conforming royal parables.

> Or: "It is like a widow." . . . R. Ḥama bar Ukba said: [The city is like] a widow who asked only for her living [from what belonged to the orphans], but not what was owing to her. But the rabbis said: [It is like] a king who

became angry at his consort *[matrona]*. He wrote her a bill of divorce *[get]*, and gave it to her, but then he returned, and grabbed it from her. Whenever she wished to marry someone else, the king said to her: Where is the bill of divorce with which I divorced you? And whenever she claimed support from him, he said to her: I have already divorced you. Similarly, whenever Israel wishes to worship idolatry, the Holy One, blessed be He, says to them: "Where is the bill of divorce of your mother whom I have dismissed?" (Isa 50:1). And whenever they ask Him to perform a miracle for them, He tells them: I have already cast you off, as it is written, "I cast her off and handed her a bill of divorce" (Jer 3:8).[31]

The parable tells of the meanness of a husband, who need not necessarily be a king but is called such in the parable. The husband has a legal obligation to give his wife a writ of divorce so that, after the divorce, she will be free to marry another man. For that reason women always took great care of their divorce writs. This mean husband robs his divorced wife of her writ of divorce and then treats her badly and does her an injustice because she, in her condition as a divorced wife without a writ of divorce, is helpless and at the mercy of his whim. She cannot marry again, but she no longer has a claim to support from him. In this parable the mean husband is portrayed as a lawbreaker, a thief, and a liar who keeps his wife dependent on him and does her injustice. This parable is an exegesis of the expression "like a widow" in Lam 1:1. The midrash transmits this parable in a series of other explanations of the expression "like a widow." All these explanations speak of women to whom injustice is done. "Like a widow" means: like a woman whose "spouse has gone to a seaside town and knows that he will return to her." She is tied to him, but he does not take care of her. Or a woman is a widow who asks for her livelihood, it is true, but not for "what is owing to her," her *ketubah*. She is thus a widow who is kept in financial dependency.

Before I discuss the question of whether God is set in relationship to the mean husband-king, it must be said that here Lam 1:1, "like a widow," is used in different ways to make visible the injustice that is done to women. The parable of the mean husband also refers to such a legal instance. Its interest is not in describing personalities, but in structural violence and the misuse of power against women; in this it is comparable to Matt 25:1-13 and Luke 18:1-8. The *nimshal* following the parable of the mean husband applies it to Israel's relationship to God. The two statements by the mean husband are paralleled with God's sayings in Isa 50:1 ("Where is your mother's writ of divorce?") and Jer 3:8 ("I have sent [Israel] away and given him a writ of divorce"). In Isaiah and Jeremiah, God's separation from Israel leads to profound pain: "Return, O faithless children" (Jer 3:14), "for the LORD has called you like a wife forsaken and grieved in spirit" (Isa 54:6). The parable and its *nimshal* leave us with the question: Has God abandoned Israel?

"Have you utterly rejected us?"—so end the Lamentations of Jeremiah. Stern makes it clear that this parable reflects Israel's suffering after 70 c.e. Israel's suffering is "like that of a widow," worse than that of a widow. The mean husband-king is not an image of God; his actions are unmistakably different from God's jealous wrath over Israel as depicted in Lamentations, Isaiah, and Jeremiah. The parable, to follow Stern's language, has an "ulterior message," but is not to be read action-by-action as a parallel with God as king. Stern calls the parable "bizarre."[32] It certainly would be if God were presented as a liar, a lawbreaker, and a thief. I read the parable of the mean husband as an antithetical parable. God is not like that. God desires neither to humiliate people nor to make them suffer.

An unbroken parallelism between the structural violence depicted in the parables and God's power is a misunderstanding. In the New Testament many parables describe such structural violence with obvious disgust—as do many rabbinic parables. Early Christianity, like the Judaism contemporary with it, used certain words from the political language of the Roman empire for experiences of salvation and hope; thus Jesus and God are called *kyrios* ("Lord"). But they are different from the lords of this world (see 1 Cor 8:5, 6). The Good News here is the Gospel of the Poor (Luke 4:18-21), and not the gospel of the birth of the world ruler in Rome, celebrated in lavish triumphal arches and inscriptions.[33] This antithetical reversal of key imperial concepts in the religious language of Judaism and early Christianity can help us to understand that the conforming royal parables only appear to conform when their content is not placed in relationship to social reality and taken seriously as a statement about the world in which human beings were really living.

My discussion of dualism in parable theories is intended to help draw attention to a hermeneutical presupposition that is seldom discussed and not often even noticed. Despite my criticisms regarding a basic hermeneutical shortcoming, I am deeply indebted to all the contributions discussed here. From the point of view of the history of research, William Herzog's *Parables as Subversive Speech,* which I discussed in connection with Mark 12:1-12 (chap. 2 above), offers a decisive new beginning. In this initiative the parable narratives, or images, are rightly evaluated as texts that make their own theological statements.

10

Metaphor or Not Metaphor?
That Is the Question

AGAINST ACCEPTING EXISTING METAPHORS

A consensus has emerged in parable research that the parables of Jesus contain metaphors and nonmetaphorical narrative sections. For example, with regard to Matt 25:3-4 it is said that oil is a metaphor for good deeds, but there is no additional significance to the lamps. I am using the word *metaphor* here in the sense of the traditional definition.[1] According to this, metaphors speak at two levels: one that offers images and one that receives them. Thus, for example, in the expression *basileia tou theou* ("kingdom/reign of God") the word *basileia* ("kingdom/reign") is a metaphor for God's action. God's action is receptive of imagery; kingship as a social and political reality yields imagery. A metaphor can consist of a word or of larger units of language. Adolf Jülicher's critique of metaphors as inexact discourse and as out of harmony with Jesus' parables[2] has led to a situation in which parables like Matt 25:1-13 or Mark 12:1-12 are suspected of belonging to subsequent redaction—for example, by the evangelists—that introduced metaphors into original Jesus parables. This supposition is contradictory to the consensus of researchers (against Jülicher), mentioned above, that parables always contain metaphors. Nevertheless, what is crucial to my understanding of metaphors is that they cannot be understood in isolation from their social context. The metaphor "the human being is a wolf" can change its meaning according to what the hearers or readers understand a wolf to be and according to what, in context, the metaphor refers to. This "attachment to the context"[3] is so deep-seated that whether the metaphor is to be understood dualistically or non-dualistically—and what its effects are in each individual case—depends on it. Whether a metaphor is present at all depends also on the literary *and* the social context in addition to the interpretation in each individual case. Therefore all interpretations of parables are problematic if they strip the parables of their framing texts (introduction, conclusion, and so on) and try to present the parable alone. The decision whether and how a metaphor in the Jesus tradition ought to be read can only be made in relation to the text, that is, through interpretation of the text in question within its literary and social-historical context.

The assumption of existing metaphors that had a particular meaning in the context of Judaism at the time of Jesus has strongly influenced parable interpretation. I, too, for a long time supposed that, for example, the metaphor "king" in this context was a clear indication that the parable was about God's action. But over time this acceptance of existing motifs or metaphors has come to appear inaccurate to me. The parable narratives in many cases arrange the same "fields of imagery"[4] (e.g., king and king's son or banquet) again and again in new ways. Each new version also gives the words a new meaning. Hence we need to note carefully what is said in each individual case (about a king, for example), what the literary context says, and how the parable narrative is to be applied to the present circumstances of the hearers or readers.

I would like to discuss the context dependency of parable discourse and metaphorical discourse by using an example, the rabbinic *mashal* of the caravansary.

> A caravan was traveling. At dusk it came to a caravansary. The head of the station said to them: Come into our station so that you will be protected from the wild beasts and robbers. But the caravan leader said to him: I don't usually go into caravansaries! He continued on, but night fell and it became dark. So he turned back and came to the leader of the caravansary, calling to him and asking that he open for him. Then the head of the station said to him: We don't usually open the station at night, and the head of the station does not ordinarily open for people at this hour! When I asked you, you did not want to come in, and now I cannot open for you. So says the Holy One to Israel: "Return, O faithless children" (Jer 3:14). And: "Seek the Lord now, while he may be found" (Isa 55:6). But none of them seeks to return. The Holy One said: "I will return again to my place" (Hos 5:15). Because they were handed over to the world empires and the nations, they cried: Why, O Lord, do you stand afar off? The Holy One said to them: When I asked you, you did not accept; now, when you ask me, I am not listening to you. Measure for measure! For it is written: "When he called, they did not hear, so, when they called, I would not hear" (Zech 7:13).[5]

Flusser has connected this parable to Matt 25:1-13. For him the closed door in this parable and in Matt 25:10 is a "symbolic image" and designates, if I understand Flusser correctly, "God's wasted . . . offer to humanity."[6] But the idea of a fixed symbolic image or even of an established metaphor (e.g., "closed door") is little help in interpreting the parables; it is not the "hook"[7] on which the interpretation can be hung. In Matt 25:10 Flusser sees a warning about wasted opportunity in the context of eternity. Thus the closed door would be a metaphor for God's eschatological condemnation to death. Matt 25:10 has often been read that way. But when the social and literary context of the two texts is examined closely, the closed door has a different meaning in the two cases: In the parable of the caravansary, the closing application reflects Israel's situation within the Roman empire, "handed over to the world empires and the nations." The closed door is interpreted as God's refusal to hear Israel's cry for help "now," after Israel has previously rejected God's invitation. In a deviation from the parable narrative it is even said that God called the people to come back, but no one came. However, the closed door is not finally sealed, for Israel is and remains God's people and under God's promise. This is not said, but it is a matter of course within this tradition. In Matt 25:10 the bridegroom's sentence sounds ultimate—on the social level or, if Matt 25:10 is regarded as a metaphor for God's eschatological judgment (something I do not do, but it is very common), in the relationship between God and those who have no good works. The meaning of the closed door depends on the situation in which it is applied. The head of the caravansary does not represent God, either. His motive for not letting anyone else in after nightfall is not stated, nor is that of the leader of the caravan in refusing the invitation to enter the caravansary in the evening and then returning after all. Here the narrative draws its logic from experiences with caravansaries, not from the experiences of God and Israel with one another. The narrative in the *mashal* aims toward the closing scene, and *that* is what is reflected in the application.

Jülicher's devaluation of metaphors and allegories or allegorical elements rested on his rejection of arbitrary Christian dogmatic interpretation of the parables. That devaluation has, correctly, not been retained in the current discussion among scholars. But that the alternative is to be measured poetically rather than rhetorically, as developed in the critique of Jülicher by Paul Ricoeur (see pp. 91–92 above), for example, is doubtful.[8] Likewise, the metaphor as an element in early Christian and rabbinic parables is overloaded when it is declared to be, as such, an indispensable medium of revelation.[9] Parable discourse and mythological discourse (or other methods of discourse that do not have the character of parables) are found alongside one another and with equal value in the Gospels: for example, Matt 25:1-13, 14-30 contains two parables: Matt 25:31-46 is a mythological discourse, and Matt 24:37-41 is a prophetic judgment discourse. The content of the parables in Matt 25:1-13, 14-30 could very well be told in different ways.

Many parables have a long history of being interpreted in terms of real or supposed metaphors. That the kings, property owners, and slaveowners represent God has been questioned by very few interpreters of the parables, and it has been repeatedly accepted throughout the flood of interpretations. Social-historical analysis of the parable narratives should, in fact, have led to a different way of dealing with the parables. But as it happens, the most obvious point, the construction of social reality in the parable narratives, has been overlooked.

My father used to tell a little story that ridiculed, self-critically, the thirst for metaphors in churchy language: The pastor wants to enliven the children's liturgy on Sunday morning, so he says: "Imagine! Just now, as I was on my way here, I saw something amazing: a little brown thing with a bushy tail, very fast. It ran up a tree. Can you guess what it was?" Little Fritz answers: "Normally I would say it was a squirrel. But the way things go around here, it must have been the Lord Jesus."

Parable images are fictional narratives. Among their elements, which ones contain a bridge or a connection to the application must be determined from the literary context in each case. But on the whole the parable imagery is much less rich in metaphors than is supposed by the traditional interpretations. In many essential parts they really are talking about squirrels (to stick with the above image)—or about the Roman empire.

11

What Is a Parable?

In this section I will be talking only about the parables in the Synoptic Gospels, and I will try to describe the literary form of the parable as I find it there. The word *parabolē* ("parable") is the term used to identify this literary form in the following text, but it is not definitively distinguished from other forms of discourse that could be described by the same word.[1] I will restrict the word *parable* to the literary genre that is typical for the Jesus tradition in the Synoptic Gospels and is in the form of a narrative.

Jesus' parables are made up of three linked parts: a parable narrative, an application of the parable, and a response, usually only implicit, from the hearers or readers.

THE PARABLE NARRATIVE

The parable narrative, which the scholarly tradition often calls the "image," tells a fictional story that is meant to be recognized as such. These narratives are often reshaped from related image fields by the use of similar figures, but in each individual case they contain a specific story (and application). Therefore it does not make sense to try to find an "original form" of a parable (e.g., by a synoptic comparison). To do so would be to lose the specificity of the various versions.

These fictional narratives make a statement about the world of human experience at the time when the oral and written tradition about Jesus of Nazareth, and therefore also the "historical" Jesus, originated (see chap. 12 below). Even the "nature" parables refer to the world of humans' lives, their work to gain their nourishment and their reverence for creation, which sustains the life of the human race. The parable narratives are not intended to describe a particular historical event but a structure, the structure of political rule or the structure of the world of work and social relationships (e.g., the injustice of wealth and the suffering of poverty; the role of the patriarchal father in relationship to sons). Social-historical research is a necessity for understanding the parable narratives. The relationship between the parable narrative and the social world needs to be investigated. The parable narratives as such provide a social analysis that, through the application of the parable, is placed in a theological context. In this way the parable narrative also makes a theologically relevant statement. It is not merely imagery in the service of something else. The parable stories work with narrative means—exaggerations, compacting, the rule of three, or contrasts of opposites, for example. It is a serious and consequential misunderstanding to read these antitheses in the parables ecclesiologically. In all the Gospels they stand in relationship to eschatology, the expectation of the just judgment of God, and therefore they are to be read eschatologically. This eschatological interpretation is usually presented in explicit applications of the parables.

PARABLE APPLICATIONS

The applications of the parables have long been regarded as "frames" and often as secondary to the parable, as later interpretations that often miss the point. But in fact they are an integral part of the parables.[2] The invitation to compare the parable narrative with the kingdom of God is aimed at a reflection on the content of God's action, God's will, of action in past, present, and future. Present and future are understood eschatologically. It thus makes sense to unpack the parable—the narrative and the application together—with the following questions: Where is the Gospel, the liberating message? The reference to the Torah, for example, hearing in the sense of the *Shema' Israel,* is part of the Gospel, the liberating message. So we can also ask: Where is the Torah? (but *not* in the sense of an opposition to the Gospel). And so comes the third question: What does the parable say about God's promise?—that is, the eschatological question, which was already outlined in the content. These three questions—Gospel, Torah, eschatology—are points of aid for understanding the parable applications. Many parable narratives present social structures that stand in opposition to God's will and action, God's kingdom. I will call them "antithetical parables." It is a misunderstanding to read the "comparison" *(homoioun)* as requiring a formal equation, either in the sense of allegorization or in the sense of a parable theory from post-allegorical scholarship since Jülicher. Whether a metaphor is being used in the parable must be determined separately in each case. We should not begin with the assumption that there are fixed, existing metaphors.

RESPONSE

The parable—narrative and application—presumes the active participation of the hearers and their understanding *response* in words and deeds. Understanding, words, and deeds are the expression of their relationship to the God of Israel.

The response of the hearers and readers is asked for in many parables, for example, through rhetorical questions or an open conclusion to the parable. Independent of whether elements of this response can be discerned in the text, the parable is incomplete without this third part. The response is always a part of the parable. In my interpretation I have sometimes attempted to reconstruct implicit responses from Scripture, from the Jewish prayer tradition, and from the praxis of the Torah at the time of the Jesus tradition.

The Synoptic Gospels present Jesus as a teller of parables. He tells parables in order to teach and to be understood. The parables are described as comprehensible discourse intended to evoke not only intellectual understanding, but the kind of understanding that follows from hearing the voice of God. It is a misunderstanding to conclude from Mark 4:10-12 and the parallels in Matt 13:10-17 and Luke 8:9-10 that parables are discourse that obscures.

The literary form *parable* is part of the history of postbiblical Jewish parable culture. It cannot be found, as such, in the First Testament or in Greco-Roman culture. It is true that related genres can be found there (e.g., fables, especially those in the Aesop tradition), but the commonalities of the rabbinic parables and those of Jesus are greater than their links to First Testament, Near Eastern, and Greco-Roman material.

12

The Historical Jesus
and the Jesus in the Gospels

Parables are typical of Jesus in the New Testament. Paul occasionally attempts an image, but his efforts are usually clumsy (e.g., the similitude of the body and its members in 1 Cor 12:12-28, which was a very common bit of material in Greco-Roman literature). Besides, there is no parable in Paul's work using the form of discourse typical of Jesus. The imagery of the Gospel of John, likewise, does not belong within this genre of parables. About one-third of the Jesus tradition in the Synoptic Gospels consists of parables, and there are shifting boundaries between parable narratives and logia using imagery. Jesus is presented as a master of public parable discourse. The variability of the synoptic parallels between parables shows that many people who contributed either in written or in oral form to the development of the Synoptic Gospels carried on Jesus' parable discourse on their own and in creative ways. We cannot determine which parables go back to the historical Jesus and which were reworked (how?) or newly added.

The assumption regarding the content of the parables that has been intensively discussed in Western biblical scholarship since the nineteenth century is this: The parables of the historical Jesus are to be distinguished, as regards their content, from their later redaction. This assumption has led to a fundamental theological distrust of the parables in the form in which we find them, as literary components of a larger text. "Community action," "evangelist," "redaction," "author"—depending on one's methodological concept these are accused of allegorization and deviation in the content, sometimes of falsification. Even if literary-critical exegesis does not desire to go behind the text, as a rule it also displays such a concept of theological distrust of the existing text. This distrust is an inheritance left us by the nineteenth- and twentieth-century discussions about the historical Jesus, about "genuine" and "nongenuine." This assumption of the difference between the historical Jesus and the theology of the Gospels presupposes an image of a church whose interests, rhetoric, and ideas dominate this theology. The underlying thought model is that of sect versus institution. The literary text before us is said to belong to an institution.[1] I will cite here only one example of this presupposition and its consequences for the interpretation of the text: "Increasingly in the Gospel we observe the acknowledgment of

Jesus as Christ. The Gospel is not merely a simple report of Jesus' life, teaching, works, death, and resurrection, but a depiction that enables the reader, on his or her part, to respond with the same acknowledgment that happens in the text."[2] According to this theory it is the church's christological confession that the readers of the Gospel accept.

I dispute the adequacy of this sociological assumption, which underlies most interpretations of the literary texts and the Gospels as a whole. In place of the sociological model of sect versus institution, I prefer to apply the thought model of a Jewish liberation movement within the Pax Romana[3] to all levels of the Jesus tradition in the New Testament, including the Gospels. The differences among the three Synoptic Gospels rest on differences among communities that, nevertheless, were all part of such a liberation movement. The differences are less relevant politically and theologically than the commonalities are. Even if the parable discourse of the historical Jesus cannot be reconstructed, it is in its essentials reproduced similarly in the three versions of its literary presentation. The parable discourse of the historical Jesus can no longer be reconstructed, and yet we know a great deal about it. The Gospels contain three believable versions of Jesus' parable discourse. They are not believable because the tradents wanted to be historically accurate but because the conditions of life and methods of expression of Jesus' work of liberation and that of his group of followers during the time of his earthly life were not essentially different from those of the groups that came after and speak to us in the Synoptic Gospels. Therefore in the next part of this book I will discuss the parables in the sequence of their literary contexts (Mark, Matthew, Luke). In the first, exegetical, part of this book I attempted to develop a theory through interpreting some parables that are as different from each other as possible; in what follows I will try to test the theory thus developed.

In this book I have omitted the parables from the *Gospel of Thomas*. There are studies that have concluded that the sayings and parables in the *Gospel of Thomas* reflect a stage of tradition corresponding to that of the (hypothetical) Sayings Source Q. Therefore, from this point of view, the parables of the *Gospel of Thomas* are regarded as part of the very ancient tradition that can help us to reconstruct the "original form" of the parables, that of the historical Jesus. I have a different view of the history of the *Gospel of Thomas*: It presumes material known to us from the canonical Gospels and, on that basis, presents its own later Christian-Gnostic version of Jesus' parables. The parables in the *Gospel of Thomas* should be interpreted out of their own literary context (that of the *Gospel of Thomas* as a whole) and the theological context of Gnostic religious thought and praxis.

13

The Genre of Parable Discourse

The parables in the Synoptic Gospels are part of a discourse of Jesus the teacher, aiming at dialogue and directed at the crowd, or rather groups among the people that also included female and male disciples (see chap. 7 above on Mark 4:1-20). In the Gospels they are written texts that, nevertheless, reveal their relationship to oral discourse, for example, when a parable like Luke 15:11-32 is open-ended, or when it poses a question as does Mark 12:9. In Mark 4:1-2, 10-12 and the parallels in Matthew (13:10-17) and Luke (8:9-10), the social location of the parable is described: public teaching, that is, teaching about the Torah, and continuation of prophetic discourse in the sense of the biblical book of Isaiah. A parable is not to be regarded as a genre of its own, but as part of the genre of public Torah teaching and prophecy. The purpose of this discourse is: hearing, seeing, understanding, repenting (Mark 4:10-12 *parr.*). The *Shemaᶜ Israel* clarifies, in its universal conception (see chap. 7 above), that each of these acts of hearing or seeing is meant comprehensively; doing the Torah in the concrete situation is included. People who in this sense hear and see are part of the People of God, which in the Synoptic Gospels includes the Jewish people and its companions drawn from among the nations. The notion of the people is not exclusive. The people is represented by the crowd *(ochlos)* that is present, and it has a universal, human eschatological perspective: the gathering of those who are scattered from all the ends of the earth (Mark 13:27 *parr.*) and the proclamation of the Gospel for all the peoples of the earth (Mark 13:10; Matt 28:16-20; Luke 24:47). The function of individual parables in public discourse cannot be captured in general categories or subcategories—for example, in the sense of Adolf Jülicher's division of parables (parable, similitude in the narrower sense, example story). David Stern's grouping of rabbinic parables—apologetics, polemics, eulogy and consolation, complaint, regret, and warning[1]—would be difficult to apply to the synoptic material. His general characterization of the social location of parable discourse, however, shows how close Jesus' parable discourse is to that of the rabbis: "The most frequent occasions for the recitation of *meshalim* . . . were the delivery of the sermon in the synagogue and the study of Torah in the academy."[2] In addition, however, *meshalim* were to be found in political discourse, in conflict situations with Gentiles, in speeches of consolation for relatives of those who have died, and in other situations.[3] In any attempt to organize Jesus' parables according to forms of oral or written discourse and poetics, their concrete reference to the lived context of the People of God and the Torah must be taken into account.

14

Toward a Synthesis of Methods

The movement of a substantial number of North American biblical scholars from historical criticism to literary-critical methods is described by many of those involved as a radical reversal. There is talk of a paradigm shift, and it is said that historical criticism is "outdated." "Cutting edge" now, for the last thirty years, are methods of textual analysis based on literary-critical theories: literary criticism (often seen as the overarching concept), narrative criticism, rhetorical criticism, reader-response criticism. These methods have placed the analysis of the text's structure at the center of scholarly treatment of biblical texts. But in doing so we have not made unnecessary a good many steps in historical criticism. They are still used by most of those involved, and often are silently presumed.

Historical criticism as a whole is not "outdated." What is out of date is source criticism. The obsession of historical-critical scholars with dissecting the text and inventing theories about the prehistory of the written text has become superfluous because its results were based on arbitrary assumptions, often transparently so. The crucial innovative step, then, lay in the move from redaction criticism to literary-critical methods. These methods offer valuable instruments for understanding the existing text as a complete work and as a work of language. But they do not render superfluous most of the steps in historical criticism: the studies in philology, in the history of religions and philosophy, social history, and textual criticism. As knowledge of ancient languages disappears, the exegetical task of making new translations of texts and the critical analysis of existing translations becomes more and more important. A synthesis of historical and text-analytical methods is therefore already present in most exegetical works, sometimes explicitly, often implicitly. A summary disqualification of historical criticism is inadequate to the factual state of the discussion and to a further development of methods. I believe that a policy of multiple methods is more appropriate. Wherever results are developed that help us to understand historical texts like those of the New Testament I will build on them. A claim of exclusivity for a method or group of methods is to be regarded as an attempt at oppression. The variety of methods corresponds to the state of the discussion as reflected in monographs that list the various methods in individual articles[1] or treat them each, in critical fashion, separately.[2] The next step should really be the systematization and metacritique of these methods.[3] I see such a metacritique as involving a hermeneutical analysis of the presuppositions and results of the different methods.[4] At the beginning of this chapter I have attempted, in this sense, to systematize the content of the presuppositions of biblical interpretation in multi-methodological fashion. The results of all methods must be subjected to a hermeneutical test.[5]

15

The Literary Context: The Gospels

I consider the literary context indispensable for the interpretation of parables. This means, then, that I always have in mind the gospel as a whole when I interpret an individual parable in its narrower literary context. The decision about the relationship of individual texts in their literary context is closely bound up with the evaluation of the genre of the overall gospel text. If I locate the Gospels within a genre of ancient literature (e.g., ancient novels or biographies) I will try to understand them as literature coming from a circle of educated people. But I see the Gospels as texts for general use, to be employed in community assemblies. Thus their situation in life is described by Justin Martyr: "On the day called Sunday there is a meeting in one place of those who live in cities or the country, and the memoirs of the apostles or the writings of the prophets are read as long as time permits. When the reader has finished, the president in a discourse urges and invites [us] to the imitation of these noble things."[1] The memoirs (*apomnē-moneumata*) of the apostles are the Gospels, whose authorship was attributed to apostles. We can scarcely suppose from this text that a whole gospel would be read; the following explication in terms of practical life by the person who presided at the assembly also points rather to the reading of limited amounts of text. On the other hand, it seems that these were longer texts than mere snippets of narrative because it appears to be the ability of the audience to receive that sets limits to the reading.

In legends of the ancient church the Gospels were attributed to men who were regarded as apostles. This referred not so much to eyewitness character as to their spiritual authority as preachers and teachers[2] of the Good News, the Gospel, in the sense intended by Jesus. The texts are not intended to entertain or educate their audience or readership, but to move them to follow Jesus or strengthen them in their commitment. They are to see, hear, and understand in the sense of Mark 4:10-12 *parr.* The Gospels are thus intended to communicate with people in the public forum of the community assembly. Because at that time the majority of people in these messianic groups following Jesus belonged to the ranks of the poor, especially in the cities of the Roman empire, we should not proceed on the assumption that all of them could read, write, and purchase long texts. The Gospels are, in view of their situation in life, a genre intended for oral communication.

The coherence in the content and theology of the individual Gospels requires an explanation if I am not presuming an elaborated literary character for the genre. Add to this that I consider it inappropriate to presume each had a single author. We should rather suppose that individual persons wrote down texts that were in use, orally and as written material, in communities, so that the concept of an "author" must be regarded critically. Thus their coherence appears to me to require a social-historical explanation. The Gospel of Mark reflects a historical situation of persecution of Christian groups by Roman authorities;[3] the Gospel of Matthew reflects the situation of economic scarcity and illness in the years after the Jewish-Roman War of 66–70;[4] the Gospel of Luke sketches a radical social Gospel of the Poor directed to well-to-do people.[5] The individual indicators of these social locations have already been discussed in other places. Despite the internal coherence of each gospel, distinguishing it from the other two neighboring synoptics, I do not want to overemphasize their differences, since eschatology, the common basis of all three Gospels, links them together.

PART 3

JESUS THE PARABLE-TELLER

THE PARABLES
IN THE LITERARY CONTEXT
OF THE GOSPELS

16

Political Prophecy

TRANSLATION

26 And he said: The kingdom of God is like this: Someone throws seed on the ground.

27 And lies down to sleep and gets up again, night and day. And the seed germinates and grows tall, the person does not know how.

28 All by itself the ground brings its yield: first the stalk, then the ears, then mature grain in the ears.

29 When the grain is ripe, the person puts in the sickle, for the harvest is ready.

30 And he said: To what shall we compare the kingdom of God, or what parable shall we make?

31 It is like a mustard seed. When it is sowed on the ground it is smaller than all the grains on earth.

32 And when it is sown it grows and becomes taller than all the plants and produces great branches, so that the birds of the air find shelter in its[1] shade.

SOCIAL-HISTORICAL ANALYSIS AND ESCHATOLOGICAL INTERPRETATION

Both these parables tell about farmers' experiences with plants that produce human nourishment: grain and mustard. Mustard leaves were braised or eaten raw as salad; mustard seed was often used as a seasoning or for healing purposes.[2] Wheat and barley were the most important basic foods. The perspective here is that of farmers, women and men, who sow a field and harvest its produce. The ground appears to belong to them. The sufferings, so obvious elsewhere in the Gospels, of those who cultivate the land are obscured. There appears to be no debt, enslavement, dispossession. "They shall all sit under their own vines and under their own fig trees, and no one shall make them afraid" (Mic 4:4). Since— for the people of that time, also the time of the Gospel of Mark—a healthy world for farmers was only a distant ideal, these texts tell of the pleasure of agrarian life with the plants that, despite the desperate economic conditions, they know and love. God causes the wheatfields to grow, as if miraculously, without people's needing to work for the growth or even being able to (vv. 27 and 28). In the verses at the center of the text the miracle of creation is painted in broad strokes, almost chanted. The ground brings forth its yield "all by itself," because God gives the growth (1 Cor 3:7). The human work that is necessary for this to happen is not mentioned at all—different from the beginning and end of the parable. Now all that matters in the narrative is the miracle of the working of God's earth, which brings forth food that there may be life.

The unusual size of the mustard bush is measured against the small size of the seed and the expanse of other vegetation. The reason why the mustard seed is said to be "smaller than all the grains on earth" is not natural observation, but the needs of the narrative and its attempt to express amazement at the contrast between the seed and the plant. That birds find shelter in the shade of the plant could be drawn from observation. However, the text seems to think of locations for birds' nests, and such a plant could be unsuitable for that purpose. In any case, the formulation of the last part of the sentence in v. 32 is so clearly grounded in biblical tradition that it was clear to the hearers at the time that this was about a bush or tree that symbolized rule. Among the endearing curiosities of the history of interpretation of Mark 4:32 and its parallels is that people have tried to find a mustard tree.[3] Pilgrims attest to having seen big mustard plants that make it plausible that one can find in nature the height of the bush (Mark) or tree (Matthew and Luke) that the narrative portrays.[4] I am not convinced that in the Markan version the mustard bush is not deliberately portrayed as a tree in order to make fun of the great world tree of biblical tradition or to contrast the modest image of the mustard bush with the majesty of a cedar.[5] Mark also emphasizes the impressive size of the bush and uses the imperial image of birds that find shelter there. But in fact what is talked about here is not a cedar, but a mustard seed and a mustard bush. We are therefore right to ask whether the mustard bush (Mark) or a tree (cedar [?], Matthew and Luke) that grows out of a mustard seed is meant to indicate the different quality of God's cosmic majesty in contrast to the imperial world powers. For the image of the world tree, in whose branches the birds find shelter, is a widely used imperial symbol.

In the tradition of interpretation there has been much discussion of whether this is a contrast parable or whether, within it, growth is *also* important. Connected to this is the question of what *notion of biology* is found in such texts. The background of this discussion is the critical confrontation with ideas of the reign of God in the nineteenth century: The reign of God will be brought about by moral development; therefore many interpretations emphasize the contrast. "The modern man [*sic*], passing through the ploughed field, thinks of what is going on beneath the soil, and envisages a biological development. The people of the Bible, passing through the same plough-land, look up and see miracle upon miracle, nothing less than resurrection from the dead."[6] The narratives themselves emphasize the contrast, but they also report the growth (vv. 27, 28, 32). However, the biological notion is not that of a nature separated from God, solely the object of natural science: God gives the growth and the yield. The reign of God and the growth in the fields are related in content; they are two spheres of divine action. The theological biology of these texts contradicts every interpretation that rests on a dualistic parable theory and regards "nature" in these texts as merely a neutral factor through which something else is illustrated or from which metaphors can be drawn. I placed the word *nature* in quotation marks because the word could be misunderstood either in terms of natural science or of romanticism. I would prefer to summarize the understanding of nature in these parables as follows, altering somewhat the quotation from Joachim Jeremias: The women and men of the Bible, passing through a plowed field, see God's creative work in the plants and the produce from which they live, one divine miracle after another. For them, the plants are transparent to the greatest divine miracle: the beginning of the kingdom of God in their midst.

Both these parables contain political prophecy in their concluding statements; each of them integrates a short biblical quotation or an allusion in the narrative about agriculture. Mark 4:29 takes up thoughts and words from Joel 3:13: "Put in the sickle, for the harvest is ripe."[7] The context in the book of Joel is a prophecy that God will repay the nations that have enslaved and oppressed Israel. "Egypt shall become a desolation and Edom a desolate wilderness, because of the violence done to the people of Judah, in whose land they have shed innocent blood" (Joel 3:19). In Rev 14:15, also, Joel 3:13 is taken up and expanded into a powerful mythical image: "Another angel came out of the temple, calling with a loud voice to the one who sat on the cloud, 'Use your sickle and reap, for the hour to reap has come, because the harvest of the earth is fully ripe.'" The Son of Man is to judge all humanity, but God's wrath is directed only at those "who worship the beast" (14:9), that is, those who submit to the Roman imperial cult and the structures of Roman imperialism. For the "harvest" and "sickle" we should not assume fixed metaphors; each context must be examined for its own meaning. For Mark 4:29 the context is the entire Gospel of Mark and the literary context of the quotation from Joel within that book.

It is difficult, in Mark 4:29, to see the harvest as divine judgment on the nations, as Joel 3:13 and the history of its interpretation in Judaism would demand.[8] The image of the miraculously growing field of grain seems to contradict this. Hence this verse is often interpreted as a "cry of jubilation."[9] But since the allusion to Joel 3:13 is clear enough here and speaks its own message, the "harvest" and "sickle" cannot be separated from God's judgment of the nations—despite the hope-filled imagery. Thus we are faced with the task of inquiring about the political vision of the Gospel of Mark for the nations of the world. Like Jewish tradition in general, the Gospel of Mark distinguishes between the elect (13:20, 22, 27) and the nations. There is no elaboration on the judgment of the nations. The Son of Man will gather the elect. The Gospel will be preached to the nations until the very end (13:10; see also 14:9). The great ones among the peoples are described as tyrants (10:42) who bring the elect to judgment (13:9). But the judgment of the nations is presumed, implicit in statements like 13:10: Only after the proclamation of the Good News throughout the world will come "the end" (*telos,* 13:7, 13). The judgment of the nations is mentioned explicitly in 13:24-26 and 14:62; also in 8:38: The coming of the Son of Man on the clouds is his coming to the universal judgment of God on humanity. Those who "will see" him (13:26; 14:62) are primarily those for whom this judgment brings a confrontation with the injustice they have done. Thus Mark 4:29 is to be read in conjunction with prophecies like 13:26 and 14:62. The divine judgment on the nations will come, but they still have time for repentance, and time to hear and see. Jesus' teaching and preaching and the preaching of those who follow him call the nations to repentance. Their testimony before the judgment, with which they seek to win over their judge even when they are being threatened with condemnation to death (13:9), shows that the communities of Mark have a political vision that will not regard anyone as lost, even when they themselves are experiencing the worst of persecutions. Although the expression "love of enemies" is not mentioned in the Gospel of Mark, what is here described is the praxis of love of enemies. This is the praxis that comes out of the expectation of God's judgment and the hope for the "end."

Mark 4:32 is also not a proper quotation, but an allusion to biblical language. What seems most likely is a reference to Ezek 17:23 (17:22-24), for there Israel is promised a world empire planted by God's very self. In Daniel 4 and Ezekiel 31 the metaphor of the world tree is employed critically against Nebuchadnezzar or Pharaoh: Their world empires will be brought to an end by God. That the birds nest in the branches of the world tree (Ezek 31:6; Dan 4:9, 18; Ezek 17:23, in the shade of the branches) means, in the biblical sense, a protecting rule over other nations; it thus deprecates imperial self-concepts. The nations have been subjected, and the new rulers are their "protectors."

Mark 4:32 expresses a political vision: God will reign over all peoples. But that means that there will be no more great empires like those that have dominated little Israel for centuries. At the time of the Gospel of Mark, 4:32 was a political prophecy that announced the end of the Roman empire and its Pax Romana. There will no longer be any nation that subjects other nations; all the nations are subject, in the same way, to God's dominion, and by it they will be protected.

The question is whether the ideology of power and dominion contained in this metaphorical tradition is able to express a critique of that power. Ivone Gebara has posed this critical question in fundamental fashion for the metaphor *basileia tou theou* ("kingdom/reign of God").[10] She considers the oppressive and authoritarian content of such metaphors impossible to overcome. This

critical question is unavoidable in the case of Mark 4:32, since here the imperial self-concept of the great empires appears in the use of the metaphor of the
world tree, despite its application to a mustard bush instead of a cedar. There is
no question that for twenty-first-century people, talk of the "kingdom of God"
and of "God's dominion" is problematic. Kings belong in fairy tales and in the
supermarket tabloids. But experiences with unfettered power are a bitter reality. The critique presented by Gebara must be considered at two levels: for the
historical material and for the religious language of the twenty-first century. The
crucial historical question is that of the quality of divine ruling power, in which
the people of that time hoped. In those hopes, did God replace the emperor in
Rome, or did God's rule mean a different quality of power, a participating in
God's dominion for the benefit of all living things? The word *dynamis* refers to
God in Mark 14:62, and to the sharing in God's power in the so-called miracle
stories. "Miracle" stories speak of the power of God that people can bestow on
one another and thus help one another, mutually, to a new and fulfilled life (see,
for example, Mark 5:21-43).[11] The historical material cannot be cleansed of the
language of power and dominion. What needs to be done is to name the inner
quality of this power, so clear in its literary and social contexts, in such a way that
it cannot be misunderstood or misused. For twenty-first-century religious language the problem is most acute not so much in biblical interpretation, which
describes the texts as historical material, as in Bible translations and the liturgical use of this language. Here the continued use of imperial language is, as a rule,
intolerable : It legitimates arbitrary power, and it is oppressive.

What does it mean that these political prophecies (4:29, 32) sound like a cry
of jubilation? They are the conclusion and climax of two nature parables that
view the growth of plants with joy. These two climaxes follow, narratively speaking, after the joy over a rich harvest in 4:8, 20: A field that bears a rich harvest
is transparent to the promised fruitfulness of the suffering disciples, those who,
in the end, do hear, see, and understand (see chap. 7 above). They hope for the
"end" (*telos,* 13:7, 13). God's judgment on humanity (v. 29) and the establishment of universal justice (v. 32) are hope for the suffering, hope directed at the
repentance of the nations. The "end," from the perspective of the suffering, is a
word of hope. The consequence of the expectation of judgment on the nations
is the praxis of love of enemies.

In the eschatological "time scheme" that is visible in the Gospel of Mark,
the "now" of the listeners is the time before the end, when the Gospel is being
preached. In both parables the end, the kingdom of God, the judgment and
world dominion of God are promised (4:29, 32). The listeners are not urged
by the parables to some action or other, although the broader literary context
presupposes their work of preaching and healing. It would be inappropriate to
the Markan context and also to the parable narrative in 4:26-29 to emphasize
the passivity of the listeners. The narrative in 4:26-29 reports activity (sowing

and cutting the grain) and the reverent waiting of the people of the land. The parable of the seed growing secretly emphasizes the miracle of God's working in the plants; the parable of the mustard seed paints the miracle of the gigantic bush that grows from a tiny seed. Both parables teach seeing. The gaze is directed to the growing fields of wheat and the mustard bushes and beholds the hand of God, which gives growth and produces marvelous plants. The happy gazing at this nature is an experience of God and a source of hope: The end will come. The word *end* is a word of hope. It does not mean the collapse of the world and the victory of those who imagine they are on the "right" side. It brings justice (4:29) and the end of all oppression (4:32).

The separation of reverence for nature from belief in God, something that affects Christian theology even now, has prevented us from seeing Jesus' nature parables as a school for appreciating God's creation. It is not the Enlightenment's untouched "Nature" in which God's presence is found here; it is the miracle of the growth of plants, seen by people who need those plants for food. They know how hunger can destroy a people, for that was present experience in the time of Jesus, and in the time of the Gospels.

The community's response could have been praise of God and of creation, which always plays a central role in the Psalms and other Jewish prayers. In the New Testament we find praise of creation only when we look for it: It was such an obvious part of the praxis of prayer as they lived it that it was often simply presupposed: in prayers at meals and in the Lord's Supper[12]; in the fourth petition of the Lord's Prayer; and in Matt 6:25-34 (Luke 12:22-32): "Look at the birds of the air; they neither sow nor reap nor gather into barns, and yet your heavenly Father feeds them. Are you not of more value (to God)?" (Matt 6:26). Seeing creation with new eyes creates peace and composure for careworn people. The difference between the value, in the eyes of God, of the human world and the value of the rest of living creation is expressed in biblical tradition not in an unbridled exploitation of nature, but in the confidence that bread for the coming day will grow in the fields, and that human life is in God's hand, not in the hands of those who grow rich on the bread of the hungry.

METHODOLOGICAL CLARIFICATION

The basis for the interpretation presented here of the parable narratives is their reference to the kingdom of God (4:26, 30) and the two references to the First Testament in 4:26, 32. The parables can be interpreted through these references, even though no explicit application follows. The literary context of the Gospel of Mark makes it possible to describe the eschatology of the parables more precisely.

An allegorizing reading has often seen the farmer as the figure for identification by the listeners—or the one who puts in the sickle at the end as the judge of the world. Both these allegorizations are inappropriate, even if the sickle speaks metaphorically of judgment. In terms of the history of scholarship it is interesting that, despite the affirmation of Jülicher and his critique of allegorization, the biblical scholarship of the twentieth century found allegorical interpretation so unavoidable that many interpreters regarded Mark 4:29 as secondary. It was not possible that at the beginning of the parable the farmer reflected the listeners and at the end the same farmer, as God, was swinging the sickle!

In "ecclesiological" traditions of interpretation we find numerous interpretations of Mark 4:26-29 that see the content of the parable there as the promise that the proclamation (that of Jesus or that of the community) will succeed.[13] For Mark 4:30-32 there is an openly triumphalistic ecclesiological tradition of interpretation: Verse 32 is said to be the promise of the universal dominion of the church; the birds represent the "pagan" peoples.[14] Quite frequently I have found in the exegetical history of the twentieth century, and still today, a variation on this interpretation that compares the insignificance of the mustard seed with the insignificance of the Jesus movement or the church of a particular time. To this insignificant beginning is promised the great and glorious future of the kingdom of God.[15] Thus the kingdom of God becomes the future of the church, an ominous misunderstanding. Even when Jesus' presence and the little group around him are interpreted allegorically as the insignificant mustard seed, this little group appears as the kernel of the church of whatever present moment— even if only implicitly. It must be clearly said that what is spoken of here is not some future church, but God and God's future, nothing else. This future is present strength for human hope, for all who learn to see creation with new eyes.

FOR FURTHER READING

C. H. Dodd, *The Parables of the Kingdom,* 131–45
V. J. John, *The Ecological Vision of Jesus,* 208–30
Luise Schottroff, "Die befreite Eva," 125–51
Rainer Stuhlmann, "Beobachtungen und Überlegungen zu Markus 4:26-29"

Springtime and the Night Watchers

Mark 13:28-37

TRANSLATION

28 From the fig tree learn (through) a parable. When its twigs are tender and it puts forth leaves, you know that summer is near.

29 So you, when you see this happening, know that God[1] is near, at the door.

30 I promise you that this generation will not pass away until all this happens.

31 Heaven and earth will pass away, but my words will not pass away.

32 No one knows that day or the hour, not even the angels in heaven, and not even the son, but only the Father.

33 Watch and stay alert! You know not when the time is coming.

34 A parable: Someone went on a journey and left the servants at home. He gave his female and male slaves the right to act, each within her or his own set of duties; and he ordered the doorkeeper to keep alert.

35 So stay alert, for you know not when the householder will come, in the evening, or at midnight, at cockcrow, or early in the morning.

36 When he suddenly comes, he must not find you sleeping.

37 And what I say to you, I say to everyone: Stay alert!

SOCIAL-HISTORICAL ANALYSIS

The parable of the fig tree sketches a picture of spring comparable to that in Song of Songs 2:11-13: "The winter is past, the rain is over and gone. The flowers appear on the earth. . . . The fig tree puts forth its figs. . . ." The barren fig tree is a typical part of winter in this country. The parable draws our attention to the changes in the twigs and their bark as the sap rises, and to the emergence of the new leaves in spring. The buds of the first round of fruit can then be seen.[2] August is the time for the principal harvest of figs. During that time people live in the orchards to guard them, and there are joyful summer festivals. Grapes and figs are *the* joys of summer (Joel 2:22).

The parable of the doorkeeper focuses our attention on the moment when a householder gives his slaves their assignments for the time when he will be absent. He is going away but does not know exactly when he will return. It may be night. He is the head of a large patriarchal household with many slaves, and they all have different areas of responsibility. Such a household would have multiple spheres of work, from farming and household maintenance to personal care and the entertainment of the master's family.[3] Many slaves, both men and women, specialized in particular kinds of work; besides these, there were also enslaved workers who lacked any skills or training. This specialization was also the basis of a hierarchy among the slaves. There is a scene in Plautus's comedy *Asinaria*[4] in which the slave who acts as doorkeeper is the center of the action. The slave steward *(atriensis)* Leonidas has instructed the doorkeeper *(ianitor)* Libanus to meet him at the barber. He beats him because he did not come. We learn incidentally from this scene that it was the doorkeeper's job "to remove the filth from in front of the door . . . / And didn't I say to get out of sight / The cobwebs on the doorposts? And furthermore / That I wanted the door knocker polished bright?"[5]

In John 10:1-2 it is clear that the doorkeeper was responsible for distinguishing the shepherds belonging to the household from thieves and robbers and not admitting the wrong people. The woman doorkeeper in John 18:16 only lets Peter pass because she knows another of Jesus' disciples who is with him. In Acts 12:14 the slave Rhoda recognizes Peter by his voice. The doorkeeper in Plautus is not permitted to receive any payments for his master. Only the slave steward may do that. It thus appears that a doorkeeper, male or female, who might be in charge at night, while not absolutely at the top of the slave hierarchy, still had an important position.[6] In Mark 13:34 this slave is ordered to remain awake all night in order to hear the returning householder's knock and his voice and to let him in. This is not an unusual situation. It would probably have been typical of the work of slave doorkeepers. Also typical would have been the accusation that the doorkeeper slaves would sleep when others were working.[7]

In Mark 13:35 the voice of Jesus, the narrator, mingles with that of the householder in the parable image. The plural address is directed at the listeners, Jesus' disciples and beyond them, "all" (13:3, 37): "Stay alert!"

In the parable image of the household slaves, however, we still have the appointment of the night watchers and are presented with the situation of the doorkeeper, who must stay awake at night to let the householder in. Thus the parable turns our attention to the work of a doorkeeper and his probable daily struggle with sleep. In today's world I associate this situation with the weariness of people who have to work swing shifts. They know about fighting the sleepiness that suddenly overwhelms them. The parable narrative culminates in a challenge to the slaves, but the world of their experience is not the interest of the householder; it is that of slaves who have to stay awake because they do not know when their master will come. For them the night is divided into four long watches.

ESCHATOLOGICAL INTERPRETATION

The basis for the interpretation of both parables is the application given in their literary frame. In 13:4 the four disciples, Peter, James, John, and Andrew had asked Jesus: " when will *this* be, and what will be the sign that *all these things* are about to be accomplished?" It is the question about the "birthpangs" of the end ("this") and the "end" itself ("all these things"). In apocalyptic language "end" is a word filled with hope: The end of suffering and oppression is anticipated with longing. The terrible experiences of the present and the near future, such as war and famine (13:8), will come to an end. They are preliminary stages of the birthpangs of the end (13:8). After the sufferings have been named in this eschatological prophecy (13:5-25), Jesus speaks of the next-to-last event: the universal divine judgment by the Son of Man and the assembling of the elect (13:26-27). The parable of the fig tree is the answer to the yearning question about the end in 13:4. The preliminary signs of the complete fulfillment, God's kingship in heaven and on earth, are already present: God's presence is already palpable for you (13:29) because you need not absolutize the sufferings of the present and can hope for their end. So will the present become a moment of happiness in the midst of suffering. God is near. This experience is associated in the parable with the joy of spring. The fig tree in spring shows people more than just that summer is near. It is transparent. The moment of thrill at the tender leaves on the tree gives new eyes to those who see creation, new eyes that can see God. Verse 30 again promises the presence of God to this generation. It is not about counting days, but about encouragement and strengthening.

From the joyful experience of the presence of God comes the strength to stay alert. The closing admonition to stay awake like the doorkeepers who watch through the night is linked to the warnings that run throughout Jesus' eschatological predictions (13:5, 7, 9, 11, 13, 23). They are to beware (13:33): of false messiahs (13:5), of their own sufferings (13:9), of the whole situation (13:23). The caution to "see" runs through the prophecy. It is "seeing" with new eyes, seeing that comes from turning back to God (4:10-12), for "to you is given the mystery of the kingdom of God" (4:11).

The parable of the doorkeeper is not to be read allegorically. God is not represented by the householder, and the work of the slaves does not reflect the tasks of the community that follows Jesus. Instead, the daily lives of slaves who must and want to remain awake are transparent to the time of waiting for God, which is a time to keep alert, beware, and listen actively to Torah (see chap. 7 above on 4:1-20). The concern that being a disciple of Jesus could be misunderstood as something exclusive, shutting others out, leads to the clarification in the last sentence of the prophecy: This is not an exclusive way, but is for everyone.

The response of the community that "sees" and "hears" is a petition that God's kingdom may come quickly and an assent to Jesus' promise: "The kingdom of God has come near" (Mark 1:15). This interpretation of the parable of the fig tree in terms of the nearness of God is connected with a decision about the relationship between the kingdom of God and the coming of the Son of Man for judgment. In v. 29b we read: "know that . . . is near." The subject of the nearness is not named. Many interpretations add "the Son of Man" here.[8] In that case the parable would be a promise of the nearness of judgment by the Son of Man (Mark 13:24-27). Verse 29a is no help: "When you see this happening . . ." In the context of Mark 13 "this" is everything predicted in 13:5-22: the preliminary signs of the end, the beginning of the birthpangs of the end-time (13:8). "This" precedes both the coming of the Son of Man and the coming of God. For me, this exegetical decision is grounded in the literary context and the formulations in Mark 13:4, as well as in the eschatological significance of the word *near* (and the word group to which it belongs). In Mark 1:15 the message of Jesus, which changes everything, is: "The kingdom of God has come near." In Mark's gospel the Son of Man who comes for judgment is a mythical figure with whom the Risen Jesus is identified. But his coming for judgment is not equated with God's coming as king. Thus in 13:32 the Son is clearly distinguished from God. The judgment of the nations is the task of the risen Messiah; only then will God come. But when all (destructive powers) have been conquered by him—the Messiah—then the Son himself will hand over his power to God, who has given it into his charge, "that God may be all in all" (1 Cor 15:28). This paraphrase of 1 Cor 15:28 is grounded in the content of 1 Cor 15:23-28. Now we need to ask where 1 Corinthians 15 may be employed for the exegesis of Mark 13:28-29. "Son" in Mark 13:32 is a good argument for doing so, but much more relevant is the location of Markan *and* Pauline eschatology in the idea of God that belongs to the First Testament and contemporary Judaism of the time, a God who will finally bring salvation to the creation. God's kingdom is the content of the hope; judgment precedes the kingdom of God. In the judgment the destruction of creation will come to an end as a final limit is set to the powers and the people who are the enemies of life. One of these life-hating powers is death. This is not the good dying of creatures at the end of their lives, but death as a humanly-created structure for destroying life. Nevertheless, the disempowering of death, to speak with 1 Cor 15:26, is not yet salvation itself. However the judgment may be portrayed in various individual texts—the differences are great—it is always clear that the judgment is terrible. The images for divine judgment are often drawn from experiences in war. For this linkage between the experience of war and divine judgment let me point to the book of Joel, or the Targum to Joel.[9] The Son of Man brings the judgment and gathers the elect (Mark 13:27); he thus preserves them in the midst of these terrible events. But this preservation is not divine salvation itself. The vision of this eschatology is of a human world and a creation living in peace and justice. Before this, there must be an end to death as a life-hating power.

METHODOLOGICAL CLARIFICATION

The basis for this interpretation of the parable narratives is explicitly contained in the text itself, in vv. 29, 33, 35, 36, and 37. There is no reason to allegorize these parables. They portray clear situations that are made transparent to the real lives of the speakers and hearers in their relationship to God. The hermeneutically decisive factor in interpreting these parables is the concept of eschatology that is applied.[10]

There is more of an ecclesiological, allegorizing tradition of interpretation for the parable of the doorkeeper than for the parable of the fig tree. The assignment of different tasks to the slaves in 13:34 has in recent times been frequently seen as allegorization, to be evaluated negatively and assigned to the ecclesiology of "Mark" or "the primitive church" (Joachim Jeremias).[11] Whereas the allegorization is regarded critically in this instance, the interpretation of the slavemaster as a parable of the Son of Man is usually taken for granted.[12] But here, too, the narrated situation as a whole should be understood as a parable. The *kyrios* is not meant to represent the Son of Man as the returning Lord of the church. He is a slaveholder and is presented as such. The multiple motif relationships with other slave parables in the Gospels have often insinuated the conclusion that Mark 13:34-37 is a "failed composition" (Jülicher), a later compilation of elements from other parables in the Jesus tradition.[13] But in Jesus parables and rabbinic *meshalim* similar material is repeatedly used; each time a unique new content results.

FOR FURTHER READING

Luzia Sutter-Rehmann, *"Geh, frage de Gebärerin . . ."* 32–68
John R. Donahue and Daniel J. Harrington, *The Gospel of Mark*
Rudolf Pesch, *Naherwartungen*
Kevin J. Cathcart and Robert P. Gordon, *The Targum of the Minor Prophets*
Luise Schottroff, *Lydia's Impatient Sisters*, 228–57

18

God Is Near:
Jesus the Parable-Teller in the Gospel of Mark

Summary

The Greek word *parabolē* has a broader meaning than the English word *parable* (or German "Gleichnis") in biblical scholarship, as does the Hebrew word *mashal*. In the Gospel of Mark it is used for a discourse about Satan that is only in part composed of imagery (3:23-27, 30). On the other hand, Jesus tells a parable—about a bridegroom (2:19-20)—without its being called a parable. Still, the word *parable* reveals a particular characteristic of Jesus' discourse: He speaks in parables because they are impossible to misunderstand, and he wants to be understood (4:12a, b; 4:23; 12:12). They characterize his discourse as a child of God or a man of God[1] whose message effects an existential decision in the hearers: Either they come to see or they harden themselves (Pharisees in 3:5; the high priest, scribes, and elders in 12:12, as it appears). But this does not mean that these groups as such consist only of those who are hardened. Jesus addresses people from these groups in order to win them over; sometimes his success is even mentioned (the scribe in 12:28-34; the leader of the synagogue in 5:21-42). That Jesus does not speak "except in parables" (4:34) is not meant to say that all his words are parables, but that his speech typically contains parables.

Jesus' work as a whole is the mighty intervention of God in a world tortured by life-hating powers: He frees people from evil spirits, from sins, Satan, sickness, and hunger. These powers are "legion" (5:9). Satan exercises dominion (3:23-27), and Jesus is there "to bind him" (3:27).

From the disciples, female and male, the groups that read or heard the gospel could learn that the way to freedom is not just a game. Even the community of those who follow Jesus can be hardened (8:17), full of anxiety and treachery, like Peter (4:17); it can sleep instead of keeping watch (14:32-42), or fall victim to the power of wealth (4:19). These themes return again and again in the interpretations of parables as well as in the narratives. Thus the interpretations of the parables are fully integrated into the content of the gospel as a whole.[2]

The parables interpreted here contain most of those parts of Jesus' discourse that are called parables in the gospel and that are related to the rabbinic parable culture: Mark 4:1-20 with the parable of the fruitful and unfruitful seed (4:3-9), the parables of the fertile ground (4:26-29) and the mustard seed (4:30-32), the parables of the vineyard (12:1-12), the fig tree (13:28-29), and the doorkeeper (13:33-37). The interpretive texts that surround the fictional parable narratives are included; I regard them as an inseparable component of the parables.

I will present my conclusions in the sequence of the gospel text. The parable of the sower and its interpretation (4:1-20) speak of the event of hearing Jesus' words as a hearing of God's voice, the Torah. The life situations of the hearers are often destructive—and yet to the hearing, seeing, and understanding of God's voice and the doing of God's word belongs the great promise: The kingdom of God will thus be revealed, and life will be changed. The judgment of the nations will come (4:26-29), but before that they will be invited to hear. The kingdom of God looks different from the great imperial kingdoms; it puts an end to the dominion of some people over other people (the mustard seed: 4:30-32). God's vineyard, Israel, has been destroyed by violence from above and from below. But God accomplishes the miracle of rescue (12:1-12). The Son of Man will judge the nations and preserve the elect in the judgment (13:24-27). Already the nearness of God, who is coming, can be seen by those who have eyes to see (13:28-29). They keep alert (13:33-37). Jesus the parable teller is a teacher of Torah with power that causes people to hear God's voice (4:1-20); he is a political prophet (4:26-32) and an interpreter of the present of the people of God (12:1-12). He is the proclaimer of God's nearness (1:15; 13:28, 29), and thus an eschatological prophet. His parables are understood because they are understandable (4:33). They are part of his authority to bind Satan, to drive destructive spirits out of human beings, to forgive sins on God's authority, to heal sicknesses. For the Gospel of Mark they are not rhetorical or poetic language, but speech with authority, filled with God's power and arising out of a faith that can move mountains (11:23). The disciples will be commissioned for this same preaching with authority. It is said that they heal the sick and drive out demons (3:14; 6:7-13). But it is not said that they tell parables as Jesus does. Why not?

19

Loving God: The Merciful Samaritan

Luke 10:25-37

TRANSLATION

25   And see: A Torah scholar stood up and posed a question to test him:
      Teacher, what must I do to have life in its eternal fullness?

26   [Jesus] said to him: What is in the Torah? How do you read it?

27   He answered: You shall love Adonai, your God, out of your whole heart
      and with your whole life and with your whole strength and with your
      whole mind, and your neighbor as yourself.

28   He [Jesus] said to him: You have answered rightly. Do that and you will
      live.

29   [The Torah scholar] wanted to defend his question and said to Jesus:
      And who is my neighbor?

30   Jesus took this up and said: A man went down from Jerusalem to Jericho
      and fell into the hands of robbers. They stripped him, beat him, and left
      him lying there half dead.

31   As it happened, a priest was going down by the same way and he saw
      [the wounded man] and passed him by.

32   In the same way, a Levite also came to the place and saw [the wounded
      man] and passed him by.

33   A Samaritan who was traveling came to him and saw him and took pity
      on him.

34   And he went to him, bound up his wounds and poured oil and wine on
      them. Then he placed him on his own donkey and brought him to the
      inn and took care of him.

35   The next morning he took out two denarii, gave them to the innkeeper
      and said: Take care of him, and if you have additional costs, I will com-
      pensate you for them when I come back.

36   What do you think? Which of these three became a neighbor to the one
      who fell among the robbers?

37   [The Torah scholar] said: The one who showed mercy to him. And Jesus
      said to him: Go your way and do likewise.

SOCIAL-HISTORICAL ANALYSIS
AND ESCHATOLOGICAL INTERPRETATION

Jesus and the Torah Scholar

In the Gospel of Luke this story about Jesus and a Torah scholar is told in more detail than in its synoptic parallels (Mark 12:28-31; Matt 22:34-40). Each of these stories must be read for itself and in its own literary context. Attempts to discover pre-Lukan material in the Lukan text remain hypothetical and do not help us to understand the text.

There is a rich dialogue here between Jesus and the Torah scholar. The scholar inquires of Jesus; he makes Jesus his teacher (v. 25)—like the rich man in a prominent political position in Luke 18:18: "What must I do, that I may inherit life in its eternal fullness?" The Torah scholar has received an education. Jesus comes from poor people in a village in Galilee (Luke 2:1-20, 39). He has been presented as a highly gifted child (Luke 2:40-52). He can read the Torah in the synagogue (Luke 4:16-21). But he does not have an education like that of the Torah scholar.[1] Throughout the scene the scholar remains the questioner and the learner.

Anti-Jewish reading has drawn the picture of the Torah scholar unjustly: as if he wanted to lay a trap for Jesus (*ekpeirazōn,* v. 25) and was being self-righteous (v. 29: "wanted to justify himself").[2] Only occasionally does someone recognize in vv. 25 and 29 the characteristics of discussion and learning that correspond to Jewish tradition. At the beginning the learned man poses a question that is crucial to his own life: What must I do now, in my life situation? He sets this question before Jesus, to test the man he has chosen to be his teacher. Jesus and the learned man are in agreement that the Torah contains the answer: in the *Shemaʿ Israel* (v. 27, from Deut 6:5) and its interpretation in Lev 19:18, the command of loving one's neighbor. In v. 29 the Torah scholar poses the correct second question: What does that mean for me, concretely: Who is my neighbor? He receives from Jesus a precise answer to his question: Be a person who pays attention and does mercy.[3] This is what it means to act lovingly toward God. Now Jesus repeats his answer from the first part of the Decalogue once again: Do this (v. 37; see also v. 28). The parable of the merciful Samaritan has made Jesus' answer concrete. It is a matter of seeing (vv. 31, 32, 33) and doing (vv. 25, 28, 37, 38).

The serious question of the Torah scholar who wants to learn from Jesus should not be projected onto the same level with Luke 18:9 and 20:20, two passages that are also to be distinguished from one another. The people addressed in 18:9 are subjectively of the opinion that they are keeping the Torah, that is, that they are righteous. Jesus disputes it. In 20:20, on the other hand, these seem to be people who have come as provocateurs and are pretending to be righteous, although they really do not believe that they are. In the interpretive tradition these two passages are often taken together and interpreted as a moral reproach of Pharisaism. I understand the question from the teacher of the Law in analogy to Luke 3:10, 12, 14: "What should we do?" That is the fundamental question in learning from Torah, which is not aimed at a timeless ethical doctrine but at the concrete situation of those who ask. What is the action God expects, here and now?

The discussion and the parable belong within the rich Jewish tradition of active compassion as an expression of love for God. Love for God and doing justice go together. This can be seen in the exegesis of the *Shema' Israel*[4] or in the traditions that underlie Matt 25:31-46:[5] "just as you did it to one of the least of these who are members of my family, you did it to me" (Matt 25:40). In Acts 10:2, Cornelius, a man of non-Jewish descent who lives as a Jew, is characterized as "a devout man who feared God with all his household; he did many righteous deeds[6] among the people and prayed constantly to God." Let me mention two rather randomly selected rabbinic stories to illustrate the tradition of acting and teaching within which Luke 10:25-37 belongs. Both are taken from a midrash on the book of Leviticus *(Leviticus Rabbah)*. This section is about reflecting on people who care for the poor.

> R. Huna said, "This refers to one who visits the sick."
>
> For R. Huna said, "Whoever visits the sick takes away one sixtieth of [whatever ails the patient]."
>
> They objected to R. Huna, "If so, let sixty people visit him and let him climb down [from his bed and go] with them to the marketplace."
>
> He said to them, "It is indeed one-sixtieth, but that is on condition that each loves him as much as he loves himself. But in any event they help him."[7]

It is possible to give a sick person so much love that it takes away a sixtieth of the illness. Rabbi Huna treats the subject carefully. Even if the care and concern are not so intensive, it is good to visit the sick. It helps them. But sometimes the miracle of love happens, and it is a miracle, even if it can only take away a little of the sickness. Rabbi Huna's words give encouragement to enter into such a love of neighbor. In the same section we find a teaching from Rabbi Abin:

> Said R. Abin, "When a poor man stands at your door, the Holy One, blessed be he, is standing at his right hand.
>
> "For it is written, 'For he stands at the right hand of the poor man' [Ps. 109:31].
>
> "'If you have given him [a worthy gift], know that my Name stands at his right hand and is going to give you your reward.
>
> "'And if you do not give him, know that my Name is standing at his right hand and is going to exact punishment from that man [that is, from you].'"[8]

God stands at the side of those who need love. Love for God happens when a poor person comes to your door. The intensity required by such love is described over and over again. Nothing about it is a matter of course. The problem of Christian interpretation of Luke 10:25-37 is that mercy appears as something so obvious,[9] while the text is telling us precisely that it is anything but obvious. The text means to make us see the miracle: It is possible to love God and other people in the deepest sense of the word *love*. Instead, the text is usually dealt with at a very general and noncommittal level: Jesus teaches love for all humankind. And that is supposed to be what is special about Christianity[10]—that, in contrast to Judaism, it does not teach only love for people of one's own nation in particularist fashion, but general and unrestricted love for all people. I doubt that this notion of generalized love of humanity is found anywhere in the New Testament. The parable of the merciful Samaritan is always introduced as the chief proof of it. But the parable does not reflect at all on the ethnic relationship between the Samaritan and the victim. It does *not* say that the victim is a Jew, so that the Samaritan's love overcomes a barrier.

The interpretation of Luke 10:30-37 as an example of loving one's enemies (in the relationship of the Samaritan to the victim) is thus not persuasive. The text would have to make it clear that the man who was attacked was a Jew. Another version of this interpretation is to assume that love of enemies is the message of the text for a Jewish audience. In fact, the parable presumes an audience that is Jewish or practices the Jewish way of life. For such people the Samaritan's action and his role as a positive model is a challenge. But love of enemies does not seem to me the appropriate interpretation of such a challenge. What is at stake in the parable is learning to do the deeds of love.

Interpreting this parable in terms of generalized love of humanity or love of enemies misses the point of the text in a significant way: This is not about notions and ideas of love, but about how a "teaching" of love can become deed. The priest and Levite fail at this, but the Samaritan "does" the deed.

From a social-historical point of view, then, the dialogue between Jesus and the Torah scholar is to be located within the Jewish culture of discussion, and its primary content in the Jewish tradition of doing righteous deeds. At the beginning Jesus asks the Torah scholar: What does the Torah say to your question? The Torah scholar answers with the *Shema' Israel*, the interpretation of which he clarifies in terms of Lev 19:18, the command to love one's neighbor. The expression "double command" of love in exegetical literature is misleading because it gives the impression that here something new (and Christian) is being added to the *Shema' Israel*.[11] That love for God is made concrete in love for other people is a matter of course for the First Testament and the postbiblical tradition. What is reflected upon is how such love can become deed, and how it can create a relationship between two people that is life-giving for both of them: the miracle of love.

Why Did the Priest and the Levite Look Away?

In vv. 30 and 31 the failure of the priest and the Levite is described in parallel formulations: "and he saw [the wounded man] and passed by on the other side."[12] They saw and looked away. The text does not say why. Their behavior is often interpreted in anti-Jewish fashion when they are said to be representatives of a Judaism that is faithful to the Torah.

A priest, by his lineage, belongs to the closed status of priesthood, those who alone are permitted to offer sacrifices in the Temple in Jerusalem. The Levite also belongs to a closed status, grounded in lineage, of those who serve in the Temple, but at this period he was located one step lower than the priest in the Temple hierarchy. Both men are on their way down from the Temple in Jerusalem to Jericho, where they probably live.

Why do they look away? There has been a broad discussion about whether they did not wish to defile themselves with a corpse.[13] But the wounded man is not dead. This whole discussion works with the anti-Jewish contrasting of life-hating Jewish notions of purity and impurity versus Christian love of human beings. Another answer to the question of why they looked away has been sought in the generally bad reputation of priests and Levites. But despite some critical statements about them,[14] there are no generally negative judgments either in Jewish literature or in the New Testament—and none in the Gospel of Luke. The two are closely described as part of the narrative contrast between them and the Samaritan. This contrast resembles that between the Pharisee and the toll collector in Luke 18:9-14.[15] The listeners would sooner have expected a priest or Levite than a Samaritan to know how to live according to the Torah. The Samaritan is presented in contrast to the priest and Levite. Samaritans lived in a conflictual proximity to the Jewish people, which worshiped the God of Israel in the Temple in Jerusalem. They worshiped the same God in a temple on Mount Gerizim. There were continual attacks and exclusions from both sides.[16] However, the contrast between the Samaritan and the cultic personnel from Jerusalem in this parable should not be interpreted in ethnic terms, as though the Samaritan were a member of a different people, hated by the Jews. The Samaritan is a member of a cultic community that worships the same God differently from the way that God is worshiped by the Judaism oriented to Jerusalem. The relationship between Jewish and Samaritan people was at times hostile, on religious grounds that are explicable precisely because of the closeness of the two cults.

In any case, the Samaritan also regards the Pentateuch as a holy book; nevertheless, at this period a Jewish audience would be more inclined to expect misbehavior from him than from their own people.[17]

I consider the answer to the question of why the priest and Levite look away to be closely bound up with Jesus' challenge at the end: Go and do likewise—do just as the Samaritan did (v. 37). It is not said whether the Torah scholar did so, because what is important is how the story continues in the hearers. They can answer the question of why the priest and Levite looked away when they should have paid attention because they themselves have already looked away. Now they must take the next step: in their own lives, to look and to act.

In Romans Paul laments before God about the violent power of sin that corrupts Jewish people as well: "You, then, that teach others, will you not teach yourself? While you preach against stealing, do you steal? You that forbid adultery, do you commit adultery? . . ." (2:21-22). All are caught in the deadly structures of sin, Jew and non-Jew alike (3:9). Paul is not accusing individuals of doing wrong out of base motives here; he is lamenting the structural power of sin, which prevents people from really looking, even when they see, and from acting and loving even when they know what is God's will.

The parable of the merciful Samaritan is often accused of banality: It is only an ethical example story without any deeper dimension. But if the hearers of this story begin to reflect on it and to talk with one another about what each needs to do here and now, the specter of supposed superficiality vanishes. What does it mean today to see what is happening with raw materials from poor countries? And if the deed of love is even a tiny one, if it really helps to protect the life of the victim, it is a miracle. This, hopefully, makes it unnecessary to discuss whether the Samaritan's idea, binding up wounds, does not represent something that remains on the surface and tends rather to sustain the structures of injustice than to change them. As long as the soup kitchens cause us not to make light of the structural injustice of violence to the poor, they are a necessary first step.

The Samaritan

The eschatological interpretation of this parable is oriented to the Samaritan's action, which is to be imitated. His acts are described in detail. At this point the parable narrative is very precise (vv. 34, 35). He dresses the wounds[18] and binds them up. He puts the wounded man on his donkey and brings him to an inn, where he procures a bed and food for him. He does continue his own journey, but makes certain that the wounded man will be allowed to recuperate. And he will come back. For centuries the Samaritan has been interpreted christologically: It is Christ who comes to the aid of the suffering and sinful people of this world.[19] Even if I do not consider the figure of the Samaritan in the narrative to be a veiled description of Jesus as Messiah, the christological interpretation is relevant for me: It reveals the eschatological dimension of the Samaritan's action. Even if it only takes away a sixtieth of the wounded man's suffering—I am referring to the rabbinic story quoted above—it makes both the sufferer and the Samaritan people of full dignity. In them God's new creation can be seen.

The Samaritan's compassion is represented as *imitatio Dei* ("imitation of God"), as indicated by the verb in v. 33, "he was moved with pity." People can bring the divine pity to earth. So God's year of release, proclaimed by Jesus according to Luke (4:19), will become reality. The Jewish tradition contains reflection on the presumption of imitating God. "Is it possible for a human being to follow after the Holy One? Was it not said long ago: Adonai, your God, is a devouring fire (Deut 4:24)? This means only that one should follow the actions of the Holy One. As he clothes the naked . . . so shall you also clothe the naked" (b. Sotah 14a).

METHODOLOGICAL CLARIFICATION

The ecclesiological tradition of interpretation is found here especially in the contrast between love in Jesus' sense (generalized love of humanity) and particularistic love of neighbor in the sense of Judaism. Thus the church becomes an institution that has a better ethics and theology. But the parable asks about deeds.

Besides this anti-Jewish stereotype, this parable is, as we have already indicated, interpreted in Christian tradition in still other anti-Jewish ways: the priest, the Levite, and the Torah teacher are understood as representatives of a Judaism true to the Torah, with the Torah teacher appearing as self-righteous, the priest and Levite as lacking in compassion because cultic purity is more important to them than a person in need.

The classification of the parable as an exemplary narrative is problematic because it reduces the text to the supposition that it is a simple matter to do likewise (one must only want to). But the text tells of the failure of those who do not want to fail, and of an action that brings the love of God to earth. The wounded man is not released from the inn as cured; the Samaritan will come back. It ends with an open action in the narrative and an open conclusion after Jesus' challenge to action. The Torah teacher will act; the audience will act. The parable becomes a window through which the new creation becomes visible. Therefore it is a parable like the others.

20

The Great Messianic Feast of Rejoicing, or, The Partying Neighbor Women

---

Luke 15:1-32

In this section I will begin with an exposition of Luke 15:11-32 because the parable of the lost son has always dominated the reading of Luke 15:3-7 and 15:8-10, and, thanks to its positioning in the text—at the end of a discourse by Jesus—it is probably meant to dominate. The two parables in Luke 15:3-7 and 15:8-10 will be discussed afterward.

TRANSLATION OF LUKE 15:11-32
"God's Hand Is Always Open":
The Father and Two Difficult Sons

11   And he said: A man had two sons.

12   The younger of them said to his father: Father, give me the part of the property that belongs to me. And he divided his property between them.

13   And a few days later the younger son gathered everything together and went away to a far distant land; and there he wasted his property in dissipated living.

14   When he had spent everything, there was a severe famine in the land; and so he began to suffer want.

15   He left there and placed himself in the service of a citizen of that country, who sent him into the fields to herd his pigs.

16   And he longed to fill himself with the pods of the carob tree, which were fed to the pigs, but no one gave him anything.

17   He said to himself: How many people in my father's employ have more bread than they need! And here I am, starving.

18   I will get up and go to my father. And I will say to him: Father, I have sinned against God and against you.

19   I am no longer worthy to be called your son. Make me one of your laborers.

20   And he got up and went to his father. When he was still far away, his father saw him and had pity on him and ran and fell on his neck and kissed him.

21   Then the son said to him: Father, I have sinned against God and against you; I am no longer worthy to be called your son.

22   Then the father said to his slaves: Quickly, bring the best clothes and put them on him; put a signet ring on his hand and sandals on his feet.

23   And bring the fatted calf and kill it, and we will feast and celebrate.

24   For he, my son, was dead and has come to life again. He was lost and is found! And they began to celebrate.

25   But his older son was in the field. And as he was coming home and approaching the house he heard musical instruments and singing.

26   And he called one of the slaves and asked what was going on.

27   He said to him: Your brother has come. Your father has killed the fatted calf because he has received him back in good health.

28   Then he was angry and would not go inside. But his father came out and begged him to come in.

29   He said to his father: So, all these years I have served you and never opposed any of your wishes. And you never gave me even a goat to celebrate with my friends.

30   But now comes this son of yours, who has devoured his property with prostitutes, and you have killed for him the fatted calf.

31   But he said to him: My child, you are always with me and everything I have is yours.

32   Now it was and is[1] important to celebrate and rejoice, because he, your brother, was dead and has come to life; he was lost and is found.

SOCIAL-HISTORICAL ANALYSIS

It is the task of social-historical analysis to explain the details of the narrative. In a second step, it is supposed to analyze the social function of the literary text: Does it intend to teach a right attitude toward property,[2] does it mean to tell about the Wisdom-directed order of the patriarchal household and how the *paterfamilias* disrupts it,[3] or does it—deliberately or accidentally—divinize the patriarchal father? This patriarchal father governs male and female slaves, male and female laborers, his wife, his daughters, and the other female members of the household, who are so unimportant in the mind of the narrator that, insofar as they are female, they remain invisible.[4]

I will trace the details of the text in order: The younger son can expect a lesser inheritance than the firstborn. He asks, during his father's lifetime, for the share of the property that will come to him.[5] "And he divided his property between them" (v. 12). The text gives no indication that the son's request is in any way reprehensible.[6] The father fulfills his request. Thus it makes sense to him also. The legal basis of this division is often labeled in scholarly discussions with a term from modern law, such as *compensation*.[7] This can be regarded as a known phenomenon in Jewish and Hellenistic legal contexts. In particular, Sir 33:20-24 and Tob 8:21 show that there was such a legal practice. The text says that the property is divided between the two sons. However, the rest of the narrative shows that the older son cannot dispose of his share as the younger can. Instead, the father remains the owner and can give gifts to the younger son on his return without asking the elder. In v. 31 the father says to the older son: "You are always with me, and everything I have is yours." But apparently the older son did indeed have the expectation of inheriting, before the younger had been received back again, and yet during his father's lifetime nothing yet "belongs" to him. And now the father has taken the younger son back again and, it seems, has also promised him another share in the inheritance.

There is discussion about *how* Luke 15:11-32 is oriented to the legal situation: whether the text holds up a mirror to it in order to confront it with a new and entirely different law, that of the kingship of God.[8] Taking back the younger son is said to be a deliberate narrative "extravagance" in Ricoeur's sense.[9] This assumption encounters two difficulties: (1) The extravagance could also be intended to illustrate a paternal love that is altogether earthly (see below), one that crosses legal boundaries; (2) in that case the father who displays such otherworldly love would be lying to his elder son (v. 31). With the taking back of the younger son, at the latest, the father's property no longer "belongs" to the older son. And as the story shows, it had never belonged to him in the sense that the younger had been able to dispose of his share of the property. We will come back to the question of how the text addresses ideas about the right to property.

Verses 13-16 describe in rich narrative detail the descent of the younger son into extreme poverty. He converts his share of the property into money[10] and travels "to a far distant land." If I presume that the text depicts the rural situation in Judea or Galilee, the distant land would be found somewhere in the Jewish Diaspora. Like many other Jewish people, the young man emigrates in search of a new economic existence, something much more difficult to find in the increasingly impoverished Jewish homeland. If his father had been a great landowner in the Roman style, the younger son's share of the property would have been adequate for a farm of his own. The emigration of the younger son remains—from a social-historical point of view—within the framework of the experiences of Jewish people in the first century, especially that of those with little property. In the Roman empire emigration for economic reasons was a common phenomenon.

He wasted/dissipated his property, because he lived beyond his means, wastefully (*asōtōs;* on this see the discussion of v. 18 below). This is the only word in the narrative about his decline that makes any moral accusation against him. His brother (v. 30) reproaches him with having spent his money on prostitutes, but the narrative does not talk about a moral downfall;[11] instead, it speaks of stupidity and its economic consequences. A famine—something that happened repeatedly in different regions of the Roman empire—brings him to starvation, because he can no longer pay the high prices for basic foodstuffs (see Rev 6:6). He tries to help himself out of this crisis by becoming the client[12] of a wealthy citizen of that country. This person apparently has (Roman?) citizenship, which the young man lacks. Thus the text also tells indirectly of his situation as an economic refugee, a foreigner with no rights. This powerful man gives him work as a herdsman, something that was regarded as degrading in all societies of that era.[13] Added to this, for a Jew, was that he could not eat pork (Lev 11:7; Deut 14:8).[14] In his hunger, he envies the swine their feed,[15] but does not dare to eat it. "No one gave it to him"—that is, he was closely watched.

The wages he receives are thus not adequate to sustain a minimal existence. Now a day laborer himself, he compares himself to his father's laborers. For their work they earn a more than adequate living (v. 17). He is about to die of hunger. He makes a second attempt[16] to save his own life. He will go to his father and beg him for forgiveness, so that he will employ him as a day laborer. His confession of "sins" is reported twice, once as an internal monologue (vv. 18, 19) and then as it is spoken (v. 21). What "sin" had he actually committed against God[17] and his father? It is plausible that the father could have regarded his failure as sin. But why, exactly, is self-incurred poverty a sin in the eyes of God? In the New Testament vice lists, which reflect the Jewish *halakah*, i.e., applied, practical interpretation of Torah, greed *(pleonexia)* is regarded as sin, but not *asōtia* in the sense of wasting money. In two of three occurrences in the New Testament the word refers to excessive use of alcohol (Eph 5:18; 1 Pet 4:4; unspecified "debauchery" in Titus 1:6).[18] The younger son's confession of sin seems probably to refer to his bad behavior, which is called "dissipated" *(asōtōs,* v. 13) and is not specified.

There exists a second-century C.E. letter from a son to his mother that tells a similar story. It was introduced into the discussion of Luke 15:11-32 by Adolf Deissmann in 1923.[19] The Egyptian Antonis Longos writes to his mother, Neilus: "I am ashamed because I am behaving shabbily. I write you that I am naked. I beg you, forgive me! Moreover, I know all that I have brought upon myself. I belong among the riffraff. I know, I have sinned *(hēmērteka)*. . . . Do you not know that I would rather become a cripple than to know that I owe anyone even an *obolos*? . . . Please come yourself! . . ."[20] Deissmann reconstructs from the letter, which is in tattered condition, that the son asked his mother to come and pay his debts. It is not really clear what this son sees as his "sin" against his mother. He seems to have left his village and his mother. That he left in anger, as Deissmann reconstructs, is possible but is not said. The conflict the son wants reconciled could also be that he does not want to return to his mother in the village. It is easier to imagine what the "sin" of the lost son against his father consisted of than why he has sinned against God.

The weight the narrative in Luke 15:11-32 places on this confession of sin by repeating it is unmistakable—just as is the meaning of the father's cry of joy

(v. 24), which is repeated in v. 32. The confession of sin links the content of the parable narrative to Luke 15:1, 7, 10. It is told in such a way that it implies the application: This is how the repentance *(metanoia)* of a sinful human being looks. In the same way, the father's cry of joy establishes soteriological relationships to the literary context: Luke 15:4, 7, 8, 10; 19:10 (key words "lost," "joy"). The two-fold confession of sin and the cry of joy make sense within the framework of the story as told,[21] but they point unmistakably to an application. Thus the parable can stand without a frame that offers an application. The implicit application is made clear from the literary context.

The narrative about the meeting of the father and son and the great and joyous festival (vv. 20-24) establishes a new focus. The son's hunger in the foreign place is now countered by the lavish banquet at his homecoming. The text is full of detail. The father runs to meet his son. Brad H. Young points to a rabbinic parable that contains a comparable motif in a context whose content is also comparable:

> "Return, O Israel, to the Lord your God" [Hos 14:2]. This can be compared to the son of a king who was far from his father—a journey of 100 days. His friends said to him: Go back to your father. He answered them: I cannot. Then his father sent to him with the message: Go as far as your strength allows; the rest of the way I will come to you. So the Holy One, blessed be he, spoke to them [Israel]: "Return to me, and I will return to you." (Mal 3:7).[22]

In another comparable rabbinic parable the son does not want to go to the father because he is ashamed. The father sends him the message: "Is there a son who is ashamed to return to his father?"[23] Thus it may be that the king's son in the rabbinic parable quoted above is also too weak with shame to travel the whole way. That God goes to meet the returning people is derived here from Mal 3:7. I cannot judge whether a Near Eastern patriarch in such a situation would not also run to meet his son. But, since Joachim Jeremias,[24] Luke 15:20 has frequently been read in this way: The father runs to meet him, which really is beneath the dignity of an "aged oriental."

In any case, the narrative means to express that the father does not insist on his patriarchal position. He meets his son on the same level. It is just this mutuality that is expressed in the rabbinic parable in *Pesikta Rabbati* 44. God needs the beloved people just as they need God. In regard to the people, God does not stand on the divine superiority. This is a frequent *topos* in rabbinic literature. For me, in the first place, this observation does not have anything to do with the relationship between the figure of the father in the narrative and God. I am using the rabbinic parable here in connection with the social-historical analysis of Luke 15:20 as a social-historical source for a hierarchy-critical awareness in regard to the relationship between father and son in a patriarchal household. Verse 20 remains within the framework of the narrative. The father loves his child. When the father goes to meet the son, the son's confession of sin acquires a different role than it had in the son's internal dialogue. It no longer expresses the subjection whose purpose was to put an end, finally, to hunger. It expresses his relationship to his father. Hence the plea for work as a day laborer disappears in v. 21.

However, the critical consciousness of the narrative is limited as regards patriarchy. The text sees no problem in maintaining silence about the presence of women and female slaves in this household, without whom it would scarcely have been possible to prepare the great feast (vv. 23-27). Likewise, the fact that the patriarch employs male slaves and day laborers (vv. 17, 22, 26) is as much a patriarchal matter of course for the narrative as is its silence about all the women in the household.

The father has slaves give his son a new outfit, probably in a festal ceremony. The quality of the outfit is important both for the interpretation of the father's love and for the understanding of the situation of the elder brother. A cleft seems to appear between the love of the father for the younger and older sons.

"The first robe," like the finger ring, the sandals, and the festival banquet with meat are presented as an expression of the overwhelming reversal of the younger son's situation: a festal banquet for the starving, handsome garments for the ragged—even though to this point rags or nakedness[25] have not been expressly mentioned. However, the fact that the robe is called the "first" *(prōtē),* plus the finger ring, could mean more than merely the honoring of the dishonored, namely his visible integration into the social status of the propertied (robe)[26] and his sharing in the authority of the patriarch of the household (ring).[27] With the ring, financial transactions could be authorized. It is not said whether the older son also has had a signet ring all these years, but that is implied by the father in v. 31 as understood. The returning son receives a share in the paternal power.

The presumed property relationship makes sense as a sharing of the sons in the father's authority in good faith. In that case 15:12 would apply only insofar as the "compensation" of the younger son means that from then on the remainder of the property was to be regarded as the future inheritance of the elder. Verse 31 would be incomplete because in the meantime, through a unilateral act of the father, the younger son again had a share in authority over the property and presumably could count on inheriting a second time. The text does not relate these details because it is not interested in a complete clarification of the legal aspects of the property relationships.[28] It is not sufficiently clear to me that the text means to portray an ideal patriarchal household with a community of goods.[29] In this regard Acts 2:42-47 and 4:32–5:11 speak a different language: Here we have a class of community property that is no longer in private hands,[30] and from which the needy are supplied. In Luke 15:11-32 there is no idea of a community of goods in the sense of social justice, but rather the idealization of a patriarchal household *with* its orientation to property and all its injustices toward women and dependents. The order of a patriarchal household is not disrupted, from the perspective of the *paterfamilias,* by the renewed acceptance of the younger son. If the intent had been that the order of the Wisdom-directed house would really be confronted with God's quite different order of things,[31] the goal of the paternal action would have to have been something other than the harmony of the father with the two sons, both of whom are in agreement as regards property questions. This is a patriarchal father of "flesh and blood," to use a rabbinic expression, which makes the distance between God and his designation as father quite clear. His love is magnificent, but it does not disrupt earthly relationships, not even the power relationships of a patriarchal household. He embodies neither the divine order nor the ideal of the generous sage.[32] He is presented positively, but not as a model for dealing with property. The rich man in Luke 18:18-23 and the many critical statements in the Gospel of Luke about the destructive power of wealth cause this father to appear as what he is: a patriarch who keeps order in his house and property in the interests of his sons. There is plenty of material in the Gospel of Luke that is critical of this patriarchal order.[33] The parable of the lost son remains within the horizon of patriarchy. The legal bases of vv. 22 and 31 are fuzzy because the father has absolute power in the house. He defines what is just and what is merciful.

The elder son stands at the center of vv. 25-32. The scene should probably be understood to show him returning in the evening from his work in the fields; it is to be expected of him that he will go into the house and join in the feast and in the rejoicing. A slave tells him what is going on in the house. He becomes angry and refuses to go in. Then the father comes out to him and asks him again and again[34] to come inside. His rejection is related in great detail in direct speech. Verse 29 describes his life as a son in a patriarchal household: He works and obeys his father. There has never been any celebration for him. This would have been an accurate description of his life, not an exaggeration. In v. 30 he speaks disdainfully of the younger son's lifestyle, though he cannot actually know any of its details. The festival for the younger son is, in his eyes, both inappropriate and unjust toward himself. The father answers this criticism: Because he was always there, there was no particular reason to celebrate. He is not disadvantaged, because he is the heir and possesses authority.[35] The parable ends with the renewed invitation in direct speech: You should be happy to celebrate and rejoice with us, for this brother (is) your brother, who was dead and has now come to life again. The father repeats for him the festive invitation with which he had inaugurated the feast (v. 24). The parable breaks off. Now it is the audience's turn[36] to step into the elder brother's shoes, to respond to the father and to participate in the feast. The narrative does not intend to portray the older brother as a negative character, but to make his wrath understandable and to win over those who identify with the elder brother.

The behavior of the elder brother and the father remains within the frame of the story as told. We can consider whether a "flesh and blood" father would have gone out to the angry son. But while it may be that not every patriarch would have been prepared to do so, this one was. Paternal love is a frequent theme in ancient literature and rhetoric.[37] It is true that the rabbis say in *Pesikta Rabbati* 44 that God differs from flesh-and-blood fathers in that God is in a position to retract a sentence once spoken. Or: God first turns back in order to model for Israel how to turn back. Or: When human beings have pronounced a severe judgment, a great deal of money has to be produced to change that judgment. But God can be persuaded to repent with just a tiny word.[38] But the stories about fatherly love really all move within this framework: Fathers can act out of love to save their sons, and not out of calculation and personal interest.[39] The father in Luke 15 is a flesh-and-blood father. The older son is not condemned in the story; he is invited. His story, too, is not to be read allegorically.

ESCHATOLOGICAL INTERPRETATION

There are hundreds of rabbinic "father" stories—some of them also stories about kings[40] or husbands—that speak of the love of God and Israel's return to its God. Eckhard Rau and Brad H. Young have presented particularly detailed discussions of Luke 15:11-32 and some of these rabbinic parables in context.[41] Without doubt the rabbinic parables, as well as this one (and other parables in the Synoptic Gospels), show links to rhetorical and other traditions in Hellenistic culture.[42] The cultural context of the ideas about paternal love as patriarchal ideal and praxis is—as we have shown—important for this parable, just as rabbinic parables about Israel's repentant return are fundamental for understanding it. But every parable says something unique in its literary context. Discovering that unique point helps us in applying the parable.

In this case there is no explicit introduction to the parable and no closing application. The immediate context consists of two other parables—the lost sheep and the lost drachma—and a fictional situation in the life of Jesus in which Jesus is supposed to have told these three parables to the male and female Pharisees and scribes, as well as the toll collectors and sinners who are also probably presumed to be present (Luke 15:1-2). This fictional situation in itself points to the context of the two-volume Lukan work as the framework of interpretation for the three parables[43] because the narrative of this fictional situation presumes that it will be understood to be exemplary in character. Why do the Pharisees and scribes grumble that Jesus is receiving sinners and eating with them? Why do the toll collectors and sinners of both sexes "draw near" to hear Jesus?

Against the background of Christian history of interpretation of this parable, in order to avoid misunderstanding, let me first clarify the notion of sin and forgiveness of sin in the context of the First Testament, contemporary Judaism, and the New Testament: Sin is a concrete violation of the Torah, and not a condition of human life. Forgiving sins is an act of God that people should emulate. The conflict between Jesus and the Pharisees cannot be about Jesus' forgiving sinners their sins for God's sake. Both parties would have agreed on that score.

Jesus is the Messiah of Israel, the longed-for liberator of the people—that is made clear in two chapters at the beginning of the Gospel of Luke. The gospel returns to that point again and again. Jesus' praxis leads to the liberation of Israel from hunger, sickness, and political oppression (see especially 4:16-21): It is a praxis of healings, the Gospel of the Poor, and Jesus' table fellowship with toll collectors and sinful people. The Gospel of Luke tells some stories about Jesus' (table) companionship with sinners and toll collectors: Luke 5:1-11; 5:27-32; 7:36-50; 19:1-11. It also says that Pharisees did not agree with Jesus' praxis in this regard (5:30); they "grumble," or "complain" (as in 15:2); they are filled with incomprehension and consider what they should do with him (6:11).[44] "The people of this generation"[45] reject Jesus as a "friend of toll collectors and sinners" and in the same breath accuse him of being "a friend of eating and of wine" (7:34).[46] At a banquet in a Pharisee's house, to which Jesus has been invited, he makes a speech critical of Pharisees (and teachers of the Law), who react to it after his departure (11:39-54). This reaction of the scribes and Pharisees (11:53, 54) is described at some length; it cannot be precisely translated, but it contains no planning for a denunciation that could lead to a charge, much less to a sentence of death. The Gospel of Luke depicts a conflict between Jesus and the Pharisees, but it is not a mortal conflict; they are not complicit in his execution.[47] Once they even warn him that Herod means to kill him (13:31). Scribes, however, do appear in the Passion story. Probably as members of the Sanhedrin, they play a part in handing Jesus over to the Romans, which leads to his execution.[48] It appears that, despite the generalizing language (*the* scribes, *the* teachers of the Law, *the* Pharisees), in the intention of the text Jesus' critics who were Pharisees or scribes are not to be regarded as a homogeneous and closed group of hostile "opponents" to Jesus. They "grumble," says 15:2 (5:30; see also 19:7), as the people Israel grumbled in the wilderness against its God.[49]

What is the content of this conflict that permeates Jesus' public activity, according to Luke? Its most important aspect is Jesus' table fellowship with toll collectors and sinners. This table companionship is part of Jesus' call to everyone, the whole people, to return to its God: Luke 13:1-9. In 7:29 Jesus says that the Pharisees and teachers of the Law rejected the baptism of John the Baptizer, which was associated with the challenge to the whole people to repent. The "people" *(laos)* and the toll collectors, however, let themselves be baptized. I read 7:29-35 to say that Jesus is like the Baptizer in that he calls the people to repentance,[50] even though his attitude toward food differs from that of the Baptizer. Jesus calls sinners to repentance. But sinners are not only those who violate the Torah and are criticized for it by self-proclaimed righteous people; they are precisely also the righteous themselves (Luke 18:9-14). The Pharisees think that they keep the Torah, but in the view of the Gospel of Luke they keep it only superficially and fail in regard to the essential content of the Torah (11:37-44). The teachers of the Law take part in the killing of prophets and messengers of God (11:45-51) and prevent people from gaining insight into the Torah instead of helping them to see (11:52). I understand Luke 5:32 to mean that there are only a few righteous,[51] and that Jesus calls the people to repentance. The ninety-nine righteous who have no (more) need to repent (15:7)[52] are in any case not the Pharisees, teachers of the Law, or the mass of the people, and not the disciples either (5:1-11). After all, Jesus makes it clear to them that doing the Torah demands more than they have heretofore been willing to comprehend. Jesus has a more radical understanding of sin and fulfillment of the Torah than his critics. His (table) companionship with sinners of both sexes is felt by his critics to be a provocation because it calls into question the righteousness of the righteous. The Pharisaic position regarding sinful people within the nation is comparable to that of Paul in 1 Cor 5:9. Jesus' vision is different. His table companionship expresses his vision of the kingdom of God and the messianic banquet: Sinners who, if possible, change their false behavior (i.e., repent) show those who are supposedly true to the Torah (though in Jesus' eyes they are not so at all) that they themselves must first of all, and immediately, change their own behavior. The refinement of cultic purity in daily life, such as washing hands before eating (11:38),[53] is in Jesus' eyes another sign of an inadequate praxis of Torah—not wrong, but inadequate as long as justice and love for God are not being lived (11:42).

How does the sinners' repentance look in real life? Luke 7:36-50 tells a story of a sinful woman. She is known in the city as a sinner, and Simon, Jesus' Pharisaic host, thinks it is wrong[54] that Jesus lets her touch him, anoint him, and kiss his feet (7:39). In Jesus' eyes, too, she is a sinner (7:47). Her loving and desperate anointing of Jesus expresses her disgust at the reality of her life. The text does *not* say that she can and will change her life. She has loved God;[55] God has forgiven her sins. The text is told more like a story of healing than a story of repentance. In a world in which single women without means can wring a living only from prostitution, a story about the moral remorse of a prostitute would not be very persuasive. God loves her, and she loves God, whether she goes on working as a prostitute or finds a family in a Christian community.[56] God's forgiveness, which gives her the dignity to be a daughter of Abraham, like the bent-over woman (13:16), is here, as in the healing of the victim of palsy, a response to need and to a cry for help.[57] Jesus' vision is of the healing of the people, beginning with the most miserable, the poor, the sick, those who are treated as sinners. God's pardon of sins renews the whole nation.

The Gospel of Luke considers sin, or violation of Torah, as destructive of life for a variety of different groups of people. "Sinners" are those who notoriously violate Torah—but also those who refuse to believe that they are not "doing" Torah. The life situations of those concerned are viewed in their concrete reality. Sin is not a general human condition.

The toll collector Zacchaeus (19:1-10) changes his life. He gives half of his property to the poor and repays (with the other half?) fourfold what he, as a chief toll collector, has gained by extortion. Jesus' public announcement that he will spend the night at Zacchaeus' house is taken by him as an expression of God's love, which includes him in the people Israel and no longer regards him as a notorious sinner, a condition associated with his profession. He changes his life; now he is a son of Abraham. Does he, but still more, do the poorer toll collectors (5:29)[58] abandon their work? The model appears to be the toll collector Levi, who abandons everything and follows Jesus (5:28), thus finding a new community.

The conflict between Jesus and his community of disciples and (some) of the Pharisaic movement, as Luke presents it, is a conflict over the praxis of Torah in real situations. Jesus challenges people living the Pharisaic mode of life to act toward sinners in light of God's love, in order to help the kingdom of God break through into the world. They are to imitate God's forgiveness of sinful people, even when the latter are not in a position to live according to Torah. The political dimension of the praxis and vision of the Jesus movement is clearly expressed in the Gospel of Luke from the outset.[59] The young girl Mary, pregnant with Jesus, is a political prophet (Luke 1:46-55) in the tradition of the political prophets of Israel. Her vision is lived and handed on by Jesus.

Luke 15:1-2 puts Jesus in a fictional situation in which his praxis of healing and his vision are embodied, as they are in the conflict with other Jewish people about real-life praxis of Torah. The speech by Jesus that follows consists of three parables. The first two have a brief application (15:7, 10). It, or something like it, need not be repeated after 15:32. It is Jesus' vision for the people—made up of a few righteous and many unrighteous—that is presented in these parables.

So what should the audience of Luke 15:11-32 learn and apply? If they are among the toll collectors and sinners, their repentance, or their love for God and their doing of Torah, looks different than if they are among those who believe sinners, as they understand them, to be lost, excluded from salvation. The invented story of the father and his two sons awaits a continuation in the lives of the listeners. Those who see their failure with respect to the Torah join the disciples of Jesus or work against demons, sickness, and hunger where they live. Those who are offended by Jesus' vision of the kingdom of God should turn back to the praxis of Torah in the sense of 11:42. They should understand that the people of God can only live *together*. The joy of the elder son over the rescue of the younger in the parable story is yet to come.

An allegorizing reading identifies the two sons with religious groups[60] and the father with God.[61] Such identifications remain within the framework of theological conceptions, for example, doctrine of justification versus works-righteousness.

This allegorization, which has shaped interpretations almost without exception, is as a rule filled with anti-Judaism. The only protest I have found against this allegorizing is that of Amy-Jill Levine: "There is no compelling reason to equate the younger son with Christians or the older son with Jews. Indeed, there is no compelling reason to see the parable as an allegory. Not all fathers, rich men . . . or judges . . . must represent God."[62] However, if it is not allegorizing but Luke 15:1-2 and its Lukan interpretive background that guide the application of the parable, the people in the audience are being asked how they will change their own way of life, their actions, wherever they happen to be. The purpose of this change is the healing of the whole people and all humanity (Acts 1:8).

How, then, can this parable be interpreted? An application in the sense intended by the text can be accomplished in light of 15:1-2, 7, 10, even though such an application is not made explicitly at the end of the text. Add to this that the younger son's confession of sin and the father's invitation to rejoice so massively dominate the narrative that they indicate what the application must be.

Luke 15:3-7 tells a parable about a lost sheep, and the key word, *lost,* links the three parables in Luke 15, as well as Luke 19:1-11. This key word has a prehistory in the Bible that is so clear that all those concerned would know that this is about God's liberation of Israel as God's people: see, for example, Jer 50:6; Num 27:17; Ezek 34:1-16; see also Matt 10:6; 15:24. This metaphor is very often related to the people's suffering, caused by the failure of those with political responsibility.

Despite the network of interpretive elements in Luke 15, the parable in 15:11-32 is told as a fictional story from human life, and it contains its own logic derived from human experience. It does not attempt to give an illustration of the love of God dressed up as allegory. The father is a patriarch and is to be distinguished from God (see also the distinction in vv. 17 and 20).

The vision of this text is the renewal of Israel as a people that lives with God's Torah and does God's will. A touching story of paternal love that brings the two sons together for a joyful feast is meant to awaken this vision among the hearers. The meals of the Jesus movement were a tangible expression of that vision. Longing for the return of the son—or the sons—continued as a theme in rabbinic parable culture in later generations.[63] Liberation from Roman exploitation was a vivid theme in the first century as in those later generations. If the whole people would live according to the Torah, the suffering would end. Jesus had announced God's jubilee year, in which God forgives all sins (Luke 4:19). God's forgiveness of sins, which Jesus promises to the sick and suffering, changes people and makes the healing of the nation palpable. This healing includes the poor being filled, their release from debt, and community with sinful people. In Luke 13:1-9 (see above) Jesus set up this hope against the threats of the Roman overlords. That is precisely what the present parable is about. It calls for an answer in the life of those who hear it and their joyful praise of God: "God's hand is always open."[64]

The history of the interpretation and influence of this parable has imposed on today's Christians not only the heritage of an anti-Jewish and triumphalistic reading, but also the divinizing of the patriarchal father[65] and the romanticizing of the patriarchal household. Also problematic is the presentation of repentance and confession of sin as an act of subjection, something that is read into vv. 18, 19, and 21.

A piece by Bertolt Brecht, "Die dumme Frau" ("The Foolish Wife")[66] can offer us extraordinary help for translating Luke 15:11-32 into stories about the love of God that leave behind the patriarchal household and its often violent power systems.

A man had a wife who was like the sea. The sea changes in response to every breath of wind, but it does not grow larger or smaller, nor does it change colour, nor taste, neither does it grow harder, nor softer; but when the wind has passed then the sea lies still again and has grown no different. And the man had to go on a journey.

When he went away, he gave his wife everything that he had, his house and his workshop and the garden round his house and the money he had earned. "All of this is my property and it also belongs to you. Take good care of it." Then she threw her arms around his neck and wept and said to him: "How shall I do that? For I am a foolish woman." But he looked at her and said: "If you love me, you can do it." Then he took leave of her.

Now that the wife was left alone, she began to fear for everything that had been entrusted to her poor hands, and she was very much afraid. And she turned to her brother, who was a dishonest man, and he deceived her. Thus her possessions dwindled, and when she noticed it she was in despair and resolved to stop eating lest they decrease still more, and she did not sleep at night and as a result fell ill.

Then she lay in her chamber and could no longer take care of the house and it fell into ruin, and her brother sold the gardens and the workshop and did not tell the wife. The wife lay on her cushions, said nothing and thought: if I say nothing, I shall not say anything foolish, and if I eat nothing, then our possessions will not decrease.

And so it came about that one day the house had to be auctioned. Many people came from all around for it was a beautiful house. And the wife lay in her chamber and heard the people and how the hammer fell and how they laughed and said: "The roof leaks and the walls are falling in." And then she felt weak and fell asleep.

When she awoke she was lying in a wooden chamber on a hard bed. There was only a very small window high up, and a cold wind was blowing through everything. An old woman came in and snapped at her viciously, telling her that her house had been sold but her debts were not yet met, that she was feeding on pity, although it was her husband who deserved it. For he had nothing left at all now. When she heard this the wife became confused and her mind was slightly touched and she got up and began to work in the house and the fields from that day on. She went around in poor clothes and ate almost nothing, yet earned nothing either, for she demanded nothing. And then one day she heard her husband had come back.

Then she was seized by a great fear. She went indoors quickly and tousled her hair and looked for a clean shift but there wasn't one there. To cover up she ran her hand over her chest and found her breasts had shrivelled. And went out through a small back door and set off, blindly.

After she had been walking for a while it occurred to her that he was her husband and they had been joined together and now she was running away from him. She turned round at once and walked back, not thinking any longer of the house and the workshop and the shift, and saw him from afar and ran towards him and clung to him.

But the man was standing in the middle of the road and from their doorsteps the people laughed at him. And he was very angry. His wife was clinging to him and would not lift her head from his chest nor take her arms from around his neck. And he felt her trembling and thought it was from fear because she had lost everything. But then she finally raised her face and looked at him, and he saw it was not fear but joy, she was trembling because she was so glad. Then he realised something and he too faltered and put his arm around her, felt unmistakably that her shoulders had grown thin, and kissed her on the middle of her mouth.

In this story the foolish wife is in the situation both of the younger son and of the father. She loses the whole property while her husband is away. When he returns home, she first runs away—in fear. Then she turns back and runs to meet him: "And he saw it was not fear but joy . . . and kissed her on the middle of her mouth." Nearly all the details in Luke 15:11-32 are found in this piece. Brecht probably wouldn't have called it a story of the love of God. I quote the text so that the two stories can interpret each other mutually. Happily, Brecht's story is told in such a way that no one is tempted to identify the husband with God.

TRANSLATION OF LUKE 15:3-7
The Lost Sheep

3   He spoke to them in this parable:

4   What man among you who has a hundred sheep and loses one of them will not leave the ninety-nine in the wilderness and go after the lost one until he has found it?

5   And when he has found it, he lays it on his shoulders—rejoicing.

6   And he goes into the house and calls his friends and neighbors together: "Rejoice with me, for I have found my sheep that was lost."

7   I tell you: So there will be joy in heaven over a sinful person who repents—more than over ninety-nine righteous who need no repentance.

SOCIAL-HISTORICAL ANALYSIS

A shepherd is tending a relatively small flock[67] in the wilderness—not far from a village where he makes his home. The story does not say whether he is the owner of the flock or whether he tends it for wages, but it seems probable to me that he is an employee. The way the parable begins, with a question, presumes that those addressed are familiar with this shepherd's world of experience. Obviously not one sheep is to be surrendered. There has been a lot said about the fact that he leaves the flock alone in the wilderness. But the story does not say that. The ninety-nine are cared for; that is simply presumed. The obviousness of the search and the joy over the finding presuppose that one sheep out of a hundred represents a value for the person affected, perhaps not only a material value, but certainly that. After all, the shepherd depends on the sheep to live, and perhaps his family does as well, at least in part. It is not important to the story that shepherds have a bad reputation.[68] The milieu described is that of rural and small holdings, perhaps nomadic conditions. The shepherd brings the sheep with him into the house—or the tent—and invites his friends and neighbors. Since the parable of the lost drachma tells a parallel story with women friends and neighbors, this appears to be a pure stag party. The feast is not depicted, but it is a joyful one. The application, which the Jesus who tells the story introduces expressly as its conclusion, parallels the joyful feast in the village house with God's joy over a sinner who repents. The ninety-nine righteous who need no repentance are mentioned more for rhetorical than for theological reasons: That is how infinitely important one lost sheep is.

ESCHATOLOGICAL INTERPRETATION

The metaphor of the lost sheep has a long prehistory in the First Testament. Here in Luke 15 the metaphor is not applied to bad political leadership by the shepherds,[69] but to finding the way back because of a good shepherd and the repentance of sinners. It is true that God is the good shepherd who seeks the lost sheep (in Ezek 34:11-16), or Moses in a legend (*Exodus Rabbah* 3:1),[70] but the figure of the shepherd does not return in the application, only his joy. The "lost sheep" metaphor for a desolate condition of the people Israel is obviously addressed here. What does that mean for the application? Is the returning sinner the people, or is it an individual among the people? I find this question hard to answer, since the vision in the Gospel of Luke of the healing of the nation[71] and the nations also means talking about individual lost ones, as in Luke 19:1-11.

The repentance of the sinful people is their return to God, and that means a return to the doing of the Torah.

METHODOLOGICAL CLARIFICATION

An allegorizing ecclesiological reading here would use the same model as in Luke 15:11-32: the salvation of the Gentile church in contrast to the non-salvation of Israel, or that of the justified sinner in contrast to self-righteous Pharisaism. As discussed in connection with Luke 15:1-2, 18-32, Luke 15:1-2, 7 gives a clear basis for the intended application.

TRANSLATION OF LUKE 15:8-10
The Lost Drachma

8   Or what woman, who has ten drachmas and[72] loses one drachma, will not light a lamp and sweep the house carefully until she has found it?

9   And when she has found it, she calls her friends and neighbors together: "Rejoice with me, because I have found the drachma I lost."

10   So, I tell you, there will be joy among[73] the angels of God over one sinful person who repents.

SOCIAL-HISTORICAL ANALYSIS

Except for two changes from v. 7 to v. 10, this text is told in parallel to the parable of the lost sheep. The parallelism has even led to the proposal that the parable is incidental and secondary,[74] as well as allusions to Luke's bias toward parallel stories involving men and women (see Luke 13:18-21; 17:34-35). I would add: The fact that women's work is presented as having equal status with men's work is really remarkable in a social context that notoriously makes women's work invisible.

This parable has irritated many exegetes because it centers on a woman and because the drachma resists many favorite allegorizations: It is easier to say of a sheep that the shepherd loves it than to say that a woman loves a drachma. On this topic of women, Adolf Jülicher wrote an inspired caricature of the exegetical discussion of his time that I would like to mention. He sees the sinners referred to in 15:1 as both male and female; that is, he recognizes androcentrism. He then mocks a colleague, Alfred Plummer, who supposes that the formulation in 15:8, "what woman . . ." shows that Jesus is here addressing only men, since it deviates from 15:4, "what person/man *among you.*" Thus, according to Plummer, Jesus only taught behind women's backs that they should help in working to win back sinners. I will quote from Jülicher's text: "Nothing prevents us from assuming that there are also sinful women . . . among them [the sinners in v. 1], despite the fact that PLUMM. sees 8, where there is no *ex hymōn* [among you] after *tis gynē* [what woman], as there is in 4 after *tis anthrōpos* [what person/man], as permitting us to suppose that perhaps there were no females present! But if, according to him, Jesus in 8-10 intends to teach that females should also work to gain sinners, Jesus could scarcely have offered this teaching only behind their backs."[75] Thanks to newer insights into androcentric language, I can only support Jülicher: The text presumes that women are addressed and are present in the listening crowd.

That the nine drachmas do not appear in v. 10 as righteous, as in v. 7, only confirms that in vv. 4-7 as well the ninety-nine sheep and ninety-nine righteous have only a rhetorical function.

The ten drachmas, apparently the entire property of this woman, draw us once more into the lives of poor people. The value of a drachma corresponded to that of a Roman denarius. Nothing is said about how the woman acquired this money, but if we consider the situation of married women or women living alone in that time the most likely supposition—and the obvious one in terms of the narrative—is that the woman herself earned the money by her daily labor. Married women among the poor, the majority of the population, had to add to the family income, and single women scarcely managed to survive on the tiny wages accorded to women. As a rule women's wages did not amount to the one denarius (Matt 20:1-6) earned by male day-laborers, but something less than half of a man's wage.[76] The one lost denarius is part of the bitterly necessary money for her daily bread. With it the woman might have been able to buy food to last two days. The parable shines a spotlight on a rural situation in which people have no land of their own and are dependent on money and on being able to buy their food. The woman needs the money to survive, even more than the shepherd needs his hundredth sheep. Neither parable fits well within romantic folklore. The woman's careful search is narrated in detail, even more than in the case of the shepherd. The tiny windowless house, the hard floor of stone or tamped earth, the intensity of the search are all easy to imagine. How should the listeners, then, picture the joyful feast? A drachma would not buy a festive banquet. The text says nothing about that, simply presuming that the listeners can imagine the women's feast of joy—like that of the men in v. 6. The women would have been happy, they would have gathered to chat, to laugh, and to sing. Perhaps they all brought something from their own tables. Neighborhood groups of women have an important social role in village life. The women have their own network that makes possible the sharing of information and solidary mutual aid.[77] Their shared joy is the bridge to the application—as in v. 4.

ESCHATOLOGICAL INTERPRETATION

The hearty stag party of the shepherds and the joyous neighbor women's social are made an image of God's joy (v. 7) and that of the angels (v. 10). God, according to v. 10, is not alone; joy must be shared. The devaluation of women's community and women's chatting and laughing together in patriarchal societies makes this parable noteworthy. It uses happy neighbor women to paint a picture of God. If you want to see the angels' happiness, look at happy women. The parable imagery has its own message, one that is theological as well. This becomes clear in the application.

That application again speaks of the single precious sinner who repents. In this case there is no further opportunity to insert allegory. The coin has not repented.

There is a rabbinic double parable that is often rightly mentioned as a parallel to Luke 15:8-10:

> As with a king who had lost a gold coin from his house or a lovely pearl—does he not find them by means of a wick worth only an assarius [a small Roman coin]? So let this parable not be minor in your eyes. For through the parable one attains to the words of the Torah. And this is a witness for you that this is so: Solomon, through this parable, arrived at the precise details of Torah . . . Rabbi Pinchas ben Jair began [to speak]: (Prov 2:4) "'If you seek it like silver etc.': If you seek the words of the Torah as you seek these treasures, the Holy One, blessed be He, will not withhold your pay. As someone who has lost a selah or an obolus somewhere in his house lights lamp after lamp and wick after wick until he finds [comes upon it]. And see, the things [are] as in the conclusion from the lesser to the greater: If someone will light lamp after lamp and wick after wick for something that preserves life in this world for an hour, until he comes upon it and finds it—must you not seek after the words of the Torah, which are the life of this world and the life of the world to come, as for these treasures?"[78]

The first parable speaks of the contrast between the tiny value of the wick by means of which the king seeks and the great value of the coin or pearl he is searching for. The parable is about parables, or better *meshalim,* which have a lesser value in comparison to the infinite value of the Torah they help to unlock. Parables about the telling of parables are very common.[79] After this first parable, a second is told on the theme of "finding the Torah," also linked to Prov 2:4. The son is to seek wisdom: "When you seek her like silver and hunt for her as for lost treasures. . . ." But the parable imagery shifts into a different social situation. The person seeks not precious treasures, as in Prov 2:4, but a tiny coin—with great effort. This effort of a poor person in search of money for survival is the bridge to the application to the Torah as the words of life.

This rabbinic double parable speaks of searching for the Torah and the significance of parables in that search, using an image similar to that in Luke 15:8-10. The sinful person's repentance, as it is thought of in the Gospel of Luke and in Jewish and early Christian tradition generally, is understood as a return to God, which means that now the Torah will become one's word of life. Even though this double parable has a different accent from that in Luke 15:8-10, it is useful not to lose sight of the connection of these parables in Luke 15 and, I would add, of all the parables in the Jesus tradition with the Torah. The parables in the Jesus tradition, too, as they are understood in the synoptic tradition, are "handles" by which to grasp the Torah, lamplight by which to seek it. The metaphor that calls parables "handles" for the Torah is found repeatedly in the rabbinic writings: "At first the Torah was like a basket without handles, till Solomon came and added handles to it" (*b. Erubin* 21b).

SUMMARY OF LUKE 15

These three parables together refer explicitly (in 15:4, 8) and implicitly (in 15:11)[80] to the world of experience of those addressed. The social circumstances are different: from the poverty of the woman to a perhaps not quite so poor shepherd's life to a farm that, in relation to the first two, looks rather prosperous, but whose economic situation cannot be confused with the comfort of rich landowners of the period. All three parables end in a joyous feast that is transparent to the feast of God's joy when the people of Israel and all nations have found the way to life. These happy experiences in the midst of a hard daily grind are transparent to the experience of this comprehensive healing. Who then (as now) could have dared (or dare) such visions of the magnificent healing of humanity? This unbelievable vision is not only laid out here in the face of a hard world of human experience, but even related to the small or great joys found in the midst of life's hardships. The great messianic feast of God's joy is grounded: The little party of happy neighbor women is a foretaste, promise, and assurance of the great healing.

FOR FURTHER READING

Brad H. Young, *The Parables* 130–57 (Luke 15:11-32); 187–98 (Luke 15:4-10)

Wolfgang Pöhlmann, "Die Abschichtung des Verlorenen Sohnes (Lk 15:12f.), und die erzählte Welt der Parabel"

Pesikta Rabbati 44, in William G. Braude, *Pesikta Rabbati: Discourses for Feasts, Fasts, and Special Sabbaths*

Klaus Berger and Carsten Colpe, *Religionsgeschichtliches Textbuch zum Neuen Testament*

Luise Schottroff, "Das Gleichnis vom verlorenen Sohn," (Luke 15:11-32)

Luise Schottroff, *Lydia's Impatient Sisters*, 91–100 (Luke 15:8-10)

21

"Once There Was a Rich Man": Money and the Torah

Luke 16 tells two parables that both begin "Once there was a rich man . . ." (Luke 16:1-7; 19-31). Between the two, Jesus interprets the first parable (Luke 16:8-13); the interpretation shifts to a rather generalized discourse about dealing with money and the meaning of the Torah regarding such dealings (Luke 16:14-17). How Luke 16:18 fits in this context is something we shall have to ask about. What does the interpretation of remarriage as adultery have to do with the subject? The parable of the rich man and poor Lazarus then begins at v. 19, and again focuses on the theme of money and Torah.

TRANSLATION OF LUKE 16:1-13
Betrayal on a Grand Scale: The Crafty Manager

1   Now he said to his disciples: Once there was a rich man who had a manager. The latter was accused of having squandered the rich man's property.

2   He called him and said to him: What is this I hear about you? Give an accounting of your management, for you cannot be my manager any longer.

3   The manager said to himself: What shall I do, since my master is taking the management out of my hands? I am not strong enough to dig, and I am ashamed to beg.

4   I have an idea what I will do, so that—when I am fired as manager—people will receive me into their homes.

5   And he called his master's debtors one by one. He said to the first: How much do you owe my master?

6   He said: a hundred *bat* of oil. He said to him: Here, take your bill, sit down quickly and write fifty.

7   Then he said to the next: How much do you owe? He said: a hundred *cors* of wheat. He said to him: Here, take your bill and write eighty.

8   And Jesus praised the unjust manager, because he had acted shrewdly. For the people of this world are more shrewd in relation to their own generation than the people of the light.

9   And I say to you: Make friends with unrighteous mammon so that, when
       it is exhausted, you will be received into the eternal tents.
10   Those who are faithful in small things are also faithful in great things;
       and those who are unjust in the smallest things are also unjust in the
       great ones.
11   If you act irresponsibly with unrighteous mammon, who will trust you
       with genuine life?
12   And if you do not act responsibly with what is foreign to you, who will
       give you what belongs to you?
13   No one can serve two masters. Either you will hate the one and love the
       other, or you will cling to one and despise the other. You cannot serve
       God and mammon.

SOCIAL-HISTORICAL ANALYSIS

The rich man's *oikonomos* is his business manager, who takes care of his finances
and is able to make decisions on his own, as the text presupposes (vv. 6, 7).
Normally the business managers in the Roman empire, even at the highest levels of statecraft, were slaves.[1] It was simply presumed that business managers
cheated. Slaves could be tortured; free men could not. But in this text it appears
that the rich man's manager is not a slave. He expects to be fired. A slave would
be sold or forced to do a different kind of work—unless he were so old or disabled that the owner had not expected to get any more use out of him. But v. 3b,
"I have no strength to dig, and I am ashamed to beg," is connected with the plan
to buy hospitality and a new occupation for himself. So one does not get the impression that he is too weak for physical labor, simply that he rejects it. Here we
are dependent on the information in the narrative itself. Whoever the audience
may have been, it would have consisted for the most part of people who had to
live by physical labor, who knew what it meant to "dig." Their fear of becoming poor beggars was an everyday matter. The manager's reflection would have
made it very clear to them that he himself, even after being fired, would go on
living in a different world, the world of the wealthy. In v. 8 and indirectly in v. 10
the business manager is called "unjust," that is, he acts against the law. Even if it is
not completely clear which law is meant here—the Torah, Roman law, provincial
law—according to all those laws he was a cheat, because he gave away financial
obligations due to his master for his own interest. In the sense of the narrative
and the accompanying meaning, he is a lawbreaker. So we would have to conclude that he was not suspected in the first place without reason (v. 1) of having
"squandered" the property of the rich man—only in part, of course—that is,
that he had taken money or other property from his master's possession through
treacherous dealing.[2]

       The forgiveness of debts that he carries out in his own interest, without his
master's knowledge, is often ennobled by interpreters. Thus we find the reflec-

tion that the forgiveness of 50 and 20 percent of the debts (vv. 6, 7) would have canceled the usurious interest contained in the total debt.[3] Thus the forgiveness of the debt appears in a somewhat rosier light, because in the end it at least accords with the First Testament's prohibition of usury. But the narrative and the interpretation do not intend in any way to present the manager in a positive light; he is a cheat—in the sense of the law and in the mind of the rich man.

The hospitality he purchases for himself by his treacherous release of debts was a social institution in the ancient world. Business acquaintances provided hospitality to one another that was much more comprehensive than merely a roof and a meal. They defended the rights of the person who was a foreign guest in the place before public officials and so on.[4] His expectation is completely realistic. He can anticipate that he will be integrated in their society and find a new occupation.

The narrative ends[5] with the treacherous forgiveness of the debts. It leaves open whether and how the owner will attempt to secure his claims or retrieve his money. The interpretation implies that the cheat can carry out his plans and the rich man cannot stop him.

The "master's debtors" (v. 5) owe the rich man enormous sums: a hundred *bat* of oil and a hundred *cors* of wheat, about 36, 500 litres of oil and 364,400 litres of wheat. It is important for understanding the narrative to know the order of magnitude of these debts. Is it imaginable that these are the debts of tenants, or are they, rather, the contractual deliveries of (wholesale) dealers?

Lease agreements between landowners and tenants were mutual legal contracts and "in their form attempt to meet the interests both of the lessor and the tenant."[6] But the situation here narrated does not refer to lease agreements; it is about bills, which contain the debtor's obligation to bring a specified amount or delivery to the creditor at a specified time.[7] "Take your bill, sit down quickly and write . . ." (v. 6; see also v. 7). The bill is a one-sided legal document. The creditor keeps the document written or signed by the debtor. If the required delivery of 100 *bat* of oil or 100 *cors* of wheat[8] is not interest *in naturalia* (in this case, in produce) what is it? Prices varied, sometimes wildly. The quantities are too great to be interpreted as consumer debts. A poor family that had to buy food on credit would scarcely borrow such quantities of a single product, or receive so much on credit.[9] One possible explanation of the case described could be that the debtors sold the creditor their wares at a particular time and must deliver an agreed quantity at a future time, independent of variations in price that may occur in the mean time: in other words, a futures contract.[10] And what is the rich man going to do with these quantities of oil and wheat? He will sell them again. Both the nature of the bills and the quantities required to be delivered fit better within the realm of (wholesale) merchandising than in that of tenants, leases, and landowners. Commerce had enormous significance in the Roman empire. The Pax Romana had produced a uniform currency, and the roads and other commercial routes were conceived in terms of worldwide trade. The Roman military forces guaranteed the security of commerce.[11] Evidence of Roman merchants has been found even far beyond the borders of the Roman empire.

The text says nothing about whether those involved were Jewish or not. Either is possible, although most merchants appear to have been Roman citizens. "Not a penny tinkled in Gaul that was not recorded in the books of Roman citizens," Cicero said.[12] It would not have been any different in Roman Palestine. The role of world commerce is clearly evident in Revelation 18, where Rome, the center of world merchandising, is sharply criticized. Aelius Aristides depicts the same situation in his praise of Rome.[13]

Verse 8 has been often and heatedly discussed: Is the "master" the rich man, who is also called master in the narrative (vv. 3, 5), or is it Jesus, as, for example, in 18:6, where he interprets the narrative? Attempts to explain that the rich man praised his treacherous business manager, for example because the relieved debtors have already started praising him,[14] are not persuasive. They want to avoid having to imagine that Jesus praised the cheat. But that is exactly what the text says, and v. 8b gives the reason: "for the people of this world are wiser in their generation than the people of light." Seeing this expression as a secondary addition does not help us to solve the problem that v. 8b presents the reason for Jesus' praise in v. 8a. For methodological reasons I consider it necessary to read the existing text as a unity—independently of the question of whatever prehistory it may have. The same is true of the following vv. 9-13: They must be read in connection with vv. 1-7 and 8. Verses 8-13 are the explanation of the parable in vv. 1-7.

If I consider v. 8 from a social-historical perspective, it presumes two different social systems: that of this era and that of the people of light. Paul's first letter to the community at Corinth presents a good clarification of this distinction of two social systems: 1 Cor 5:10; 7:31-34 distinguishes between the social order "of the world" *(kosmos)* and that of the community. The phrase "this era" *(aiōn houtos)* appears in 1 Cor 1:20 and elsewhere as interchangeable with "world": It is the social world of the non-Jewish peoples, whose way of life, from a Jewish or early Christian perspective, separates people from God, that is, the God of Israel. Christian men can, certainly, participate in it "as if not" *(hōs mē):* Their marriages and the way they "use" the world distinguish them from those of the nations (1 Cor 7:29-35). This difference is defined by *halakah,* an explanation of the Torah that defines for Jewish and Christian people how they are to act in respect to marriage, sexuality, money, and the ever-present contact with foreign deities. *Porneia, pleonexia,* and *eidōlolatria*[15] are the cardinal sins of this world: sexual behavior rejected by the Torah, greed for money, and serving idols, that is, practicing another religion. Luke 16 is a chapter of *halakah* on the subject of money, from the perspective of the Lukan communities. Not surprisingly in a Jewish context, there are other interpretations of the Torah that do not agree with this *halakah*. These are criticized in v. 14 as Pharisaic greed. So then, how does this *halakah* envision the attitude of Christian communities toward money (vv. 8-13)?

ESCHATOLOGICAL INTERPRETATION

Jesus praises the cheat because he—unwillingly—models a praxis that can be applied by Christian communities: to use money to build friendships—in this life and in the life to come (v. 9). Friendships in this life (v. 9a), "faithfulness in small things" (v. 10), faithfulness in dealing with unrighteous mammon (v. 11), faithfulness in dealing with what belongs to the other sphere—that is, this era—(v. 12) are other ways of describing the praxis in regard to money that corresponds to the eschatological promises (vv. 9b, 10, 11, 12). The concreteness of this praxis is indicated in the two parables in Luke 16 and appears repeatedly in other parts of the two-volume Lukan work.

According to v. 9 the model character of the cheat consists in the fact that he establishes friendships (by forgiving debts). Forgiveness of debts is only implicitly addressed in the interpretation, but it is a central theme of Luke's gospel: The community of Jesus' disciples are to give credit to one another without expecting repayment (6:30-38). The parable tells of a cheat in the world of (wholesale) merchandising. Not every detail is to be covered in the interpretation, but only those that appear there: dealing with money and the establishment of friendships.[16] The system of (mutual) hospitality was of crucial significance for Christianity in this period, as Acts shows. With regard to money, what is primary is accepting the obligation to prevent hunger and extreme poverty for other members of the community, if necessary at the expense of one's own economic substance. This is shown by the examples of the so-called community of goods in Acts 4:36-37; 5:1-11 (though 5:1-11 describes a failed example). Luke 18:28-30 and Acts 2:24-27 and 4:32-35 formulate this in general terms as a fundamental Christian practice: The structures of the world are left behind; people find a new house and a new family "now, and in the world to come life everlasting." The Gospel of Luke has a radical message about the way one deals with money and with marriages, which, after all, are part of the economic system of "this era." Luke 20:34-36 is not just about the "other" world, any more than is Luke 16:9 or 18:28-30. The people in the Christian communities do not marry, and they use their money on behalf of those in the community who suffer want[17]—and probably others as well (12:33-34). Calling this practice "giving alms" weakens it severely.[18] The goal is not ascetic poverty, but an economic solidarity that prevents hunger and the social suffering and impairment of health that are the result of poverty. The "people of light" in Luke 16:8 are the "people of the resurrection" (20:36),[19] who are like the angels.

The people of light and the resurrection are faithful *(pistoi)* in small things and with unrighteous mammon (vv. 10-12), which belongs to the alien sphere "of this world" and is a realm foreign to them (v. 12). These statements are often taken in the sense of faithful management (in contrast to the cheat in the parable). But it is not a question of someone else's money entrusted to one, but of money as part of the world transformed by God, the mammon that in principle is inimical to God. The sharp critique of the money economy (v. 13 and in the expression "unrighteous mammon") and the *pleonexia* associated with it, the endless wanting-more, is shared by the Gospel of Luke with other parts of the New Testament and postbiblical Judaism—but with many Hellenistic-Roman authors as well.[20] The misery of poverty, which in this period was more severe in Palestine than elsewhere in the Roman empire, is attributed to the boundless greed of the rich and the opportunities opened for them by the money economy.

The eschatological perspective is again stated in the interpretation of the parable (vv. 8-13) in every sentence: God will receive you into the everlasting tents (v. 9); you will be faithful "in many things" (v. 10); the true thing will be entrusted to you (v. 11); you will receive your own, what belongs to you. The believers are, to speak with Luke 20:35, those "who have been considered worthy of a place in that world and in the resurrection from the dead." The promise transforms them, now already, into "people of the resurrection" (20:36). Their new praxis in dealing with money frees them from unrighteousness, and that also means from violation of the Torah. Unrighteousness *(adikia)* in vv. 8-13 should be referred to the Torah; that is the law that the unrighteous break. Paradoxically, the people of light can learn something from a treacherous money man: that it is a matter of using money to establish friendships—in this world and with God.

METHODOLOGICAL OBSERVATION

The ecclesiological tradition of interpretation has accepted primarily the idea of faithful household management and honest dealing with money. The radical critique of the money economy in 16:8-13, and indirectly in the parable narrative in 16:1-7, is not taken seriously. The widespread interpretation of the parable narrative in terms of eschatological resolution has the kingdom of God only indirectly in view: Because the judgment is coming, Christians will act quickly, decisively, and wisely. In this, the crooked household manager is a model for them. The concrete meaning of that is either described as almsgiving or not enlarged upon at all.

Here again, the methodological basis of my explication is reading the text as a unity and as part of the Gospel of Luke, using a social-historical analysis. It enables me to begin to understand the "economic assumptions" of the text and so to reconstruct the "world of the audience" for this text. In doing so, I refer to John S. Kloppenborg's "The Dishonoured Master (Luke 16:1-8a)," especially pages 479 and 486, because his essay is a model for describing the task of social-historical analysis. Justin S. Ukpong's essay "The Parable of the Shrewd Manager" reads the debtors as small farmers and the manager as poor and without rights. The rich man is converted in v. 8a to a recognition of the farmers' need and an acceptance of the forgiveness of debts on their behalf. Although I have come to a different social-historical estimation of the situation described, nevertheless this interpretation is useful to me as the expression of a liberation-theological reading against the background of West African small farmers' experience. Ukpong rightly sees in Luke 16:1-8 the expression of a concept of justice that contradicts that of the exploitation represented by the rich man. But for me this contradiction is not found in the narrative of vv. 1-7; rather, it is in the interpretation in vv. 8-13. The manager is not the hero of righteousness in the kingdom of God, but the unwilling teacher of Christian communities regarding their praxis of justice.

TRANSLATION OF LUKE 16:14-31
The Rich Man and Poor Lazarus

1   The Pharisees heard this, and because they were greedy for money, they ridiculed him.

2   Jesus said to them: You are those who present yourselves as just in the sight of others, but God knows your hearts. For God regards the self-exaltation of people as an abomination.

3   The law and the prophets were in effect until John; since then the good news of the kingdom of God is proclaimed, and everyone tries to enter it by force.

4   Heaven and earth will pass away before one stroke of a letter of the Torah will be dropped.

5   Anyone who divorces his wife and marries another commits adultery, and whoever marries a woman divorced from her husband commits adultery.

6   Once there was a rich man who dressed in purple and fine linen and lived in luxury and happiness every day.

7   But a poor man named Lazarus lay before his great gate; he was covered with sores.

8   And he longed to satisfy his hunger with what fell from the rich man's table; even the dogs would come and lick his sores.

9   But it happened that the poor man died and was carried away by the angels to Abraham's bosom. The rich man also died and was buried.

10   And when he was in the underworld and lifted up his eyes, because he was being tortured, he sees Abraham from afar, and Lazarus in his bosom.

11   He called out: "Father Abraham, have mercy on me! Send Lazarus to dip the tip of his finger in water and cool my tongue, for I am in agony in these flames."

12   Abraham said: "Child, remember that during your lifetime you received
     your good things, and Lazarus in like manner evil things. Now he is
     comforted here, and you are in agony.
13   And besides: Between us and you a great chasm has been fixed, so that
     those who might want to pass from here to you cannot do so, and no
     one can cross from there to us."
14   He said: "I pray you, father, that you send him to my family.
15   For I have five siblings; let him warn them, so that they will not also
     come into this place of torment."
16   Abraham answered: "They have Moses and the prophets, and they
     should listen to them."
17   He said: "Yes, Father Abraham, but if someone comes to them from the
     dead, they will repent."
18   Abraham said: "If they do not listen to Moses and the prophets, neither
     will they be convinced even if someone rises from the dead."

The Sequence of Ideas in Luke 16:14-31

This parable follows a critical speech by Jesus addressed to Pharisees. In 16:14
it is said that they had ridiculed Jesus after hearing his parable about the unjust manager and his radical critique of the money economy. The narrative calls
them money-hungry. Thus they represent a different opinion about dealing with
money and therefore also a different praxis. In Judaism at that time there were
conflicts about the money economy. Jesus' teaching and that of other Jewish
teachers,[21] that money presses one into the service of mammon, something not
compatible with belonging to God, was opposed by other more or less pragmatic
positions. The opposite extreme may well have been represented by people who
advocated the *prosbol*.[22] The concept of *prosbol* was intended to make it possible
for rich people, in spite of the Torah laws regarding the sabbatical year and the
prohibition of usury, to give credit to poor people at high interest, and these debts
need not be forgiven in the year of release. In the Mishnah (*Šeb.* 10:3) it is said
that the release of debts in the seventh year (Deut 15:1-2), in particular, caused
"people to refuse to lend to one another." The *prosbol* was supposed to remedy
this. Since the *prosbol* is not mentioned in Luke's gospel, the opposing position
of the Pharisees in 16:14 is probably to be sought rather in a middle course. We
cannot tell how well off they themselves are. The banquets given by Pharisees are
not those of the rich, but also not those of the poor (7:36-50; 11:37-52; 14:1-24).
Pharisees invite Jesus and listen to his radical critique, though not unresistingly.
They themselves would have had only modest wealth at their disposal, but they
propounded a teaching that did not offend the truly rich.[23]

When they ridicule Jesus because of his teaching about money, Jesus criticizes them as those who regard themselves as righteous, that is, faithful to the
Torah, and portray themselves thus in public as well. Jesus now explains to them

that in their hearts they have distanced themselves from God and God's Torah, and that God turns away from them because they place value in being regarded as righteous, but they are not (16:15). Here, as in 18:9, this criticism is not about a moral charge of self-righteousness, but rather, as in Luke 18:9-14; 11:37-44, about the objection that people who think they are keeping the Torah are really not doing so, and are closing their eyes to the need to recognize the extent of their own violations of Torah.

It is astonishing to what an extent Jesus' radical position has been watered down in the history of Christian interpretation of these Lukan texts, and on the other hand the Pharisaic position has been morally disqualified. The position of the Pharisees that we must presume here is actually closer to the content of the Christian history of interpretation of these texts than the latter is to Jesus' position. A radical critique of the money economy, as Jesus presents it, was probably as hard to hear on the part of those who think "realistically" and in terms of *Realpolitik* as it is today. This is a conflict about the interpretation of the Torah—not on the level of learned disputes about the historical correctness of Torah interpretation, but on the political level. Jesus' vision of the reign of God includes, for example, well-to-do people's renunciation of the repayment of debts owed to them.[24]

The law and the prophets were and are the expression of God's will. John the Baptizer and then Jesus himself proclaim God's year of release and the kingdom of God[25] with great success among the people, as is repeatedly said. "And everyone tries to enter [the kingdom of God] by force." But everything depends on fulfilling the Torah (16:16, 17). The proclamation of the kingdom of God is the interpretation of the Torah that is necessary now. The Jesus saying in 16:18 asserts: A second marriage after a divorce is adultery. That the theme of marriage *halakah* appears at this point can only mean that marriage and economic questions were regarded as connected.[26] Jesus and the Pharisees are apparently in disagreement on this question also. The Lukan Jesus criticizes people who marry and thus surrender themselves to the economic situation of exploitation.[27] A second marriage after divorce is adultery, says the Lukan Jesus. In the Gospel of Luke—different from the other Gospels—people also give up marrying for the sake of the kingdom of God (14:26; 18:29). The climax of this critical discourse on money, Torah, and marriage is the parable about the rich man and poor Lazarus. Its application is already clear beforehand: It is to be associated with this teaching of Jesus, and will clarify and sharpen it still further.

SOCIAL-HISTORICAL ANALYSIS

The parable contains a fictional narrative about events in the life of two people (16:19-21) and after their deaths (16:22-31), when the rich man is in the underworld and poor Lazarus in Abraham's bosom. That a parable should tell a story about life after death is not without parallel.[28] This is a fictional story about life after death that reflects and comments on life before death. Both halves of the parable are fictional and apply to reality. In addition, vv. (26), 27-31 should be read with 16:19-25 as a unit.

The narrative is constructed in strict parallels: The earthly fate of the poor and that of the rich stand in sharp contrast: gorgeous clothing and a life of happiness and luxury characterize the rich (see Luke 6:24, 25). The poor man lies hungry, helpless, and ill outside the gate, covered with sores licked by stray dogs (see Luke 6:20, 21). After their death the fate of both is reversed: The rich man suffers thirst and longs for a drop of water as previously poor Lazarus had hungered for the crumbs from the rich man's table (v. 24). Poor Lazarus sits comfortably protected in Abraham's bosom; he is consoled for his life of misery (v. 25; see also the indirect parallel to Luke 6:24: The rich have already received their consolation in this life). The invisible barrier between the rich and the poor in life becomes an impassable gulf in the world of the dead.[29] The rich man's first plea to Abraham, and Abraham's answer, show the insurmountability of the chasm between poor and rich in the world of the dead. The closing scene (vv. 27-31) makes it clear how that chasm can be crossed: only in life before death, if the rich listen to Moses and the prophets, and that means repentance (vv. 29, 30). Even a messenger from the world of the dead[30] can change nothing if the rich do not listen to the Scriptures.

Although the messenger from the world of the dead is represented as someone who has risen, this is not about the resurrection of Jesus. In Luke 24:44-47 the Risen Christ expounds the Scriptures. Here, too, the miracle of faith comes through understanding Scripture. In fact, it should not have required the Risen One as teacher of Scripture; the disciples should have been able to understand Scripture and repent without him. Now they will have to go on their way without the living presence of the Risen One. Luke 24:44-47, like 16:27-31, points to the central significance of Torah, which should not require any additional support, not even from someone risen from the dead.

The conclusion in vv. 27-31 links back to the beginning,[31] to life before death. That is when the rich people's decisions are made. Social-historical analysis must consider whether and how the picture of poverty and wealth that is drawn here is related to reality. For an eschatological interpretation the crucial question is what the rich man's error is, in the sense intended by the text. Did he use his wealth in a morally irresponsible manner, or is his wealth as such an unforgivable sin in God's eyes? The question contains a social-historical dimension: In the intention of the text, does wealth as such derive from the evil of the exploitation of other people? Is that evil avoidable, and how can it be prevented?

Martin Goodman[32] has sketched the social situation in Judea before 66 c.e. that led to the first Jewish revolt. He describes a Jewish upper class, including many priestly families, who were so excessively wealthy that they could not spend what they had through consuming and even by erecting large buildings.

They were looking for opportunities for investment. An enormous source of further wealth for them was the extension of credit to small farmers and acquiring their land when they were unable to repay. Even the people themselves were frequently enslaved and became the property of these new masters. The end of this ruling class came with the revolt that led to war with Rome. This conflict, reconstructed from nonbiblical sources, can help us to understand Luke 16:19-31. It is true that this text may not necessarily have (only) this prewar situation in view, but even after the war there was a comparable exploitation, now primarily through Roman aristocrats, but including a number of wealthy Jews.[33] Heavy obligations were imposed on the small farmers, and they were driven from their land. And it was not only in Judea and Galilee that the wealth of the rich was the cause of the economic misery of the majority of the population; the same was true throughout the Roman empire.[34]

The discussion of possible literary parallels to Luke 16:19-31 has revealed that the contrast between wealth and poverty plays a part in the literature of the period, for example in Lucian. The poor man and the rich man thus became a literary motif in declamations, that is, rhetorical exercises.[35] But this literary motif does not relieve us of the obligation to inquire about the relation of Luke 16:19-31 to reality.

That beggars suffer from illnesses is clearly documented in the Synoptic Gospels themselves. It was the usual thing for them to wait at the gates of the wealthy in hope of receiving gifts of food.[36] The crumbs that fall from the rich person's table (Luke 16:21) are the subject of magnificent floor mosaics in Hellenistic-Roman palaces throughout the Roman empire: Here lie the scattered bones of fowl, fruit, and pieces of bread. Those at table used bread to wipe their fingers. The mosaics are vivid, colorful, and lively. They give the dining room a fine atmosphere.[37] They proudly display wealth in the mirror of its garbage.

Luke 16:19-21 sketches a fictional picture of a reality that was omnipresent in the cities of the Roman empire. That the wealth of the rich is connected to the poverty of the poor is not explained with the aid of economic analyses, but with the literary means of antithetical parallelism. The rich man in Luke 16:19-31 is a Jew, because he is advised to read the Scriptures. This rich man is presented as if he had refused the poor man the garbage from his table, which is really scarcely imaginable for a Jew. But the text is not at all interested in that question. The misery of the poor person who dies from hunger and the illness that goes with it are the fault of the rich person. He could and should have prevented this misery, and that would involve more than giving a piece of bread as alms now and again.

The parable of the rich farmer (Luke 12:16-21) need not be discussed in detail here, since it is within the same horizon of thought. At the same time, it must not be read in an individualizing sense. It does not describe a regrettable single instance of moral failure, but a driving up of prices on a grand scale for the sake of maximizing profit, and the hoarding of grain, which was one of the causes of famine. Thus the rich farmer drives the poor to starvation and for that reason is punished at God's judgment.

ESCHATOLOGICAL INTERPRETATION

Attempts to individualize the guilt of the rich and the salvation of the poor are numerous. Let me mention just two examples: The poor man is said to be a devout person who can rest in Abraham's bosom because of his piety. This is shown by his name, "Lazarus,"[38] that is, "God helps." Or: The rich man has used his wealth immorally; he has thrown lavish banquets, even including sexual orgies.[39] But the text does not speak of a devout poor man and a godless rich man. It is an uncompromising and radical text.[40]

The text sketches a situation after death, in the underworld and, on the other side of the gulf, in the sheltering arms of Abraham. The eschatological idea is that of the reversal of fortunes: In his lifetime the rich man had everything; now he must suffer. This is a scene of eschatological punishment and reward. How God's judgment takes place is not stated. Its result is the reality immediately after the death of a human being. There is no call to speculate about the life beyond; instead, conclusions are to be drawn for life before death: listening to the Scriptures and repentance, for God's year of release has come. The Gospel of Luke has a radical social analysis, and a grand vision.

METHODOLOGICAL CLARIFICATION

The idea that Luke 16:(26), 27-31 is a later addition to the earlier parable, which I previously shared, I now consider inaccurate. The texts must be read in their literary context. But I also no longer share the theological assessment of the text that is associated with this hypothesis, namely that the reference to the repentance of the rich (vv. 27-31) deprives the text of its radicality. This would only be true if repentance were to be seen as the repenting of the individual sins of the rich. But what the text in fact says is that the service of mammon, which destroys one's relationship to God, consists simply in the possession of wealth at the expense of the poor. There are substantive parallels outside the Bible, especially in Pliny the Elder and in the *Testaments of the Twelve Patriarchs*. I will quote these texts here; unlike the motif parallels to Luke 16:19-31, these really offer a comparable position, in their content, to the Lukan analysis of the guilt of the rich and the brutality of the money economy.

Pliny the Elder speaks of the crime committed by the one who first made a gold denarius. He criticizes the violence of the money economy: "But from the invention of money came the original source of avarice when usury was devised, and a profitable life of idleness; by rapid stages what was no longer mere avarice but a positive hunger for gold flared up with a sort of frenzy."[41]

The Testaments of the Twelve Patriarchs (*T. Judah* 18:2–19:1) also offers a fundamental critique of the money economy:

2   Beware, therefore, my children, of fornication and the love of money,
    and hearken to Judah your father.

3   For these things [i.e., greed] withdraw you from the law of God,
    And blind the inclination of the soul,
    And teach arrogance,
    And suffer not a man to have compassion upon his neighbour.

4   They rob his soul of all goodness,
    And oppress him with toils and troubles,
    And drive away sleep from him,
    And devour his flesh.

5   And he hindereth the sacrifices of God;
    And he remembereth not the blessing of God,
    He hearkeneth not to a prophet when he speaketh,
    And resenteth the words of godliness.

6   For he is a slave to two contrary passions,
    And cannot obey God,
    Because they have blinded his soul,
    And he walketh in the day as in the night.

19:1   My children, the love of money leadeth to idolatry; because, when led
    astray through money, men name as gods those who are not gods, and it
    causeth him who hath it to fall into madness.[42]

Ecclesiological interpretations of this parable appear in two forms: First, in the de-radicalizing of this uncompromising text, for example when the behavior of the rich man is interpreted as greedy or immoral and Lazarus is seen as devout. Such individualization relieves the middle-class churches of the West of their bad conscience: It is true, we are well off, but we act responsibly with our wealth. The second ecclesiological reading interprets Lazarus as representing the church,[43] or only the group of the devout poor in Judaism[44]—a kind of precursor form of the church. Then even Pharisaic Judaism can be read into the wealthy who will suffer in Hades.

SUMMARY OF LUKE 16

I will summarize my conclusions regarding the whole of Luke 16 as a chapter about money and the Torah: The parable of the unjust manager makes a corrupt employee from the world of the super-rich the unwilling model for people who follow Jesus. They are to use the economic resources they possess to build up friendships. This does not refer to giving alms, but to freely chosen, but sometimes thoroughgoing, renunciation of private possessions (v. 9). This way of dealing with money merits God's promise. In v. 13 and the Lazarus parable the underlying analysis of contemporary experience with money and wealth is explicated. This analysis is radical and uncompromising. Those who are rich serve mammon and live in opposition to God. The appearance of this kind of wealth is characterized briefly and—for the nature of the wealth of elites in the Roman empire—accurately in 19:19. A good life is based on the misery of the poor. The Pharisees (or better: some Pharisees) are not really being addressed as representatives of this wealth, but rather as those whose interpretation of Torah legitimates this wealth and indirectly profits from it. The Lukan Jesus presents his social analysis in accordance with Torah. It is his vision that Pharisees and wealthy Jews should remember the Torah—and that means its idea of social justice—so that the universal liberation of the people can become a reality. It is no simple thing to translate this message of the Lukan Jesus, which presumably was also that of the historical Jesus, into the present world of globalized money. Translations into moralizing and individualizing warnings to deal responsibly with money, should it happen that some people have too much wealth, are not very convincing. This message from Jesus is still accurate in its analysis. I see the work of making visible the structures of the present-day money economy, critiquing them, and taking small or large steps toward changing them, as the task of those who follow Jesus.

FOR FURTHER READING

Richard J. Bauckham, "The Rich Man and Lazarus"
John S. Kloppenborg, "The Dishonoured Master (Luke 16:1-8a)"
Luise Schottroff and Wolfgang Stegemann, "Der Sabbat ist für den Menschen da," 38–41
Justin S. Ukpong, "The Parable of the Shrewd Manager"

22

"He Lived the Life of a Slave": Slave Parables in the Gospel of Luke

Luke 12:35-48; 17:3-10; and 19:11-27

The parables that describe the lives of female and male slaves have been read for centuries, and still are read at present, as allegories or parables with allegorical elements. This tradition of interpretation has justified slavery and identified the slaveowners with God. More recently there have been interpretations that distance themselves from justifying violence against slaves by saddling the evangelists with this allegorization. But the allegorization itself is not questioned. I will attempt to read the slave parables in the context of the particular gospel—here, to begin with, the Gospel of Luke—without allegorizing them. And I am not prepared to justify violence against female or male slaves. My questions arise out of my theological refusal to believe that the same people who recognize God's Son in the tortured body of Christ could have looked right past the tortured bodies of slaves. I cannot believe that the slave parables justify the sufferings of slaves, willingly or unwillingly. That is why I have chosen the quotation from the Christ hymn in Phil 2:6-10 as the title for this section. It does not say that Jesus was only superficially or externally like a slave ("he took the form of a slave"). The Greek word *morphē* ("form") describes the whole person: He lived the life of a slave. The word *slave* in this statement is no metaphor, for Christ died the death of a slave.

TRANSLATION OF LUKE 12:35-48
Obedient Day and Night
35 Let your loins be girded and keep your lamps burning.
36 And you are to be like people who wait for their owner to return from the banquet, so that, when he comes and knocks, they may immediately open to him.
37 Blessed are those slaves whom the owner, when he comes, finds watching. I tell you, it will be so: He will gird himself and have them recline at table, and he will come and serve them.
38 And if he does not come until the second or third watch of the night, blessed are they!

39   Know this: If the owner of the house knew at what hour the thief was
     coming, he would not let his house be broken into.
40   And you: Be ready, for the Son of Man is coming at an unexpected hour.
41   Then Peter said: Teacher, are you telling this parable for us or for
     everyone?
42   And their teacher continued: Who is the faithful and wise manager
     whom his owner puts in charge of his slaves, to give them their
     allowance of grain at the proper time?
43   Blessed is that slave whom the owner will find at work when he arrives.
44   I tell you, he will surely put that one in charge of all his possessions!
45   But if that slave says in his heart: My master is delayed in coming, and if
     he begins to beat the other slaves, men and women, and to eat and drink
     and get drunk,
46   then the owner of that slave will come on a day when he does not
     expect him and at an hour that he does not know, and will cut him in
     two pieces, and mete out to him the punishment of unfaithful slaves.
47   A slave who knows the will of the owner and does not show concern for
     it or carry it out will be severely beaten.
48   The one who does not know the owner's will and does something that
     deserves a beating will be punished less harshly. From all to whom God
     gives much, God will expect much; and from all to whom God has given
     great tasks, God will also ask great things.

In this speech to disciples (the Lukan) Jesus employs two parable narratives (12:36-38 about the night shift and 12:42-46 about faithful and unfaithful
managers) and two brief sketches of a situation that should be read as parables
(12:39, the thief in the night; 12:47, 48a, the well-informed and the badly-
informed slave). The applications to the situation of disciples are clearly delin-
eated: these are found in vv. 35, 40, and 48b. Peter's question in v. 41 is answered
in v. 48b in such a way that all those who receive great gifts and tasks from God
are addressed. I understand these great gifts and assignments in the meaning
of the Gospel of Luke as God's Torah and the Holy Spirit. Thus the address is
for all those who have the duty of hearing the word of God and doing it (Luke
8:21). The word "slave" does not appear in these applications, even though the
images are exclusively drawn from the life of slaves. If the applications are to be
related to the idea of God's children as "slaves of God" in the sense of the First
Testament's tradition for this metaphor, nevertheless the absence of the word
"slave" must be considered. I will return to these applications.

SOCIAL-HISTORICAL ANALYSIS
Luke 12:36-40

Here it is not only the porter who must remain awake all night (as in Mark 13:34) to open the door for the returning slaveowner, but a whole group of slaves. Who they are is not specified. They are all supposed to open the door when the master comes, whether in the evening, before, or after midnight (v. 38). The Roman painting from Trier of a slaveowner being greeted by two—or possibly more[1]— slaves shows, just as in Luke 12:36-38, what this is about: greeting the master, who wishes to be received. He needs his slaves' greeting to be assured that he is master in the house. It is not just about opening the gate; there is more. And it is not enough that a porter should be awakened by the sound of the knocker[2] to open the gate. The slave men and women must remain awake in order to show that they are slaves. Such behavior on the part of human beings can only be compelled through violence and the permanent threat of violence.[3] While in Mark 13:35 the strain on the night watcher is evident, we can perceive here also that the slaves want to or have to please their master. For people who themselves were slaves, or who knew such persons as their brothers and sisters in Christ in the congregation,[4] the latent violence would have been clear. In a society that used slave labor in all spheres of life, the violence and degradation suffered by slaves were hidden from no one. This slaveowner comes into his house, is greeted, and then rewards his slaves, though he has no need to reward them. He hitches up his gown so that he can work, tells his slaves to recline at table, and then serves them. He apparently exchanges roles with them, because otherwise it is he who reclines at table and is served by slaves.

This amazing deed of a slaveowner has caused this passage to be read as an allegory of Christ. In Luke 22:24-27 Jesus says that there are to be no power relationships in the community of his followers that resemble the relationships of political power in the Roman empire. "Those who have the tasks of leadership are to become servants." Since the Greek word *diakonein* ("serve") refers to household work and care for others, things a free man would never do,[5] I would not put too much emphasis on the fact that in this Jesus saying Luke, different from Mark and Matthew, does not use the word *slave*. "Serving" is slaves' work. A metaphorical usage of the word *serve* that does not refer to any real surrender of power and privilege, is not (yet) in play here. Jesus then says of himself: "I am in your midst as one who serves"—and I believe we are justified in understanding "one who serves" as the equivalent of "slave." The one who serves at table is subordinate in rank to those who recline at table (22:27), Jesus says.

Against this background, an allegorical reading of Luke 12:37 seems likely. And yet the social-historical question should be posed nevertheless, and the frame for Luke's understanding of 12:37 not simply be drawn from Luke 22:27.

Seneca describes the treatment of slaves who serve at meals very critically and realistically. It is his idea that fate has placed them in this state but that they could have a noble character. Therefore the slaveowner should treat them decently and even, if they are well behaved, invite them individually to eat at table with him:

> I am glad to learn, through those who come from you, that you live on friendly terms with your slaves. This befits a sensible and well-educated man like yourself. "They are slaves," people declare. Nay, rather they are men. "Slaves!" No, comrades. "Slaves!" No, they are unpretentious friends. "Slaves!" No, they are our fellow-slaves, if one reflects that Fortune has equal rights over slaves and free men alike. That is why I smile at those who think it degrading for a man to dine with his slave. But why should they think it degrading? It is only because purse-proud etiquette surrounds a householder at his dinner with a mob of standing slaves. The master eats more than he can hold, and with monstrous greed loads his belly until it is stretched and at length ceases to do the work of a belly; so that he is at greater pains to discharge all the food than he was to stuff it down. All this time the poor slaves may not move their lips, even to speak. The slightest murmur is repressed by the rod; even a chance sound—a cough, a sneeze, or a hiccup,— is visited with the lash. There is a grievous penalty for the slightest breach of silence. All night long they must stand about, hungry and dumb. The result of it all is that these slaves, who may not talk in their master's presence, talk about their master.[6]

Seneca writes this for people like himself, educated members of the upper class in the Roman empire. This text can help us to picture how such an audience would react to Luke 12:37: Even Seneca himself found it excessive to give up the position of master even symbolically and for a short time. His concern was to encourage masters to behave cordially toward their slaves. Here in Luke 12:37 a slaveowner gives up his status as master, symbolically and for a limited time. He lowers himself to the social status of a slave.

This would not prevent a "normal" slaveowner from having slaves who do not carry out his orders beaten—or beating them himself. It would also not prevent him from expecting servility and subjection from them, as is evident in the body language of the slaves in the Trier painting. Nor would it prevent him from conceding to slaves, in the pictorial conventions of the time only half the size of free persons, as shown also in the Trier painting. They are slaves, the property of their masters and mistresses, who could do with them whatever they wanted—even exchange roles for a short time.

Jennifer A. Glancy has confronted the romanticization of Luke 12:37 with the social history of slavery in the Roman empire. She links the analysis of Luke 12:36-38 with that of Luke 17:7-10: Why are these two parable images different? The difference lies in the attitude of the master, not that of the slaves. It depends on the slaveowner's mood whether he has the slave working until late in the night without a word of thanks or whether he rewards the slave with a meal at which the master serves. Luke makes it clear that normally masters would never serve. Still, "the structure of these parables rests on the recognition that the welfare of chattel slaves depends on the caprice of the slaveholder and not on the intrinsic merits of the slave."[7] Glancy's book is a milestone for New Testament research on the slave parables in the Gospels. There has been ongoing critical discussion of Paul's attitude toward slavery, but the slave parables have for the most part been spared such criticism.[8] The sweet poison of allegorization has immunized readers of the Bible.

The brief parabolic saying in v. 39 emphasizes a single thought from the preceding parable: the uncertain time of the Lord's appearing. The house owner does not know when the thief will break in; otherwise he could successfully defend himself. This parabolic saying did not suffer allegorization in subsequent interpretation. The thief is not identified with Christ. That happened only in the case of the slaveowner. Therefore the parable about the night watchers (Mark 13:28-34) should also be spared allegorization. Christ is not reflected either in the thief or in the slaveholder who serves his slaves at night. The application of the parable in vv. 35 and 40 also makes only one connection with the parable: Believers should be prepared at all times for the coming of the Son of Man. The Son of Man comes for judgment. Prepared for this event are those who "hear the word and do it" (Luke 8:21; 11:28): Jesus' words and the words of the Torah, which he teaches with authority.

Luke 12:41-48

To Peter's question about whether Jesus is addressing only his community of disciples or the whole crowd (12:1, 13, 16), Jesus replies with another parable. He asks who is really the faithful manager. This question is forgotten in what follows because the text contrasts two possible attitudes of a slave (v. 45): the faithful and the unfaithful slave.[9] The faithful slave proves to be a wise manager. He is ordered by his master to distribute the grain ration to his fellow slaves. He accomplishes his task correctly. On his arrival, the slaveowner rewards him for his correct behavior and gives him charge over his whole property. This is a rapidly rising career, but it remains within the realm of the imaginable. Many of the financial managers, even of great estates or institutions, were slaves. Because slaves could be tortured by their owners at any time, they were preferred for such work as financial management. They could assure themselves of a great deal of power and influence, but always remained in the unconditional dependent state of slavery, with their bodies at the owner's disposal.[10] The unfaithful slave takes advantage of the master's absence. Instead of distributing the grain ration, he beats the other slaves. Here, despite its pervasive androcentrism, the text goes out of its way to mention slave women. Instead of giving the others their food,

he himself eats and drinks and gets drunk. When the owner unexpectedly returns, he cuts the unfaithful slave into two pieces; that is, he kills him in a horrible manner. "And he gives him what belongs to the unfaithful." I understand
this expression not as eternal punishment that God will bestow on him after his
death,[11] but as a clarification of what it is that legitimates his being killed. As an
unfaithful slave he has forfeited his life, if his owner wishes it so. This text about
the obedient or disobedient slaves describes the life of slaves, their unconditional
subjection to the will of their master, the brief and short-sighted opportunities
for disobedience—and even then at the expense of other enslaved people. By
its contrast of obedient and disobedient behavior the text makes its own the
slaveowner's ideology of proper upbringing.

A parabolic saying inserted in vv. 47 and 48a remains within the same logic of
the slaveowner. It presents the case of slaves who do not know their master's will,
and do something he finds deserving of punishment; then they are beaten, if not
as severely. On the other hand, the slave who knows the master's will and does
not act accordingly receives a severe beating. This sounds like a legal principle. If
so, it is the self-made law of a slaveowner, the law of his whip.

The application in v. 48 takes up only one feature of the parable and the
added parabolic saying: that of the assignment of a great responsibility. It is even
repeated: the one to whom much is given . . . the one to whom much has been
assigned. These are divine passives. What the text says is: You have been given
great gifts by God; you have received a great task. God expects much, indeed,
very much from you. God is not identified with the punishing slaveowner and
his ideology of upbringing and his law of the whip. All that is reported without
any explicit indication about how it should be evaluated.

I consider it absolutely impossible that the Gospel of Luke tells these stories
to God's slaves in order to say something to them allegorically about their relationship to God as God's slaves.[12] "Even upon my slaves, both men and women,
in those days I will pour out my Spirit; and they shall prophesy . . ." (Acts 2:18).
Nor do the ideas about how slaves belonging to the Christian community are
to be treated run in that direction. We do not learn much about this, but Acts
12:13-17 tells a story that offers a clear alternative to the treatment of slaves in
Luke 12:38-48. The slave woman Rhoda participates in the community assembly in the house of her owner, Mary. She also has the task of opening the door.
Peter, who has miraculously escaped from prison, knocks at the gate. She goes
to the door, recognizes his voice, and for sheer joy is incapable of opening the
door. The gathered community cannot believe it. The slave woman insists that
it is Peter. Peter is still standing outside, knocking. According to the standards
of the slaveowner in Luke 12:41-48, she did not obey, because she did not open
the door and she apparently contradicted other people. We cannot even imagine
what kind of punishment a normal slaveowner would have thought was obvi-

ously called for! But she was a respected member of the Christian community, who admired and handed down the story of her deed.

Where, then, do the criteria for the hearers of these slave parables come from?—these parables that so brutally depict the reality of slave life, often including the ideology of the slaveowner. Those criteria must be so obvious that these slave stories could be told without any explicit guide to their evaluation.

With the expansion of the Pax Romana this form of slavery also expanded, in Palestine also. Many Jewish people were enslaved after becoming prisoners of war in the Jewish-Roman war of 66–70 c.e. Since Christianity spread as a house-church movement, there were probably no Christian communities, from the very beginning, without enslaved members. That Christ lived as a slave and was hymned as such made him a companion of slaves. And it made this movement suspect to slaveowners.[13] In Luke's gospel we hear, from the very beginning, God's great promise, which is also for slaves, male and female: God has sent his anointed one "to proclaim release to the captives" (Luke 4:18). That can refer to prisoners of war or debt slaves but also to other enslaved people. The Messianic year of release in Jesus' preaching (Luke 4:19), like Mary's vision in the Magnificat, is comprehensive, worldwide: The arrogance of the masters of the world will have its end. The slaveowner's lowering of himself in 12:37 is, in this context, a sign of hope, even if the parable is only a fictional story with particular emphases and if this feature is not particularly emphasized. The humiliation[14] of the lowly, which Mary (1:48) embodies, has been "regarded" by God, who has put an end to it. In the slave parables of the Gospels we have a representation of slavery in the Roman empire. The Gospels apply them to a relationship to God that is also described in the First Testament with the word ʿebed. But this word does not imply the subjection to violent authority that characterized Roman slavery. Being the ʿebed of God does *not* mean being subjected to other human beings. It is the idea, unique in antiquity, that slaves of God reject all subjection to earthly masters.[15] The Gospel of Luke describes the children of God, in the tradition of the First Testament, as slaves of God, as we have already said. That this metaphor is only implicitly present in the applications is something I regard as an expression of critical awareness with regard to slavery in the Roman empire.

ESCHATOLOGICAL INTERPRETATION

"Let your loins be girded . . ." (v. 35), "be ready" when the Son of Man comes for judgment (v. 40), "God has entrusted a great task to you" (v. 48b)—that is the message addressed to the community of Jesus' disciples and likewise to the nation.[16] Those belonging to the people of God are God's slaves. What it meant to be enslaved in the Roman empire was a matter of daily experience, though perspectives on it differed. Jesus teaches what it means to be God's slave (as in the First Testament): God liberates women and men from subjugation and gives them the spirit of prophecy. God lifts up the lowly. As slaves of God they have the great task of hearing and doing the word. The metaphor "slave" of God in the New Testament is an antithetical metaphor to the reality of slavery in the Roman empire, just as God's kingdom is an antithetical metaphor. The critical view of slavery in the introductory v. 35, with its citation from the Exodus tradition (Exod 12:11), is especially concrete: Let your loins be girded. This is the manner in which the people is to eat the Paschal lamb while remembering its escape from slavery in Egypt. It is already part of the allegorical immunization to identify Luke 12:35, of all verses, with the subsequent image of the waiting slaves instead of reading the verse as a critical superscription for the parable that follows: How different it is to be God's "slave," freed from the degradation of slavery.

METHODOLOGICAL CLARIFICATION

The basis for the interpretation of the parables in Luke 12:35-48 is the applications in vv. 35, 40, 48b. The answer to Peter's question in v. 41 depends on an understanding of the task of God's slaves as Luke sees it. The ecclesiological tradition of interpretation, which referred the duty of the manager-slave to the special duties of the community leadership[17] as distinct from those of the people of the church, is out of line. It has no basis in the text, and it legitimates slavery and violence against slaves.

TRANSLATION OF LUKE 17:3-10
"We Are Worthless Slaves . . ."

3   Be on the alert for one another! If your brother or your sister has sinned,[18] criticize them clearly. And if they repent, forgive them.

4   And if they wrong you seven times a day and seven times come to you and say "I repent," forgive them.

5   And the apostles said to Jesus: Increase our faith!

6   Jesus said to them: If you had faith the size of a mustard seed, and if you would say to the mulberry tree "Pull up your roots and plant yourself in the sea" it would obey you.

7   Who among you, if you have slaves plowing or tending sheep, when one of them comes home from the field will say "Come here at once and take your place at the table"?

8   Would you not rather say "Prepare supper for me; put on your apron and serve me while I eat and drink. Later you may eat and drink"?

9   Do you thank the slave for doing what was commanded?

10   So you also, when you have done all that you were ordered to do, say "We are worthless slaves; we have done only what we ought to have done!"

SOCIAL-HISTORICAL ANALYSIS

The merciless obedience demanded of slaves is the theme of the parable in Luke 17:7-10. The opening question to the audience, "Who among you . . ." suggests that the slaveowners present, like all free persons, can identify the event narrated in the parable that follows as a social structure in which they unavoidably participate. In Luke 7:8 the centurion at Capernaum describes the same structure: "when I say to my slave, 'Do this,' he does it." This is the unconditional obedience that is compelled by violence, often with the whip.

This parable tells about a small farmer who has a slave working for him as a field hand and employs the same slave in household work. Slave labor had enormous dimensions in the agriculture of the Roman empire, and working in the fields was feared by slaves in great households.[19] This slave has to cook for his master in the evening, after his field work, then serve him and wait until his master has finished his meal before he himself can eat. The exploitation of slaves through endless workdays was the rule.[20] Verse 9 again asks the audience: Would a slaveowner thank the slave? It is clear that the slave must do what the master wants. Thanks would defy the system. The Lukan audience may know the parable in Luke 12:36-38. They know that here—unlike there—the structure of slavery is being described in all its bitterness.

Verse 10 applies the parable to the lives of the hearers. But this application remains within the imagery of the parable just related. The listeners are to identify with the self-degradation of the slave who calls himself worthless, because even in his own consciousness he is only the product of his master. The master calls him worthless, so he calls himself worthless. From earliest times it has irritated interpreters that here a parable and parable application that sound not at all "Christian" are attributed to Jesus.[21] It would be "Christian" in this sense if the master expected unconditional obedience, but graciously gave thanks for it and called the enslaved people "brother" or "sister." But this so-called Christian love-patriarchalism is only an especially effective justification of slavery.

ESCHATOLOGICAL INTERPRETATION

As in Matt 18:21-35, the issue is that Jesus' teaching obligates the people who follow him to an infinite readiness to forgive one another. In Luke 17:4 the limitlessness of this readiness to forgive is expressed this way: "And if your brother or your sister wrongs you seven times a day and seven times repents and says: 'I am sorry,' you must forgive."[22] To this, the apostles say: "Strengthen our faith," our ability to live according to God's will. Jesus responds with the saying about the infinite power of faith, even if it is as tiny as a mustard seed (17:6). The parable then follows. The apostles expect unconditional obedience from their slaves and should put themselves in the place of a slave who has lost all self-confidence: "We are worthless slaves" (17:10). The reference here to the readiness to forgive is clear. Those who find it hard to forgive without limit are given an exercise: to identify with a broken slave at the end of his or her too-long workday. The reference point between this application of the parable and the readiness to forgive is the renunciation, connected with faith, of the claim to define before God when the limit of forgiveness has been reached. It is *kenosis,* the surrender of one's security as God's child, in Jesus' life and death (Phil 2:7). The humiliation of a slave becomes, in Luke 17:10, an image for self-surrender to love and to God, the self-forgetting God who asks nothing more. The humiliation of a slave becomes the image for self-surrender. Consciousness of injustice and the violence that brings people to the point of calling themselves worthless slaves is evident in the Gospel of Luke, and especially in this parable. The identification with this humiliation creates a solidarity with the lowly—not a justification of the violence that humiliates them. In Luke 1:48, Mary's humiliation is coupled with that of a barren woman in a patriarchal society (1:25). Mary's humiliation is that of a pregnant woman whose child has no father.[23] The self-humbling that is so important in the Gospel of Luke (18:14; 14:11) leads to an encounter with the most extreme degradation in society and to solidarity with the lowly.[24]

I find in a text by Dorothee Soelle a description of this kind of mystical solidarity that I see in the Gospel of Luke.

All these forms of refusal, boycott, renunciation, and alternate life that is lived out already here and now have a mystical ground. It becomes manifest in a dream that John Woolman [U.S., 18th century] had when he was seriously ill and could not even remember his own name.

"Being then desirous to know who I was, I saw a mass of matter of a dull gloomy colour, between the south and the east, and was informed that this mass was human beings in as great misery as they could be and live, and that I was mixed in with them and henceforth might not consider myself as a distinct, or separate being. In this state I remained several hours. I then heard a soft, melodious voice, more pure and harmonious than any voice I had heard with my ears before, and I believed it of an angel who spake to other angels. The words were *John Woolman is dead.* . . . I was then carried in spirit to the mines, where poor and oppressed people were digging rich treasures for those called Christians, and heard them blaspheme the name of Christ, at which I was grieved, for his name to me was precious. I was informed that these heathens were told that those who oppressed them were the followers of Christ, and they said amongst themselves: 'If Christ directed them to use us in this sort, then Christ is a cruel tyrant.'"[25]

At times, the mysticism of simple needs sounds somewhat homespun or even doctrinaire. But behind this moralism there is something that is set alight by the decisive question raised by possessions and the obsession with them. Slavery is the radical, most gruesome consequence of the craving for possessions. In slavery, disenfranchised human beings, robbed systematically of all autonomy and dignity, are turned into commodities, into things to be used as objects to be sold. This absurd division of people who are born as slaves and destined to be such and those who are masters and owners who have no sense of wrongdoing is based on a philosophy of life that regards having, ownership, and the individual's self-interest as the sole foundation of the economy. The mystical view of the unity of all life contradicts that technological-rationalistic view.

Something of this different thinking that arises from the perspective of God can be seen in John Woolman's dream. Mystical thinking is rooted in a sense of not being different from the "others," those who have no possessions and no rights, those of different color and the other sex. The indistinguishable mass of fellow creatures that the dreaming John Woolman saw in the mines is integrally part of the inextinguishable longing for oneness. Possession separates just as Ego does. God, of whom Eckhart says that she is the only reality that we ought to have as a possession and which renders all else unnecessary, binds together all who set themselves apart by means of possessions and the lusting after them. This is what Woolman saw in his dream: in the state of "as great a misery as . . . could be," he saw those who had nothing and himself "mixed in with them." In the sense of contemporary mysticism, this can mean nothing other than that they who make up the 20 percent of the owners of the world belong together with the remaining 80 percent "in the state of as great a misery as . . . could be."[26]

TRANSLATION OF LUKE 19:11-27
We Do Not Want a King Like Herod

11   As they were still listening, he went on to tell a parable, because he was near Jerusalem, and because they supposed that the kingdom of God was to appear immediately.

12   He said: A man of noble lineage went to a distant country to obtain the kingship and then return.

13   He summoned ten of his slaves and gave them ten *minas* of gold and said to them: Do business with this until I come back.

14   His subjects hated him and sent a delegation after him with the message: We do not want this man to rule over us.

15   And it came to pass that he returned with the kingship. Then he summoned the slaves to whom he had given the money, to find out what they had gained by trading.

16   The first came and said: Master, your *mina* has made ten *minas*.

17   He said to him: Well done, faithful slave! Because you have been obedi-
     ent in small things, you shall take charge of ten cities.

18   The second came and said: Master, your *mina* has made five *minas.*

19   He said to him, too: You shall take charge of five cities.

20   And the next slave came and said: Master, here is your *mina,* which I
     kept safe in a napkin.

21   For I was afraid of you, because you are a harsh man; you take what you
     did not deposit and reap what you did not sow.

22   He said to him: With your own words I will judge you, you wicked slave!
     If you knew that I am a harsh man and take what I did not deposit and
     reap what I did not sow,

23   why did you not at least put my money into the bank? Then I could have
     come and collected it with interest.

24   And to those standing around him he said: Take the *mina* from him and
     give it to the one who has ten *minas.*

25   And they said to him: Master, he already has ten *minas.*

26   I say to you: The one who has will receive still more, and from the one
     who has nothing, even what he has will be taken away.

27   And these my enemies, who did not want me to rule over them: bring
     them here and slaughter them in my presence.

SOCIAL-HISTORICAL ANALYSIS

The parable of the "entrusted pounds," as it is called in the Luther Bible, tells
a highly political story containing elements drawn from the experience of the
Jewish people in the first half of the first century c.e. A man from an elite family
goes to "a distant country" to be installed as king of his native land and return
as its ruler (19:12). Against the background of Jewish history, this "distant land"
is Rome, where all the Herodian kings received their vassal kingships: Herod the
Great, his sons Archelaus and Antipas, and his nephew Herod Agrippa.[27] There
was always Jewish resistance to the royal regencies of the Herodians. We are especially well informed about the Jewish resistance to the kingly aspirations of
Archelaus. I will quote here the text of Josephus about the Jewish delegation to
Rome that tried to prevent his kingship. The delegation spoke to the emperor,
and Josephus describes the scene:

So when Varus had settled these affairs, and had placed the former legion
at Jerusalem, he returned back to Antioch; but as for Archelaus, he had
new sources of trouble come upon him at Rome, on the occasions following: for embassage of the Jews was come to Rome, Varus having permitted
the nation to send it, that they might petition for the liberty of living by
their own laws. Now, the number of the ambassadors that were sent by

the authority of the nation were fifty, to which they joined above eight thousand of the Jews that were at Rome already. Hereupon Caesar assembled his friends, and the chief men among the Romans, in the temple of Apollo, which he had built at a vast charge; whither the ambassadors came, and a multitude of the Jews that were there already came with them, as did also Archelaus and his friends; but as for the several kinsmen which Archelaus had, they would not join themselves with him, out of their hatred to him; and yet they thought it too gross a thing for them to assist the ambassadors [against him], as supposing it would be a disgrace to them in Caesar's opinion to think of thus acting in opposition to a man of their own kindred: Philip also was come hither out of Syria, by the persuasion of Varus, with this principal intention to assist his brother [Archelaus]: for Varus was his great friend; but still so, that if there should any change happen in the form of government (which Varus suspected there would), and if any distribution should be made on account of the number that desired the liberty of living by their own laws, that he might not be disappointed, but might have his share in it.

Now, upon the liberty that was given to the Jewish ambassadors to speak, they who hoped to obtain a dissolution of kingly government, betook themselves to accuse Herod of his iniquities; and they declared that he was indeed in name a king, but that he had taken to himself that uncontrollable authority which tyrants exercise over their subjects, and had made use of that authority for the destruction of the Jews, and did not abstain from making many innovations among them besides, according to his own inclinations; and that whereas there were a great many who perished by that destruction he brought upon them, so many indeed as no other history relates, they that survived were far more miserable than those that suffered under him, not only by the anxiety they were in from his looks and disposition towards them, but from the danger their estates were in of being taken away by him. That he did never leave off adorning these cities that lay in their neighborhood, but were inhabited by foreigners; but so that the cities belonging to his own government were ruined, and utterly destroyed: that whereas, when he took the kingdom, it was in an extraordinary flourishing condition, he had filled the nation with the utmost degree of poverty; and when upon unjust pretenses, he had slain any of the nobility, he took away their estates: and when he permitted any of them to live, he condemned them to the forfeiture of what they possessed. And, besides the annual impositions which he laid upon every one of them, they were to make liberal presents to himself, to his domestics and friends, and to such of his slaves as were vouchsafed the favor of being his tax gatherers, because there was no way of obtaining a freedom from unjust violence, without giving either gold or silver for it. That they would say nothing of the corruption of the chastity of their virgins, and the reproach laid on their wives for incontinency, and those things acted after an insolent and inhuman manner; because it was not a smaller pleasure to the sufferers to have such things concealed, then it would have been not to have suffered them. That Herod had put such abuses upon them as a wild beast would not have put on them, if he had power given him to rule over us: and that although their nation had passed through many subversions and alterations of government, their history gave no account of any calamity they had ever been under, that could be compared with this which Herod had brought upon their nation; that it was for this reason that they thought they might justly and gladly salute Archelaus as king, upon this supposition, that whosoever should be set over their kingdom, he would appear more mild to them than Herod had been; and that they had joined with him in the mourning for his father, in order to gratify him, and were ready to oblige him in other points also, if they could meet with any degree of moderation from him: but that he seemed to be afraid lest he should not be deemed Herod's own son; and so, without any delay, he immediately let the nation understand his meaning and this before his dominion was well established, since the power of disposing of it belonged to Caesar, who could either give it to him or not as he pleased. That he had given a specimen of his future virtue to his subjects, and with what kind of moderation and good administration he would govern them, by that his first action which concerned them, his own citizens, and God himself also, when he made the slaughter of three thousand of his own countrymen at the temple. How, then could they avoid their just hatred of him, who, to the rest of his barbarity, hath added this as one of our crimes, that we have opposed and contradicted him in the exercise of his authority? Now, the main thing they desired was this: That they might be delivered from kingly and the like forms of government, and might be added to Syria, and be put under the authority of such presidents of theirs as should be sent to them; for that it would thereby be made evident, whether they be really a seditious people, and generally fond of innovations, or whether they would live in an orderly manner, if they might have governors of any sort of moderation set over them.[28]

The parable also tells of such an embassy: "We do not want this man to rule over us" (Lk 19:14). While Archelaus received only limited power from Rome, the nobleman in the parable is given the kingship. After his return home as king he builds up his government and establishes his power. Before his departure he had commissioned ten slaves to increase his wealth during his absence. Ten *minas* are distributed among them. One *mina* is a small amount, corresponding to a hundred drachmas or denarii. In Josephus's text Herod's slaves collect taxes and take in large amounts in return for a favorable apportionment of taxes. Since they are slaves, they act in the interest of their master's business.[29] In the parable the slaves make large profits with very little money: ten and five times the original sum (19:16, 18). In doing so, they have proved to the satisfaction of the new king that they can form the backbone of his administration. They receive the governorship of cities according to their potential: one gets ten cities, the other five. The details about the remaining successful slaves of the total of nine are not related. The audience can imagine all that for itself. Now the slaves can relate in grand style what they have so successfully accomplished on a small scale: exploiting people and land to increase the wealth of their master—as Herod's slaves did in the quotation from Josephus.

One of the slaves, however, was disobedient. He did not increase the sum given him; he did not even lend it at interest to brokers.[30] He says that he feared his master, a harsh man who takes people's property from them.[31] He has kept the money in a handkerchief. The king has it demonstratively and publicly taken from him and given to the most successful slave. In this way he can demonstrate the rule that, in his opinion, should govern the economy: Those who have something will be given more, and those who have nothing will be squeezed.[32] Finally he acts against the people who wanted to prevent him from becoming king. He has them publicly executed (katasphazein) in his presence. The narrative is absolutely clear. It describes the economic and political structure of an exploitative kingship. The perspective of the description is that of the people that reluctantly bear this governance and desire an end to it. What is described is not a particular, individual historical event, but a structure. The historical application is so clear that an allegorizing interpretation that saw the obedient slaves as obedient servants of God[33] and the journey to Rome as Jesus' ascent into heaven occasionally reveals some uncertainty. François Bovon says: "However, one may not confuse Rome and heaven, Italy and the kingdom of God."[34] But then he posits an "allegorizing reflex" by the author of the Lukan special material, who sees the journey to Rome as Jesus' ascent into heaven. So are we, after all, to confuse Rome and heaven?

Adolf Jülicher[35] insists that the distant land is not Italy, but heaven. It is widely noted that the embassy (19:14) is hard to allegorize. Nevertheless, the parable is read throughout as an allegory. I really cannot understand how Jesus' messiahship could ever have been interpreted in this way—as if Jesus' journey to God could be described and recognized in terms of Archelaus' journey to Rome, or that of some comparable ruler. After all, these interpreters have always recognized the connection with political history. And in spite of that the real history has been made into neutral illustrative material for something that is supposedly altogether different: Jesus' messiahship. And the Jewish embassy, so inimical to the king, is made into a revolt of his "fellow Jews in their blind hatred" against Jesus' kingship.[36] It is also sometimes noted that the allegorization encounters some difficulties,[37] yet most interpreters cling to it.

ESCHATOLOGICAL INTERPRETATION

Verse 11 says why Jesus is telling the parable. He is in Jericho, shortly before his arrival in Jerusalem. He has said to the chief toll collector, Zacchaeus: "Today salvation has come to this house. For the Son of Man has come . . . to save the lost" (19:9, 10). This scene and these words of Jesus are heard by those standing around. They could be disciples, but also other interested persons. They conclude from Jesus' words and the fact that he is about to enter Jerusalem that God's kingship will very soon be revealed, that God will rescue the lost: the people that dwells in darkness (1:79). Desperate people's hope for the kingship of God was, at that time, very often connected with a prophetic action that would introduce God's coming. Josephus tells of such messianism, which in his eyes was anti-Roman and criminal. But if we leave aside his polemic, his report permits us to sketch a picture of the messianic groups.

> These works, that were done by the robbers, filled the city with all sorts of impiety. And now these impostors and deceivers persuaded the multitude to follow them into the wilderness, and pretended that they would exhibit manifest wonders and signs, that should be performed by the providence of God. And many that were prevailed on by them suffered the punishments of their folly; for Felix brought them back, and then punished them. Moreover, there came out of Egypt about this time to Jerusalem, one that said he was a prophet, and advised the multitude of the common people to go along with him to the Mount of Olives, as it was called, which lay over against the city, and at the distance of five furlongs. He said farther, that he would show them from hence, how, at his command, the walls of Jerusalem would fall down; and he promised that he would procure them an entrance into the city through those walls, when they were fallen down. Now when Felix was informed of these things, he ordered his soldiers to take their weapons, and came against them with a great number of horsemen and footmen, from Jerusalem, and attacked the Egyptian and the people that were with him. He also slew four hundred of them, and took two hundred alive. But the Egyptian himself escaped out of the fight, but did not appear any more. And again the robbers stirred up the people to make war with the Romans, and said they ought not to obey them at all; and when any persons would not comply with them, they set fire to their villages, and plundered them.[38]

The expectation of the kingdom of God that Jesus teaches is different from this expectation of a miraculous liberation of Jerusalem: He hopes for the repentance of the whole nation (Lk 13:1-9), and that is what he works for. But even his disciples misunderstand his message about the kingdom to the very end:

They hope that God will now, "immediately" (*parachrēma*, 19:11) "in these days" (Acts 1:6) intervene to free the people (see Lk 24:21). Jesus, in contrast,[39] sees the danger that is approaching Jerusalem and the people. Jerusalem will be destroyed because the people have not recognized the times (Lk 19:44). But the message of repentance and return to God will continue, even after Jesus' death, and God will establish God's kingship (Luke 24:47; Acts 1:8). God's kingship is near (Lk 21:30, 31).

The parable thus clarifies for those standing around him why Jesus regards their messianic hopes as false. His political analysis is radical: The Roman *imperium* is brutally erected on money and power. You know how this *imperium* functions. Those who aspire too high will be killed (19:27). Jerusalem will be destroyed (19:41-44; 21:5-6, 20-24).

Jesus gives no explicit concluding interpretation of the parable. His interpretation is his previous encounter with Zacchaeus and his departure for Jerusalem (19:28), where he will be killed by this same imperial power and where—according to "Luke"—he will rise again. The meaning of the truth that Jesus is a king is shown in his Passion, for which he is greeted, on his entry into Jerusalem, as a king (19:38).

METHODOLOGICAL CLARIFICATION

In this exegesis—as throughout this book—I have interpreted the text in its literary context. Thus I have not inquired about the prehistory of this parable in oral or written tradition, although I assume that all the elements of the synoptic tradition have such a prehistory. But in this case it is clearer than almost anywhere else that it is destructive to segment the text in terms of its possible prehistory. This segmentation destroys the total picture as it stands in its context, the Gospel of Luke. Such a deconstruction has been discussed very emphatically in the case of Luke 19:11-27. In particular, the comparison with Matt 25:14-30 has led to attempts to find an original form that preceded both of these texts. In the process the fact that in Matt 25:14-30 and Luke 19:11-27 we have before us two completely different parables that sometimes make use of identical motifs becomes invisible or incidental. Luke 19:11-27 tells a very different story from Matt 25:14-30. In addition, Luke 19:11-27 does not combine two independent parables about slaves and a claimant to a throne; it tells a story that is coherent in itself, about the beginning of the reign of a vassal king, his management of the administration of his kingdom, and the establishment of his power.

FOR FURTHER READING

Jennifer A. Glancy, *Slavery in Early Christianity*
William R. Herzog, *Parables as Subversive Speech*
Klaus Wengst, *Demut* (ET *Humility*)

23

Crying to God:
The Insistent Friend and the Stubborn Widow

Luke 11:5-13 and 18:1-8

TRANSLATION OF LUKE 11:5-13

The Insistent Friend

5   And he said to them: Suppose one of you has a friend, and you go to him
    at midnight and say: Friend, lend me three loaves of bread.

6   For a friend of mine who is traveling through has stopped with me, and I
    have nothing to set before him.

7   And he answers[1] from within: Do not bother me. The door has already
    been locked, and my children are with me in bed. I cannot get up and
    give you [bread].

8   I tell you: If he does not get up and give him[2] what he asks because he is
    his friend, because of his impertinence he will get up and give him ev-
    erything he needs.

9   And I say to you: Ask, and God will give to you; seek, and you will find;
    knock, and God will open to you.

10 All who ask, receive, and those who seek, find, and those who knock, to
    them the door is opened.

11 Which of you who is a father, if his son asks him for a fish, will give him
    a snake instead?

12 or if he asks for an egg, will give him a scorpion?

13 So then, if you, who are evil, are able to give good gifts to your children,
    how much more will your Father in heaven give the Holy Spirit to those
    who ask him.

SOCIAL-HISTORICAL ANALYSIS

The parable and its application (11:8-13), which first operates within the parable imagery (v. 8) and then adds another parable (vv. 11, 12), refer to two of
life's situations: (1) Someone wakes his friend at night to borrow bread; (2)
Children ask their father for food, a fish and an egg. The first situation is unusual. Someone has a visit from a friend during the night. The friend is traveling.
Normally travelers try not to be on the road at night, but there are situations that
force a traveler to go farther, for example, if he or she finds no room in a lodg-

ing place (Luke 2:7). It is part of friendship to offer hospitality. The host now attempts to scare up some dinner for his late-arriving guest during the night. He goes to his friend who lives nearby and who is already in bed. The latter is not so eager to do a friendly deed in the middle of the night. It is hard to determine here whether he thus offends against the social rules that define friendship or not. The text does not intend to paint him negatively and makes it clear that he does not feel obligated by friendship to get up and bring the bread; he only does it because he wants to get rid of this importunate visitor. While someone traveling at night can count on a friend to show hospitality and not send him back onto the streets, a friend can be annoyed if he is hauled out of bed in the middle of the night because someone is missing a meal. The social conditions presumed here are those of people who live from hand to mouth and have no provisions beyond those for today. The text also presumes that people help each other: the traveling friend and the neighbor who has no bread—but not necessarily at night.

The parable describes the solidarity of friends who provide each other shelter at night and, if necessary, are also prepared to demand solidarity beyond the boundaries of decency. The rhetorical question "Who among you?" expects neither swift refusal nor agreement, but reflection on whether the hearers would make such urgent demands or not. The situation describes how people network and the transparency of that networking for the relationship to God.

ESCHATOLOGICAL INTERPRETATION

The subject is prayer and the gift of God, the gift of the Holy Spirit. If even a friend and neighbor who is quite annoyed about it will give bread in the middle of the night, how much more will God hear your prayers. I regard the conclusion *a minore ad maius* (from the less to the greater), which follows in v. 13, as applying to vv. 8 and 9 also. If children can count on their fathers not to put them in danger, how much more can you rely on God, who will give you the Holy Spirit if you ask. The Spirit of God is the power given us by God for the renewal of life according to the will of God. The Spirit of God enables us to heal the sick, to spread the Gospel to the poor, and to be courageous in the face of judgment. In the Gospel of Luke, Jesus himself, the Baptizer, Mary, Elizabeth, Zechariah, and Simeon are all described as people filled with the Spirit (Luke 1:15, 25, 41, 67; 2:25-27; 3:22; 4:1, 18, etc.). The Acts of the Apostles is full of stories about the power of the Spirit of God. In the Gospel of Luke the community of disciples is only associated explicitly with the Spirit here and in 12:12. But their power to heal and their authority to speak prophetically about the kingship of God (see only 10:1, 17, 21) is implicitly nothing other than an expression of God's gift of the Spirit. This Spirit of God is not a characteristic that is always and everywhere associated with discipleship, but the expression, wherever it appears, of the living experience of divine revelation. Luke 11:5-13 relates a parable to encourage the disciples to persistence and audacity in their prayers to God. The relationship to God expressed in the application of the first parable (v. 8) is not a bit subservient; it is prepared to go almost to the point of embarrassment. Stories of such a relationship to God are also told in the First Testament and by the rabbis.

METHODOLOGICAL OBSERVATION

The parable in Luke 11:5-8, 9-13 has many similarities to Luke 18:1-8, but it is not a parallel story saying the same thing in different words. Luke 11:5-13 is about the power of the Holy Spirit, which believers must sometimes struggle to obtain from God; it is not something that is simply their due. The persistence (*anaideia*) in Luke 11:8 has been the subject of much discussion because the word has negative connotations. Attempts have been made to develop a positive interpretation of the word or to attribute the persistence to the friend who wants to stay in bed,[3] not the one who disturbs him. But the word has a negative connotation, and v. 8 is, in its language, quite clear that the one disturbing the peace is the persistent one. This is the very strength of the parable: that through its depiction of persistence in a situation of solidarity it invites us to persistence toward God. The discussion of "persistence" or "obstinacy" that tries to weaken it misses the unique character of this parable.

TRANSLATION OF LUKE 18:1-8
The Stubborn Widow

1   He told them a parable so that they might learn to pray always and not to lose heart.
2   He said: In a certain city there was a judge who neither feared God nor had respect for people.
3   In that city there was a widow who kept coming to him and saying: Grant me justice against my opponent.
4   For a while he refused. Then he said to himself: Though I have no fear of God and no respect for anyone,
5   yet because this widow keeps bothering me, I will grant her justice. Otherwise, in the end she may come and give me a black eye.
6   Then Jesus said: Listen to what the unjust judge says!
7   Will not God grant justice to his chosen ones who cry to him day and night? Will he delay long in helping them?
8   I tell you: He will quickly grant justice to them! And yet, when the Son of Man comes, will he find fidelity to God anywhere on earth?

SOCIAL-HISTORICAL ANALYSIS

Both the figures in this parable should be read in the light of Torah. The unjust judge embodies the misuse of Torah law. This figure continually plays an important role in Torah: see, for example, Isa 5:7: "[God] expected justice, but saw bloodshed; righteousness, but heard a cry!" The judge embodies the opposite of what a judge in Israel should be: "'You judge not on behalf of human beings but on the Lord's behalf.... Now, let the fear of the Lord be upon you; take care what you do, for there is no perversion of justice with the Lord our God, or partiality, or taking of bribes'" (2 Chr 19:6-7). God also embodies the opposite of the unjust judge: "Do not offer him a bribe, for he will not accept it ... for the Lord is the judge, and with him there is no partiality. [God] will not show partiality to the poor.... He will not ignore the supplication of the orphan, or the widow when she pours out her complaint. Do not the tears of the widow run down her cheek as she cries out against the one who causes them to fall?" (Sir 35:14-19).

In the Torah, widows and orphans are placed under the special protection of divine law. In the patriarchal societies of the ancient world they were structurally the first victims of economic and social injustice and of legal maneuverings, and they were the objects of treachery and attempts at exploitation.

The injustice done to this widow is on two levels. She has been victimized by a man who has infringed on the economic basis of her life, and against whom she seeks to defend herself with the aid of a judge. She accuses him before the court. In the parable he appears as the "opponent." But in addition, she becomes the victim of an unjust judicial decision that has no regard for her rights. The judge has repulsed her many times, as the parable says. The twofold injustice done to this woman is the object of the Hebrew Bible's continual lament against the perpetrators of injustice and the people in whose midst such injustice occurs. We can draw both from the Old Testament material and from the parable itself that these texts regard this double injustice against widows as structural. The Old Testament texts address this injustice as structural through the very fact of their constant repetition of this accusation. The New Testament parable does the same by presenting the crisis situation as a typical case. Thus it becomes clear from this text that in early Christianity as elsewhere in the Jewish tradition there was an awareness that a patriarchal society involves structural injustice against which God intervenes. The parable says that the judge did not fear God (vv. 2, 4), but it also documents his deficient fear of God in his attitude toward the widow, for the God of the Hebrew Bible demands just judgment on behalf of widows.

The widow's resistance to the twofold injustice done to her, and to many other widows, consists in her going to court on account of the infringement on her livelihood and not allowing herself to be put off by the unjust judge. She comes back so often (and apparently behaves more objectionably every time) that the judge says she is making trouble for him (v. 5). He does justice for her so that her persistence will not shine even more light on him.[4]

Resistance through the courts is a frequent theme in ancient texts of all types: An early Egyptian story tells of an "eloquent farmer" who returns to the judge nine times, even though he has no success and once is even beaten with whips by the judge's servants. In his speech he reminds the judge of his duty to do justice for the weak: "Trust was placed in you, and you have become wicked. You were set up as a dam for the suffering to prevent them from drowning—and look, instead, you are their lake." He accuses the judge again and again of having himself become a thief: "The one who should lead in [obedience to] the law, instead commands robbery." He invokes evil on the judge himself and on his livestock. He regards himself, in his resistance, as the representative of what is right, who will never close his mouth: "The one you have caused to speak will not (will no longer) be silent; the one you have awakened will not (will no longer) sleep; . . . the one to whom you have given knowledge is not (is no longer) ignorant. Such are they who drive out evil."[5]

In an Oxyrhynchus papyrus from the beginning of the first century c.e. there is a petition from a "weak widow" who had previously entered a petition against her son-in-law because of an infringement. The evildoer "succeeded in rendering the petition void, so that no one could proceed against him." She does not allow this catastrophe to prevent her from mentioning the old misdeed again and bringing a new petition against a new injustice.[6]

The widow in the parable in Luke 18:1-8 resists by drawing the judge's attention to her rights, that is, to the Torah.[7] Her obstinate persistence is possible because she knows that God's law is on her side. She also expresses her resistance by violating her social boundaries: She behaves loudly and aggressively in public; she may even scream and shout (v. 7 could be understood in this way). Women's resistance through public clamor and other violations of the boundaries that are placed around women, especially widows, is also attested in other sources.[8] The judge's internal conversation reflects her transgression of boundaries: He can even expect this woman to attack violently, to hit him in the face.[9] Attributing violence to women who exercise resistance is a sexist stereotype and a deliberate exaggeration. The woman and her action are at the center of the parable. The hearers are to learn from her. And so the interpretation of the parable, in the introduction and the conclusion, also refers to her alone, and not to the judge (vv. 1, 7, 8).

ESCHATOLOGICAL INTERPRETATION

The parable closes an eschatological discourse of Jesus to the disciples (17:22) that had been initiated by a question from Pharisees. They ask (17:20): When will the kingdom of God come? The group of disciples asks "where" it will come (17:37). As in 19:11, Jesus responds to longings for a rapid beginning of liberation that seem illusionary to him. Now is the time of the Son of Man's suffering, not that of the judgment of the world (17:25). These are the days of Noah before the great flood, and of Lot before the catastrophe of Sodom. People are living their short-sighted and violent lives (17:26-33) as if they would go on this way forever.

In 18:1-8 Jesus closes the discourse with an admonition to do what is necessary in this situation, in which so much violence is their experience: continually, with their whole existence, to pray and to cry to God for justice (vv. 1, 8). God will act soon and with justice. The Son of Man will come for judgment. This is the time of repentance because all are disdaining God's will, the Torah (18:9-14). Fidelity to God has become rare on earth (18:8). The unjust judge is the image of what is diametrically opposite to God. At the same time, he embodies the structures of oppression from which the people to whom Jesus is speaking are suffering.

Prayer and crying to God against injustice suffered describe the whole life of believers, their efforts, their protest against injustice, their trust in God, for they know that God acts altogether differently from the unjust judge. Romans 8:15, 26 also speaks of this prayer as what believers do. They cry out like women in labor, they do not give up, they maintain the patient power of resistance *(hypomonē)* that comes from hope in the nearness of God. The parable concentrates its view on this resistant behavior of believers, for which the persistent behavior of the widow is the model. This kind of prayer and stubborn hope, however, does not remain within an isolated relationship of individuals to God, as modern dualism categorizes prayer. This prayer characterizes the action and prayer of the community in its environment as well: It constitutes its power and persistence in dealing with human beings also. They hope that God's judgment will create justice.[10]

METHODOLOGICAL OBSERVATION

Only rarely in the history of interpretation has anyone been willing to assert that God is to be equated with the unjust judge; it was too clear that he represents a counter-image to God. Nevertheless, the conclusion has very often been taken as an *a minore ad maius*: If even an unjust judge does justice, how much more will God. But the judge is not a miniversion of God; he is God's opposite. This parable presents an admirable aid for practicing a reading of parables that overcomes allegorization. The application of the parable in vv. 1, 7, and 8 does not refer in allegorizing fashion to the parable, but interprets the widow's behavior as a clarification of what resistance against injustice and crying to God day and night means. At the same time, the "image" of the unjust judge illustrates the injustice under which people suffer: The judgments that are given betray the Torah and represent the interests of the economically powerful.[11]

The unavoidable eschatological interpretation of the parable has been ecclesiologically revised under the influence of the idea that Jesus expected an imminent end and the actual delay of God's coming: Now is the time of the church, during which God is waiting because God's kingship has been removed to a distant time. God's patience *(makrothymein, v. 7)* has been interpreted temporally since the nineteenth century: God is waiting.[12] But this word has a well-developed biblical history. God abandons divine wrath over human injustice (Exod 34:6-7);[13] that is God's patience. God's "elect" (Luke 18:7) are not the church, but the people from all nations who cry to God for justice on earth and are accorded their rights by God. Election is an eschatological promise.

Luke 18:1-8 is frequently read together with Luke 11:5-13. I, too, have put the two parables together. Although they both speak about prayer, they should be appreciated for their difference. Luke 11:5-13 speaks of the strength and endurance of networks of solidarity among human beings, and 18:1-8 of resistance to structures of injustice. And both parables open our eyes to the reliability of God's closeness and mercy for those who call to God day and night, urgently and boldly.

FOR FURTHER READING

William R. Herzog, *Parables as Subversive Speech,* 215–32
Luise Schottroff, *Lydia's Impatient Sisters,* 101–18

24.

Parables in the Gospel of Luke

Summary

In the Gospel of Luke two themes are made the focus of individual chapters made up of parables: (1) the vision of a messianic feast of the renewal of Israel and the nations, which is in the three parables about the lost (Luke 15), and (2) a radical analysis of the money economy and social justice that corresponds to the Torah (Luke 16). The parables reveal Jesus' radical interpretation of the Torah in respect to other themes as well: sin (Luke 18:9-14) and loving one's neighbor (Luke 10:25-37). Political (Luke 19:11-27) and socio-political themes are especially prominent in the Gospel of Luke. The text addresses slaveowners (17:7) and the wealthy (12:13-21; 14:12-14), but its perspective is shaped by the suffering of enslaved and impoverished people.

In the Gospel of Luke, as in the other synoptics, Jesus is presented as a teacher who tells parables because they are easy to understand. They are also understood by those who decide against Jesus' words, because for them "temptation," "cares," "riches," and "the pleasure of life" are more powerful forces than the Spirit of God (8:9-15).

25

God's Forgiveness and the World of Finance

TRANSLATION

21   Then Peter came and said to him: Master, how often must one of my sisters or brothers sin against me and I in turn forgive her or him? As many as seven times?

22   Jesus said to him: I tell you, not seven times, but seventy-seven times.

23   For this reason the kingdom of God is to be compared to the following story about a human king who wanted to settle accounts with his slaves.

24   When he began the reckoning, one who owed him ten thousand talents was brought to him.

25   Since he could not pay, the master commanded that he, his wife, his children, and his whole property be sold and payment made.

26   The slave fell on his knees before him, and said: Have patience with me, and I will pay you the whole debt.

27   The master had mercy on this slave, released him, and forgave him the debt.

28   As this slave was going out, he met one of his fellow slaves who owed him a hundred denarii. He seized him, throttled him, and said: Pay what you owe.

29   Then his fellow slave fell down before him and begged him: Have patience with me, and I will pay you.

30   But he refused, and he went and threw him into prison until he should pay the debt.

31   His fellow slaves saw what had happened, and they were greatly distressed. They went and told their master everything that had happened.

32   Then his master called him and said to him: You wicked slave! I forgave you that whole debt because you pleaded with me.

33   Should you not also have had mercy on your fellow slave, as I had mercy on you?

34   And his master was furious and handed him over to the torturers until he would have paid the whole debt.

35   How is this, then, to be compared to the kingdom of God? My heavenly

father will call you to account if you do not forgive all your sisters and brothers with your whole heart.

SOCIAL-HISTORICAL ANALYSIS

The king in this parable is a ruler who need not trouble himself with any legal process in pursuing his objectives.[1] He is thus not only a rich man, but the ruler of a whole country. A rich man would have had to make use of judicial bodies to force repayment, at least from freeborn debtors (Luke 12:57-59; Matt 5:25-26). This master can order the sale of a family and a slave's property (18:25) and have him tortured until he—that is, his family—has paid the debt (18:34).

The slaves are not only his servants, but slaves who have no rights against their master. As king and slaveowner he has a double power over them. Slaves can be tortured,[2] and for that reason people liked to put them in charge of finances. Even if they rose to high positions, as in the case of the first slave here, they remained slaves and could be tortured. These slaves could also have their own property and families (*peculium* and *contubernium*), but their legal status still did not correspond to that of freeborn persons, nor did they have the same rights in their marriages and over their property. We can recognize that this story is about royal slaves, that is, slaves in the household and under the power of a ruler, especially from the fact that the first slave can throw the second slave who owes him money into prison (18:30) without involving any legal or judicial body. Here we can perceive a financial system managed by slaves that also involved access to means of coercion.

The money at stake in this parable is called "debt." The Greek word group (*opheilō*) is generally applied to financial obligations and also, at the same time, to obligations toward God, as, for example, in the Lord's Prayer (Matt 6:12). What financial obligations are in play here? Given the huge magnitude of the sum of ten thousand talents owed by the first slave, we can eliminate private debts for the cost of living or the economic needs of a private household or business. The size of the debt points clearly to sums gathered by taxation and other payments within the ruler's jurisdiction.[3] For taxes and imposts to be administered by financial "officials" who were slaves was rather the rule than the exception.[4] The first slave is comparable to the one in Luke 19:17 whom the newly crowned king placed in charge of ten cities. His duty is clear: He is to advance the interests of the ruler in those cities, especially his financial demands. It was no accident that the area in which he qualified for this assignment was his management of his master's money (Luke 19:16, 17). It is plausible that the duty of collecting money appears in Matt 18:23-35 as a "debt" to the king. The debt did not result from loans, but from the obligation to collect funds.[5] Control over the work of slaves in financial administration was exercised through their reckoning with the king (18:23, 24). Suetonius writes about Augustus: "In a third [document Augustus gave] a brief overview of his whole empire: how many soldiers were stationed where at what time, how much money was in the state treasury and the [impe-rial?] treasuries, as well as late payments. In addition, he mentioned by name the freedmen and slaves from whom an accounting could be demanded (*ratio exigi*)."[6] The Vulgate uses the word *ratio* also as a translation for Matt 18:23: *qui voluit rationem ponere cum servis suis.*

The second slave belongs on the lower end of the hierarchy among the king's slaves, just as the first slave represents the upper end. He only owes a hundred denarii, about half a year's earnings for a day laborer in agriculture (Matt 20:1). Since the narrative suggests a clear internal connection between the situations of the first and second slave, this debt would also stem from an assignment to collect money for the king. The second slave is probably a subordinate of the first slave in a hierarchy of slaves. His task is to coerce money from poor people. The parable presumes two fundamental situations in the ancient financial economy that were feared by those concerned because of their brutality: the collection of taxes and the collection of debts. Philo describes the brutality of the collection of taxes:

> Not long ago a certain man who had been appointed a collector of taxes in our country, when some of those who appeared to owe such tribute fled out of poverty, from a fear of intolerable punishment if they remained without paying, carried off their wives, and their children, and their par-ents, and their whole families by force, beating and insulting them, and heaping every kind of contumely and ill treatment upon them, to make them either give information as to where the fugitives had concealed themselves, or pay the money instead of them, though they could not do either the one thing or the other; in the first place, because they did not know where they were, and secondly, because they were in still greater poverty than the men who had fled. But this tax-collector did not let them go till he had tortured their bodies with racks and wheels, so as to kill them with newly invented kinds of death, fastening a basket full of sand to their necks with cords, and suspending it there as a very heavy weight, and then placing them in the open air in the middle of the market place, that some of them, being tortured and being overwhelmed by all these afflictions at once, the wind, and the sun, and the mockery of the passers by, and the shame, and the heavy burden attached to them, might faint miserably; and that the rest, being spectators, might be grieved and take warning by their punishment, some of whom, having a more acute sense of such mis-eries in their minds than that which they could receive through their eyes, since they sympathised with these unfortunates as if they were themselves suffering in the persons of others, put an end to their own lives by swords, or poison, or halters, thinking it a great piece of good luck for persons, li-able to such misery, to be able to meet with death without torture.

But those who did not make haste to kill themselves, but who were seized before they could do so, were led away in a row, as in the case of actions for inheritance, according to their nearness of kindred, the nearest relations first, then those next to them in succession, in the second or third place, till they came to the last; and then, when there were no relations left, the cruelty proceeded on to the friends and neighbours of the fugitives; and sometimes it was extended even into the cities and villages, which soon became desolate, being emptied of all their inhabitants, who all quitted their homes, and dispersed to places where they hoped that they might escape detection.

But perhaps it is not wonderful if men, barbarians by nature, utterly ignorant of all gentleness, and under the command of despotic authority, which compelled them to give an account of the yearly revenue, should, in order to enforce the payment of the taxes, extend their severities, not merely to properties but also to the persons, and even to the lives, of those from whom they thought they could exact a vicarious payment.[7]

This description can help us to imagine the situation hinted at in Matt 18:23-35. The parable sketches, without glossing it over, the structure of the collection of public moneys, from the perspective of those who depend on the forgiveness of their debts—people who are comparable to the second slave with his debt of one hundred denarii. The sympathy of the narrative is directed to his situation.

The king's forgiveness of debt certainly affects not only the first slave, but his whole administrative district. Such remissions by rulers are attested and were certainly reasonable, in certain situations, for the preservation of power.[8] The parable does not idealize this forgiveness of debts. At the end of the narrative the king again demands the ten thousand talents from the first slave. But at that point the pressure for payment falls once again on the people. We cannot suppose that the slave or his family could produce that much out of their own property. Thus at the end the king mercilessly withdraws the release of debt in order to punish his top financial slave, who did not imitate his forgiveness of debt in miniature. To sharpen the point: Matt 18:34 describes a situation that will also affect the second slave, who will surely have to pay his debt now. The ruler has the absolute power; his mercy and his wrath have consequences for the population, not only for his slaves. The end of the narrative does not show a merciful ruler, but a man of power who mercilessly pursues his own interests. According to Matt 18:22 he should at least have given the slave a second chance.[9] Even if one were to locate the social-historical situation of the parable not in public financial administration, but in the realm of private indebtedness,[10] the theological problem that 18:34 is contradicted by 18:22 remains fully present.

ESCHATOLOGICAL INTERPRETATION

The application of the parable in 18:35 sounds like a brutal lesson if we read the parable as usual—allegorically: The heavenly Father will treat you "thus," as the king treated the slave who did not forgive, if you do not forgive (18:35). Will God torture the unforgiving until they have "paid" for their sins? The contradiction to the parable's introduction in 18:21, 22 could not be more blunt. Is forgiveness to be taught by threats from a God who is merciless (in the end, anyway)?

Pardon between persons is the clear purpose of the closing application. But apparently it was obvious to the text, that is, to those who told the story at that time, that no one would bring God into this analogy, as is common in current interpretation. There are many rabbinic parallels for this nonallegorical application of parables,[11] including a parable with comparable imagery:[12] A city is unable to pay its taxes to the king. He moves with his palace officials "against it," that is, apparently with his soldiers. As he is approaching, the city leaders meet him and beg him for mercy; then the simple people come, and finally all the inhabitants. The king first forgives part of the debt, and then all of it. "For your sakes I forgive all of it. But a new calculation starts now." In Billerbeck's translation the attached application then reads: "The 'king' is the king of all kings. . . . The 'inhabitants of the city' are the Israelites, who pile up the debt of sins every day of the year." God says to them: Do penance. They fast in groups and in stages during the year. Finally, on the Day of Atonement, all Israelites fast and pray for mercy, "and God forgives them everything." They praise God. A new reckoning of sins begins. There is nothing in the application corresponding to the fear and the (military) pressure. Parallels are found primarily in the division into groups within the population, the universal forgiveness of debt, and the new beginning with a new reckoning of guilt or debt. The parable intends to establish analogies, but the narrative is completely clear: there are two worlds, that of the political ruler and that of God. So when the application says, "The 'king' is the king of all kings" this formulation does not point to an allegorical interpretation in which the king in the parable is an image of God. God does not come with military power to destroy those unable to pay, as the king in the parable does. God expects that, because of their sins, people will pray to God for mercy. God releases them from their guilt. The parable and its application speak of two completely different contents. The two parts are joined only by a few bridges that are mentioned in the application. An interpretation of the king in the parable as a parable of God is not intended.

God's release from guilt in Matt 18:23-35, as in this rabbinic parable, takes its visible image from rulers' forgiveness of debts—as is also true in the First Testament.[13] It is no accident that the forgiveness of guilt is connected to the world of finance. The fact that people are required by God to forgive the credit, debt, and loans of their fellow human beings is true also in the material sense,[14] in both the First Testament tradition and the New Testament. It is not by chance that financial metaphors play a central role in language about sin, guilt, and forgiveness. The hearers of the parable know that they are not to understand it allegorically and that God is not to be equated with a human king. They understand that there are certain features of the narrative that play a part in the application. These features acquire clarity and weight from the parable. And at the same time God's mercy is distinguished from that of a political ruler. The violence, pressure, and fear in political affairs are not comparable to God's loving care. In the rabbinic parable it is said of that care that it comes again and again, in the end, universally—and is always renewed when the new reckoning of guilt has piled up high. In the story of the "king" and the city, as in Matt 18:23-35, certain things can be applied to God, but the king in the parable and his actions are not an image of God. That would be blasphemy in the eyes of Jewish tradition.

Matthew 18:21-22, 35 presents an eschatological interpretation. This is about forgiveness among human beings and its absolute importance. I will use a text from the Mishnah to clarify the horizon of understanding this interpretation addresses. In rabbinic literature Deut 13:18 is applied to the relationship between God's forgiveness and pardon between human beings.[15] This forgiveness of other human beings is imperative, as is unmistakably and emphatically stated in the Mishnah (*Yoma* 8:9): "For transgressions that are between man and God the Day of Atonement effects atonement, but for transgressions that are between a man and his fellow the Day of Atonement effects atonement only if he has appeased his fellow." In Sir 28:1-9 there is a warning in the same vein: "Forgive your neighbor the wrong he has done, and then your sins will be pardoned when you pray." The question in Christian dogmatics about whether human forgiveness is some kind of condition for God's forgiveness misses the point of these texts. They are filled with praise of God, whose mercy is without end. At the same time they make it clear that forgiveness between human beings is a sign of the presence of this God: "Let this be a sign in your hand: As often as you are merciful . . . the Almighty has mercy on you."[16] The Mishnah text, after making it clear that even the Day of Atonement cannot expiate sins against other people, continues: "R. Akiba said: Blessed are ye, O Israel. Before whom are ye made clean and who makes you clean? Your Father in heaven." The negative formulations of the relationship between human and divine forgiveness (if you do not forgive . . .), like the statement about the Day of Atonement in *m. Yoma* 8:9, say that God's will to forgive is powerless when people harden themselves. And at the same time it is true that God's pardon, for which the whole people may hope, is already the basis of their life.

In the Gospel of Matthew, eschatological reconciliation is especially connected to God's "Father" title. The kingdom of God is the kingdom of the Father, who is like no human father (23:9): "For you have one Father—the one in heaven." God's "Father" title expresses hope for the healing of the world. This healing can be experienced already when the hungry are filled, the sick are healed, and enmity is overcome (on this see only 5:48). We cannot tell what concrete situations of interhuman offense and forgiveness are intended in Matt 18:35 and Matt 18:21-22 (6:14-15), but it does seem that something concrete is indeed at stake. That is why the imperative of forgiveness between human beings is so important that the Jesus of Matthew's gospel tells the parable about the king and his slave administrator. Verse 35 applies the parable to only one idea, that of the imperative of forgiveness between human beings. The Gospel of Matthew pictures the process of forgiveness not as a covering up of conflicts, but as a public clearing of the air that changes both sides (18:15).

The parable and its application would be misunderstood if the king in the parable were identified with God. That is why I have given a different rendering of the Greek word *houtōs* ("so") in my translation (how is . . . to be compared?). The traditional interpretations of Matt 18:34 have rightly been found, quite often, to be alienating.[17] The parable is told in order to deepen the thought in Matt 18:22, 35 (6:14-15). The image of the king in the parable differs fundamentally from that of God. God's fatherhood brings humanity into universal salvation. The king in the parable is, in the end, precisely where the parable began: in a situation in which he is overburdening an individual—and the whole population—with payments that are extorted from them through violence. The "so" in the parable application in the Greek text of Matt 18:35 concentrates our attention on the necessity of human forgiveness and at the same time contains the huge difference: God is not like this king. In the end, God will exclude the unmerciful from salvation (see, e.g., Matt 25:41; 8:12), but now there is time for repentance.

"Come and see what a difference there is between the acts of the children of humanity and the acts of God: They begin fighting when someone cannot pay a debt. But God is not so: In God's creation the day borrows time from the night (in the summer) and the night from the day (in winter) without any quarreling and backbiting."[18] The content of the Gospel of Matthew is very closely related to the later rabbinic ideas about the necessity of forgiveness between human beings and its basis in God's promise. This promise is made visible when God is called "Father." Indeed, the Father also sets limits in the eschatological judgment—for those who do evil. But now is the time for repentance and forgiveness, which is a sign of the presence of God, who wills the salvation of all humanity. Verse 35 points out how human beings can perform saving acts. Verse 34, in contrast, sketches a hopeless cementing of violence within the system of taxes, debts, and the release from debt.

That forgiveness and release from debt between human beings must be without limit (seventy-seven times: 18:22) is not repeated in 18:35. Here the word is: Forgive one another "from the heart," that is, universally. The Gospel of Matthew, like the whole Jesus tradition, expresses a hope that envisions the beginning of a new world where financial debts and guilt will be radically forgiven. That—and the God whose mercy and justice are without end—is what it is all about. Matthew 18:23-35 is also an antithetical God-parable. Its basis is, on the one hand, the First Testament idea of God (Ps 103:32, 51; Deut 15:1-5), and on the other hand political experience of rulers' collection of taxes and tolls. Matthew's gospel emphasizes, from the very beginning, the people's suffering because of political power and its significance for Jesus' task. Herod is a child-murderer (Matt 2:16-18). The devil tempts Jesus with "all the kingdoms of the world." Jesus answers with the *Shemaᶜ Israel*: "Worship Adonai, your God, and serve only him" (Matt 3:10; Deut 6:13). There is no reason to confuse the king in the parable with God. This happens only when "so" *(houtōs)* in 18:35 is completed by applying an allegorical theory.

Under the influence of the centuries-old reading of "so" in 18:35 as an invitation to an allegorical equation of the king with God, it is hard to read "so" in a new way. It contains an invitation to compare the places where parallels exist between the parable and its application, and where there are differences. Parallel is the necessity of forgiveness between human beings. That is why the parable is told. At the same time, it calls the hearers to consider God's difference. It is no accident that the kingdom of God is not painted in full in the Gospels. The kingdom of God is spoken of in parables that make it possible to speak about God—in the depths of the difference between God and the experience we have of domination and violence. Nothing is said explicitly about God, not even in analogies. Speaking of God remains the property of the hearts of the hearers. Their explicit speech is their response in praise of God. Therefore in my translation I have rendered "so" in such a way that its invitational character is clear: "How is this, then, to be compared to the kingdom of God?"

The eschatological interpretation of 18:35 says: God will call you to account at the judgment if you have not forgiven each other. But now is the time to forgive. According to Matthew, that forgiveness is all-encompassing: It includes material debts and hatred between persons. The Gospel of Matthew expresses a comprehensive vision of God's fatherhood, the vision of a healed and saved people. Now the people suffer from illnesses, debts, violence, and hatred. "The bruised reed" will not be broken (Matt 12:20). Other parables in the Gospel of Matthew will reveal this same vision.

FOR FURTHER READING

Frank Crüsemann, "'Wie wir vergeben unseren Schuldigern'"
William R. Herzog, *Parables as Subversive Speech*, 131–49
Martin Leutzsch, "Verschuldung und Überschuldung, Schuldenerlaß und Sündenvergebung"

26

Bread and Hope

Matthew 13

SOCIAL-HISTORICAL ANALYSIS AND ESCHATOLOGICAL INTERPRETATION OF MATTHEW 13:1-35

Hearing and Understanding:
Jesus Speaks to the People in Parables

From this section of the discourse I want to take a closer look only at its conclusion, the parable of the leaven. For the parables of the fertile and infertile seed and of the mustard seed, see chapter 7 above.

In the first part of this parable discourse Jesus confronts the fact that there are persons within the people of God who rigidly reject his prophetic message and refuse to repent. They have "made their hearts impenetrable and stopped up their ears . . ." (13:15) to prevent themselves from hearing and understanding. They are unwilling to repent and let God heal them.[1] Jesus generalizes his and the Baptizer's experience with Pharisees, scribes, and elders. They are among "those" (13:11) to whom God has not revealed his kingdom. By "generalizing" I do not mean that they are made representative of the whole Jewish people, but that the experience with certain leadership groups, including the Pharisees, is detached from these groups and presented as the attitude of all the people who, while they hear Jesus and the Baptizer, deliberately refuse to "understand," that is, to surrender themselves to this message and change their way of life, to repent. Jesus speaks in parables because they (13:13) do not want to understand, but he wants them to. Jesus' parables are the revelation of the salvation prepared by God from the beginning of the world,[2] the revelation of the "secrets" of the kingdom of God (13:11, 35). They are a promise for those who understand, and a second chance for those who are unwilling to understand. Jesus makes it emphatically clear in a parable that it cannot be the duty of human beings to pull up the "weeds." God alone, in judgment, is permitted to judge those who have lived lawlessly and led others to fall (13:41, as a subsequent clarification of 13:29-30).

In his parable discourse Jesus is practicing the love of enemies he taught in the Sermon on the Mount (5:43-48). He does not avoid the conflict in which he finds himself, but he makes it clear that he will not hit back with the same methods and that it is his task to imitate God's love for creation (5:45), and not to react with hatred or violence.

For those who hear and understand, the parables signify the thrilling experience of seeing the salvation of the world before their very eyes. Their understanding means living with their whole existence according to the will of God. Whoever surrenders to it will see the kingdom of God, its beginnings and its great promise of salvation for all peoples (13:32, 33). The disciples are first of all those who understand in the full sense (13:11). But neither are the promises of salvation restricted to them, nor can they weigh their discipleship with confidence.[3] The thrilling promises of this discourse (13:11a, 12a, 16, 17, 23, 31-33) are for all who "understand"—with their whole hearts—as the *Shema' Israel* says (22:37).

Jesus' conflict with the Pharisees and other groups who lead the Jewish people is depicted in Matthew's gospel as sharper than what we find in the other Gospels.[4] This reflects historical recollection of Jesus' conflicts. But the sharpness comes from experiences of Jewish people who found themselves among the followers of Jesus at the time when the Gospel of Matthew came into existence. The Pharisees want to kill Jesus (12:14; cf. 21:45-46) and participate in the attempt to prevent the theft of Jesus' corpse: No one is to be able to say that he is risen (27:63, 64). They have completely different ideas about how the Jewish people is to find its way into the future than these Jesus people.

The parables chapter has for a long time been read in anti-Jewish fashion: In 13:36 Jesus finally turns away from the people and toward the disciples as representatives of the church. The parables are obscure discourse that is meant to prevent the people, who in any case are already cut off, from understanding. I have no need to go into a detailed critique of this anti-Jewish tradition of interpretation here.[5]

TRANSLATION OF MATTHEW 13:33-35
The Parable of the Woman Baking Bread

33   He told them another parable: The kingdom of God is to be compared to leaven, which a woman took and hid in three *sat* of flour, till all the flour was leavened.

34   Jesus told the crowds all these things in parables; and without a parable he told them nothing.

35   This was to fulfill what had been spoken through the prophet: I will open my mouth to speak in parables; I will proclaim what has been hidden from the foundation of the world.

SOCIAL-HISTORICAL ANALYSIS
AND ESCHATOLOGICAL INTERPRETATION

A basic life situation is here sketched in a single sentence. A woman is preparing bread dough. At that time and in that society bread was the basic staff of life. The word *bread* can represent all the food on the table or all the nourishment people need (Matt 6:11). When the Creator, who has given bread, is blessed over the bread, human life is experienced as part of creation. The miracle of human life and its dependence on creation are brought to awareness. The sounds of kneading bread have deeper meaning than other sounds. They assure those listening that life will go on—even and especially in situations in which life is endangered. That is how the situation of the Jewish people is being described in the Gospel of Matthew.

The people to whom Jesus is speaking here are so described in Matthew's gospel: The people are so impoverished that their relationship to God is breaking (Matt 5:3),[6] and hunger is suppressing the Sabbath (12:1-8).[7] The illnesses spoken of in the Gospel of Matthew are connected to the state of hunger. In three great scenes the sick become representatives of the people before the "throne" of the messianic king, Jesus (4:23–5:1; 7:28; 15:29-31), a mountain in Galilee.[8] Jesus invites the weary and heavy-laden (11:28-30). The people suffers from bad political leadership,[9] "like sheep without a shepherd" (9:36; 10:6; 15:24). The feeding miracles (14:13-21; 15:32-39) transform the starving people into guests at the richly laden table of the messianic future, the reign of God.

To these starving people Jesus, in Matt 13:1-35, tells four parables about the fruits of the earth: two about grain and one about mustard, then, at the end, the parable about the leaven. The first two parables report the failure and success of farm work. The two at the end speak only of success, the miracle of the earth and its products. People, both men and women, must work[10] for their food. They have to sow; they have to knead bread.

The parable of the leaven focuses on the work of the woman baking bread. She "takes" the leaven and "hides"[11] it in a large quantity of flour.[12] She is preparing the dough for many people, bread for several families. The parable draws our attention to a particular moment in the preparation of the dough: The mixture of leaven, flour, and water must stand in a warm place, covered, while it rises, "until the whole of the flour is leavened." Then the dough will be kneaded again and shaped into bread. It is not only the work of the woman baking bread, it is also the miracle of creation that the dough is leavened and rises. The woman lets her hands fall and waits.[13]

That it is a gift of God when people hold steaming bread in their hands is a familiar experience in Jewish religion, one that is expressed in prayer and gesture. The solemn breaking and sharing of bread[14] at the beginning of the meal continually give ritual expression to it. For people who struggle with hunger this gift is not a matter of course. It gives a hint of how God wants creation to be, of how it will be when only God "reigns."

In the Jesus traditions of all the Gospels the common meals of the gathered "community" *(ekklēsia)*[15] are presented as a foretaste of the eucharist. In the daily prayer Jesus teaches his community of disciples the community prays for the bread that people need in order to live. The parable of the woman baking bread challenges us to compare the kingdom of God to the leaven, to recognize in the miracle of the rising dough the traces of the messianic world. A dualistic parable theory that interprets this image "from the kitchen"[16] as purely illustrative of something completely different does not do justice to the materiality of our experiences with bread and to the messianic hopes that are bound up with bread and meals.

SOCIAL-HISTORICAL ANALYSIS AND ESCHATOLOGICAL INTERPRETATION OF MATTHEW 13:36-52
Jesus Speaks in Parables to His Community of Followers

Verses 36-52 say that in this discourse Jesus addresses the community of his followers so that they may understand. To them, too, he speaks in parables, because they can be understood: not so much because they are intellectually easier to understand, but because they can open us to understanding with the heart, to a praxis of life according to the will of God. The disciples are not fundamentally in a different situation, as regards the parable discourse, from the mass of the people or Jesus' critics.

Jesus explains to them the preceding parable about the weeds and adds another parable about divine judgment, the one about the fishnet (13:47-50). Both times an explicit explanation is added to the judgment parable (vv. 40-43, "so will it be at the end of the age"; vv. 49-50, "so it will be at the end of the age"). Both times what is at stake is the division between the righteous and the "wicked" (v. 49), who have caused sin and have acted lawlessly (v. 41). But only God's judgment will show who that is. This in itself makes the two parables in this part of the discourse—as previously the parable of the weeds in vv. 24-30—clear. "Righteous," "sons of the kingdom" (v. 38), and "evil" (v. 38, sons of the evil one; see also v. 49) are all eschatological concepts. The long tradition of ecclesiological interpretation of these contrasts can only be called a misunderstanding of these transparent parables. The parables have the whole human world in view (v. 38). The kingdom of God will include all nations.

Between the two parables about God's judgment two short parables without explicit explanation are inserted: the treasure in the field and the valuable pearl (vv. 44, 45-46). Both end in almost the same words: He sells everything he has and buys that field, or the pearl. In context this is about the understanding that follows from hearing. Both parables are meant to encourage understanding with the heart and living in accordance with God's will. To sell everything one has is part of both stories, but it is also the bridge to the implicit explanation of the parables. Both the one who finds the treasure and the pearl merchant take a radical step in order to obtain something of great value. If the two parables meant to challenge the listeners to renounce their own possessions (sell everything you have; see Matt 19:21), they would be bizarre. They draw the picture of a person who owns a treasure he has found—perhaps gold and jewels—and a pearl merchant who owns a pearl of more than ordinary value. Both rejoice in their valuable possessions, something unattainable by ordinary people. I could imagine instead that people who could only dream of such riches would call their "treasure in heaven" (Matt 6:20) that kind of wealth, something that even "normal" rich people only rarely have: We have an infinitely valuable pearl and a treasure chest. In v. 52 those who are learned in Scripture and are studying for the kingdom of God are told that they are "to be compared to a householder who brings out of his treasure new things and old," that is, great knowledge of scripture and the hope for God's kingdom, the "new covenant" (Matt 26:28). "Old" and "new" are not contrary concepts here. Knowledge of Torah and hope for the kingdom belong together. The "new" is an eschatological concept.[17] This, too, is a parable from the world of the well-established, about a rich householder. How rich you are, you people, you women and men disciples, who in your lifetime can already recognize the kingdom of God because you understand with all your hearts. The three little parables are, in their content, an intensification of the blessing of those who already hear and see (13:11a, 12a, 16, 17).

The social situations pictured in the parables are, as to content, in contrast to what ought to be learned from the parable. There is a similar tension in content in Mark 4:25 and Matt 13:12, a saying that reveals the brutal laws of the money economy.[18] The hope for God's kingdom is compared to the possession of luxury and the wealth of a householder. Again the parables convey a twofold message: God's coming makes you infinitely rich—but this wealth is precisely not to be experienced if you hoard treasures and pearls. But in any case such a thing is outside the scope of the community of Jesus' followers or the majority of the Jewish people after the destruction of Jerusalem in 70 c.e., the time of Matthew's gospel.

FOR FURTHER READING

Anthony J. Saldarini, *Matthew's Christian-Jewish Community*

27

"Am I Not Allowed to Do What I Choose with What Belongs to Me?"

Matt 20:1-16

TRANSLATION

1   The kingdom of God is to be compared to the reality in the following story about a human being, a person who owned a piece of land. He went out early in the morning to hire workers for his vineyard.

2   When he had agreed with the workers to pay them a denarius for the day, he sent them into the vineyard.

3   And when he went out about the third hour, he saw others standing in the marketplace, unemployed.

4   He said to them, too: Go into the vineyard, and I will give you what is right.

5   And they went. Around the sixth and ninth hours he went out again and did the same.

6   When he came at about the eleventh hour he found others standing there and said to them: Why are you standing here unemployed the whole day?

7   They answered him: Because no one has hired us. He said to them: You also, go into my vineyard.

8   When it was evening the vineyard owner said to his manager: Call the workers and pay them their wages. Begin with the last and continue to the first.

9   So those from the eleventh hour came and each received a denarius.

10   When the first came, they thought that they would receive more. But they, too, received one denarius.

11   They took it and complained to the landowner:

12   "These last have worked one hour, and you have made them equal to us, who had to bear the burden of the day and the heat."

13   He said to one of them: "Friend, I am doing you no injustice. Did you not agree with me for a denarius?

14   Take what is yours, and go! For I will give this last one what I gave to you.

15   Or am I not permitted to do with my property what I want? Are you perhaps envious because I am generous?"

16   How is that, then, to be compared with the kingdom of God? The last
      will be first and the first, last.

SOCIAL-HISTORICAL ANALYSIS

The owner of the vineyard (*kyrios,* 20:28), the "householder" (*oikodespotēs,*
20:1, 11), is presented in this narrative from two perspectives: First, he is the
owner of the land and has the unrestricted right to dispose of it as he will. Verse
15a summarizes the concept of private property, particularly in terms of Roman
law: An owner can do whatever he wants with what is his. For freeborn householders and landowners there is no superior law.[1] William R. Herzog is correct
in contrasting v. 15 with the tradition of the Torah, according to which God is
the owner of the land. Verse 15 is a blasphemy in which the Roman definition
of private property contradicts the Torah and its laws. The landowner's power
to dispose of his property is also broadly painted in the narrative as well, in the
sequences of his agreements with the laborers: Only the first group learns in
advance what their pay will be; the later groups are subject to the "generosity" of
the landowner. He defines "what is right" (*dikaion,* 20:4). It is the householder's
absolute right of disposal in Roman law that gives him this "right." For Cicero
and many other political theorists of the period the householder's right to dispose of property, family, slaves, and bequest is the basis of the ideal ordering
of a state. I also agree with Herzog in a further aspect of this depiction of the
landowner: During this period the experience of the small agricultural enter-
prises losing their land through debt was an open wound for many people. It
was precisely the planting of vineyards on land that previously was the source
of life for families that made visible the economic changes wrought by Rome's
expanding world commerce. Wine brings higher profits than grain in relation
to the land cultivated.[2]

The second perspective in which the landowner is portrayed is that of his
"generosity." He is "generous" (20:15), as he himself says. He sees unemployment (20:3, 6). He decides to give those who could only work part of the day a
full day's pay. The text juxtaposes this generosity with his profit orientation: He
brings in workers at later hours of the day in order to keep his labor costs as low
as possible.[3] The hiring of laborers throughout the day makes it possible for him
to estimate exactly how much labor he still needs to achieve his goal for the day,
probably the complete harvesting of the vineyard. This process also allows him
to exploit unemployment in order to buy the labor of those hired later for less
than a denarius. After the story told in vv. 1-7, his generosity surprises—and yet
it remains within the framework of the concept of a landowner in the Roman
imperial era.

Pliny the Younger gave money for the support of needy children.[4] In doing so,
he was acting within the tradition of aristocratic *liberalitas* ("liberality").[5] This
liberality primarily serves one's own social and political interests. In the Gospel

of Luke this liberality of lordly "benefactors" is explicitly criticized (Luke 22:25): "The kings of the Gentiles have absolute power over them, and those who misuse their power are called benefactors." This detail is lacking in Matt 20:25. But what is said about the misuse of power in Matthew's gospel is no less sharp. It is also anything but an accident that the parable of the landowner in Matt 20:1-16 is followed by one of Jesus' Passion predictions, and that in turn is followed by the so-called pericope about the quarrel over rank with its fundamental critique of the Roman empire.

In regard to this question about the generosity of the landowner in Matt 20:1-16, I need to expand my own social-historical analysis of this parable.[6] I was convinced in 1990 that I could follow the exegetical tradition that saw God's generosity in Matt 20:8-15. My altered view is the result of Herzog's further analysis and the clear social-historical material on the liberality of the big and little "emperors" *(imperatores)* in the Roman empire—the emperor, and the rich statesmen and private persons. Release from debt and other good deeds lay entirely within the compass of their cool political calculations, as the parables in Matt 22:1-14 *par.* and Matt 18:23-35 show. So I can no longer say: "Matthew 20:1-15 represents the reality of life in every respect—except for one point: the attitude of the employer at paytime."[7] The attitude of the employer/landowner also and especially fits within the frame of contemporary ideas. It does not disrupt them. God's generosity is fundamentally different—even according to the world of ideas expressed in this parable. This is an antithetical parable, which does not equate God's kingdom with the attitude of the landowner, but seeks to compare them. I had a hard time drawing this conclusion from my social-historical analysis. I can understand those who refuse to follow Herzog's analysis of this figure in the parable. Arland J. Hultgren criticizes Herzog: "But all this is to ruin a good story. It is difficult to deny that the employer is portrayed as unusually generous."[8] But unfortunately he is not unusually generous; he is a benefactor within a limited range. And it is not unusual. Herzog has found very little support,[9] but legal history and the history of ethics give further strength to his point of view—as shown above.

The one denarius represented in this parable as the usual day's wage of a farm laborer needs to be related to the unemployment of the day laborers. Arye Ben-David calculated that at full employment a day laborer could earn two hundred denarii per year and with this a family of six could live at the lower "limit of the contemporary standard of living."[10] But Ben-David himself sees that such earnings, while they could enable people to survive, would not make them capable of working. So what was lacking had to be made up by the work of women and children, through small service businesses and their own, much lower paid labor.[11] Therefore we may certainly not suppose that one denarius is mentioned as the usual family income at the lower end of society; rather, it is the earnings of a male day laborer, who cannot feed a family with it. Matthew 20:1-16 is an androcentric text from which we cannot see that these day laborers' wives and children also had to work, perhaps in the home of the same householder. The landowner's generosity is thus exercised within a narrow sphere. He pays the wage that is usual in that locality, and pays it correctly at the end of the work-day.[12] But the unexpected full day's pay eases the unemployed men's fight for survival for only one day.

Why does the owner of the vineyard himself go into the marketplace to employ day laborers when he has a manager (*epitropos*, 20:8)? He appears not to be one of the great landowners who live in the cities and no longer on the land. In this he is comparable to the farmer who is the father of the "lost son" (Luke 15:11-32). He, too, lives on the farm, and his elder son works in the fields. Nevertheless, he employs slaves and day laborers.

It is more difficult to answer the question of why the owner of the vineyard wants the laborers hired at the first hour to see the last hired receiving their denarius. The answer has to be found in the argument that follows. That dispute is presented at extraordinary length. The laborers from the first hour expect that the vineyard owner will be equally generous to them: that is, that he will pay more than the one denarius they had agreed upon. The vineyard owner answers one of the protesting group by pointing to the legality of his behavior: (1) He has paid in accordance with their agreement, and (2) he has the right to do with his property as he chooses. He accuses the complaining laborers of being greedy. Of course, he could have appealed to them also to join in rejoicing at the gift he is giving to the last-hired. He wanted to provoke the protest. He wanted the dispute. Herzog calls his attitude "blaming the victim."[13] The parable narrative leaves the ending open. We are not told how the disappointed workers reacted. The vineyard owner had the last word. The story is not satisfying. The hearers cannot do anything but go on discussing it.

The situation of free farm laborers in the Roman empire at that time is very realistically presented in this parable. Day laborers for the harvest are attested in Roman agriculture in analogical ways, so that the information from various sources is mutually supporting, and in this matter at least one can call upon Roman agrarian writers to clarify the situation in Palestine. Moreover, the book of Ruth reveals similar relationships. The reapers who work in Boaz's field and are managed by an overseer (Ruth 2:3-7) are presumably just such harvest workers earning daily wages or a colony of harvesters who are hired for the harvest, something also known in Roman agriculture.[14]

Varro wrote his *De re rustica* when he was eighty years old. It is true that, as far as workers in agriculture are concerned, he was primarily interested in the managers, and he gives advice to owners on how to deal with managers in the interests of greater profit from their land. He speaks more incidentally about the laborers themselves:

All fields are cultivated by people, either slaves or free persons or both; free persons cultivate the land themselves, something done by many poor people and their children, or day laborers (*mercennarii*), if one has the harder work, for example grape harvesting or haying, done by renting free labor; and those whom our ancestors called *obaerarii* (who are working off a debt through their labor), and of whom there are still many in Asia and Egypt and in Illyricum. My opinion of all this is that it is better for unhealthy areas to be worked by day laborers than by slaves, and even in healthy regions it is better to have the hard labor done by them, for example the bringing in of the fruits of the grape harvest or the [grain] harvest.[15]

Cato also employed free day laborers (*Agr.* 1, 3) and recommended: "(The land-owner) should not hire the same workers and day laborers and farm servants for more than a day."[16] That is, he will attempt by this means to be sure that the day laborers themselves are in as weak a position as possible when it comes to their wage demands. Keeping the day laborers down was attempted in other ways as well. Columella writes (3, 21.9-10) that different types of grapes should be planted in separate, fenced-off vineyards.

One who separates the various sorts by sections has regard to these differences as to situation and setting. He also gains no small advantage in that he is put to less labour and expense for the vintage; for the grapes are gathered at the proper time, as each variety begins to grow ripe, and those that have not yet reached maturity are left until a later time without loss; nor does the simultaneous ageing and ripening of fruit precipitate the vintage and force the hiring of more workmen, however great the cost.[17]

With the aid of these sources, to which others could be added,[18] we can generally reconstruct the situation of the day laborers. The picture matches that in Matt 20:1-15. At harvest time, also and especially at the grape harvest, day laborers are hired on large estates and farms. Less care is paid to their health than to that of slaves. A smart farmer sees to it that, under the pressure of the harvest, he does not need to pay too much for day laborers. Occasionally it is supposed that contracting with day laborers played only a small part in the economy of the Roman imperial period because slaves did most of the work.[19] Undoubtedly there were local differences in the numbers and status of day laborers. Columella, for example, presumes a shortage of such labor at harvest time. Matthew 20:1-15 presumes an oversupply. We need not be surprised that this group of people, who in fact were less well-protected than slaves, received little attention (in law, for example). But we should not conclude from this fact that they were few in number. Their numbers would correspond directly to the local and current situation of the rural population. As the size of estates increased, the number of day laborers was likely to increase also. The fact that the suffering of slaves is better known than the still greater misery of day laborers may be connected directly with the fact that the slaves were an object of both economic and legal interest to ancient landowners. The harvest laborers and their misery play only a minor role in their calculations. To that extent the concept of a "slaveowning society" is incomplete. It reflects only the awareness of the ruling classes in antiquity. The owner has an interest in the profitability, that is, the ability to work and the life expectancy of slaves. They are his property, which can be amortized and must also yield a profit. If the slave dies too soon or too quickly becomes incapable of working, the owner's capital account suffers. The day laborer, on the other hand, is a kind of slave working at his or her own risk.[20]

Jewish and Roman legal sources confirm the image of the day laborers' social situation. In the First Testament the Law (Lev 19:13; Deut 24:14-15) prescribes that the laborer's wages are to be paid at the end of the day. That is, there are employers who attempt to hold back their laborers' wages, even though the worker needs them right away. The day laborer and his family live from hand to mouth. The Mishnah regulates in great detail the rights of wage laborers to meals during the time they are working. For example, they must be prevented from demanding food of too high quality or eating too much of the produce they are harvesting.[21] On the other hand, the employer must be prevented from giving a lesser food ration than what is customary in the place. The Mishnah, like the First Testament, requires that the wages are to be paid in the evening, although the Mishnah qualifies this by saying that the employer may withhold the wages if the worker has not asked for them.[22] In this way the First Testament prescription is severely attenuated, since day laborers, at least, if they can hope to be hired frequently by the same employer, may under those circumstances not always dare to demand their wages. The neediness of day laborers is especially well illuminated by a rule in the Tosefta: "A worker has no right to do his own work by night and to hire himself out by day . . . on account of the robbery of his labor, which belongs to the householder [who hires him]."[23]

We can thus conclude in several ways from the legal regulations how threatened day laborers' wage demands were in reality and how desperate their social situation. The prophet Jeremiah's saying was probably valid for the whole ancient world: "Woe to him . . . who makes his neighbors work for nothing, and does not give them their wages" (Jer 22:13; see also Job 7:1; Sir 34:22).

ESCHATOLOGICAL INTERPRETATION

᠁ v. 16 the parable is given an eschatological interpretation by the narrator, Jesus.
᠁ᵉ kingdom of God "the last will be first, and the first, last." This is a prophecy

about the kingdom of God. The parable has been introduced as a grounding (20:1) for this prophecy. In 19:30 Jesus had said: "Many who are first will be last, and the last, first." There the prophecy was applied to the fate of Jesus' community of followers (19:27-29). The disciples, unlike the rich young man (19:16-26), have left their families and their lands to follow him through all Galilee and even to Jerusalem. The closing prophetic statement is not meant to say: And you disciples are those who will be the first. In that case it would not be an eschatological statement. It is a promise for those who have abandoned families and lands, just as it is a warning for those who act like the rich young man. But he, too, will stand before God's judgment, and will not be treated now, already, as someone condemned by God, for with God all things are possible (19:26).

Only one of the thoughts in the parable narrative is evaluated in the interpretation: In God's kingdom, too, there will be those who are last and will become first, as in this story. Thus v. 16 links to the fate of the last group in the parable. How will it be, when the last become first in the kingdom of God? The statement is a promise that extends far beyond what is narrated in the parable.[24] Who are the "last"? The Gospel of Matthew as a whole draws a tender picture of the people's suffering. The statement in 20:16 is a promise for the whole people, as are the Beatitudes in Matt 5:3-10. That is where we can find the explanation for 20:16. Jesus is speaking in public. We are to imagine the crowd present (19:2)—even when he is speaking with the rich young man and with the disciples. This public discourse concludes with 20:1-16, after which he withdraws with his own (20:17).

In the Beatitudes the kingdom of God is promised (5:3) to those who suffer from poverty, sickness, and the destruction of their relationship to God.[25] For them, there is already a way out of their misery: the way of renunciation of violence (5:5), of hunger for (God's) righteousness, of mercy (5:7), of purity of heart (5:8), and of peacemaking. This people will "inherit" the earth and dwell on it in righteousness. Matthew 20:16 invites all the hearers to join in following this way. But it is not only in Matt 19:30 and 20:16 and the Beatitudes that the Gospel of Matthew expresses hope for the oppressed people. The promise of eschatological healing of those who are now on the bottom runs throughout the whole gospel: Matt 9:36; 10:6; 15:24—Jesus has pity on the lost sheep of the house of Israel, a mercy that expresses God's will to heal Israel and the nations. Matthew 11:2-6, 25-30 and 12:20 also express this promise, already visible in Jesus' calling. Matthew 20:16 belongs within this context of the eschatological perspective for the people Israel and the nations.[26]

V. George Shillington presents an interesting interpretation: He regards the parable itself, because of its second part (vv. 8-15), as a promise for the unemployed: "How can a destitute Israelite honour his religious heritage in the Holy Land given to sustain life?"[27] Injustice and hunger rob the poor of their ability to celebrate the Sabbath. I regard this interpretation as accurate for 20:16, though not for 20:8-15.

What is the message of the parable image, not exclusively given in the explicit interpretation in 20:16? The image itself also has meaning with respect to the kingdom of God. In 20:15 the parable narrative ends with the landowner's assertion that he is "good" *(agathos)*. In the preceding story about the rich young man, Jesus corrects him when he asks about what "good" he should do: God alone is "good" (19:17). This linking of the parable to its context is usually interpreted as confirmation that the householder is to be read as an image of God. But then God's freedom for goodness and generosity would have to be equated with the freedom of a landowner in the Roman empire.[28] The parable image is—again—proposed as an antithesis to the kingdom of God. It shows the world of landowners and its flip side, the misery of the unemployed and the day laborers. The generosity of this landowner offers only a weak hint at what God's generosity means. God desires that the "meek," those who live in righteousness,[29] will inherit the earth (Matt 5:5). A landowner who on one occasion pays unemployed people a denarius is a counter-image to this God. This is just what 20:16 says, and the hearers have learned to remember God's deeds and draw hope from them, for that is the content of many prayers in the Jewish tradition.[30] Those who pray these prayers will not recognize God in the landowner. On the contrary, the parable, with its sharp analysis, illuminates economic misery and its causes at the time of the Gospel of Matthew. Private property in the sense of Matt 20:13-15 directly contradicts God's Torah. When God's Torah secures the freedom of a free man who owns land, it does so only in order that life in this land may be blessed, when everyone—the unfree, women, foreigners—has a share in that blessing.[31]

Matthew 20:16 is an eschatological promise that has consequences for common life. This is evident from the context of chapters 19 and 20. Jewish people at the time of Matthew's gospel were scarcely in any position to thank God for their nourishment and their land, as the prayer after meals *(Birkat Hamazon)* probably said even at that time. Matthew 20:16, in contrast to the parable, shows the way out of this destruction of the bases of life. I will quote a few lines from the table prayer, which could be for the hearers a response to the parable, a response of hope and trust:

> Blessed art thou, Adonai our God, king of the universe,
> who feeds the whole world through your goodness!
> . . .
> We give you thanks, Adonai our God, that you gave to our ancestors the
> beloved, good, and broad land for a heritage,
> that you, Adonai, our God, led us out of the land of Egypt and freed us
> from the house of slavery.[32]

METHODOLOGICAL CLARIFICATION

The ecclesiological interpretation of Matt 20:1-16 has a powerful tradition. In the twentieth century the parable was almost universally read in anti-Jewish fashion: The God of Israel is a God who demands deeds, while the God of Jesus is merciful (Matt 20:8-15). The Pharisees or Law-observant Jews are portrayed in the workers hired at the first hour; the toll collectors and sinners or the Gentile church are represented by those last hired. This anti-Jewish tradition of interpretation[33] has given way increasingly in recent years to an interpretation critical of the disciples being equivalent to the church. But this does not abandon the hermeneutical model of ecclesiological interpretation. The Gospel of Matthew in particular, with its heavy emphasis on God as the sole judge in the eschatological judgment, contradicts such ecclesiological interpretive models.

FOR FURTHER READING

Warren Carter, *Households and Discipleship*
William R. Herzog, *Parables as Subversive Speech*
Luise Schottroff, *Befreiungserfahrungen* (ET *Let the Oppressed Go Free*)
Luise Schottroff and Wolfgang Stegemann, "Der Sabbat ist für den
    Menschen da"
V. George Shillington, "Saving Life and Keeping Sabbath (Mt 20:1b-15)"

28

The End of Violence:
Jesus' Discourse in the Temple

Matt 21:23—22:14

Jesus teaches in the Temple (21:23); he teaches the people. It is not said specifically that a crowd of people is present, together with his community of disciples; it is simply presumed (see only 21:26, 46). This is about the future of the people Israel and all other nations. In the first part of the discourse Jesus shows the high priests and elders, that is, the political leadership in Jerusalem, how he regards them and what he considers necessary for them to do. In doing so he makes use of a parable, the one about the two children (21:28-32). In a second part of the discourse he describes structures of violence, first within the Jewish people (21:33-46), then in the Roman empire (22:1-14). He uses a parable for each. In his application of the parables Jesus develops his hope for the future of the people and the nations. In this section I will discuss the first parable and sketch the whole train of thought in this discourse of Jesus according to Matthew. The two parables in 21:33-46 and 22:1-14 were already analyzed in chapters 2 and 4 above.

TRANSLATION OF MATTHEW 21:28-32
The Two Children

28   What do you think of the following case? A man had two children. He came to the first and said: My child, go and work in the vineyard today.

29   The boy answered: I will not. But later he felt sorry, and he went.

30   The father came to the second and said the same thing. This boy answered: Yes, master. But he did not go.

31   Which of the two did the will of the father? They answered: the first child. Jesus said to them: I say to you in all seriousness: The toll collectors and the prostitutes will go into the kingdom of God before you.

32   John came to you with the praxis of righteousness, and you did not believe him. The toll collectors and the prostitutes believed him. And you—even though you saw this—have not repented, so that you might at last believe him.

SOCIAL-HISTORICAL ANALYSIS

For the second time Jesus tells a parable about children in order to win over people who have decided against his message. In Matt 11:16-19 it was children who complained about someone who spoils their play. There, too, the rejection of the Baptizer's message and that of Jesus are lamented in the parable and its application. Here it is two children, neither of whom wants to work in the vineyard. But the two behave differently toward their father and their duty. There are rabbinic texts from which we learn that children were supposed to work, beginning at the age of six.[1] It is not said that the vineyard into which the father is sending his boys to work belongs to the father. It is possible that the text presumes this, but the milieu is that of poor families, where it is a matter of course that children have to earn money and hand it over to their father. The text does not say that the father reproaches the first boy, who openly defies him. The sympathy in the narrative falls to him, and not to the devout child who speaks with exaggerated subservience and conceals his resistance.

ESCHATOLOGICAL INTERPRETATION

The application of the parable begins with a question to the hearers about which has done the father's will. They give the expected answer: the first child. Then Jesus turns the parable onto the leaders in Jerusalem he is addressing: You would have done better to act like the first child. You rejected the Baptizer's message from the start. When you saw that the toll collectors and prostitutes were following him, you should have thought better of it. But you did not want to. Therefore you are—he could have followed with Matt 13:14—like those who see and yet do not see. And now Jesus tells them the parable in order to win them anew.[2] They now, at last, should believe the praxis of righteousness and walk the path into the kingdom of God. Jesus does not say: You will not find the way; you are already lost. The parable and its application are intended to open up a difficult situation. The leaders should follow behind the toll collectors and the prostitutes; they should learn from them. The judgment remains for God to make. Jesus practices the love of enemies he taught, a love that never ceases to fight for people even if they repeatedly turn away.

The widely adopted ecclesiological interpretation has two primary versions: The Jewish leadership is already lost, excluded from the reign of God which the church, either the Gentile church or a church of Jews and Gentiles, embodies. The second version of the ecclesiological interpretation is in the manuscripts that reverse the sequence of the children, so that the devoted child is first. This first child is then interpreted, in terms of salvation history, as Israel, which did not do the will of God.[3]

THE TWO PARABLES IN MATT 21:33-46 AND 22:1-14
IN THE CONTEXT OF JESUS' TEMPLE DISCOURSE
IN 21:23—22:14

In spite of the unresolved conflict with the leaders of the Jewish people, Jesus is repeatedly pictured in dialogue with them. The parable of the violent tenants applies to the whole people, but it is rightly understood by the "high priests and the Pharisees" (21:45) as a critique of their politics. They have let things go so far that the victims of economic violence are beginning to kill the slaves of their torturers.[4] The nation is afflicted with a hopeless, violent rage. The second parable describes the structures of imperial power within the Roman empire.[5] According to this parable the leaders want to force Jesus to make a political sacrificial oath (22:15-22). He is to say that he rejects the Roman poll tax because it cannot be reconciled with confession of the God of Israel. But Jesus, in the situation as given, regards the confession of Israel's God and payment of the poll tax as compatible—as did many Jewish and Christian people at the time.[6] Only when the Roman state demands religious submission is the limit drawn by the *Shema' Israel* reached.

But the two parables in 21:33-46 and 22:1-14 are not told for the sake of the leadership alone.[7] Their applications speak of hope for the end of this violent power. They are spoken before the crowds and develop a perspective toward the kingdom of God. The nation portrayed in its subjugation "has become the cornerstone" (21:42). God has lifted up the lowly. The "wonder in our eyes" (21:42) has become visible: God's kingdom, in which will live the people who bring forth fruits corresponding to God's righteousness—the people drawn from all nations.

The second parable, on the Roman empire, coming after the parable of the vineyard tenants, is all the more gloomy in its impact because it again describes violence. No one can have any further illusions about a peaceful life. How different is God's kingdom, which is already here to be seen! The brief application, in v. 14, of the parable in Matt 22:1-13 recalls God's promise for all the nations and especially for Israel. All the nations are called, and little Israel is God's beloved child.

The two parables of violent power evoke a longing for God's kingdom, for the God who fed the people with manna in the desert and delivered then from endless slavery. Every prayer in the Jewish tradition paints a picture counter to Matt 21:33-41 and Matt 22:1-13: Blessed art thou, O God, for you have lifted up the lowly.

FOR FURTHER READING

Anthony J. Saldarini, *Matthew's Christian-Jewish Community*
Luise Schottroff, *Befreiungserfahrungen*

The Parable of the Talents
and God's Judgment on the Nations

TRANSLATION

14 For you should compare the kingdom of heaven with the story of a man who, as he was leaving on a journey, called his slaves and gave them his fortune to manage.

15 To one he gave five talents, to the next two, to the third one, each according to his ability. Then he departed. Immediately

16 the one with the five talents began and traded with them and gained five more.

17 In the same way, the one with the two talents made two more.

18 The one with the one talent went out, dug a hole in the earth, and hid his owner's money.

19 After a long time the owner of these slaves returned and held a reckoning with them.

20 The one with five talents came and brought five more, saying: Master, you gave me five talents, and here are the other five I have gained.

21 His owner said to him: Well done, good and faithful slave. You were reliable in a small thing, and now I will give you a great task. You are a joy to your owner.

22 The one with the two talents came and said: Here are the other two that I have gained.

23 His owner said to him: Well done, good and faithful slave. You were reliable in a small thing, and now I will give you a great task. You are a joy to your owner.

24 The one with the one talent also came and said: Master, I knew that you are a hard man, who reaps where he has not sown and gathers what he has not scattered.

25 Out of fear of you, I went out and hid your talent in the ground. Here is your money back.

26 The owner answered him: You wicked, lazy slave! You knew, then, that I reap where I have not sown and gather what I have not scattered?

27   Then you should have put my money in the bank, so that I could now receive my property back with interest.

28   Take the talent from him and give it to the one with ten talents.

29   To those who have something, more will be given, even to superfluity. Those who have nothing will have taken away from them even the little that they have.

30   Throw this useless slave into a dark dungeon. There he will weep and gnash his teeth in fear of death.

31   But when the heavenly Human One comes in his divine glory, and all the angels with him, then he will sit down on the heavenly throne of judgment.

32   And all the nations will gather and stand before his judgment. He will separate people as a shepherd separates the sheep from the goats.

33   He will set the sheep on his right hand and the goats on his left.

34   Then the Royal One will say to those on his right: Come; you belong to God, my Father and my Mother; you will live in the kingdom that God has created for you from the beginning of the world.

35   I was hungry, and you gave me to eat; I was thirsty, and you gave me water; I was a stranger, and you received me.

36   I was naked, and you clothed me; I was sick, and you cared for me; I was in prison, and you came to me.

37   Then the righteous will answer him: Jesus, when did we see you hungry and give you food, or thirsty and give you water?

38   When did we see you in the stranger and receive you, or naked and clothed you?

39   When did we see you sick or in prison and come to you?

40   And the Royal One will answer them: Truly, I tell you, everything you did for one of these, the least of my sisters and brothers, you did for me.

41   Then he will say to those on his left: Go from me; you are far from God; go into the endless fire that God has prepared for the devil and those who serve him.

42   I was hungry, and you gave me nothing to eat; I was thirsty, and you gave me no water.

43   I was a stranger, and you did not receive me; I was naked, and you did not clothe me; I was sick and in prison, and you paid no heed to me.

44   Then they, too, will answer: Jesus, when did we see you hungry or thirsty or a stranger or naked or in prison and did not care for you?

45   Then the heavenly Human One will answer them: Truly, I tell you, everything that you did not do for one or another of these least ones, you did not do for me.

46   And they will go forth into endless punishment, but the righteous into life with God.

The parable of the talents (Matt 25:14-30) was the one that for a long time made me doubt the possibility of interpreting the kings and masters in parables as God. The third slave tells the truth. He accuses the slaveowner of theft.[1] And the slaveowner does not feel insulted by it. He criticizes the slave for not having invested the money in such a way that it would double—or at least gain interest in the bank. The third slave is thrown into prison,[2] where he will weep and gnash his teeth in fear of death. He has acted as Jesus taught in the Sermon on the Mount. He has not served mammon (Matt 6:24). He has refused to be a henchman in the dispossession[3] of small farmers. To see this third slave as the embodiment of people who reject God's righteousness and God's Torah is simply unbearable to me. Such an interpretation is only possible if the imagery in the parables is read without any reference to human life, as almost abstract symbols for something else—that is, allegorically. This tradition of interpretation is so powerful that I continually fall back into it if I do not stay alert to social history—and to the internal contradictions between the message of Jesus, in this case according to the Gospel of Matthew, and the behavior of the kings and masters in the parables.

The parable is told in Matthew without any explicit application. It is followed immediately by the great mythic vision[4] of the eschatological judgment of the Son of Man over all the nations (v. 32).[5]

The hungry, the thirsty, the refugees, the naked, the sick, and the prisoners are the least of all, and they are Jesus' sisters and brothers (vv. 25, 40). As in Matt 28:19-20, the reference is to all nations; Jews and non-Jews will be judged by the Son of Man. All that matters is what they have done. It makes no difference whether they thought Jesus was the Messiah or knew that they belonged to the God of Israel. All people are to hear Jesus' message, his interpretation of Torah, and act accordingly (see also 13:38; 24:14). The Gospel of Matthew certainly retains the vision that the righteous from among the Jewish people and from all peoples will share in the messianic banquet (see only 8:11-12).[6] God's judgment will separate the just from the unjust. The criteria are the Torah and Jesus' interpretation of the Torah, and that means the deeds of righteousness. Jesus calls the sick, the weary, and the heavy-laden, the "last," the lost sheep of the house of Israel and the poor in spirit, and welcomes them with God's mercy. The listing of those who suffer in Matt 25:31-46 corresponds to what the gospel has told of Jesus' deeds (see also the summary of the Messiah's works in 11:2-6). The universal interpretation of Matt 25:31-46 that I am presenting here corresponds to the message of the Gospel of Matthew itself. It is just this vision of God's judgment, which will be conducted by the Son of Man, that is the basis of all the individual stories and parables in Matthew's gospel.

The fact that Matt 25:31-46 follows immediately after the parable of the talents shows that this vision is to be read as an application of the parable (and those that precede it). The third slave in the parable of the talents would be among those who ask in astonishment: When did we see you hungry? He had refused to participate in the unjust expropriation of the lands of small farmers. The vision of the messianic judgment is obviously narrated in the awareness that this is a story that tries to illustrate something that no one can really know. The text is almost playfully staged. But it depicts something that in Israel was ancient tradition and the basis of life: God will be a just judge. What is at stake now is to draw the conclusion from that. Jesus the parable teller speaks about salvation for all peoples. No one is now denied the opportunity to hear and see what is to be done. Parables are also to be understood by those who, up to this point, have obstinately refused. They are texts of eschatological hope, and telling them is practical love of neighbor.

The social injustice that mishandles young girls and causes slaves to become complicit in the expropriation of small farms (Matt 25:1-30) is confronted with the anticipation of divine judgment (Matt 25:31-46). The drama is comparable to that in Rev 18:2. "Babylon," the mighty city, embodied in the power and wealth of Rome and the Roman empire, is confronted with God's justice: The angel "cried with a loud voice: Fallen, fallen is Babylon the great. . . ." God's judgment is still anticipated. But the voice of the world judge, or of this angel, can already be heard. God's justice cannot be annulled.

Appendix
How Should I Read a Gospel Parable?

1. I understand a parable narrative as a stylized and fictional combination of experiences from daily life. I attempt to recognize the connection to social structures. The parable narratives frequently contain depictions of violence and injustice in society.

2. I look within the literary context for the explicit or implicit statement about God's action that belongs to the parable narrative. It can appear in the form of a "saying" as application, or in many other forms.

3. God's story is connected to the narrative by only a few bridges. The narrative often contains an antithesis to God's story. "So" *(houtōs)* or "like" *(homoios)* are to be read as a challenge to critical comparison, not as an invitation to equation (e.g., not: God is like a king, who . . .). I ask: Where is the God of the Torah, and the Torah itself, to be seen—alongside, behind, and/or in the parable?

4. The parable narrative and the story of God connected to it are part of a dialogue. This dialogue took place in oral form—in Jesus' time and thereafter. Its written traditions in the Gospels presume oral responses that often are not written down. These are to be sought in Jewish traditions of address to God or praise of God. I attempt to flesh out this dialogue for myself.

5. I try to unlearn the triumphalistic ecclesiology of the Christian tradition of interpretation, which works by contrasting us against them, good against evil, Gentile church against Judaism. This kind of interpretation rests on the identification of groups and their association with or opposition to "us," the church, which is always on the right side.

6. I attempt to think eschatologically, to pray, and to speak with and about God. That means: (1) leaving it up to God to judge good and evil and (2) understanding the present as the hour when God's justice begins in the world, which makes it my responsibility to do good—that is, to keep the Torah.

Notes

CHAPTER 1

1. Sanders, *Judaism.*

2. Social-historical material on toll collectors, the activities of customs officials, and hatred of them can be found in L. Schottroff and W. Stegemann, *Jesus von Nazareth,* 16–24.

3. For female tax or toll collectors see L. Schottroff, *Lydia's Impatient Sisters,* 243n110.

4. Bovon, *Das Evangelium nach Lukas,* 3:200–218.

5. Culpepper, "The Gospel of Luke," 9:340–43.

6. Examples from rabbinic literature are in Billerbeck, *Kommentar zum Neuen Testament aus Talmud und Midrasch,* 2:240–41.

7. See the collection in ibid., 2:240.

CHAPTER 2

1. Hengel, "Das Gleichnis von den Weingärtnern"; W. Schottroff, *Gerechtigkeit lernen.*

2. Columella, *On agriculture* 1.7.6-7; W. Schottroff, "Das Gleichnis von den bösen Weingärtnern (Mk 12,1-9 parr.). Ein Beitrag zur Geschichte der Bodenpacht in Palästina," in idem, *Gerechtigkeit lernen: Beiträge zur biblischen Sozialgeschichte,* ed. Frank Crüsemann and Rainer Kessler (Gütersloh: Kaiser, 1999), 188, with information on sharecropping.

3. W. Schottroff, "Das Gleichnis von den bösen Weingärtnern," 169n16. John S. Kloppenborg Verbin rejects this interpretation, writing that the parable would otherwise have said that in the first years of planting, before the vines bore fruit, the owner paid wages to the tenants. But the parable skips over that time because it is unimportant to the narrative ("Isaiah 5:1-7, the Parable of the Tenants and Vineyard Leases on Papyrus," 129–30).

4. W. Schottroff, "Das Gleichnis von den bösen Weingärtnern," 191.

5. Columella, *On agriculture* 1.1.20. W. Schottroff, "Das Gleichnis von den bösen Weingärtnern," 182; rabbinic material in Snodgrass, *The Parable of the Wicked Tenants,* 38–39.

6. Hengel, "Das Gleichnis von den Weingärtnern," 26–27; W. Schottroff, "Das Gleichnis von den bösen Weingärtnern," 189.

7. An eschatological interpretation of Matt 21:43 that overcomes the still-widespread anti-Jewish/ecclesiological reading can be found in Wendebourg, *Der Tag des Herrn,* 233; and Jones, *The Gospel of Matthew,* 389. See also part 3 below on Matt 21:43 (21:23—22:14).

8. Herzog, *Parables as Subversive Speech,* 21. Without reference to Herzog, Arnal ("The Parable of the Tenants and the Class Consciousness of the Peasantry," 135–57) develops a similar interpretation for a hypothetical nonallegorical primitive form of the parable as found in *Gospel of Thomas* (logion 65); the original parable told of class-conscious resistance by the tenants against the landowner.

9. Jeremias, *Die Gleichnisse Jesu* (ET *The Parables of Jesus*).

10. Horne, "The Parables of the Tenants as Indictment," 111–16.

11. Targum Ps, 118:22-29; Billerbeck, *Kommentar zum Neuen Testament aus Talmud und Midrasch,* 1:876; Milavec, "A Fresh Analysis of the Parable of the Wicked Husbandmen in the Light of Jewish-Catholic Dialogue," 108; Derrett, *Studies in the New Testament,* 62.

12. I am adopting here the image from 1 Pet 2:5, developed in connection with Ps 118:22.

13. See Horsley, *Jesus and the Spiral of Violence.*

14. For this tradition, see Klawans, *Impurity and Sin in Ancient Judaism.*

15. Oldenhage, *Parables for Our Time,* 65.

16. Ibid. 65, 67.

17. Ibid., 142.

18. Ricoeur, *Figuring the Sacred,* 165 (see also chap. 9 below); Oldenhage, *Parables for Our Time,* 142.

19. Oldenhage, *Parables for Our Time,* 143.

20. Ibid., 144.

21. Ibid.

CHAPTER 3

1. Wegner, *Chattel or Person?* 21–23, 27–28, 221.

2. Ilan (*Jewish Women in Greco-Roman Palestine,* 83) interprets this tradition as attesting "the freedom to choose one's marriage partners," more common among the poorer classes. Unlike Ilan, I do not see this tradition as showing that here women could choose their partners.

3. See Maier, "Das Buch der Sprichwörter," 208–20.

4. There is a collection of material on marriage customs in Billerbeck, *Kommentar zum Neuen Testament aus Talmud und Midrasch,* 1:500–517. For the lamps see especially Luz, *Das Evangelium nach Matthäus,* 3:469–71 (see the forthcoming volume from Fortress Press).

5. The exception to this rule is Balabanski, "Opening the Closed Door," 71–97.

6. Luz, *Das Evangelium nach Matthäus,* 3:467, is illuminating on this point.

7. The bridegroom emphasizes his statement with a preceding *amen,* as Jesus often does in the Gospels. Previous discussion among scholars concerning Jesus' emphatic formula has proceeded on the assumption that there are no Jewish parallels to this formula of self-assertion, only the (widely attested) responsory use of *amen* to confirm the speech of an interlocutor. The stylization of the bridegroom's speech is then regarded as an argument for the allegorization of the parable: Here it is not a human bridegroom who speaks, but the eschatological judge, the Son of Man. But such an individual usage, a special expression used only by Jesus, intended also to be christologically amplified, is problematic on the basis of fundamental methodological considerations. The allegorical character of this verse cannot be demonstrated in this way; rather, what this shows is that the narrator of this parable regarded the confirmatory usage of *amen* for this solemn social death sentence to be appropriate on the lips of a bridegroom in a parable (see Luke 14:15: "I say to you"). Eta Linnemann has rightly disputed the assumption of an allegorical text in Matt 25:1-13: "But it is also argued against its being a parable that 'a mass of individual features of the parable' cannot be explained from the procedure of an ordinary wedding. But one must distinguish between what is not the rule, and what crosses the bounds of possibility" (*Jesus of the Parables. Introduction and Exposition,* 193). I would add that this is all the more the case when, as here, a marriage celebration is the framework for making visible

the oppressive dualism of a distinction between good and bad, clever and stupid women in all its harshness.

8. Luz, *Das Evangelium nach Matthäus.*

9. Balabanski, "Opening the Closed Door."

10. Ibid., 96–97.

11. For this understanding of eschatology and time see chap. 8 below.

12. For this text see L. Schottroff, *Lydia's Impatient Sisters,* 152–73.

13. Jeremias, *Die Gleichnisse Jesu* (ET *The Parables of Jesus*), 100–103. However, Jeremias understood *hōmōioun* to mean "equate," not "compare," though the latter is more common in Christian parable interpretation (see part 2 below).

14. For the meaning of "the kingdom of God" see chap. 4 below.

15. For the question of a "closed" door metaphor see chap. 10 below.

CHAPTER 4

1. Friedländer, *Darstellungen aus der Sittengeschichte Roms in der Zeit von Augustus bis zum Ausgang der Antonine,* 1:98–103; 2:381–82.

2. For an extensive collection of material see Ziegler, *Die Königsgleichnisse des Midrasch beleuchtet durch die römische Kaiserzeit.*

3. See L. Schottroff, "Das Gleichnis vom großen Gastmahl in der Logienquelle," 200n21.

4. With BAGD and LSJ, I understand the word *diexhodos* as the place where roads or streets lead outward through a narrow passage, that is, the exits of various streets from the city.

5. Ziegler, *Die Königsgleichnisse des Midrasch beleuchtet durch die römische Kaiserzeit.*

6. Ibid., 321; Marquardt, *Das Privatleben der Römer,* 208; Friedländer, *Sittengeschichte,* 1:98.

7. Juvenal, *Satires,* 5, 10ff.

8. Friedländer, *Sittengeschichte,* 1:258.

9. Seneca, *De ira* XXIII, 3–4.

10. Ziegler, *Die Königsgleichnisse des Midrasch beleuchtet durch die römische Kaiserzeit,* 323, 325; Billerbeck, *Kommentar zum Neuen Testament aus Talmud und Midrasch,* 1:878.

11. For a summary of these punishments see Ziegler, *Die Königsgleichnisse des Midrasch beleuchtet durch die römische Kaiserzeit,* 404–7. For private prisons see also Krause, *Gefängnisse im Römischen Reich,* 59–63.

12. Ziegler, *Die Königsgleichnisse des Midrasch beleuchtet durch die römische Kaiserzeit.*

13. Krauss, "Griechen und Römer."

14. Attributed to Johanan ben Zakkai in *b. Ber.* 28b; see the discussion in Billerbeck, *Kommentar zum Neuen Testament aus Talmud und Midrasch,* 1:730–31. Sugranyes de Franch (*Études sur le droit Paléstinien à l'époque Evangélique,* 26–29) tries to read the expression *anthrōpos basileus* differently: a certain (*quidam,* "un certain" in French) king. Linguistically that is possible, but the critical awareness in these texts of the difference between God and the king in a parable points in the direction of the rabbinic formula of a king "of flesh and blood."

15. Further examples of this explicit distinction are found in Billerbeck, *Kommentar zum Neuen Testament aus Talmud und Midrasch,* 1:170; Krauss ("Griechen und Römer," 1, 60) makes a comparable distinction between a human father and the "father in the heavens." On this see G. F. Moore, *Judaism in the First Centuries of the Christian Era,* 204; and Luz, *Das Evangelium nach Matthäus,* 1:444.

16. Schürer, *The History of the Jewish People in the Age of Jesus Christ*, 2:531–32. See also G. F. Moore, *Judaism in the First Centuries of the Christian Era*, 401. Camponovo offers good information on the First Testament and postbiblical Jewish material in *Königtum, Königsherrschaft und Reich Gottes in den frühjüdischen Schriften*.

17. *Pesiq. Rab Kah. 3b, c* (parallels in *Shir. R.* 8, 12; at 8, 14 [II, 82b]), quoted in the translation and arrangement of the text provided by Thoma and Lauer, *Die Gleichnisse der Rabbinen*, vol. 1: *Pesiqta de Rav Kahana*, 123–24; Ziegler, *Die Königsgleichnisse des Midrasch beleuchtet durch die römische Kaiserzeit*, 185.

18. Thoma and Lauer criticize Ziegler on the basis of a dehistoricizing literary-critical theory. "[Ziegler] could not understand that the rabbinic parables, much like the NT parables, are adopted or newly constructed units with the 'dramatic quality of fiction' (Via, *The Parables*). As such they are not an adequate reflection of social-historical situations" (*Die Gleichnisse der Rabbinen*, vol. 1: *Pesiqta de Rav Kahana*, 69). What is here understood to be "adequate"? Both the rabbinic parables and those in the Jesus tradition are the reflection of social-historical situations. What kind of reflection they represent is something that has to be clarified through individual analyses. For parable theory, see below.

19. Chrysostom, *Commentarius in sanctum Matthaeum Evangelistam*, 57, 58.

20. Luz, *Das Evangelium nach Matthäus*; many commentators have interpreted similarly.

21. Summary information on this can be found in Seebaß, "Erwählung I: Altes Testament."

22. From the translation by Dexinger in "Erwählung II: Judentum," 190. For the Hebrew text and a translation see Heidenheim, *Gebete für das Neujahrsfest*, 81. For further postbiblical material see Billerbeck, *Kommentar zum Neuen Testament aus Talmud und Midrasch*, 3:293–94; 1:397–98.

23. For a collection of material see Park, *Either Jew or Gentile*, 9–20.

24. Billerbeck, *Kommentar zum Neuen Testament aus Talmud und Midrasch*, 3:293–94.

25. *Pesiq. Rab Kah.* 99a (see Billerbeck, *Kommentar zum Neuen Testament aus Talmud und Midrasch*, 1:869).

CHAPTER 5

1. Bolkestein, *Wohltätigkeit und Armenpflege im vorchristlichen Altertum*, 264, 270, 338–39, 366, 370ff.

2. Haenchen, "Das Gleichnis vom großen Mahl," 154: "The God whom Jesus proclaims does not turn to the poor because the rich have insulted him." He therefore doubts that the parable of the banquet is to be traced to Jesus.

3. L. Schottroff, "Das Gleichnis vom großen Gastmahl," 200n19.

4. Bolkestein, *Wohltätigkeit und Armenpflege im vorchristlichen Altertum*, 56–66; F. Crüsemann, *Die Tora*, 424; Esler (*Community and Gospel in Luke-Acts*, 194) rightly emphasizes the connection between the practice here demanded and eschatology: "Salvation for Luke is not a purely eschatological reality, for within the Christian community it begins here and now."

5. See L. Schottroff, "Vom Mut, Gott nachzuahmen."

6. See Crüsemann and Crüsemann, "Das Jahr das Gott gefällt," 19–24.

7. *p. Ḥag. 2.77d, 38* (parallel in *p. Sanh. 6.23c, 26*), quoted from Billerbeck, *Kommentar zum Neuen Testament aus Talmud und Midrasch*, 2:231–32.

8. Friedländer, *Darstellungen aus der Sittengeschichte Roms*, 1:160; see Acts 3:2; Luke 16:19.

9. See Bolkestein, *Wohltätigkeit und Armenpflege im vorchristlichen Altertum,* 412–13; Billerbeck, *Kommentar zum Neuen Testament aus Talmud und Midrasch,* 2:206–7; Krauss, *Monumenta Talmudica,* 3:56. The Talmudic story cited above about the toll collector's son from *p. Sanh. 6.23c* (Billerbeck, *Kommentar zum Neuen Testament aus Talmud und Midrasch,* 2:23ff.) also belongs to this tradition.

10. See Bolkestein, *Wohltätigkeit und Armenpflege im vorchristlichen Altertum,* 413; L. Schottroff, "DienerInnen der Heiligen," 222–42. For the problems presented by the word *almsgiving* in this context see pp. 157–63 below on Luke 16:1-13.

11. L. Schottroff, "Das Gleichnis vom großen Gastmahl in der Logienquelle," 200–201, n22.

12. See in detail L. Schottroff, *Lydia's Impatient Sisters,* chap. 4, section B.

13. In "Das Gleichnis vom großen Gastmahl in der Logienquelle." I considered the framework of the parable that underlies the different versions in Matt 22:1-10 and Luke 14:16-24 to be available to interpretation as God's invitation to the poor. For that reason I also considered this statement to be taken from Q. This interpretation rests on the interpretation of the king (Matthew) and householder (Luke) as God. In the meantime I have been forced to abandon the metaphorical plausibility posited by the exegetical tradition.

14. Bovon, *Das Evangelium nach Lukas,* vol. 2.

15. For the banquet at the end of days see G. F. Moore, *Judaism in the First Centuries of the Christian Era,* 364–65; and Priest, "A Note on the Messianic Banquet," 222–38.

CHAPTER 6

1. Lémonon (*Pilate et le Gouvernement de la Judée,* 273) is interested in freeing Pilate as a person from the accusation of bloodthirstiness, but he does not gloss over the means Pilate employed against people whom he considered political insurrectionists (for example, see 203). Unfortunately Lémonon does not analyze Luke 13:1 because the text cannot be verified outside the Bible (134). But there is an extensive examination of the historical sources that can be connected to Luke 13:1 in Blinzler, "Die Niedermetzelung von Galiläern durch Pilatus," 49. He comes to the conclusion "that the simple note in Luke 13:1, non-tendentious but nevertheless often underestimated, misunderstood, or set aside as of no value, also withstands a stringent historical critique." Even if I do not accept all the details of his reconstruction, I join him in regarding Luke 13:1 as a reliable historical source.

2. Bailey, *Poet and Peasant and Through Peasant Eyes,* 75.

3. Josephus, *B.J.* 2.189–74; *Ant.* 18.55-59; *B.J.* 2.175-77; *Ant.* 18.60-62. See the analysis of the sources in Lémonon, *Pilate et le Gouvernement de la Judée.*

4. Parallels to the mingling of blood are discussed by Blinzler, "Die Niedermetzelung von Galiläern durch Pilatus," 28–29.

5. Flusser, *Die rabbinischen Gleichnisse und der Gleichniserzähler Jesu,* 81.

6. See also Isa 63:17-19; 4 Macc 17:20-22; *Prayer of Azariah* 14–16.

7. Klawans, *Impurity and Sin in Ancient Judaism,* 26; idem, "Notions of Gentile Impurity in Ancient Judaism," 289.

8. *b. Yoma 39b*; see Michel and Bauernfeind, *Flavius Josephus, De Bello Judaico,* 2:2, 180.

9. See only the discussion of the signs of the coming destruction in *B.J.* 6:288-315.

10. See, for example, Josephus, *B.J.* 2:192-203.

11. Flusser, *Die rabbinischen Gleichnisse und der Gleichniserzähler Jesu,* 81. He refers to Grotius, *Annotationes in Novum Testamentum,* on Luke 13:3.

12. Oldenhage, *Parables for Our Time.* On this see pp. 21–25 above regarding Jeremias.

13. Billerbeck, *Kommentar zum Neuen Testament aus Talmud und Midrasch,* 2:194.

14. A random selection of exegeses that represent this tradition of interpretation: "In

such catastrophes one should only consider that one must do penance in good time" (Klostermann, *Das Lukasevangelium,* 142); "far more important is the fact that all sinners face the judgment of God unless they repent" (Marshall, *The Gospel of Luke,* 554); "their fate stands as a warning to everyone of the urgency of repentance" (Lieu, *The Gospel of Luke,* 106); "he contrasts an objective and disinterested teaching with a faith that recognizes its errors and turns to God" (Bovon, *Das Evangelium nach Lukas,* 2:376).

15. Josephus, *B.J.* 6:300–315.

16. For an analysis of the cases alluded to in Luke 12:57-59, when debtors are trapped by debt, see Marshall, *The Gospel of Luke.*

17. There is further biblical material in Bovon, *Das Evangelium nach Lukas,* 2:373n16; for rabbinic material see Flusser, *Die rabbinischen Gleichnisse und der Gleichniserzähler Jesu,* 83–84.

18. Dodd, "The Fall of Jerusalem and the 'Abomination of Desolation,'" 47–54, on Luke 19:42-44; 21:20, 24, 28.

19. Tertullian, *Marc.* III 23, 3-4.

20. Stern, "Rhetoric and Midrash," 261–91; see also idem, *Parables in Midrash,* 37–42.

21. Stern ("Rhetoric and Midrash") presents two slightly different versions (one from the edition by Salomon Buber and one from the standard editions of *Lamentations Rabbah*). I have quoted from the German translation of the version in the standard editions by Wünsche, *Bibliotheca Rabbinica, 13. und 14. Lieferung: Der Midrash Echa Rabbati,* 140. See also Stern, *Parables in Midrash,* 37–42.

22. Stern, "Rhetoric and Midrash," 273.

23. Ibid., 274.

24. Ibid., 275.

CHAPTER 7

1. Gerhardsson, "The Parable of the Sower and Its Interpretation," 165–93. According to *m. Ber.* 3.3, women, slaves, and children are freed from the recitation of the prayer.

2. The *Shemaʿ Israel* includes and summarizes Deut 6:4-9; 11:13-21; Num 15:(37-)41. On the *Shemaʿ Israel* see Billerbeck, *Kommentar zum Neuen Testament aus Talmud und Midrasch,* 4, excursus 9; Bradshaw, *The Search for the Origins of Christian Worship,* 39–40; and see chap. 19 below (n4).

3. See the collected material and analysis in L. Schottroff, "Die Befreiung vom Götzendienst der Habgier," 137–52; see also chap. 21 below.

4. See the analysis of the situation of persecution discernible in the Gospel of Mark in L. Schottroff, "Die Gegenwart in der Apokalyptik der synoptischen Evangelien," 73–95.

5. Kögel, *Der Zweck der Gleichnisse Jesu im Rahmen seiner Verkündigung,* 75; see also Jülicher, *Die Gleichnisreden Jesu,* vol. 1: *Die Gleichnisreden Jesu im Allgemeinen,* 133.

6. The German word group *Verstockung* ("obstinacy," "unrepentance") owes its theological career to Luther's Bible translation, which summarized complicated biblical terminology in a unified vocabulary. On this see the article by Schmidt and Schmidt, "*pachynō, ktl.,*" 5:1023–24.

7. The extensive exegetical discussion rests primarily on possible uses of language that would avoid the idea of God's *intent* to harden them and keep open the possibility of repentance. Even the ancient history of translation of Isa 6:9-10 was influenced by this difficulty.

8. This so-called determinism does not justify violence and injustice, but consoles those who suffer from it: God is not disempowered by injustice. "In such situations of persecution, a theology of apocalyptic determinism functions to assure the hard-pressed faithful that their suffering does not signal a loss of divine control" (Marcus, *Mark 1–8,*

307). Of course, Mark is concerned that in the text itself determinism should not have the last word (307; see also 321, where Marcus laments Mark 4:25b). But the condemnation of the perpetrators of injustice at the divine judgment cannot be separated from this notion of God. Nevertheless, it is God's judgment, and it can in no way be anticipated by human beings. Those who suffer injustice are delivered from hatred and vengeance by trusting entirely in God's justice.

9. I see this also as the reason why the apparently separate teaching to the disciples is so inconsistently presented in the narrative. The text presumes that, starting at v. 21 (?), the crowd is again (?) present, without explaining how the situation in 4:10 is to be reconciled with 4:1-2.

10. Kögel, *Der Zweck der Gleichnisse Jesu im Rahmen seiner Verkündigung*; see L. Schottroff, "Verheißung und Erfüllung aus der Sicht einer Theologie nach Auschwitz," 93–100.

11. Young, *The Parables*, 263.

12. One of the reasons for the misunderstanding that parables, in the sense of Mark 4:10-12, 33, 34, are veiled speech is the interpretation of the parallelism in Mark 4:11-12 as a contrast between two methods of proclamation (first, in parables; second, without parables or with parables that receive an extra explanation) or as a contrast between revelation and concealment, with *parabolē* translated as "riddle." But the parallelism represents two different encounters with the *one*, understandable revelation: rejection (not seeing, not understanding) and receiving as gift (*dedotai*).

13. Stern, "Imitatio Hominis," 164; idem, *Parables in Midrash*, 16–18.

14. Gerhardsson, "The Parable of the Sower and Its Interpretation."

15. Young, *The Parables*, 252. See Flusser, *Die rabbinischen Gleichnisse und der Gleichniserzähler Jesu*, 63.

16. Stern, "Imitatio Hominis," 165; idem, *Parables in Midrash*, 16–19. See also Young, *The Parables*, 270, on Mark 4:14-20 as *nimshal*.

17. See in more detail L. Schottroff, "Wir sind Samen und keine Steinchen," 112–33. Young (*The Parables*, 265–68) sets Mark 4:3-8 in the context of Jewish traditions about four different kinds of Torah students. But Mark 4:1-20 does not describe four different reactions to the "word," but two. On this subject see also McArthur and Johnston, *They Also Taught in Parables*, 182–83.

18. See White, "The Parable of the Sower."

19. Dalmann, *Arbeit und Sitte in Palästina*, 194–95.

20. Sonnen, "Landwirtschaftliches vom See Genezareth," 77–78; see also Mell, *Die Zeit der Gottesherrschaft*, 82–109.

21. See White, "The Parable of the Sower."

22. Applebaum, "Judaea as a Roman Province," esp. 365; Strange, "First Century Galilee from Archaeology and from the Texts," 46–47.

23. See, for example, Marcus, *Mark 1–8*, 320.

24. See Billerbeck, *Kommentar zum Neuen Testament aus Talmud und Midrasch*, 1:660–61 for further material.

25. Billerbeck, *Kommentar zum Neuen Testament aus Talmud und Midrasch*, 1:661.

26. See, for example, the critique of Roman markets, bridges, and baths in *b. Sabb.* 33b.

27. Schniewind, *Das Evangelium nach Markus*, 74.

28. Weder, *Die Gleichnisse Jesu als Metaphern*.

29. Dietzfelbinger, "Das Gleichnis vom ausgestreuten Samen," 92.

30. Donahue and Harrington, *The Gospel of Mark*, 144–46.

31. Ibid., 145.

32. Gerhardsson, "The Parable of the Sower and Its Interpretation."

33. Donahue and Harrington, *The Gospel of Mark,* 144 (The "disturbing element is the determination and sectarian theology put on the lips of Jesus").

34. Kögel, *Der Zweck der Gleichnisse Jesu im Rahmen seiner Verkündigung,* 69.

35. Beavis, *Mark's Audience.*

36. Ibid., 150: "Elsewhere in the Gospel 'those about him' and 'those outside' are not absolutely rigid categories: a ruler of the synagogue can be faithful. . . ."

37. Marcus, *Mark 1–8,* 307.

38. Young, *The Parables,* 268.

39. Ibid., 276.

CHAPTER 8

1. For my understanding of eschatology, see the following section.

2. See L. Schottroff, "Gesetzesfreie Heidenchristentum und die Frauen?" 227–45.

3. Robinson has already done this in *The Body.* See the extensive analyses in Martin, *The Corinthian Body*; and Ammicht-Quinn, *Körper, Religion, Sexualität,* 27–37. See also the articles by Ammicht-Quinn and Nagl-Docekal in *WBFTh.*

4. See Janssen, "Leibliche Auferstehung?" 84–102.

5. Townes, *In a Blaze of Glory*; Martin, "A Sacred Hope and Social Goal," 209–26.

6. Bloch, *Atheism in Christianity*; Metz, *Faith in History and Society*; Ebach, "Apokalypse," 5–61; Ruether, *Sexism and God Talk.* Also in this tradition are the works of Rehmann, "*Geh, frage de Gebärerin . . .*"; Janssen, *Eschatologie und Gegenwart*; and L. Schottroff, especially *Lydia's Impatient Sisters.* Ebach has repeatedly referred to the connection to Walter Benjamin. Liberation-theological initiatives toward the interpretation of eschatology also belong in this tradition; I can only refer to them here in general.

7. Borg, *Jesus in Contemporary Scholarship.*

8. Stendahl, *Paul among Jews and Gentiles, and Other Essays*; Tamez, *The Amnesty of Grace.*

9. Deutsche Bibelgesellschaft, *Die Bibel nach der Übersetzung Martin Luthers in der revidierten von Fassung 1984.*

10. Harrington, "The Gospel according to Mark," 621.

11. See L. Schottroff, *Befreiungserfahrungen,* 324–57.

12. See L. Schottroff, "Feministische Hermeneutik des ersten Briefes an die korinthische Gemeinde," 149–55.

13. Brecht, "Das Pfund der Armen"; Kazantzakis, *The Last Temptation of Christ,* 217; for Herzog see chap. 2 above; for Levine see chap. 20 below; for Balabanski see chap. 3 above.

CHAPTER 9

1. Bultmann, *The History of the Synoptic Tradition,* 198.

2. Ibid., 174.

3. Jeremias, *The Parables of Jesus,* 22.

4. For example, see ibid., 135. The *tertium comparationis* is the "key" to its meaning, the central idea that unlocks meaning for the reader/hearer, in Jülicher's theory.

5. Ibid., 12–13.

6. Ricoeur, "Stellung und Funktion der Metapher in der biblischen Sprache," 45–70. An expanded version is in Crossan, ed., "Paul Ricoeur on Biblical Hermeneutics," 27–148. See also Ricoeur, "Biblical Hermeneutics."

7. Ricoeur, "Stellung und Funktion der Metapher in der biblischen Sprache," 61.

8. Ibid., 64.

9. Black, *Models and Metaphors*, 236.

10. Ricoeur, "Stellung und Funktion der Metapher in der biblischen Sprache," 52; see also Harnisch, *Die neutestamentliche Gleichnisforschung im Horizont von Hermeneutik und Literaturwissenschaft*, 294. Erlemann (*Gleichnisauslegung*, 30) calls these "two spheres of reality" in his formulation of the new "consensus" in parables research based on Ricoeur.

11. Ricoeur, "Stellung und Funktion der Metapher in der biblischen Sprache," 51; see also Harnisch, *Die neutestamentliche Gleichnisforschung im Horizont von Hermeneutik und Literaturwissenschaft*, 293.

12. Bailey, *Poet and Peasant and Through Peasant Eyes*.

13. Dodd, *The Parables of the Kingdom*.

14. Ukpong, "The Parable of the Shrewd Manager."

15. De la Torre, *Reading the Bible from the Margins*.

16. See Schüssler Fiorenza, "The Ethics of Interpretation," 3–17; and Tolbert, "When Resistance Becomes Repression," 331–46.

17. Flusser, *Die rabbinischen Gleichnisse und der Gleichniserzähler Jesus*.

18. Stern's "Rhetoric and Midrash" and "Jesus' Parables from the Perspective of Rabbinic Literature," are earlier versions of chaps. 1, 2, and 6 in his *Parables in Midrash*.

19. Stern, "Jesus' Parables from the Perspective of Rabbinic Literature," 44; idem, *Parables in Midrash*, 188.

20. Stern, "Jesus' Parables from the Perspective of Rabbinic Literature," 45.

21. Stern, "Rhetoric and Midrash," 267; idem, *Parables in Midrash*, 21ff.

22. The most important collections and studies of the Tannaim remain those of Guttmann, "Das Masal-Gleichnis in tannaitischer Zeit," and Fiebig, *Altjüdische Gleichnisse und die Gleichnisse Jesu*, and idem, *Die Gleichnisreden Jesu im Lichte der rabbinischen Gleichnisse des neutestamentlichen Zeitalters*.

23. Stern, "Rhetoric and Midrash," 267.

24. Stern, *Parables in Midrash*, 20.

25. Stern criticizes Ignaz Ziegler, who, he says, did not recognize that the *meshalim* are "fictional narratives" (*Parables in Midrash*, 20; see also "Rhetoric and Midrash," n28).

26. This concept comes from medieval Jewish texts. See Stern, *Parables in Midrash*, 13.

27. Stern, "Jesus' Parables from the Perspective of Rabbinic Literature," 58.

28. Stern, *Parables in Midrash*, 94; see also chap. 4 above.

29. Ibid., 95.

30. Ibid., 99.

31. Wünsche, *Bibliotheca Rabbinica*, 46; English translation in Stern, *Parables in Midrash*, 99, 258 (*m. Echa Rabbati* 1:1).

32. Ibid., 100. Stern's explanation for this bizarre character as an expression of rabbinic anthropomorphism in God language is not persuasive, since this anthropomorphism, which Stern discusses in relation to other texts (apart from the royal parables) is quite different in its content. God laughs or weeps, mourns over Israel and over Godself; see Stern, "Imitatio Hominis," 151–74.

33. Deissmann spoke of a "polemical parallelism" between the imperial cult and the Christian cult (*Licht vom Osten*, 298). His remarks on the political context of fundamental Christian concepts are unsurpassed (esp. 298–324).

CHAPTER 10

1. Weinrich, *Sprache in Texten*, 276–341; see also Klauck, *Allegorie und Allegorese in synoptischen Gleichnistexten*, 141, and Erlemann, *Gleichnisauslegung*, 29–30. The traditional

definition of *metaphor* is not affected by different evaluations of metaphors as exact or inexact. Jülicher's devaluation of metaphors has not stood. For me, however, the key question in dealing with metaphors is that of the dualistic or non-dualistic relationship between the two levels.

2. Jülicher, *Die Gleichnisreden Jesu,* vol 1: *Die Gleichnisreden Jesu im Allgemeinen,* 53–54.

3. Erlemann, *Gleichnisauslegung,* 29

4. Klauck, *Allegorie und Allegorese in synoptischen Gleichnistexten,* 141–43, gives a succinct summary of the discussion of this concept; see also Theissen and Merz, *Der historische Jesus* (ET *The Historical Jesus),* 296.

5. Rabbi Hanina bar Hama in Flusser, *Die rabbinischen Gleichnisse und der Gleichniserzähler Jesu,* 25, *Midrash Teh.* on Ps 10:1 (in the edition by Salomon Buber, 92–93); there is a slightly different German translation in Wünsche, *Midrasch Tehillim,* 93–94.

6. Flusser, *Die rabbinischen Gleichnisse und der Gleichniserzähler Jesu,* 179, 25.

7. Ibid., 179.

8. Erlemann, *Gleichnisauslegung,* 55–58.

9. Ricoeur, "Stellung und Funktion," 70; Erlemann, *Gleichnisauslegung,* 29.

CHAPTER 11

1. See Stern, *Parables in Midrash,* 9–13; Donahue, *The Gospel in Parable,* 5.

2. The part of the parable that Thoma and Lauer call "novelty" in *Die Gleichnisse der Rabbinen* (see chap. 4 above), or the more frequent expression *"nimshal"* (see Stern, *Parables in Midrash,* 13), refers to the parable applications in rabbinic parables, which are just as much an integral part of the parables as the parable applications in the Jesus tradition. In the course of their development, their form has been unified. In the Synoptic Gospels they have not yet acquired a unified form.

CHAPTER 12

1. For further development of my disagreement with this thought model see L. Schottroff, *Lydia's Impatient Sisters,* 3–11.

2. Ricoeur, in Ebeling, Bar, and Ricoeur, *The Bible as Document of the University,* 68. Translation by L. Schottroff.

3. L. Schottroff, *Lydia's Impatient Sisters,* 3–11.

CHAPTER 13

1. Stern, *Parables in Midrash,* 102–51.

2. Ibid., 47.

3. Ibid.

CHAPTER 14

1. See, for example, Green, *Hearing the New Testament.* In his introductory chapter he uses the system "behind the text; in the text; in front of the text" (6–9), but this grouping, which is popular in North America, serves to disqualify historical criticism as "behind the text," in a way that is unjust. In the chapter of the book on hermeneutics (278–300) neither feminist hermeneutics nor liberation theology nor Jewish-Christian dialogue is considered.

2. See The Bible and Culture Collective, *The Postmodern Bible.*

3. For such books on method to list feminist and liberation-theological initiatives as further pearls on the string of methods represents a misunderstanding. These projects are

developing a different *hermeneutic* from mainline exegesis and not another method. They criticize mainline exegesis not because of its methods, but because of its hermeneutics. Let me mention as examples of this inappropriate ordering: Porter, *Handbook to Exegesis of the New Testament*; Green, *Hearing the New Testament*; and Oeming, *Biblische Hermeneutik*.

4. Yee's *Judges and Method* is an example of such a metacritique and synthesis of methods.

5. It is easy to find examples of brand new methods that use hoary old hermeneutical prejudices (e.g., anti-Judaism).

CHAPTER 15

1. Justin, *Apology* 1.67, 3-5, as translated in Richardson, *Early Christian Fathers*.

2. A sharp distinction between teaching and *kērygma* ("proclamation") is appropriate neither to the representation of Jesus in the Gospels themselves nor to the information we have about early Christian community assemblies; such a sharp distinction is also inappropriate between cult and teaching. For discussion of this see Beavis, *Mark's Audience*, esp. 45–67, although she gives priority to the Hellenistic cultural context and therefore interprets "seeing," "hearing," and "understanding" too little within the tradition of the First Testament as a change of life, practical repentance. I agree with her that Mark (and, I would add, the other Gospels as well) was intended also to reach a non-Christian audience.

3. See L. Schottroff, *Let the Oppressed Go Free*, 91–130; Tolbert, "When Resistance Becomes Repression," 331–46.

4. See L. Schottroff, "Das geschundene Volk und die Arbeiter in der Ernte Gottes nach dem Matthäusevangelium," 149–206.

5. See, for example, Esler, *Community and Gospel in Luke-Acts*.

CHAPTER 16

1. In v. 32 the possessive pronoun refers to the mustard seed, although what must be intended is the bush that has grown from the seed. Is the reference here to the "tree" to which the parallel possessive pronoun in Luke 13:18 and Matt 13:32 refers?

2. Dalman, *Arbeit und Sitte in Palästina*, 2:293.

3. Royle, "On the Identification of the Mustard Tree of Scripture," 136–37:

> In conclusion, it appears to me, that taking everything into consideration, *Salvadora persica* appears better calculated than any other tree that has yet been adduced to answer to everything that is required, especially if we take into account its name and the opinions held respecting it in Syria. We have in it a small seed, which, sown in cultivated ground, grows up and abounds in foliage. This being pungent, may, like the seeds, have been used as a condiment, as mustard and cress is with us. The nature of the plant, however, is to become arboreous, and thus it will form a large shrub, or a tree, twenty-five feet high, under which a horseman may stand, when the soil and climate are favorable. It produces numerous branches and leaves, among which birds may and do take shelter, as well as build their nests.

4. For example, see Wilken, *Biblisches Erleben im Heiligen Land*, 1:108:

> As we were watering our mounts at the well, my eyes fell on a garden in which a number of leafy plants with large, broad leaves were growing. These were between 2.6 and 3 meters tall. Many tiny birds, like finches, were flying out from the shade of the leaves and, after quickly snaring insects, returning swiftly be-

neath them again. Since I had not previously seen such strikingly tall plants in the Holy Land, I inquired and heard, to my astonishment, that these mighty bushes had grown from mustard seeds, the smallest type of seed in the Holy Land.

This size for a mustard bush cannot be corroborated by reference to the description of mustard in the relevant books on biology (e.g., see Zohary and Feinbrunn-Dothan, *Flora Palaestina*, 309–12: the maximum is about two meters tall).

5. Donahue and Harrington, *The Gospel of Mark*, 152: "comic irony."

6. Jeremias, *The Parables of Jesus*, 149. For the interpretive models of liberal theology (development) and dialectical theology (contrast) see Theissen, "Der Bauer und die von selbst Frucht bringende Erde," 167–82. For theological biology see Stuhlmann, "Beobachtungen und Überlegungen zu Markus 4,26-29," 153–62.

7. On this see especially Stuhlmann, "Beobachtungen," 161–62; he shows that the allusion here is not to the Septuagint version, but to the Masoretic text.

8. See *Pesiq. Rab Kah.* 3b on Joel 3 [4]:19 (quoted on pp. 43–44 above) and the Targum of Joel 3 [4]:13, 19: "Put the *sword into them, for the time of their end has arrived; go down and tread their warrior dead like grapes that are trodden in the winepress; pour out their blood,* for their wickedness is great" (Targum to Joel 4:13, *The Targum of the Minor Prophets*, 72–73; the italicized words indicate changes from the Masoretic text). The divine judgment of the nations is directed primarily at their armies.

9. See, for example, Gnilka, *Das Evangelium nach Markus*, 1:184.

10. Gebara, "The Face of Transcendence as a Challenge to the Reading of the Bible in Latin America," 172–86.

11. See Metternich, *"Sie sagte ihm die ganze Wahrheit"* and her interpretation of the miracle stories in the Gospels.

12. See 1 Cor 11:24, *eucharistesas*, Mark 14:22, *eulogesas*, and the parallels in Matthew and Luke. Janssen, *Eschatologie und Gegenwart*, presents good arguments for reading 1 Cor 15:39-41 as praise of creation.

13. For example, Marcus, *Mark 1–8*, 326: "ultimate success." There is a collection of interpretations of this type throughout the history of interpretation in Theissen, "Der Bauer," 172–73.

14. Marcus, *Mark 1–8*, 331.

15. Jeremias, *The Parables of Jesus*, 152.

CHAPTER 17

1. Regarding my translation see the "Eschatological Interpretation" section in this chapter.

2. Dalman, *Arbeit und Sitte in Palästina*, 1:379.

3. Marquardt, *Das Privatleben der Römer*, 1:137–53, presents an overview of the specializations in slaves' work; see also Paoli, *Das Leben im alten Rom*, 144–45. Inscriptions from the grave monument of the Volusii Saturnini on the Via Appia also show this specialization, in this case, that of the slaves of a senatorial family in the first century c.e. (See Eck and Heinrichs, *Sklaven und Freigelassene in der Gesellschaft der Römischen Kaiserzeit*, 52–58.) For a corresponding picture of slavery in Plautus see Spranger, *Historische Untersuchungen zu den Sklavenfiguren des Plautus und Terenz*, 76–82.

4. See translation in Ludwig, *Antike Komödien*, 390ff. (II, 3).

5. Ibid., 81 (*Asinaria*, 424ff.).

6. Wengst, *Das Johannesevangelium*, 2:207–8 (with sources).

7. Plautus, *Asinaria,* 429–30 (see translation in Ludwig, *Antike Komödien*).

8. For example, Donahue and Harrington, *Gospel of Mark,* 375: "In this context 'he' as a reference to the Son of Man seems to be the most obvious subject." See the extensive remarks on this in Pesch, *Naherwartungen,* 180, 200.

9. Joel 2:10 refers to an army sent by God, surpassing all imaginable horrors: "The earth quakes before them, the heavens tremble. The sun and the moon are darkened, and the stars withdraw their shining"; see also Joel 3:15. Targum Joel 2:10: "Before them the earth *is laid waste,* the heavens shake; the sun and the moon are darkened." "Them" refers to "armed men" in 2:9. Cathcart and Gordon, *The Targum of the Minor Prophets.*

10. For the concept I am using see chap. 3 and chap. 8 above.

11. Jeremias, *The Parables of Jesus,* 55; Pesch, *Naherwartungen,* 198.

12. France, *The Gospel of Mark,* 545; Gnilka, *Das Evangelium nach Markus,* 2: 210; Moloney, *The Gospel of Mark,* 268, for the Markan text.

13. Jülicher, *Die Gleichnisreden Jesu,* 169. This judgment has dominated the discussion ever since.

CHAPTER 18

1. "Son of God" in Mark's gospel reflects Jesus' assignment from God (see only the scenes of the baptism and transfiguration), but does not give him a christological "title" that separates him from other children of God. Favoring a translation of "son of God" as "child of God" is that the latter word includes women, but against it is that it is not clear that it includes adults. "Man" of God may better permit the association that there are also women of God. "Son" of God has become very inflexible because of its role in christological tradition.

2. On this see especially Beavis, *Mark's Audience.*

CHAPTER 19

1. For *nomikoi* ("teachers of the Law" or "Torah scholars") see Schürer, *The History of the Jewish People in the Age of Jesus Christ,* 2, §25, 2; Gutbrod, "*nomikos,*" 4:1088. The Greek word *nomikos* is also used in rabbinic writings, according to Krauss (*Talmudische Archäologie,* 169) to make it clear that the "teachers of the law" were comparable to teachers of Roman public law.

2. The moral and theological disqualification of the Torah scholar is common in Bible translations and interpretations. Exceptions include Klinghardt, *Gesetz und Volk Gottes,* 32: The Torah scholar "indicates his soteriologically-significant membership in the chosen people"—which is then set aside by Jesus through the figure of the Samaritan. Klinghardt tries not to read v. 29 in a discriminatory fashion (see 147). Clearer is Ebach's suggestion that the text be read as an expression of the scholar's justified interest in defending his question "in order to give a basis for the action of moving from universal love of neighbor to concrete love of neighbor" (Ebach, "Sozialgeschichtliche Bibelauslegung [zu Lukas 10,25-37]," 429).

3. The shifting of the word *neighbor* from the object of love (vv. 27, 29) to its subject (v. 36) should not be overemphasized, as though v. 29 were criticized in v. 37. The question in v. 29 is to be taken seriously in the sense of the text, and v. 37 is the answer to the question. The relationship between giver and receiver is repeatedly interpreted in Jewish tradition as one of mutuality, changing both parties. For example: "It was taught in the name of R. Joshua, 'More [good] than the householder does for the poor person, the poor person does for the householder" (*Lev. Rab.* 34; Wünsche, *Bibliotheca Rabbinica,* 5:240; see also Neusner, *Judaism and Scripture,* 566).

4. In rabbinic interpretation the *Shemaʿ Israel* is not restricted to an internal attitude; one's whole existence, including the material side of one's life, is included. Deuteronomy

6:5, "with all your strength," is interpreted this way in the Mishnah (*m. Ber.* 9:5, "with all you possess"), and this interpretation remains constant in many other exegeses; see, for example, *Sifre Deuteronomium* on Deut 6:5 (see Bietenhard, *Sifre Deuteronomium, übersetzt und erklärt von Hans Bietenhard*). There is a collection of materials in Gerhardsson, *The Testing of God's Son,* 71–76; see also chap. 7 above on Mark 4:1-34.

5. Wikenhauser, "Die Liebeswerke in dem Gerichtsgemälde Mt 25:31-46," 366–77; Billerbeck, *Kommentar zum Neuen Testament aus Talmud und Midrasch* 4:1, 536–610.

6. The Greek word here, *eleēmosynē,* a translation of the Hebrew word *ṣĕdākâ,* is usually translated as "alms." But that is too narrow a translation and does not maintain the connection between doing good and righteousness that exists both in the First Testament and in Judaism; see Reimer, *Women in the Acts of the Apostles,* 38–39.

7. *Lev. Rab.* §34; Wünsche, *Bibliotheca Rabbinica* 5:234; Neusner, *Judaism and Scripture,* 556.

8. *Lev. Rab.* §34; Wünsche, *Bibliotheca Rabbinica* 5:240; Neusner, *Judaism and Scripture,* 566–67.

9. Ebach, "Sozialgeschichtliche Bibelauslegung zu Lukas 10:25-37." Among attempts to drain the text of the hackneyed and taken-for-granted character it has acquired in Christianity, the remarks of Jacques Debout are especially worth reading:

> I confess that I have never considered imitating the merciful Samaritan. Instead, I have to admit that in my eyes this parable needs an explanation that will weaken its thrust. One would wish that some preacher or other would say that the Lord spoke rather strongly here, for pedagogical reasons, or that exegesis has pointed out to us that here the Vulgate translation is somewhat freer than elsewhere, and one must attribute much—in fact, most of it—to the Eastern style of exaggeration. First of all, this Samaritan is a kind of heretic, or at least a schismatic. He has no right to give a lesson in humanity to a Levite, certainly not to a priest. If the Levite and the priest passed by, they had good reasons for doing so. The Samaritan, on the other hand, seems to be a hothead. He doesn't even think twice before he goes to help the dying man. "The wise are known by their reservation," and there is no trace of that in him. I can't help thinking that he has muddied and dishonored the true notion of love of neighbor, because he surrounds it with not a trace of caution and consequently with no respect. When love of neighbor becomes instinctive, it is a very dangerous form of anarchy. This case of the Samaritan smells like communism. After all, whom is he supporting? The first one who comes along, without any kind of previous acquaintance. The first one he finds, somebody left half dead by robbers. That dying man might be a robber himself; maybe some more honorable robbers beat him up because they had a shred of conscience left. Maybe he was a quarrelsome guy or one of those careless types who risk their lives to save their money; maybe he was a bum or a sleepwalker. What was he doing when the robbers came along? I have always found that the victims of an attack are not worth much. Good people don't go out much, they don't carry much money, but they do carry a weapon. They only go to places where the police are walking the beat. This character the Good Samaritan helped was rash, in any case. And even if he had been a teacher of Israel, the one offering him help would have had to make sure of it beforehand. If better gentlemen acted like the good Samaritan, love of neighbor would just encourage people to sin and idleness, the parents of poverty. The Samaritan was not even smart enough to be satisfied with a small contribution or a kind word. He treats just any unknown person as if he were his own brother. He bestows companionship on someone who is useless, if not in fact a pest, certainly a

weakling, possibly even a revolutionary element. And it costs him time, oil, and wine, when the cost of living is so high. He puts the sick man on his horse and he himself walks, like the farmer in the fable. There are some people who just spoil everything; this one spoils love of neighbor. Besides, we have to suppose that the Samaritan is neglecting his civil or familial obligations in order to permit himself such extravagances. I'll bet that he was late to work. So he was deceiving his boss, just as he had fooled the innkeeper, leaving him stuck with an unknown, wounded man, probably filthy and full of vermin—not to mention that he was taking money from his own children and his heirs that belonged to them. I know he saved somebody from dying, but I wonder if that is enough of an excuse! (Debout, "Vernünftige Kritik des barmherzigen Samaritans," 48ff.).

10. The article on love of neighbor in Billerbeck (*Kommentar zum Neuen Testament aus Talmud und Midrasch,* 1:353–68) has probably been especially influential in spreading this anti-Jewish cliché: "It therefore seems established that the first one who taught humankind to see the 'neighbor' in every person and therefore to encounter every person in love was Jesus; see the narrative of the merciful Samaritan" (1:354).

11. The question of whether it is possible to find Jewish texts that link Deut 6:5 and Lev 19:18 has remained on a formal level that does not do justice to Jewish discussion of this theme. Flusser ("A New Sensitivity in Judaism and Christian Message") offers a good basis for a less exclusion-oriented discussion, and some of the new commentaries on Luke 10:27 work in the same direction (e.g., Nolland, *Luke 9:21–18:34*; Bovon, *Das Evangelium nach Lukas*).

12. Even if the Greek word *antiparerchomai* cannot be translated univocally (one possibility would be "pass by in the other direction"), it is clear in the context that it means the priest and Levite went on without stopping.

13. For example, see Böhm, *Samarien und die Samaritai bei Lukas,* 252, 256.

14. For a collection of positive and negative material about priests, see Billerbeck, *Kommentar zum Neuen Testament aus Talmud und Midrasch,* esp. 2:182–83.

15. See chap. 1 above.

16. See Böhm, *Samarien und die Samaritai.*

17. Böhm, *Samarien und die Samaritai,* 255–60: The Samaritan is associated with membership in the Gerizim community. It is rather improbable that he would have been regarded as a member of a mixed, syncretistic people. Böhm gives good reasons for interpreting the Samaritan not as a member of a hated alien people but as representative of a different interpretation of the Torah that had led to conflicts between Jews and Samaritans. She discusses the relevant material in detail.

18. For oil alleviating pain see Krauss, *Talmudische Archäologie,* 1:234; for wine (to disinfect?) see Bovon, *Evangelium,* 91n44. For the treatment of wounds see also Aus, *Weihnachtsgeschichte, barmherziger Samariter, verlorener Sohn,* 103–6.

19. Klemm, *Das Gleichnis vom Barmherzigen Samariter,* 20; Monselewski, *Der barmherzige Samariter,* 36–37.

CHAPTER 20

1. BAGD, *dei* 6a [BDAG 2c] on the imperfect *edei* restricts this use of the imperfect to a past event. That is neither grammatically necessary (see Blass, Debrunner, and Rehkopf, *Grammatik des neutestamentlichen Griechish,* §358,2), nor does it make sense in the context. The feast is not yet over; the son is supposed to join in it.

2. Holgate, *Prodigality, Liberality and Meanness in the Parable of the Prodigal Son.*

3. Pöhlmann, *Der Verlorene Sohn und das Haus.*

4. Wartenberg-Potter, "Über die Frage, ob der Verlorene Sohn eine Halbwaise war," 30–34.

5. Deut 21:17 presupposes that the firstborn will receive a portion double that given to subsequent sons.

6. Holgate, *Prodigality, Liberality and Meanness,* 134, reads Luke 15:12 in the context of Hellenistic moral instruction against greed and interprets the younger son's petition as "motivated by avarice." But I can see no basis for this either in the narrative or in the legal context; so also Pöhlmann, *Der Verlorene Sohn,* 200. It is an old tradition to interpret the son's petition as a rebellion against his father.

7. German "Abschichtung." Daube, "Inheritance in two Lucan Pericopes," *Zeitschrift der Savigny-Stiftung für Rechtsgeschichte,* 326–34; for detailed discussion see most recently Pöhlmann, "Die Abschichtung des Verlorenen Sohnes (Lk 15,12f.), und die erzählte Welt der Parabel," 194–213.

8. Pöhlmann, "Abschichtung," 213, in criticizing, among other things, one of my essays ("Das Gleichnis vom verlorenen Sohn," 27–52); however, neither then nor now did I evaluate the relationship to the legal context and conditions in a way that genuinely deviates from Pöhlmann's thesis. The text establishes associations with legal circumstances, but it is not consistently interested in presenting those circumstances.

9. Pöhlmann, *Der Verlorene Sohn,* 131.

10. Pöhlmann, "Abschichtung," 210n68.

11. Holgate (*Prodigality, Liberality and Meanness*) attempts to read Luke 15:11-32 this way (see n6 above), but neither his description of the decline nor the association with moral teachings against greed can be plausibly explained. The motivation for this interpretation is suggested by the title of the parable in English, "The Prodigal Son," which, however, does not do justice to the parable itself. I consider the title "The Lost Son" more appropriate.

12. The Greek word at this point, *kollasthai,* can have a sexual connotation (see Mark 10:7), but the narrative does not point that way. The special relationship of dependency on a citizen as described by the text do not fit with normal day labor. Since the young man is neither a slave nor a freedman, it seems to me that a client–patron relationship is the most adequate explanation; see Friedländer, *Darstellungen aus der Sittengeschichte Roms in der Zeit von Augustus bis zum Ausgang der Antonine,* vol. 1, chap. 3, IV §5; Marquardt, *Privatleben,* 1:200–201.

13. For the dishonorable character of the job of shepherd or herdsman see L. Schottroff, "Das geschundene Volk und die Arbeiter in der Ernte Gottes nach dem Matthäusevangelium," 194–96.

14. That as a swineherd he was cultically impure is given as a further reason for his dishonor. But if that were so, it would mean little to the young man at such a distance from the Jerusalem Temple. Impurity should no longer be misinterpreted as social isolation.

15. See Billerbeck, *Kommentar zum Neuen Testament aus Talmud und Midrasch.*

16. Verses 15 and 18 here use the verb *poreuein* ("go, travel," but also of personal conduct, "live, walk").

17. "Heaven" as a circumlocution for God, as often in Judaism and in Matthew's gospel. The text presupposes Jewish identities both in the story as told and among the audience—which does not exclude the possibility that they were of non-Jewish origin. Reverence for the name of God is important in the text.

18. Holgate (*Prodigality, Liberality and Meanness,* 146, and frequently elsewhere) does not distinguish adequately between *pleonexia* ("greed") and *asōtia* ("debauchery"), which,

when it refers to money, precisely does *not* mean greed, that is, increase of property, but its loss.

19. Deissmann, *Licht vom Osten* (ET *Light from the Ancient East*), 153–58.

20. Ibid. I have omitted the symbols in the text that show where words are incomplete.

21. See the collection of material on "death" and "life" in the moral vocabulary of Hellenism in Holgate, *Prodigality, Liberality and Meanness,* 161–64. He attributes the juxtaposition of "lost" and "found" to the link between Luke 15:11-32 and 15:3-7, 8-10. I would add that it is based on the metaphor "lost sheep" of the house of Israel; see the eschatological interpretation of Luke 15:11-32 and the exegesis of Luke 15:3-7. I doubt that the death–life contrast is to be read morally, and I see it as an expression of the father's pain and joy.

22. *Pesiqta Rabbati* 44; English translation in Braude, *Pesikta Rabbati,* 2:779; Young, *The Parables,* 151; McArthur and Johnston, *They Also Taught in Parables,*195.

23. *Deuteronomium Rabba* 2:24 on Deut 4:30; Billerbeck, *Kommentar zum Neuen Testament aus Talmud und Midrasch,* 2:216; English translation in Young, *The Parables,* 148–49; McArthur and Johnston, *They Also Taught in Parables.*

24. Jeremias, *The Parables of Jesus,* 130.

25. See the letter quoted above at nn19–20.

26. For clothing as representative of status see Wilckens, "*stolē,*" 7:689; Holgate, *Prodigality, Liberality and Meanness,* 216; Marquardt, *Privatleben* 2:552–53.

27. For the signet ring see Fitzer, "*sphragis, ktl.,*" 7:939–53.

28. See n8 above.

29. Holgate, *Prodigality, Liberality and Meanness,* 136ff.

30. Reimer, *Women in the Acts of the Apostles,* 11–12.

31. Pöhlmann, "Abschichtung," 213, and frequently elsewhere.

32. Holgate, *Prodigality, Liberality and Meanness,* 168–91.

33. Luke 14:18-20; 17:27-28; see chap. 5 above for the eschatological interpretation of 14:12-24.

34. The verb is in the imperfect tense.

35. For the vagueness of v. 31, see above.

36. Pöhlmann (*Der Verlorene Sohn,* 16) rejects such a "didactic" interpretation of the open conclusion, which he thinks instead underscores the collision of the patriarchal order, embodied in the protest of the elder brother, with God's order, embodied in the father's action. Against this interpretation I object not only that the father does not embody God, but also that all the parables are part of a partly unwritten dialogue, as has often been shown.

37. See L. Schottroff, "Das Gleichnis vom verlorenen Sohn"; Rau, *Reden in Vollmacht,* 252–71; Berger and Colpe, *Religionsgeschichtliches Textbuch zum Neuen Testament,* 137–39; see also Boring, Berger, and Colpe, *Hellenistic Commentary to the New Testament,* 224–25; Erlemann, *Gleichnisauslegung,* 283.

38. All examples are from *Pesikta Rabbati* 44 in Braude, *Pesikta Rabbati* 1:771, 776, 772.

39. See, e.g., Seneca, *De ira* XXIII, 3-4; see above on Matt 22:1-14.

40. Ziegler, *Die Königsgleichnisse des Midrasch beleuchtet durch die römische Kaiserzeit* has a section (XI) called "Die Söhne und Töchter der Kaiser," which offers a rich lode of material.

41. Rau, *Reden in Vollmacht,* 252–71; Young, *The Parables,* 148–149. Rabbinic parallels to Luke 15:11-32 are also considered, for example, in Billerbeck, *Kommentar zum Neuen Testament aus Talmud und Midrasch,* 2:216; McArthur and Johnston, *They Also Taught in Parables,* 194–95; Oesterley, *The Gospel Parables in the Light of Their Jewish Background,* 183–91; Berger and Colpe, *Religionsgeschichtliches Textbuch,* 137–40; and Boring, Berger, and Colpe, *Hellenistic Commentary,* 225–26.

42. For example, the rabbis tell fables in the style of Aesop. Hellenistic-Roman culture was dominant for centuries and influenced both Jewish culture and the beginnings of Christianity. Jewish and Hellenistic-Roman literatures are relevant for the New Testament and are interwoven in multiple ways. The discussion, of parables in particular, is still too much dominated by either/or thinking. Nevertheless, we may say that rabbinic parables, despite the fact that most of them originated later, provide the closest parallels to Jesus' parables, as regards both the parable form and the content.

43. Permit me a note of my own: In 1971 I was working with the question, What is the relationship of Luke 15 to the soteriology of the whole Lukan corpus? I came to the conclusion that Luke was the author of 15:11-32. I have been thoroughly criticized for this. Now the critique has lost its target, because in the meantime it has become commonplace to read the texts in their literary context, in this case the Gospel of Luke, thanks to the rise of literary-critical methods. For the question of the relationship of the existing texts to the "historical" Jesus see chap. 12 above. Today I am even more convinced than I was then that the existing texts are anchored in a vital orality. Consequently I have become more cautious about regarding a single person as their "author." Now, as then, I consider the congruence in content between Luke 15:11-32 and the Gospel of Luke to be quite clear, but my ideas about the soteriology and eschatology in the Lukan corpus, and in the Synoptic Gospels as a whole, have changed.

44. "What they should do with him" (Luke 6:11) is usually translated negatively: "what they should do to him" or the like. See also BDAG on *poein*, 4b, "to someone's advantage, and 4c, "to someone's disadvantage.") But the verb can also be used neutrally or positively. If the negative sense were so clear, the anti-Jewish Codex D would not have had to change the text here: "how they might destroy him" (see also Mark 3:6).

45. Here (Luke 7:31), as in Luke 19:7, the conflict between Jesus and the Pharisees is generalized; it is not only Pharisees who are included.

46. Deut 21:20 lxx is clearer about the negative connotation of such accusations. Luke 7:34 clearly implies a negative evaluation of Jesus' behavior, but the translation "glutton and drunkard" is not accurate.

47. For the depiction of the Pharisees in the Gospel of Luke see, for example, Ziesler, "Luke and the Pharisees," 146–57; Carroll, "Luke's Portrayal of the Pharisees," 604–21; Saldarini, *Pharisees, Scribes, and Sadducees in Palestinian Society.*

48. Luke 22:2, 66; 23:10. But this group of *nomikoi* or *grammateis* ("experts in the law, scribes") are not all portrayed in a negative light, despite Jesus' generalizing critique of *nomikoi* ("teachers of the Law") in 11:45-52. In Luke 10:25-37 one of these teachers of the Law becomes a pupil of Jesus.

49. This connotation, that grumbling against Jesus' deeds is interpreted as grumbling against the will of God, seems to me to be possible here; see, for example, 7:29. In that case the rejection of the Baptizer's baptism of repentance is being interpreted by Jesus as a rejection of the divine will. The conflict with the Pharisees must be healed if the people is to be healed.

50. Other interpretations come to the conclusion that the Lukan Jesus did not associate any call to repentance with his eschatological message. The preaching of repentance does not exclude the possibility that Jesus' companionship with sinners did not require their prior repentance, but promises them healing and the forgiveness of their sins. See below on Luke 7:36-50.

51. See especially Luke 1:6; 2:25; 23:50; Acts 10:22.

52. I no longer interpret them as hypocrites (L. Schottroff, "Das Gleichnis vom ver-lorenen Sohn," 70); instead, I see an interpretation like that of Bovon as more appropriate:

"The sheep that was lost and found again draws the whole herd with it into its fate. Jesus was certainly thinking of the people . . ." (Bovon, *Das Evangelium nach Lukas,* 3:29, on Luke 15:7).

53. Here let me refer in general to E. P. Sanders, and especially to his important book *Jesus and Judaism* (174–211). He considers the idea that *all* Pharisees before 70 c.e. practiced priestly purification of food in daily life (see chap. 19 above on Luke 18:9-14) to be only half right; this was done by a small group, the *haberim,* who also may have belonged to the larger group of the Pharisees. For the discussion between Neusner and Sanders on this question see Sanders, "Jesus and the Sinners," 14 and n31, and Neusner, *From Politics to Piety,* 80, 83; idem, *Das pharisäische und talmudische Judentum,* 43–51. I cannot decide this question, but I consider Sanders's position and especially his critique of the Christian interpretation of the conflict between Jesus and the Pharisees a fundamental new orientation to this question: The Pharisees roundly criticized Jesus' association with toll collectors and sinners, but from this perspective "sinners" are people who deliberately and over time violate the Torah; they are not the "poor" or *amme ha 'aretz* ("the ordinary people"). The Pharisees were not at this time a group who were able to exclude anyone from society and they also had no reason to exclude the *amme ha 'aretz,* whom they by no means regarded as sinners. For the idea of repentance in Sanders's concept, see Choi, *Jesus' Teaching on Repentance.*

54. That the woman is unclean and Jesus should therefore not let himself be touched by her is a Christian misinterpretation of Jewish notions of purity. That the Pharisee criticizes her erotic approach to Jesus may be an exaggeration. In any case, this touching and the criticism of it belong together with Jesus' table companionship with toll collectors and sinners, who symbolize the eschatological community of the people of God—without the sinners' having renounced their way of life as violation of Torah.

55. The discussion about whether repentance precedes grace in this instance, or grace precedes repentance, has its background in later Christian dogmatics. The text itself says both (7:47) and is not interested in the alternative: see L. Schottroff, *Let the Oppressed Go Free,* 138–57.

56. Stories about communities of healing and communities of sinners are to be read as call stories. "Go in peace" in Luke 7:50 would be cynical if Jesus was thereby dismissing the woman to the hard life of a prostitute. The Gospels presuppose the existence of Christian communities and a praxis in those communities that produces a solidary common life.

57. The palsied man is also, according to Luke, in need of healing and is suffering. He is not a sinner in some sense defined especially by his sickness.

58. See above at Luke 18:9-14.

59. That the Gospel of Luke presents an apologetic on behalf of Rome is a misinterpretation that is regularly traced to Conzelmann's 1954 book, *Die Mitte der Zeit* (ET *The Theology of St. Luke*). In *Jesus, Politics, and Society,* Cassidy has developed an alternative that is more commonly advocated today; see Janssen, *Elisabet und Hanna—zwei widerständige Frauen in neutestamentlicher Zeit:* Luke 1:2 anticipates the point of view of the Gospel of Luke as a whole, cannot be separated from the whole gospel, and is a politically oriented text.

60. For the history of interpretation of Luke 15:11-32 see Antoine et al., *Exegesis* (ET *Exegesis*); Wright, *Studies in the Interpretation of Six Gospel Parables.* The interpretation of the younger son as Christ in contrast to Judaism or as model of the justification of sinners in contrast to Jewish or Pharisaic Torah piety, or religion of deeds, goes back to the premodern period and is still common enough in the postmodern era. One exception is Young, *The Parables,* who sees the two sons as two "types of sinners" (156), although in doing so he has not ceased to allegorize.

61. The uneasiness that still comes over some interpreters when they interpret the slave-owner or king in parables as God usually gives way, in the case of Luke 15:11-32, to satisfaction in being able to identify God with a loving father. It is only in those associated with the new women's movement that this identification is seen as problematic; see above at n4. For the rabbinic tradition the distinction between a flesh-and-blood father and God is a matter of course. It should finally begin to be practiced in the reading of Luke 15:11-32 too. Jülicher (*Die Gleichnisreden Jesu*), keeping faith with his concept, sees the father as a patriarch and not as a representation of God (2:334), but in his interpretation the old identification creeps back in: "Like the father of two sons . . . so the way to God's fatherly heart, even for the most corrupt sinner . . . is always open . . . though this does not mean that the righteous are in any way neglected" (2:362).

62. Levine, "Matthew, Mark, and Luke: Good News or Bad?" 96.

63. See the material in the collections listed in n41 above.

64. *Deuteronomy Rabbah* II, 3:24. "So also the hand of God is always open to receive the penitent" (translated in Wünsche, *Bibliotheca Rabbinica*, 3:25)

65. Beavis ("'Making Up Stories'") reads Luke 15:11-32 from the perspective of a victim of incest. By this she is not saying that the intention of the text is to portray the lost son as the victim of the father's sexual abuse, but only that the story can be read this way by those who are such victims. But the question her essay suggests must be raised: Why can the parable be read that way? My answer is that it is because the father in the parable has a position of absolute power with respect to his sons.

66. Brecht, *Gesammelte Werke*, 11:49–51 (English: Willett and Manheim, "The Foolish Wife," 19–21).

67. Jülicher has already discussed the biblical material on this estimation (*Die Gleichnisreden Jesu*, 2:316). The Bible can be used without alteration as a handbook for nomadic and non-nomadic care of small animals. Derrett ("Fresh Light on the Lost Sheep and the Lost Coin," 36–60) rightly points to Matt 12:11-12 as a social-historical parallel to Luke 15:4-6 for the rescue of animals from danger. For the social situation of shepherds see L. Schottroff, "Das geschundene Volk," 194–95.

68. On this see Derrett, "Fresh Light on the Lost Sheep and the Lost Coin," 40; L. Schottroff, "Das geschundene Volk," 194.

69. As, for example, in Num 27:17; Jer 50:6; Mark 6:34; Matt 10:6.

70. See Billerbeck, *Kommentar zum Neuen Testament aus Talmud und Midrasch*, 2:209; Luz, *Das Evangelium nach Matthäus*, 3:27n20.

71. "The sheep lost and refound draws the whole flock with it into its fate. Jesus was certainly thinking of the nation, which was so dear to his heart, when he concerned himself primarily with the outcasts" (Bovon, *Das Evangelium nach Lukas*, 3:29–30). He correctly names this dimension of the text, which is often overlooked.

72. The majority of Greek manuscripts have here "if she loses a drachma." My translation is directed at making the text understandable in a modern language.

73. The text says "before" or "in the presence of."

74. See the critique of this tradition of interpretation in Maloney, "'Swept under the Rug,'" 34–38.

75. Jülicher, *Die Gleichnisreden Jesu*, 2:315. "PLUMM." refers to Plummer, *A Critical and Exegetical Commentary on the Gospel According to St Luke*.

76. See the detailed discussion in L. Schottroff, *Lydia's Impatient Sisters*, 91–100, including a critique of the interpretation of the ten drachmas as a bridal portion or household allowance.

77. See Krauss, *Talmudische Archäologie* 3:22.

78. *Shir ha-Shirin Rabba* on 1:1 (translation from Berger and Colpe, *Religionsgeschichtliches Textbuch,* 136–37). Another translation is in Wünsche, *Bibliotheca Rabbinica,* 2:6.

79. See the materials from *b. Erubin* 21b and the Midrash on Song of Songs 1:1 in Billerbeck, *Kommentar zum Neuen Testament aus Talmud und Midrasch,* 1:653–54.

80. The introduction to the parable of the lost son in 15:11 is linked by "and he said . . ." to the preceding parables with their questions to the listeners.

CHAPTER 21

1. See n. 10 to chap. 22 below. Beavis, "Ancient Slavery as an Interpretive Context for the New Testament Servant Parables with Special Reference to the Unjust Steward (Luke 16:1-8)," 49 argues for the proposition that the unjust manager in Luke 16:1-8 is a slave. Given the ability of the manager to plan his own future, I think it is probable that he is not a slave; on this see also Glancy, *Slavery in Early Christianity,* 108–9.

2. The verb *diaballō* in v. 1 can also be understood in the sense of a false accusation. Then he would have been accused of a betrayal that he, ironically, only begins to commit as a consequence of the accusation (Kloppenborg, "The Dishonoured Master [Luke 16:1-8a]," 487–88). But the narrative or its interpretation is not interested in freeing him from suspicion. He is the subject of a hostile accusation in v. 1, but rightly so; on this, see BDAG 226.

3. Derrett, "Fresh Light on St Luke XVI," 216. In contrast, Kloppenborg ("The Dishonoured Master," 483) objects persuasively that the amount forgiven is much greater than the usual interest. There is a variant in Fitzmyer, *The Gospel according to Luke,* 1,101: The amount the manager subtracts is his commission. But the wording of v. 5, "what do you owe my master?" speaks against this supposition, as does the evidence of ancient bills, which include no commission or other provision for agents (Kloppenborg, "The Dishonoured Master," 481).

4. See the materials in Reimer, *Women in the Acts of the Apostles,* 147–48n292.

5. Kloppenborg, "The Dishonoured Master," like many others, regards v. 8a as part of the parable narrative; that is, the *kyrios* is the rich man, who praises the treacherous manager. His arguments, which must be taken seriously: vv. 1-7 are incomplete, and v. 8a is a "narrative swerve" (477). Here the rich man steps beyond the cultural code that forces him to defend his honor (492) and renounces vengeance, in the sense of Luke 6:29. Against this interpretation is that in vv. 8b-13, which Kloppenborg regards as secondary from a literary standpoint; there is no reference to this surprise. Verse 8b already presumes that it is Jesus who is speaking in v. 8a. Even if I isolate the parable from its interpretation beginning in v. 8b, thus reconstructing a hypothetical original version, v. 8a would not be a meaningful narrative surprise or "swerve" if it is not explained. Moreover, other parable narratives also have open endings; see, e.g., Luke 15:32.

6. W. Schottroff, "Das Gleichnis von den bösen Weingärtnern (Mk 12:1-9 parr.)," 18–48.

7. See the materials in L. Schottroff, "Schuldschein," 528; Kloppenborg, "The Dishonoured Master," 490n53. Examples from Murabaat (original texts with German translations) are found in Koffmahn, *Die Doppelurkunden aus der Wüste Juda.*

8. The Greek word primarily refers to wheat, but can also mean other grains.

9. Kloppenborg, "The Dishonoured Master," 482, estimates the quantity of wheat as "a half-share rent for almost 200 acres" = "twenty times the size of an average family plot." The quantity of oil (3,500 litres) corresponds to "a very large olive grove." There is a similar estimate in Jeremias, *The Parables of Jesus,* 181. See also Ezra 7:22. For the statements of quantity in the Babatha archive, which support these estimates, see Broshi, "Agriculture and Economy in Roman Palestine," 234–35.

10. Krauss, *Talmudische Archäologie*, 2:370; Ben-David, *Talmudische Ökonomie*, 1:193–96.

11. For a survey of commerce in the Roman empire see Shelton, *As the Romans Did*, 125–37.

12. Cicero, *Pro Fonteio* 11; Shelton, *As the Romans Did*, 135.

13. Aristides, *Roman Discourse* 11-13; Shelton, *As the Romans Did*, 136.

14. Bailey, *Poet and Peasant and Through Peasant Eyes*, 99–100 (*Poet and Peasant*). Kloppenborg's view is somewhat different: on this see n5 above.

15. L. Schottroff, "Die Befreiung vom Götzendienst der Habgier," 149.

16. "Make friends with unrighteous mammon" does not recommend giving alms, but more extensive economic solidarity. Friendship is a basic model for societies in that period. It includes both personal relationships and social duties for the stabilization of the life of those befriended; on this see especially Hezser, "Rabbis and Other Friends: Friendship in the Talmud Yerushalmi and in Graeco-Roman Literature," 189–254.

17. Mineshige (*Besitzverzicht und Almosen bei Lukas*, 118–19) wishes to see the description of renunciation of possessions and celibacy in the two-volume Lukan work as restricted to the time of Jesus. For people who consider themselves the community of Jesus' followers, such a historicizing treatment of Jesus traditions is unimaginable. See, with somewhat more refinement, Phillips, *Reading Issues of Wealth and Poverty in Luke-Acts*, 180–82.

18. See only the title of Mineshige's book ("Renunciation of Possessions and Almsgiving in Luke"). This widespread softening of Luke's Gospel of the Poor is rightly contested by Esler, *Community and Gospel in Luke-Acts*, 195–97.

19. Luke 20:34-38 speaks clearly of the resurrection *in this life*—and in the other. "They cannot die any more" (v. 36) because they live in the promise of the resurrection that God has given them (v. 35), of which God has "considered them worthy." For this idea of resurrection see Janssen, *Eschatologie und Gegenwart*, 229–54.

20. See the collection of materials in L. Schottroff, "Die Befreiung vom Götzendienst," 141–45; one example is Pliny the Elder, *Natural History* 33.

21. See the materials in L. Schottroff, "Die Befreiung vom Götzendienst," 141–45.

22. For the *prosbol* (from the Greek word *prosbolē*) see Goodman, "The First Jewish Revolt," 421–23; Schürer, *Geschichte des jüdischen Volkes*, 2:60, 427–28.

23. Substantive parallels in the Gospel of Luke are especially 11:39 (accusation of "theft" on the part of Pharisees) and 20:47 (accusation of devouring widows' houses, against scribes). The accusation of "theft" cannot really mean violent robbery, but something more like "white collar" theft through explanations of Torah that are unfavorable to the poor. I understand 20:47 similarly. Often the rich man in Luke 16:19-31 is seen as an embodiment of the Pharisees: see, for example, Gowler, *Host, Guest, Enemy, and Friend*, 261, because they are addressed in v. 15. However, a glance at Jewish history of this period forces us to be more discriminating. At no time were the Pharisees part of the economic elite. In addition, the generalizing language in 16:14 is problematic because there may also have been Pharisaic positions that agreed with that of Jesus.

24. See chap. 5 above.

25. It is true that the Gospel of Luke (differently from Matt 3:2) does not say that the Baptizer preached the kingdom of God, but the forgiveness of sins in his preaching and the year of release in Jesus' preaching are good news about the "liberation of the people" of God (Luke 1:68), like the preaching of the kingdom of God. I cannot go into the history of interpretation of Luke 16:16 here, but see, for example, Prieur, *Die Verkündigung der Gottesherrschaft*, 234–41.

26. See chap. 5 above.

27. Luke 20:34, 35; 17:27.

28. See, for example, the rabbinic parable about the (son of the) toll collector Maʻjan cited in chap. 5 above.

29. For a good analysis of the narrative see Schnider and Stenger, "Die offene Tür und die unüberschreitbare Kluft," 273–83; on the gulf see 281–82.

30. See especially Bauckham, "The Rich Man and Lazarus," 225–46.

31. Ibid., 246.

32. Goodman, "The First Jewish Revolt"; see also idem, *The Ruling Class of Judaea*.

33. Applebaum, *Prolegomena to the Study of the Second Jewish Revolt (A.D. 132–135)*, 11.

34. Alföldy, *Römische Sozialgeschichte* (ET *The Social History of Rome*).

35. Hock, "Lazarus and Micyllus," 447–63.

36. See Krauss, *Talmudische Archäologie*, 3:63; Friedländer, *Darstellungen aus der Sittengeschichte Roms*, 1:160.

37. For example, see the copy of a Hellenistic original in the Vatican museum (Museo Gregoriano Profano, inv. # 10132).

38. See, for example, Horn, *Glaube und Handeln in der Theologie des Lukas*, 150.

39. Hock, "Lazarus and Micyllus." His material yields only motif parallels; none of these parallels the content of Luke 16:19-31.

40. Bauckham, "The Rich Man and Lazarus."

41. Pliny the Elder, *Natural History*, LCL 33, 42, 48.

42. Translation from Charles, *The Testaments of the Twelve Patriarchs*, 88–89.

43. Hintzen, *Verkündigung und Wahrnehmung*, 353, 380.

44. Horn, *Glaube und Handeln*, 151.

CHAPTER 22

1. A third, shadowy figure can be glimpsed in a doorway.

2. See chap. 17 above.

3. For this aspect of slavery see especially Patterson, *Slavery and Social Death*.

4. See Acts 12:13-17.

5. See L. Schottroff, *Lydia's Impatient Sisters*, 212–14.

6. Lucius Annaeus Seneca, *Ad Lucilium Epistulae Morales*, with an English translation by Richard M. Gummere, 3 vols. (London: Heinemann; New York: G. P. Putnam's Sons, 1917), 47.1–4.

7. Glancy, *Slavery in Early Christianity*, 110.

8. Exceptions are Beavis, "Ancient Slavery as an Interpretive Context"; Herzog, *Parables as Subversive Speech*; Munro, *Jesus, Born of a Slave*.

9. The word *pistos* ("faithful") appears in v. 42 and qualifies fidelity in v. 43; *apistos* ("unfaithful") appears in v. 46, about punishment, and characterizes infidelity in v. 45. See also n11 below.

10. Horsley, "The Slave Systems of Classical Antiquity and Their Reluctant Recognition by Modern Scholars," 55–56; Patterson, *Slavery and Social Death*, 307; see also above at the first footnote to Luke 16:1-8.

11. In the tradition of interpretation of v. 46 the punishment through horrible slaughter is assigned to the earthly slaveowner and the application of "the share of the *apiston*" to God's eternal punishment of the wicked. But in this context *apistos* is the unfaithfulness of a slave in contrast to faithfulness (see n9 above). Nothing is said here about eternal punishment, so long as the passage is not allegorized.

12. For the interpretation of the ʻebed as God's slave in the First Testament and the Ancient Near East and the differences between that relationship and slavery in the Roman

empire see Callender, "Servant of God(s) and Servants of Kings in Israel and the Ancient Near East," 67–82; and Wright, "*Ebd/doulos*," 83–112.

13. Beavis ("Ancient Slavery as an Interpretive Context," 54) summarizes her observations on the slave parables as follows: "The slave parables . . . do not directly attack the institution of slavery, but their tendency to dignify the role of the slave and to suggest that the slave owner identify with his/her human property might have been perceived as radical social teaching by ancient authors."

14. On this, see L. Schottroff, *Lydia's Impatient Sisters,* 58–65; for the First Testament's notion of "humility" as "solidarity of the humiliated" see Wengst, *Demut—Solidarität der Gedemütigten* (ET *Humility: Solidarity of the Humiliated*).

15. See Callender, "Servant of God(s) and Servants of Kings," and Wright, "*Ebd/doulos.*"

16. In the tradition of interpretation of v. 41 the task entrusted to the slave as *oikonomos* is frequently extrapolated into an allegorical interpretation in terms of community leadership as distinguished from the people of the church. In this interpretation Peter's question in v. 41 would be answered, according to the mind of Jesus, as follows: Now he is speaking only to the disciples (often equated with the apostles—and where are the other disciples, male and female?), who are entrusted with office in the church: see, for example, Jülicher, *Die Gleichnisreden Jesu,* 2:159–60; Fitzmyer, *The Gospel according to Luke,* on Luke 12:41, 2:48 (he attributes this interpretation in terms of the church hierarchy to the Lukan level). Tilborg, "An Interpretation [of Lk 12,35-48] from the Ideology of the Text," 205–15, reads Luke 12:35-48 as addressed to slaveowners, whom the text leads on the path of downward mobility as they learn to set aside the ideology of the ancient household, that is, of the patriarchy. But unlike in Luke 17:7-10, with its address to slaveowners, I see here an address to the community of disciples as a whole, with a message of liberation linked to the Exodus.

17. See n 16.

18. Verse 4 is about sins "against you," that is, among the sisters and brothers; in v. 3 this is *not* said—and consequently has been added in part of the manuscript tradition. What is probably intended, already in v. 3 as well, is a violation of the Torah that is damaging to one or another brother or sister.

19. See Shelton, *As the Romans Did,* 166–71.

20. There is a vivid example in ibid., 165–66.

21. A small portion of the manuscript tradition (SyrSin; Marcion) omits the verse. For the problem see also Jülicher, *Die Gleichnisreden Jesu,* 2:18–20.

22. For the Jewish tradition of mutual human forgiveness see Billerbeck, *Kommentar zum Neuen Testament aus Talmud und Midrasch,* 1:795–97; Oesterley, *Gospel Parables,* 92–93; Young, *The Parables,* 124.

23. See L. Schottroff, *Lydia's Impatient Sisters,* 58–65.

24. Wengst, *Demut* (ET *Humility*), with his interpretation of "humility and solidarity," does not focus particularly on the Gospel of Luke, but the Gospel of Luke stands within the First Testament tradition he describes. Munro (*Jesus, Born of a Slave,* 355) emphasizes that this parable is addressed to slaveholders; she reads the text as an implicit vision of the reversal of the humiliation of the slaves—thus probably as identification and solidarity of slaveholders with enslaved people.

25. John Woolman, *The Journal and Major Essays of John Woolman,* quoted in Soelle, *The Silent Cry,* 246.

26. Soelle, *The Silent Cry,* 246.

27. See Schürer, *Geschichte des jüdischen Volkes* 1, §16 (Archelaus and Antipas); §18 (Agrippa). Busse ("Dechiffrierung eines lukanischen Schlüsseltextes [Lk 19,11-27]," 423–41)

rightly emphasizes the unitary character of this text, which describes a political structure, not a single event. However, he continues to interpret the king in the parable allegorically as Christ, which does not accord with the text.

28. Josephus, *Ant.* 17.11.1-2 (§299–314). Translation from Whiston, *The Works of Josephus, Compete and Unabridged*, 471–72.

29. It is a false assessment to regard such slaves as "retainers" of the powerful and as sharers, to a certain extent, in power and wealth (Lenski, *Power and Privilege*). Herzog (*Parables as Subversive Speech*, 157–58) sees the slaves in Matt 25:14-30 and Luke 19:11-27 as such "retainers," powerful bureaucrats who could do business on their own behalf. For the fallacy of this estimation see Glancy, *Slavery in Early Christianity*, 126: The slaves, even in managerial positions, remain slaves whose bodies are subjected to their owner's absolute control. Nor do they have any legal opportunity to make their own money in their jobs. The parable also presumes this: The capital and the profit are the property of the master.

30. As pictured in this text, dealing in money brings less profit than other methods of increasing capital, for example, lending against material security (land).

31. "Take what I did not deposit" (19:21, 22) draws on an ancient maxim of unwritten law: that one may not take away what one has not put in. Thus we can hear in this that the owner of the third slave is being called a thief, because he takes high profits on his capital. For a collection of material on this unwritten law see Brightman, "S. Luke 19:21," 158.

32. See above at Mark 4:24.

33. One recent example is Kim, *Stewardship and Almsgiving in Luke's Theology*, 165, which attempts not to read the *minas* ("money") allegorically. The subject, he says, is responsible handling of money, or "stewardship." But that means that he interprets the slaves allegorically.

34. Bovon, *Das Evangelium nach Lukas*, 3:293.

35. Jülicher, *Die Gleichnisreden Jesu*, 2:486.

36. Ibid., 2:487; similarly Prieur, *Die Verkündigung*, 264 (who considers this condemnation of the Jews pre-Lukan).

37. For example: Bovon, *Das Evangelium nach Lukas*, 3:296. Herzog (*Parables as Subversive Speech*, 155) notes the insecurity in traditional exegesis. In my view he is the only one who has drawn the conclusion that the text is not to be read allegorically.

38. Josephus, *Ant.* 20.8.6 (§167–172). Translation from Whiston, *The Works of Josephus, Compete and Unabridged*, 536.

39. Jesus' expectation of the kingdom, and that of his disciples, is here a political hope. There is no basis in the text for de-politicizing the Lukan idea of the kingship of God as, for example, Prieur does, *Die Verkündigung der Gottesherrschaft*, 269–70.

CHAPTER 23

1. The rhetorical question in v. 5 is not carried through consistently. Verse 7 describes the expected reaction of the friend who has been disturbed at night: Will he not refuse? The answer to be expected is: Yes, he will refuse, as in v. 7. Hultgren, for example, thinks differently (*The Parables of Jesus*, 229): The rejection is imaginable, but "things like that simply do not occur in the usual course of events." Here we can only argue with the order of the text. Verse 7 describes the rejection in detail, while v. 8 indicates the fulfillment of the request as not happening because of friendship. Thus v. 8 presumes nonfulfillment as normal.

2. Here the rhetorical structure of the address in vv. 5-7 is abandoned.

3. This interpretation would see the one in bed as obstinate if he did not get up: "because he ought to be ashamed if he did not help his friend" (Paulsen, "Die Witwe und der

Richter [Lk 18,1-8]," 27 is one example of a widespread interpretation; see also Jeremias, *The Parables of Jesus,* 158). The text of vv. 7-8, however, presumes the rejection of the plea in the night as most likely.

4. For economic assaults on widows according to the Hebrew Bible, see Stählin, "*chēra,*" 9:445–46, and the extensive article on the situation of widows by W. Schottroff in *Gerechtigkeit lernen,* 134–64.

5. There is a German translation in Erman, *Die Literatur der Ägypter,* 157ff. Brunner (*Altägyptische Weisheit,* 359) dates the text to the period of the ninth or tenth dynasty (between 2155 and 2030 B.C.E.). According to the text, the judge and the king had intended to fulfill the farmer's petition the first time he appeared, but did not tell him so that they could hear further examples of his eloquence. A social-historical analysis of the farmer's behavior need not consider this fictional rhetorical situation.

6. P.Oxy. 8.1120. There is further material and discussion of opposition in court and women's resistance in Luise Schottroff, *Lydia's Impatient Sisters,* 101–18.

7. Herzog (*Parables as Subversive Speech,* 215–32) develops this feature especially clearly.

8. L. Schottroff, *Lydia's Impatient Sisters,* 101–18.

9. Delling (*Studien zum Neuen Testament und zum hellenistischen Judentum,* 213) discusses this word *(hypōpiazein)* very thoroughly. There is no evidence of any derived usage.

10. Luke 18:1 uses a verb, *egkakein,* that is the opposite of *hypomonē* ("patient resistance"). Both words can describe the experience of women in childbirth: see Rom 8:25 (in the context of 8:18-25) and 2 Clem 2:2. For *ekdikēsis,* vv. 3 and 7, see especially Delling, *Studien zum Neuen Testament,* 209ff. The idea is multilayered: God, or the judge, is to repay the injustice suffered by the widow, or the believers, and restore justice, helping people to obtain their rights. God, as the eschatological judge, repays injustice—an idea that was fundamental in early Christianity but is often repressed in Christian reading of the New Testament because of an anti-Jewish distinction that is drawn between the God of Israel as a God of vengeance and the God of the New Testament. Beverly Wildung Harrison's reflections on the necessity of anger in relationships are helpful ("The Power of Anger in the Work of Love," 3–21).

11. The "opponent" (18:3) as the widow's antagonist in court is preferred *de facto* by the unjust judge, either because he has paid a bribe or because this judge, like many others, generally gives preference to the interests of the rich and powerful. See especially Herzog, *Parables as Subversive Speech,* 215–32.

12. See the information in BDAG 612–13.

13. See Horst, "*makrothumia, ktl.,*" 4:376–77.

CHAPTER 25

1. Nörr, "Die Evangelien des Neuen Testaments und die sogenannte hellenistische Rechtskoine," 135–36.

2. See L. Schumacher, *Servus index.*

3. See Leutzsch, "Verschuldung und Überschuldung, Schuldenerlaß und Sündenvergebung," 112–16; Hultgren (*The Parables of Jesus,* 24) regards the sum as unrealistically high, but the material gathered by Leutzsch proves that it is realistic. Of course, the narrative sets its own accents: The first slave is a debtor on the order of a whole country's taxes, while the second slave has the typical debts of a small farmer. The narrative wants to emphasize the contrast, but it remains realistic in its assumptions.

4. See Friedländer, *Darstellungen aus der Sittengeschichte Roms,* 1:70.

5. Herzog (*Parables as Subversive Speech*, 141) analyzes this convincingly: "As a part of the ruler's strategy of exerting control, he designates the contract for collecting tribute as a 'loan' *(daneion)* that he can call in at will."

6. Suetonius, *Divus Augustus* 101.4 (on the year 14 c.e.).

7. Philo, *On the Special Laws* 3:159–63 (see Yonge, *The Works of Philo*, 610).

8. See Kloft, *Liberalitas principis*, 120–24; Leutzsch, "Verschuldung und Überschuldung," 109; Crüsemann, "'Wie wir vergeben unseren Schuldigern,'" 96. There is no reason to suppose that there is a messianic disruption of reality here (Herzog, *Parables as Subversive Speech*, 146–47; suggested by Ringe, "Solidarity and Contextuality," 210–11).

9. This contradiction between 18:22 and 18:34 is often seen, but as a rule no conclusion is drawn from it. Even so, the king in the parable is interpreted as God. See Hultgren, *The Parables of Jesus*, 30, with further examples.

10. As a rule interpreters have presumed that the indebtedness results from loans. Jülicher (*Die Gleichnisreden Jesu*, 2:3–5) cautiously connected the idea of loans with that of a high official, "treasurer, toll collector, or satrap."

11. Especially drastic is the parable of the mean husband (see pp. 96–99 above).

12. Midrash Tanḥuma on Lev 23:40: Bietenhard, *Midrasch Tanhuma B.*, 2:140–41; Billerbeck, *Kommentar zum Neuen Testament aus Talmud und Midrasch*, 1:799, with parallels.

13. See Crüsemann, "'Wie wir vergeben unseren Schuldigern,'" 96.

14. See especially ibid.

15. See Billerbeck, *Kommentar zum Neuen Testament aus Talmud und Midrasch*, 1:425, and see also (without explicit reference to Deut 13:18) Sir 28:1-9 and the material parallels in the New Testament: Matt 6:14-15; Mark 11:25, 26; Luke 17:4; 11:4; Matt 5:7.

16. *t. Baba Qamma* 9.29-30 (365–66); Billerbeck, *Kommentar zum Neuen Testament aus Talmud und Midrasch*, 1:425.

17. It is quite common to offer a tradition-critical or literary-critical solution to the problem: v. 35 or vv. 34-35 are secondary. The murky pedagogy of the usual interpretation thus attributes them to "Matthew," and Jesus is freed from them. But such an apologetic solution indirectly reveals, once again, the problem of the usual interpretation. Reid ("Violent Endings in Matthew's Parables and Christian Nonviolence," 237–55) takes us beyond this. She names the problem unmistakably: How does the God of love of enemies fit with a God for whom metaphorical language can be used that describes structures of brutal violence? Her solution is that Jesus' ethic is absolutely clear in its demand for an abandonment of vengeance and violent resistance. But God's eschatological judgment is described in metaphors of violence that must be called into question today. I share this view, but not her categorization of Matt 18:23-35; 21:33-46; 22:1-14; 24:45-51; and 25:14-30 as allegorical presentations of God's brutality in judgment. These parables speak of the injustice of violence in society, which God rejects.

18. Midrash Tanḥuma on Exod 22:24: Bietenhard, *Midrasch Tanhuma B.*, 1:380; Billerbeck, *Kommentar zum Neuen Testament aus Talmud und Midrasch*, 1:800.

CHAPTER 26

1. I read *mēpote* in 13:15 as purposeful and internally coherent with deafness, etc. They have closed their eyes so that they will not see, etc. This is the meaning suggested by the language itself. The indicative, "I will heal them" in v. 15 can also be read as a divine promise of salvation (Vahrenhorst, "Gift oder Arznei?" 162). That strengthens the interpretation presented here even further. For an analysis of the language see Karrer, "'Und ich werde sie heilen,'" 257–59.

2. Matthew 13:35 describes revelation and not concealing speech. An interpretation of

the parables as veiled speech is often wrongly inserted here, as in Mark 4:10-12 (see part 1 above). This is a consequence of the anti-Jewish tradition of interpretation that long dominated the reading of Matthew 13 as well. Matthew 13:35 is rightly seen as a revelatory discourse, for example by Hultgren, *Parables of Jesus,* 462; Jones, *The Gospel of Matthew,* 283–84; Levine, *The Social and Ethnic Dimensions of Matthean Social History,* 256; differently, for example, Luz, *Das Evangelium nach Matthäus.*

3. Although Matthew tones down the disciples' lack of understanding in contrast to Mark's gospel, he does present their misunderstanding and their "little faith"; see only 17:20; 16:9; for the image of the disciples in the Gospel of Matthew see especially Saldarini, *Matthew's Christian-Jewish Community,* 84–123.

4. This is an important new development in the interpretation of the Gospel of Matthew that fundamentally and convincingly overcomes the anti-Judaism of the traditional interpretations of Matthew: see Levine, *Social and Ethnic Dimensions;* Saldarini, *Matthew's Christian-Jewish Community;* Jones, *Gospel of Matthew;* Vahrenhorst, *"Ihr sollt überhaupt nicht schwören."*

5. I am restricting myself to the interpretation of the texts that has grown out of a critique of the anti-Judaism of the interpretive tradition, since in this critique I am largely in agreement with the arguments of Levine, *Social and Ethnic Dimensions,* and Saldarini, *Matthew's Christian-Jewish Community.*

6. Poverty "in spirit" in Matt 5:3 is wrongly interpreted as spiritual poverty that has nothing to do with material poverty. The Psalms, like Matt 5:3, speak in these or similar terms of material poverty that also destroys the relationship to God. See the detailed arguments in L. Schottroff, "Das geschundene Volk," 162–66.

7. The disciples' hunger in Matt 12:1-8, which in Jesus' interpretation of the Torah makes it necessary to override the Sabbath, is to be understood in connection with the people's situation; see L. Schottroff and Stegemann, "Der Sabbat ist für den Menschen da."

8. See further L. Schottroff, "Das geschundene Volk," 151–57.

9. Ibid., 157–58; Saldarini, *Matthew's Christian-Jewish Community,* 27–43.

10. The appreciation of women's work in preparing food as comparable to men's work in the fields is present at all levels of the Synoptic tradition and can also be observed in the Mishna. A devaluation of this work that sees it as not genuine labor finds its place especially in the middle classes in the West in the nineteenth and twentieth centuries. For women's work in the New Testament and the work of the woman baking bread see L. Schottroff, *Lydia's Impatient Sisters,* 79–90.

11. The "hiding" in 13:33 should not be seen as a disruption of ordinary life, since it is part of the process of leavening. For the recent history of interpretation of this word see ibid., 80, 90.

12. This is 39.4 liters of flour, not an unusual quantity, as is often supposed; see ibid., 80.

13. As in Mark 4:28, human work and the miracle of God's working are not set up as alternatives. In the history of interpretation there is often a struggle against human synergism, while, for the biblical text, it is completely obvious that people have to work for the reign of God—and at the same time it is God's action that thus becomes visible.

14. Both the stories of the feeding miracles and the Last Supper traditions in the New Testament tell of this Jewish ritual as a matter-of-fact part of the religious meal praxis of early Christianity (Mark 6:41, etc.; 14:22, etc.).

15. In the New Testament the Greek words *ekklēsia* and *synagōgē* describe the assembly of believers, and not buildings or institutions, certainly not separate institutions (synagogue versus church).

16. Examples from this tradition of interpretation can be found in L. Schottroff, *Lydia's Impatient Sisters*, 89–90.

17. It is not a question of a "new" teaching in contrast to an old one, as this is often interpreted (see, e.g., Saldarini, *Matthew's Christian-Jewish Community*).

18. See part 1 above on Mark 4:25.

CHAPTER 27

1. The German civil code reflects Roman law (§903): "The owner of a thing may do as he or she wishes with it, insofar as the law or the rights of a third party are not in conflict, and may exclude others from any infringement." Correspondingly, in Roman legal discussions also, the rights of a neighbor, for example, can restrict the rights of an owner. However, the legal subject is a freeborn, landowning man with a fundamentally unrestricted *dominium* and unrestricted *patria potestas*. Matthew 20:1-16 reflects the new development in the Roman empire during this period. It describes the *dominus/kyrios* in accordance with preclassical Roman law: see Diösdy, *Ownership in Ancient and Pre-classical Roman Law*, 135–36, 183. In the legal history of ancient Israel also, the free, landowning man is the legal subject. However: "The laws of God break through the economic laws when these lead to exploitation and dependency" (Crüsemann, *Die Tora*, 219, on the Book of the Covenant; see 264 on Deuteronomy). For property in Roman law see also Kaser, *Römisches Privatrecht*, 125, 448–49; for the *patria potestas* see Shelton, *As the Romans Did*, 17–20. Plato, *Laws* 922–23, characterizes a dying testator in words similar to Matt 20:15, but as an extreme negative example of caprice, which lawgivers ought to prevent. The dying man asserts that he is master of his property, but the lawgiver understands property not as private, but as common. Hezser (*Lohnmetaphorik und Arbeitswelt in Mt 20:1-16*, 240) notes the caprice shown in 20:14-15, but sees it as covered by generosity. Herzog (*Parables as Subversive Speech*) is the first to draw the conclusion from such an observation: The owner of the vineyard is not a portrait of God.

2. See chap. 2 above.

3. Only the laborers hired at the first hour receive a contract that mentions a wage amount. The next groups do not get any clear statement of what their pay will be and are dependent on the boss's decision when pay is distributed in the evening. The vineyard owner makes use of unemployment to his own advantage. The day laborers are in a totally weakened position; on this see L. Schottroff, "Die Güte Gottes und die Solidarität von Menschen," 37–38; Herzog, *Parables as Subversive Speech*, 86.

4. Pliny the Younger, *Epistulae* VII, 18; I, 8.10; XI, 30. See Kloft, *Liberalitas principis*, 65.

5. See Bolkestein, *Wohltätigkeit und Armenpflege im vorchristlichen Altertum*, 304–5; Kloft, *Liberalitas principis*; Hezser, *Lohnmetaphorik und Arbeitswelt in Mt 20:1-16*, 97, although with the idea that this "ethos of the upper classes" is to be made accessible, through the parable, to the lower classes. Holgate, *Prodigality, Liberality, and Meanness*, 168–91, gives material on liberality, although applied to a different context (Luke 15:11-32).

6. L. Schottroff, "Die Güte Gottes und die Solidarität von Menschen."

7. Ibid., 44.

8. Hultgren, *The Parables of Jesus*, 40; similarly Shillington, "Saving Life and Keeping Sabbath (Mt 20:1b-15)," 97.

9. Gottwald ("Social Class as an Analytic and Hermeneutical Category in Biblical Studies," 20) accepts Herzog's thesis. In the context of Matt 25:14-30 *par.* Rohrbaugh takes a similar tack ("A Peasant Reading of the Talents/Pounds," 32–39).

10. Ben-David, *Talmudische Ökonomie*, 292. In the last thirty years Ben-David's calculation has been followed, directly or indirectly, by a number of interpreters.

11. See the discussion of the relevant sources in L. Schottroff, *Lydia's Impatient Sisters*, 94–97, 245–46.

12. Leviticus 19:13; Deut 24:14-15; for further material see Hezser, *Lohnmetaphorik und Arbeitswelt in Mt 20:1-16*, 76–79.

13. Herzog, *Parables as Subversive Speech*, 79, 95.

14. *CIL* 8, Suppl. 11,824.

15. Varro, *De re Rustica* I, 17.2-3; see also Columella, *De re rustica* I. 7.4. I have already discussed these and the following sources on the situation of day laborers in agriculture in a 1979 essay. They were taken up by Hezser *(Lohnmetaphorik und Arbeitswelt in Mt 20:1-16)*, and she has added other sources that support this picture.

16. Cato, *Agriculture* 5, 4. There is a German translation in Krenkel, "Zu den Tagelöhnern bei der Ernte in Rom," 141; his arguments against the interpretation by Gummerus (*Der römische Gutsbetrieb*, 26–27) are correct.

17. Columella, *De re rustica* 3.21. 9-10.

18. For further information see the literature cited in n. 16 above, and Brunt, "Die Beziehungen zwischen dem Heer und dem Land," 124ff., esp. 133–34.

19. Thus, for example, Ven, *Sozialgeschichte der Arbeit*, 1:98–99; more cautiously Kaser, *Das römische Privatrecht*, 1:300–301.

20. For these questions see especially Krenkel, "Zu den Tagelöhnern bei der Ernte in Rom," 141.

21. *Baba Meṣiʿa* 7:1-7.

22. *Baba Meṣiʿa* 9:12b.

23. *t. Baba Meṣiʿa 8.2* (Neusner, *The Tosefta*, 2:1,066).

24. There has been discussion of the idea that 20:16 is a later addition to the parable in the form of a logion by a wandering prophet, with its formal reference to the sequence of payment in 20:8. This is a completely inappropriate idea. Verse 16 is the necessary interpretation of the parable and refers to the generosity of the vineyard owner toward the "last." But it sets this generosity in opposition to God's generosity in judgment, when the last will become the first.

25. On Matt 5:3 see pp. 205–7 above.

26. Matthew 20:16 (and 19:30) are often read ecclesiologically, not eschatologically, when groups are identified with the last or the first: for example, rich people or disciples. Even Carter (*Households and Discipleship*, 160) reads 20:16 as a challenge to the addressees to accept a lifestyle critical of patriarchy, without hierarchies and orientation to wealth; that is, his reading is ecclesiological. I largely agree with his analysis of Matthew 19 and 20 as a critique of patriarchy, but I evaluate the landowner in 20:8-15 differently and understand 20:16 (19:30) as eschatological: a promise for the people and the nations, all of whom are in "Matthew's" thought, and not only as an invitation to live as an alternative household.

27. Shillington, "Saving Life and Keeping Sabbath (Mt 20:1b-15)," 35–51.

28. Nützel ("'Darf ich mit dem Meinen nicht tun, was ich will?'" 279) interprets v. 15 as an expression of God's freedom, God's will, God's compassion *(eudokia)*. But I see a contrast between God's freedom and 20:15.

29. The "meek" (Matt 5:5) embody the contrast to the powerful on their thrones and their arrogance *(hybris)* (e.g., Matt 20:25; Luke 1:51-52).

30. See Bradshaw, *Two Ways of Praying*, 45–56.

31. See Crüsemann, *Die Tora*, 264.

32. M. Sachs, *Gebete der Israeliten*, 344.

33. Comprehensive information in Hezser, *Lohnmetaphorik und Arbeitswelt in Mt 20:1-16*.

CHAPTER 28

1. See Krauss, *Talmudische Archäologie*, 2, 18–21.

2. Levine (*Social and Ethnic Dimensions*, 206) understands 21:31b, *proagein* ("go in ahead") as exclusive. The Jewish leadership has had a second chance, and now they are definitively excluded from salvation. I would argue against this not only with the meaning of the word *proagein*, but primarily with the idea of God's judgment, which is coming but is not preordained even by Jesus.

3. The reversal of the text in the manuscripts could go back as early as the second century; the salvation-historical interpretation is attested since Origen. On this see Luz, *Das Evangelium nach Matthäus*, 3:213; Hultgren, *The Parables of Jesus*, 218–19. But for text-critical reasons as well as the principles of parables theory the version translated here, that of the twenty-sixth and twenty-seventh editions of the Greek New Testament by Nestle-Aland, is to be preferred: This version has a somewhat better manuscript attestation, and an allegorical reading is inappropriate to the gospel parables. The second child does not represent Jesus' opponents. Rather, they are to learn from the first child.

4. See chap. 2 above.

5. See chap. 4 above.

6. See the detailed analysis in L. Schottroff, *Befreiungserfahrungen*, 184–216.

7. The promises in Matt 21:42-43 and 22:14 are very often read ecclesiologically and thus as the rejection of certain groups. Although he critically points out the traditional ecclesiological anti-Judaism, Saldarini (*Matthew's Christian-Jewish Community*, 60) still reads 21:43 as a rejection of the Jewish leadership and understands the people *(ethnos)* that brings the fruit of the kingdom as the group of disciples in the Gospel of Matthew, who are to be Israel's new leaders. Here again I would point to the eschatological horizon of 21:43 (see chap. 2 above), which contradicts such an interpretation.

CHAPTER 29

1. See chap. 22 above on Luke 19:21. For a social-historical analysis of the duties of slaves in Matt 25:14-30 see chap. 22 above. The sums of money here in Matt 25:14-30 are higher, but the milieu and the methods of gaining such profits are comparable to Luke 19:11-27. For a social-historical analysis see also Rohrbaugh, "A Peasant Reading of the Talents/Pounds."

2. See chap. 4 above on Matt 22:13.

3. See chap. 21 above on Luke 16:14-31.

4. Matt 25:31-46 is not a parable, but in the tradition it is frequently, and wrongly, called "the parable of the great world judgment."

5. The question of who the peoples in v. 32 are should be answered in terms of the overall context of the Gospel of Matthew. These are all the nations of humanity, as in 28:19, including the Jewish people; on this see especially Levine, *Social and Ethnic Dimensions*, 233–39; Saldarini, *Matthew's Christian-Jewish Community*, 80.

6. See Saldarini, *Matthew's Christian-Jewish Community*, 42, and frequently elsewhere.

Abbreviations

AB	Anchor Bible
Ant.	*Jewish Antiquities* (Josephus)
B.J.	*Bellum judaicum* (Josephus)
BAGD	Walter Bauer, William F. Arndt, F. William Gingrich, and Frederick W. Danker, *Greek-English Lexicon of the New Testament and Other Early Christian Literature,* 2nd ed., 1979
BDAG	Walter Bauer, Frederick W. Danker, William F. Arndt, and F. Wilbur Gingrich, *A Greek-English Lexicon of the New Testament and Other Early Christian Literature,* 3rd ed., 1999
BK	*Bibel und Kirche*
BTB	*Biblical Theology Bulletin*
BZ	*Biblische Zeitschrift*
CBQ	*Catholic Biblical Quarterly*
CIL	*Corpus inscriptionum latinarum*
EKKNT	Evangelisch-katholischer Kommentar zum Neuen Testament
ET	English translation
EvT	*Evangelische Theologie*
FRLANT	Forschungen zur Religion und Literatur des Alten und Neuen Testaments
HNT	Handbuch zum Neuen Testament
HTR	*Harvard Theological Review*
JBL	*Journal of Biblical Literature*
JSNT	*Journal for the Study of the New Testament*
JSOT	*Journal for the Study of the Old Testament*
JTS	*Journal of Theological Studies*
LCL	Loeb Classical Library
LSJ	Liddell, H. G., R. Scott, H. S. Jones, *A Greek-English Lexicon,* 9th ed., 1996
LXX	Septuagint
Neot	*Neotestamentica*
NovT	*Novum Testamentum*
NTD	Das Neue Testament Deutsch
NTS	*New Testament Studies*
TDNT	Gerhard Kittel and Gerhard Friedrich (eds.), *Theological Dictionary of the New Testament* (trans. Geoffrey W. Bromiley), 10 vols., Grand Rapids, 1964–76
TRE	*Theologische Realenzyklopädie,* edited by G. Krause and G. Müller, Berlin, 1977–
WBC	Word Biblical Commentary
WBFTh	Elisabeth Gössmann et al., eds., *Wörterbuch der Feministischen Theologie,* 2nd ed.
ZNW	*Zeitschrift für die neutestamentliche Wissenschaft und die Kunde der älteren Kirche*
ZThK	*Zeitschrift für Theologie und Kirche*

Bibliography

Alföldy, Géza. *Römische Sozialgeschichte.* 3rd ed. Wiesbaden: Steiner, 1984. English: *The Social History of Rome,* trans. David Braund and Frank Pollock. Totowa, N.J.: Barnes & Noble, 1985.

Ammicht-Quinn, Regina. *Körper, Religion, Sexualität: Theologische Reflexionen zur Ethik der Geschlechter.* 2nd ed. Mainz: Matthias-Grünewald-Verlag, 2000.

Antoine, Gérald, et al. *Exegesis: problèmes de méthode et exercises de lecture (Genèse 22 et Luc 15): travaux publiés sous la direction de François Bovon et Grégoire Rouiller.* Neuchâtel: Delâchaux et Niestlé, 1975. English: *Exegesis: Problems of Method and Exercises in Reading (Genesis 22 and Luke 15),* trans. Donald G. Miller. Pittsburgh: Pickwick, 1978.

Applebaum, Shimon. "Judaea as a Roman Province: The Countryside as a Political and Economic Factor." In *Aufstieg und Niedergang der Römischen Welt* II.8. Berlin: de Gruyter, 1977, 355–96.

———. *Prolegomena to the Study of the Second Jewish Revolt (A.D. 132–135).* Oxford: British Archaeological Reports, 1976.

Arnal, William E. "The Parable of the Tenants and the Class Consciousness of the Peasantry." In *Text and Artifact in the Religions of Mediterranean Antiquity,* ed. Stephen G. Wilson and Michael Desjardins. Waterloo, Ont.: Wilfrid Laurier University Press, 2000, 135–57.

Aus, Roger D. *Weihnachtsgeschichte, barmherziger Samariter, verlorener Sohn: Studien zu ihrem jüdischen Hintergrund,* trans. Eckhard Benz-Wenzlaff. Berlin: Institut Kirche und Judentum, 1988.

Bailey, Kenneth E. *Poet and Peasant and Through Peasant Eyes: A Literary-Cultural Approach to the Parables of Luke.* Grand Rapids, Mich.: Eerdmans, 1983.

Balabanski, Vicky. "Opening the Closed Door: A Feminist Reading of the 'Wise and Foolish Virgins' (Mt 25,1-13)." In *The Lost Coin: Parables of Women, Work, and Wisdom,* ed. Mary Ann Beavis. London and New York: Sheffield Academic Press, 2002, 71–97.

Bauckham, Richard. "The Rich Man and Lazarus: The Parable and Parallels," *NTS* 37 (1991) 225–46.

Walter Bauer, William F. Arndt, F. William Gingrich, and Frederick W. Danker. *Greek-English Lexicon of the New Testament and Other Early Christian Literature.* 2nd ed. Chicago: University of Chicago Press, 1979.

Walter Bauer, Frederick W. Danker, William F. Arndt, and F. Wilbur Gingrich, *A Greek-English Lexicon of the New Testament and Other Early Christian Literature,* 3rd ed. Chicago: University of Chicago Press, 1999.

Beavis, Mary Ann. "Ancient Slavery as an Interpretive Context for the New Testament

Servant Parables with Special Reference to the Unjust Steward (Luke 16:1-8)," *JBL* 111 (1992): 37–54.

———. "'Making Up Stories': A Feminist Reading of the Parable of the Prodigal Son (Lk 15.11b-32)." In *The Lost Coin: Parables of Women, Work and Wisdom,* ed. Mary Ann Beavis. London and New York: Sheffield Academic Press, 2002, 98–122.

———. *Mark's Audience: The Literary and Social Setting of Mark 4.11-12.* London and New York: Sheffield Academic Press, 1989.

Ben-David, Arye. *Talmudische Ökonomie: Die Wirtschaft des jüdischen Palästina zur Zeit der Mischna und des Talmud.* Vol. 1. New York: Olms, 1974.

Berger, Klaus, and Carsten Colpe. *Religionsgeschichtliches Textbuch zum Neuen Testament.* Göttingen: Vandenhoeck & Ruprecht, 1987.

Bible and Culture Collective. *The Postmodern Bible.* New Haven and London: Yale University Press, 1995.

Bietenhard, Hans. *Midrasch Tanhuma B.* Vols. 1 and 2. New York: Peter Lang, 1980, 1982.

———. *Sifre Deuteronomium, übersetzt und erklärt von Hans Bietenhard.* New York: Peter Lang, 1984.

Billerbeck, Paul. *Kommentar zum Neuen Testament aus Talmud und Midrasch.* See Strack, Hermann L. and Paul Billerbeck.

Black, Max. *Models and Metaphors: Studies in Language and Philosophy.* Ithaca, N.Y.: Cornell University Press, 1962.

Blass, Friedrich, Albert Debrunner, and Friedrich Rehkopf. *Grammatik des neutestamentlichen Griechish.* Göttingen: Vandenhoeck and Ruprecht, 1975.

Blinzler, Josef. "Die Niedermetzelung von Galiläern durch Pilatus," *NovT* 2 (1957): 24–49.

Bloch, Ernst. *Atheismus im Christentum: Zur Religion des Exodus und des Reiches.* Frankfurt: Suhrkamp, 1980. English: *Atheism in Christianity: The Religion of the Exodus and the Kingdom.* Trans. J. T. Swann. New York: Herder & Herder, 1972.

Böhm, Martina. *Samarien und die Samaritai bei Lukas.* Tübingen: Mohr/Siebeck, 1999.

Bolkestein, Hendrik. *Wohltätigkeit und Armenpflege im vorchristlichen Altertum.* Groningen: Bouma's Boekhuis, 1967.

Borg, Marcus J. *Jesus in Contemporary Scholarship.* Valley Forge, Penn.: Trinity Press International, 1994.

Boring, M. Eugene, Klaus Berger, and Carsten Colpe. *Hellenistic Commetary to the New Testament.* Nashville: Abingdon, 1995.

Bovon, François. *Das Evangelium nach Lukas.* Vols. 1–3. EKKNT. Neukirchen-Vluyn: Neukirchener Verlag, 1989–2001. English (to date): *Luke 1: A Commentary on the Gospel of Luke 1:1–9:50,* Hermeneia, trans. Christine M. Thomas. Minneapolis: Fortress Press, 2002.

Boyarin, Daniel, and David Stern. "An Exchange on the Mashal Rhetoric and Interpretation: The Case of the Nimshal," *Prooftexts: A Journal of Jewish Literary History* 5 (1985): 269–80.

Bradshaw, Paul F. *The Search for the Origins of Christian Worship.* Oxford: Oxford University Press, 2002.

———. *Two Ways of Praying.* Nashville: Abingdon, 1995.

Braude, William G. *Pesikta Rabbati: Discourses for Feasts, Fasts, and Special Sabbaths.* Vols. 1 and 2. New Haven and London: Yale University Press, 1968.

Brecht, Bertholt. "Das Pfund der Armen." Appendix to vol. 13: *Dreigroschenroman.* In *Gesammelte Werke.* 20 vols. Frankfurt: Suhrkamp, 1967).

Brightman, F. E. "S. Luke 19:21: *Aireis ho ouk ethēkas*," *JTS* 29 (1927–28): 158.

Broshi, Magen. "Agriculture and Economy in Roman Palestine: Seven Notes on the Babatha Archive," *Israel Exploration Journal* 42 (1992): 230–40.

Brunner, Hellmut. *Altägyptische Weisheit*. Darmstadt: Wissenschaftliche Buchgesellschaft, 1988.

Brunt, P. A. "Die Beziehungen zwischen dem Heer und dem Land." In *Zur Sozial- und Wirtschaftsgeschichte der späten römischen Republik,* ed. Helmuth Schneider. Darmstadt: Wissenschaftliche Buchgesellschaft, 1976.

Bultmann, Rudolf. *Die Geschichte der synoptischen Tradition.* 4th ed. Göttingen: Vandenhoeck & Ruprecht, 1958. English: *The History of the Synoptic Tradition,* trans. John Marsh. New York: Harper & Row, 1963.

Busse, Ulrich. "Dechiffrierung eines lukanischen Schlüsseltextes (Lk 19,11-27)." In *Von Jesus zum Christus,* ed. Rudolf Hoppe and Ulrich Busse. New York: de Gruyter, 1998.

Callender, Dexter E., Jr., "Servant of God(s) and Servants of Kings in Israel and the Ancient Near East." In *Slavery in Text and Interpretation,* ed. Allen Dwight Callahan, Richard A. Horsley, and Abraham Smith. Semeia 83/84. Atlanta: Society of Biblical Literature, 1998.

Camponovo, Odo. *Königtum, Königsherrschaft und Reich Gottes in den frühjüdischen Schriften.* Göttingen: Vandenhoeck & Ruprecht, 1984.

Carroll, John T. "Luke's Portrayal of the Pharisees," *CBQ* 50 (1988): 604–21.

Carter, Warren. *Households and Discipleship: A Study of Matthew 19–20.* Sheffield: JSOT Press, 1994.

Cassidy, Richard J. *Jesus, Politics, and Society: A Study of Luke's Gospel.* Maryknoll, N.Y.: Orbis, 1978.

Cathcart, Kevin J., and Robert P. Gordon, eds. and trans. *The Targum of the Minor Prophets.* Wilmington, Del.: Michael Glazier, 1989.

Choi, J. D. *Jesus' Teaching on Repentance.* Binghamton, N.Y.: Binghamton University Press, 2000.

Chrysostom, Johannes. *Commentarius in sanctum Matthaeum Evangelistum.* Patrologia Graeca 57, 58. Paris: J. P. Migne, 1857–1886.

Columella, Lucius Junius Moderatus. *On Agriculture.* With a recension of the text and an English translation by Harrison Boyd Ash. LCL 361, 407–408. Cambridge, Mass.: Harvard University Press; London: W. Heinemann, 1960–1979.

Conzelmann, Hans. *Die Mitte der Zeit: Studien zur Theologie des Lukas.* Tübingen: Mohr/ Siebeck, 1954. English: *The Theology of St. Luke,* trans. Geoffrey Buswell. London: Faber and Faber, 1960; New York: Harper & Row, 1961.

Crossan, John Dominic, ed. "Paul Ricoeur on Biblical Hermeneutics," *Semeia* 4 (1975): 29–148.

Crüsemann, Frank. *Die Tora: Theologie und Sozialgeschichte des alttestamentlichen Gesetzes.* Munich: Kaiser, 1992.

———. "'Wie wir vergeben unseren Schuldigern': Schuld und Schulden in der biblischen Tradition." In *Schuld und Schulden,* ed. Marlene Crüsemann and Willy Schottroff. Munich: Kaiser, 1992, 90–103.

Crüsemann, Marlene, and Frank Crüsemann. "Das Jahr das Gott gefällt: Biblische Traditionen von Erlaß- und Jobeljahr," *BK* 55 (2000): 19–24.

Culpepper, R. Alan. "The Gospel of Luke." In *The Interpreter's Bible* 9. Nashville: Abingdon, 1995, 340–43.

Dalman, Gustaf. *Arbeit und Sitte in Palästina.* 7 vols. Hildesheim: Olms, 1964.

Danby, Herbert. *The Mishnah.* Oxford: Clarendon Press, 1933.

Daube, David. "Inheritance in Two Lucan Pericopes," *Zeitschrift der Savigny-Stiftung für Rechtsgeschichte,* Romanistiche Abteilung 72 (1955): 326–34.

Debout, Jacques. "Vernünftige Kritik des barmherzigen Samaritans." In *Gewissenserforschung eines mittleren Christen: Christ heute*. Series 1, vol. 4. Einsiedeln: Johannes Verlag, 1948.

Deissmann, Adolf. *Licht vom Osten: Das Neue Testament und die neuentdeckten Texte der hellenistisch-römischen Welt*. 4th ed. Tübingen: Mohr, 1923. English: *Light from the Ancient East: The New Testament Illustrated by Recently Discovered Texts of the Graeco-Roman World*, trans. Lionel R. M. Strachan. New York : Harper, [1922?].

De la Torre, Miguel A. *Reading the Bible from the Margins*. Maryknoll, N.Y.: Orbis, 2002.

Delling, Gerhard. *Studien zum Neuen Testament und zum hellenistischen Judentum*. Göttingen: Vandenhoeck & Ruprecht, 1970.

Derrett, J. Duncan M. "Fresh Light on the Lost Sheep and the Lost Coin," *NTS* 26 (1980): 36–60.

———. "Fresh Light on St. Luke XVI," *NTS* 7 (1960–61): 198–219.

———. *Studies in the New Testament*. Vol. 2. Leiden: Brill, 1978.

Deutsche Bibelgesellschaft. Die Bibel nach der Übersetzung martin Luthers in der revidierten Fassung von 1984. Stuttgart: Deutsche Bibelgesellschaft, 1985.

Dexinger, Ferdinand. "Erwählung II: Judentum," *TRE* 10 (1982): 189–92.

Dietzfelbinger, Christian. "Das Gleichnis vom ausgestreuten Samen." In *Der Ruf Jesu und die Antwort der Gemeinde (F. S. J. Jeremias)*, ed. Eduard Lohse with Christoph Burchard and Berndt Schaller. Göttingen: Vandenhoeck & Ruprecht, 1970, 80–93.

Diósdy, György. *Ownership in Ancient and Pre-Classical Roman Law*. Budapest: Akadémiai Kiadó, 1970.

Dodd, C. H. "The Fall of Jerusalem and the 'Abomination of Desolation,'" *Journal of Roman Studies* 37 (1947): 47–54.

———. *The Parables of the Kingdom*. New York: Scribner, 1961.

Donahue, John R. *The Gospel in Parable: Metaphor, Narrative, and Theology in the Synoptic Gospels*. Philadelphia: Fortress Press, 1988.

Donahue, John R., and Daniel J. Harrington. *The Gospel of Mark*. Collegeville, Minn.: Liturgical, 2002.

Ebach, Jürgen. "Apokalypse: Zum Ursprung einer Stimmung," *Einwürfe* 2 (1985): 5–61.

———. "Apokalypse und Apokalyptik." In *Zeichen der Zeit: Erkennen und Handeln*, ed. Heinrich Schmidinger. Innsbruck: Tyrolia, 1998, 213–73.

———. "Sozialgeschichtliche Bibelauslegung [Luke 10:25-37]," *Junge Kirche* 52 (1991): 428–29.

Eck, Werner, and Johannes Heinrichs. *Sklaven und Freigelassene in der Gesellschaft der Römischen Kaiserzeit: Textauswahl und Übersetzung*. Darmstadt: Wissenschaftliche Buchgesellschaft, 1993.

Erlemann, Kurt. *Gleichnisauslegung: Ein Lehr- und Arbeitsbuch*. Tübingen: Francke, 1999.

Erman, Adolf. *Die Literatur der Ägypter*. Hildesheim: Olms, 1971. English: *Ancient Egyptian Poetry and Prose*, trans. Aylward M. Blackman. New York: Dover, 1995.

Esler, Philip Francis. *Community and Gospel in Luke-Acts: The Social and Political Motivations of Lucan Theology*. Cambridge: Cambridge University Press, 1987.

Farbstein, David. *Das Recht der unfreien und freien Arbeiter nach jüdisch-talmudischem Recht*. Frankfurt: Kauffmann, 1896.

Fiebig, Paul. *Altjüdische Gleichnisse und die Gleichnisse Jesu*. Tübingen: Mohr/Siebeck, 1904.

———. *Die Gleichnisreden Jesu im Lichte der rabbinischen Gleichnisse des neutestamentlichen Zeitalters*. Tübingen: Mohr/Siebeck, 1912.

Fitzer, Gottfried. "*sphragis, ktl.*" In *TDNT* 7:939–53.

Fitzmyer, Joseph A. *The Gospel According to Luke*. 2 vols. Garden City, N.Y.: Doubleday, 1981, 1985.

Flusser, David. "A New Sensitivity in Judaism and Christian Message," *HTR* 61 (1968): 107–27.

———. *Die rabbinischen Gleichnisse und der Gleichniserzähler Jesu.* Vol. 1: *Das Wesen der Gleichnisse.* New York: Peter Lang, 1981.

France, R. T. *The Gospel of Mark: A Commentary on the Greek Text.* Grand Rapids, Mich.: Eerdmans; Carlisle, U.K.: Paternoster, 2002.

Friedländer, Ludwig. *Darstellungen aus der Sittengeschichte Roms in der Zeit von Augustus bis zum Ausgang der Antonine.* 4 vols. 10th ed. Aalen: Scientia, 1979. English: *Roman Life and Manners under the Early Empire,* trans. Leonard A. Magnus. New York: Arno, 1979.

Gebara, Ivone. "The Face of Transcendence as a Challenge to the Reading of the Bible in Latin America." In *Searching the Scriptures: A Feminist Introduction,* ed. Elisabeth Schüssler Fiorenza. New York: Crossroad, 1993.

Gerhardsson, Birger. "The Parable of the Sower and Its Interpretation," *NTS* 14 (1967–68): 165–93.

———. *The Testing of God's Son.* Lund: Gleerup, 1966.

Glancy, Jennifer A. *Slavery in Early Christianity.* Oxford and New York: Oxford University Press, 2002.

Gnilka, Joachim. *Das Evangelium nach Markus.* 2 vols. Zürich: Benziger, 1978–1979.

Goodman, Martin. "The First Jewish Revolt: Social Conflict and the Problem of Debt." In *Essays in Honor of Yigael Yadin,* ed. Geza Vermes and Jacob Neusner. Totowa, N.J.: Allanheld, 1983.

———. *The Ruling Class of Judaea.* Cambridge: Cambridge University Press, 1987.

Gottwald, Norman K. "Social Class as an Analytic and Hermeneutical Category in Biblical Studies," *JBL* 112 (1993): 3–22.

Gowler, David B. *Host, Guest, Enemy and Friend: Portraits of the Pharisees in Luke and Acts.* New York: Peter Lang, 1991.

Green, Joel B. *Hearing the New Testament: Strategies for Interpretation.* Grand Rapids, Mich.: Eerdmans; Carlisle, U.K.: Paternoster, 1995.

Grotius, Hugo. *Annotationes in Novum Testamentum.* Erlangen and Leipzig: Apud Ioannem Carolum Tetzschnerum, 1755–1757.

Gössmann, Elisabeth, et al., eds. *Wörterbuch der Feministischen Theologie.* 2nd ed. Gütersloh: Gütersloher, 2002.

Gutbrod, Walter. "*nomikos,*" *TDNT* 4:1,088.

Gummerus, Hermann. *Der römische Gutsbetrieb: Als wirtschaftlicher Organismus nach den Werken des Cato, Varro und Columella.* Leipzig: Dieterich, 1903.

Guttmann, Theodor. *Das Masal-Gleichnis in tannaitischer Zeit.* Ph.D. dissertation, Frankfurt, 1929.

Haenchen, Ernst. "Das Gleichnis vom großen Mahl." In eadem, *Die Bibel und wir.* Vol. 2. Tübingen: Mohr/Siebeck, 1968.

Harnisch, Wolfgang, ed. *Die Gleichniserzählungen Jesu: Eine hermeneutische Einführung.* Göttingen: Vandenhoeck & Ruprecht, 1985.

———. *Die neutestamentliche Gleichnisforschung im Horizont von Hermeneutik und Literaturwissenschaft.* Darmstadt: Wissenschaftliche Buchgesellschaft, 1982.

Harrington, Daniel J. "The Gospel according to Mark." In *The New Jerome Biblical Commentary,* ed. Raymond E. Brown et al. Englewood Cliffs, N.J.: Prentice-Hall, 1990.

Harrison, Beverly Wildung. "The Power of Anger in the Work of Love." In eadem, *Making the Connections: Essays in Feminist Social Ethics,* ed. Carol S. Robb. Boston: Beacon, 1985.

Heidenheim, Wolf. *Gebete für das Neujahrsfest: Mit deutscher Übersetzung.* Rödelheim: Lehrberger, 1892.

Hengel, Martin. "Das Gleichnis von den Weingärtnern: Mc 12,1-12 im Lichte der Zenon-papyri und der rabbinischen Gleichnisse," *ZNW* 59 (1968): 1–39.

Herzog, William R., II. *Parables as Subversive Speech: Jesus as Pedagogue of the Oppressed.* Louisville, Ky.: Westminster John Knox, 1994.

Hezser, Catherine. "Rabbis and Other Friends: Friendship in the Talmud Yerushalmi and in Graeco-Roman Literature." In *The Talmud Yerushalmi and Graeco-Roman Culture,* ed. Peter Schäfer and Catherine Hezser. Vol. 2. Tübingen: Mohr/Siebeck, 2000, 189–254.

———. *Lohnmetaphorik und Arbeitswelt in Mt 20:1-16.* Göttingen: Vandenhoeck & Ruprecht, 1990.

Hintzen, Johannes. *Verkündigung und Wahrnehmung: Über das Verhältnis von Evangelium und Leser am Beispiel Lk 16, 19-31 im Rahmen des lukanischen Doppelwerkes.* Frankfurt: Hain, 1991.

Hock, Ronald F. "Lazarus and Micyllus: Greco-Roman Backgrounds to Luke 16:19-31," *JBL* 106 (1987): 447–63.

Holgate, David A. *Prodigality, Liberality, and Meanness in the Parable of the Prodigal Son: A Greco-Roman Perspective on Lk 15.11-32.* Sheffield: Sheffield Academic Press, 1999.

Horn, Friedrich Wilhelm. *Glaube und Handeln in der Theologie des Lukas.* Göttingen: Vandenhoeck & Ruprecht, 1983.

Horne, Edward H. "The Parables of the Tenants as Indictment," *JSNT* 71 (1998): 111–16.

Horsley, Richard A. *Jesus and the Spiral of Violence: Popular Jewish Resistance in Roman Palestine.* Minneapolis: Fortress Press, 1993.

———. "The Slave Systems of Classical Antiquity and Their Reluctant Recognitiion by Modern Scholars." In *Slavery in Text and Interpretation,* ed. Allen Dwight Callahan, Richard A. Horsley, and Abraham Smith. Semeia 83/84. Atlanta: Society of Biblical Literature, 1998, 19–66.

Horst, Friedrich. "*makrothymia, ktl.*" In *TDNT* 4:376–77.

Hultgren, Arland J. *The Parables of Jesus: A Commentary.* Grand Rapids, Mich.: Eerdmans, 2000.

Ilan, Tal. *Jewish Women in Greco-Roman Palestine: An Inquiry into Image and Status.* Tübingen: Mohr/Siebeck, 1995.

Janssen, Claudia. *Elisabet und Hanna—zwei widerständige Frauen in neutestamentlicher Zeit: Eine sozialgeschichtliche Untersuchung.* Mainz: Matthias-Grünewald, 1998.

———. *Eschatologie und Gegenwart: Die Körpertheologie des Paulus als Schlüssel für das Verständnis von Auferstehung (1 Kor 15).* Marburg: Habilitationsschrift, 2003.

———. "Leibliche Auferstehung? Zur Diskussion um Auferstehung bei Karl Barth, Rudolf Bultmann, Dorothee Sölle und in der aktuellen feministischen Theologie." In *Paulus: Umstrittene Traditionen—lebendige Theologie: Eine feministische Lektüre,* ed. Claudia Janssen, Luise Schottroff, and Beate Wehn. Gütersloh: Kaiser, 2001.

Jeremias, Joachim. *Die Gleichnisse Jesu.* 7th ed. Göttingen: Vandenhoeck & Ruprecht, 1965. English: *The Parables of Jesus,* trans. S. H. Hooke. 2nd ed. New York: Scribner's, 1972. References are to the English edition.

John, V. J. *The Ecological Vision of Jesus: Nature in the Parables of Mark.* Bangalore: Christava Sahitya Samithy, Thiruvalla & Board of Theological Text Book Programme of South Asia, 2002.

Jones, Ivor H. *The Gospel of Matthew.* London: Chapman, 1994.

Jülicher, Adolf, *Die Gleichnisreden Jesu.* Vol. 1: *Die Gleichnisreden Jesu im Allgemeinen.* 2nd ed. Tübingen: Mohr, 1910. Vol. 2: *Auslegung der Gleichnisreden der drei ersten Evangelien.* 3rd ed. Tübingen: Mohr, 1910.

Jüngel, Eberhard. *Paulus und Jesus: Eine Untersuchung zur Präzisierung der Frage nach dem Ursprung der Christologie.* 3rd ed. Tübingen: Mohr/Siebeck, 1967.

Karrer, Martin. "'Und ich werde sie heilen': Das Verstockungsmotiv aus Jes 6:9f. in Apg 28:26f." In *Kirche und Volk Gottes,* ed. Martin Karrer, Wolfgang Kraus, and Otto Merk. Neukirchen-Vluyn: Neukirchener Verlag, 2000.

Kaser, Max. *Römisches Privatrecht: Ein Studienbuch I.* 2nd ed. Munich: Beck, 1971. English: *Roman Private Law.* Trans. Rolf Dannenbring. Durban: Butterworths, 1965.

Kazantzakis, Nikos. *The Last Temptation of Christ.* New York: Simon and Schuster, 1960.

Kim, Kyoung-Jin. *Stewardship and Almsgiving in Luke's Theology.* Sheffield: Sheffield Academic Press, 1998.

Klauck, Hans-Josef. *Allegorie und Allegorese in synoptischen Gleichnistexten.* Münster: Aschendorff, 1978.

Klawans, Jonathan. *Impurity and Sin in Ancient Judaism.* Oxford and New York: Oxford University Press, 2000.

———. "Notions of Gentile Impurity in Ancient Judaism," *AJS Review: The Journal of the Association for Jewish Studies* 20 (1995): 285–312.

Klemm, Hans Gunther. *Das Gleichnis vom Barmherzigen Samariter: Grundzüge der Auslegung im 16./17. Jahrhundert.* Stuttgart: Kohlhammer, 1973.

Klinghardt, Matthias. *Gesetz und Volk Gottes: Das lukanische Verständnis des Gesetzes nach Herkunft, Funktion und seinem Ort in der Geschichte des Urchristentums.* Tübingen: Mohr/Siebeck, 1988.

Kloft, Hans. *Liberalitas principis: Herkunft und Bedeutung.* Studien zur Prinzipatsideologie. Cologne: Böhlau, 1970.

Kloppenborg, John S. "The Dishonoured Master (Luke 16:1-8a)," *Biblica* 70 (1989): 474–95.

Kloppenborg Verbin, John S. "Isaiah 5:1-7, the Parable of the Tenants and Vineyard Leases on Papyrus." In *Text and Artifact in the Religions of Mediterranean Antiquity,* ed. Stephen G. Wilson and Michael Desjardins. Waterloo, Ont.: Wilfrid Laurier University Press, 2000, 111–34.

Klostermann, Erich. *Das Lukasevangelium.* HNT. 2nd ed. Tübingen: Mohr/Siebeck, 1929.

Koffmahn, Elisabeth. *Die Doppelurkunden aus der Wüste Juda: Recht und Praxis der jüdischen Papyri des 1. und 2. Jahrhunderts n. Chr. samt Übertragung der Texte und deutscher Übersetzung.* Studies on the Texts of the Desert of Judah 5. Leiden: Brill, 1968.

Kögel, Julius. *Der Zweck der Gleichnisse Jesu im Rahmen seiner Verkündigung.* Gütersloh: Bertelsmann, 1915.

Krause, Jens-Uwe. *Gefängnisse im Römischen Reich.* Stuttgart: Steiner, 1996.

Krauss, Samuel. "Griechen und Römer." In *Monumenta Talmudica.* Vol. 5: *Geschichte.* Darmstadt: Wissenschaftliche Buchgesellschaft, 1972.

———. *Talmudische Archäologie.* 3 vols. Hildesheim: Olms, 1966.

Krenkel, Werner. "Zu den Tagelöhnern bei der Ernte in Rom," *Romanitas* 6/7 (1965): 141.

Krondorfer, Björn. "Of Faith and Faces: Biblical Texts, Holocaust Testimony and German 'After Auschwitz' Theology." In *Strange Fire: Reading the Bible after the Holocaust,* ed. Tod Linafelt. New York: New York University Press, 2000.

Lémonon, Jean-Pierre. *Pilate et le Gouvernement de la Judée.* Textes et Monuments. Paris: Gabalda, 1981.

Lenski, Gerhard E. *Power and Privilege: A Theory of Social Stratification.* Chapel Hill: University of North Carolina Press, 1984.

Leutzsch, Martin. "Verschuldung und Überschuldung, Schuldenerlaß und Sündenvergebung: Zum Verständnis des Gleichnisses Mt 18,23-35." In *Schuld und Schulden,* ed. Marlene Crüsemann and Willy Schottroff. Munich: Kaiser, 1992.

Levine, Amy-Jill. *The Social and Ethnic Dimensions of Matthean Social History.* Lewiston, N.Y.: Edwin Mellen, 1988.

———. "Matthew, Mark, and Luke: Good News or Bad?" In *Jesus, Judaism, and Christian Anti-Judaism: Reading the New Testament after the Holocaust,* ed. Paula Fredriksen and Adele Reinhartz. Louisville, Ky.: Westminster John Knox, 2002.

Liddell, H. G., R. Scott, H. S. Jones. *A Greek-English Lexicon,* 9th ed. Oxford: Oxford University Press, 1996.

Lieu, Judith M. *The Gospel of Luke.* Peterborough: Epworth, 1997.

Linnemann, Eta. *Jesus of the Parables: Introduction and Exposition,* trans. John Sturdy. New York: Harper & Row, 1967.

Ludwig, Walther, ed. *Antike Komödien: Plautus/Terenz,* trans. Wilhelm Binder. Darmstadt: Wissenschaftliche Buchgesellschaft, 1973.

Luz, Ulrich. *Das Evangelium nach Matthäus.* 4 vols. Zürich: Benziger and Neukirchener, 1985–2002. English: *Matthew 1–7: A Commentary* (German vol. 1.), trans. Wilhelm C. Linss. Continental Commentaries. Minneapolis: Fortress Press, 1992; *Matthew 8–20: A Commentary on the Gospel of Matthew* (German vol. 2.), trans. James Crouch, ed. Helmut Koester. Hermeneia. Minneapolis: Fortress Press, 2001.

Maier, Christl. "Das Buch der Sprichwörter." In *Kompendium Femnistische Bibelauslegung,* ed. Luise Schottroff and Marie-Theres Wacker. Gütersloh: Kaiser, 1998.

Maloney, Linda. "'Swept under the Rug': Feminist Homiletical Reflections on the Parable of the Lost Coin (Lk 15.8.9)." In *The Lost Coin: Parables of Women, Work, and Wisdom,* ed. Mary Ann Beavis. London and New York: Sheffield Academic Press, 2002.

Marcus, Joel. *Mark 1–8: A New Translation with Introduction and Commentary.* AB 27. New York: Doubleday, 1999.

Marquardt, Joachim. *Das Privatleben der Römer.* 2 vols. Darmstadt: Wissenschaftliche Buchgesellschaft, 1975.

Marshall, I. Howard. *The Gospel of Luke.* Grand Rapids, Mich.: Eerdmans, 1978.

Martin, Dale B. *The Corinthian Body.* New Haven and London: Yale University Press, 1995.

Martin, Joan M. "A Sacred Hope and Social Goal: Womanist Eschatology." In *Liberating Eschatology: Essays in Honor of Letty M. Russell,* ed. Margaret A. Farley and Serene Jones. Louisville, Ky.: Westminster John Knox, 1999.

McArthur, Harvey K., and Robert M. Johnston. *They Also Taught in Parables: Rabbinic Parables from the First Centuries of the Christian Era.* Grand Rapids, Mich.: Zondervan, 1990.

McDonald, J. Ian H. "Alien Grace (Lk 10:30-36): The Parable of the Good Samaritan." In *Jesus and His Parables: Interpreting the Parables of Jesus Today,* ed. V. George Shillington. Edinburgh: T & T Clark, 1997.

Mell, Ulrich. *Die Zeit der Gottesherrschaft: Zur Allegorie und zum Gleichnis von Markus 4,1-9.* Stuttgart: Kohlhammer, 1998.

Metternich, Ulrike. *"Sie sagte ihm die ganze Wahrheit": Die Erzählung von der "Blutflüssigen"—feministisch Gedeutet.* Mainz: Matthias Grünewald, 2000.

Metz, Johann Baptist. *Glaube in Geschichte und Gesellschaft: Studien zu einer praktischen Fundamentaltheologie.* 2nd ed. Mainz: Matthias Grünewald, 1978. English: *Faith in History and Society: Toward a Foundational Political Theology,* trans. David Smith. New York: Seabury, 1979.

Michel, Otto, and Otto Bauernfeind, eds. *Flavius Josephus, De Bello Judaico: Der jüdische Krieg.* 3 vols. Munich: Kösel, 1959–69.

Milavec, Aaron A. "A Fresh Analysis of the Parable of the Wicked Husbandmen in the Light of Jewish-Catholic Dialogue." In *Parable and Story in Judaism and Christianity,* ed. Clemens Thoma and Michael Wyschogrod. New York: Paulist, 1989.

Mineshige, Kiyoshi. *Besitzverzicht und Almosen bei Lukas.* Tübingen: Mohr/Siebeck, 2003.

Moloney, Francis J. *The Gospel of Mark: A Commentary.* Peabody, Mass.: Hendrickson, 2002.

Monselewski, Werner. *Der barmherzige Samariter: Eine auslegungsgeschichtliche Untersuchung zu Lukas 10,25-37.* Tübingen: Mohr/Siebeck, 1967.

Moore, George Foot. *Judaism in the First Centuries of the Christian Era.* Vol. 2: *The Age of the Tannaim.* Cambridge, Mass.: Harvard University Press, 1954.

Moore, Stephen D. "Deconstructive Criticism: The Gospel of Mark." In *Mark and Method: New Approaches in Biblical Studies,* ed. Janice Capel Anderson and Stephen D. Moore. Minneapolis: Fortress Press, 1992, 84–102.

Munro, Winsome. *Jesus, Born of a Slave: The Social and Economic Origins of Jesus' Message.* Lewiston, N.Y.: Edwin Mellen, 1998.

Neusner, Jacob. *From Politics to Piety.* Englewood Cliffs, N.J.: Prentice-Hall, 1973.

————. *Judaism and Scripture: The Evidence of Leviticus Rabbah.* Chicago and London: University of Chicago Press, 1986.

————. *Das pharisäische und talmudische Judentum.* Tübingen: Mohr/Siebeck, 1984.

Nolland, John. *Luke 9:21—18:34.* WBC 35B. Dallas: Word, 1993.

Nörr, Dieter. "Die Evangelien des Neuen Testaments und die sogenannte hellenistische Rechtskoine," *Zeitschrift der Savigny-Stiftung für Rechtsgeschichte,* Romanistiche Abteilung 78 (1961): 92–141.

Nützel, J. M. "'Darf ich mit dem Meinen nicht tun, was ich will?' (Mt 20,15a)." In *Salz der Erde—Licht der Welt: Exegetische Studien zum Matthäusevangelium: Festschrift für Anton Vögtle zum 80. Geburtstag,* ed. Lorenz Oberlinner and Peter Fiedler. Stuttgart: Katholisches Bibelwerk, 1991.

Oeming, Manfred. *Biblische Hermeneutik: Eine Einführung.* Darmstadt: Wissenschaftliche Buchgesellschaft, 1998.

Oesterley, W. O. E. *The Gospel Parables in the Light of Their Jewish Background.* London: SPCK, 1936.

Oldenhage, Tania. *Parables for Our Time: Rereading New Testament Scholarship after the Holocaust.* American Academy of Religion, Cultural Criticism Series. Oxford and New York: Oxford University Press, 2002.

Paoli, Ugo Enrico. *Das Leben im alten Rom.* 3rd ed. Bern: Francke, 1979.

Park, Eung Chun. *Either Jew or Gentile: Paul's Unfolding Theology of Inclusivity.* Louisville, Ky.: Westminster John Knox, 2003.

Patterson, Orlando. *Slavery and Social Death: A Comparative Study.* Cambridge, Mass.: Harvard University Press, 1982.

Paulsen, Henning. "Die Witwe und der Richter (Lk 18,1-8)," *Theologie und Glaube* 74 (1984): 91–110.

Pesch, Rudolf. *Naherwartungen: Tradition und Redaktion in Mark 13.* Düsseldorf: Patmos, 1968.

Phillips, Thomas E. *Reading Issues of Wealth and Poverty in Luke-Acts.* Lewiston, N.Y.: Edwin Mellen, 2001.

Plummer, Alfred. *A Critical and Exegetical Commentary on the Gospel according to St Luke.* Edinburgh: T & T Clark, 1896.

Pöhlmann, Wolfgang. "Die Abschichtung des Verlorenen Sohnes (Lk 15:12f.), und die erzählte Welt der Parabel," *ZNW* 70 (1979): 194–213.

————. *Der Verlorene Sohn und das Haus: Studien zu Lukas 15,11-32 im Horizont der antiken Lehre von Haus, Erziehung und Ackerbau.* Tübingen: Mohr/Siebeck, 1993.

Porter, Stanley E. *Handbook to Exegesis of the New Testament.* Leiden: Brill, 1997.

Priest, John. "A Note on the Messianic Banquet." In *The Messiah: Developments in Earliest Judaism and Christianity*, ed. James H. Charlesworth. Minneapolis: Fortress Press, 1992.

Prieur, Alexander. *Die Verkündigung der Gottesherrschaft*. Tübingen: Mohr/Siebeck, 1996.

Rau, Eckhard. *Reden in Vollmacht: Hintergrund, Form und Anliegen der Gleichnisse Jesu*. Göttingen: Vandenhoeck & Ruprecht, 1990.

Reid, Barbara E. "Violent Endings in Matthew's Parables and Christian Nonviolence," *CBQ* 66 (2004): 237–55.

Reimer, Ivoni Richter. *Women in the Acts of the Apostles*. Minneapolis: Fortress Press, 1995.

Richardson, Cyril C., ed. and trans. *Early Christian Fathers*. New York: Macmillan, 1970.

Ricoeur, Paul. "Biblical Hermeneutics," *Semeia* 4 (1975): 27–148.

———. *Figuring the Sacred: Religion, Narrative, and Imagination*, trans. David Pellauer, ed. Mark I. Wallace. Minneapolis: Fortress Press, 1995.

———. "Stellung und Funktion der Metapher in der biblischen Sprache." In *Metapher: Zur Hermeneutik religiöser Sprache*, ed. eadem and Eberhard Jüngel. Sonderheft Evangelische Theologie. Munich: Kaiser, 1974.

Ringe, Sharon H. "Solidarity and Contextuality: Readings of Matthew 18:21-35." In *Reading from this Place*, Vol. 2: *Social Location and Biblical Interpretation in the U.S.*, Fernando Segovia and Mary Ann Tolbert. Minneapolis: Fortress Press, 1995.

Robinson, John A. T. *The Body: A Study in Pauline Theology*. 4th ed. London: SCM, 1957.

Rohrbaugh, Richard L. "A Peasant Reading of the Talents/Pounds: A Text of Terror?" *BTB* 23 (1993): 32–39.

Royle, J. Forbes. "On the Identification of the Mustard Tree of Scripture," *The Journal of the Royal Asiatic Society of Great Britain and Ireland* 8 (1846): 113–37.

Ruether, Rosemary Radford. *Sexism and God Talk: Toward a Feminist Theology*. Boston: Beacon, 1983; 10th anniversity ed. 1993.

Sachs, M. *Gebete der Israeliten*. Rev. ed. Tel Aviv: Sinai, 1988.

Saldarini, Anthony J. *Matthew's Christian-Jewish Community*. Chicago and London: University of Chicago Press, 1994.

———. *Pharisees, Scribes, and Sadducees in Palestinian Society: A Sociological Approach*. Wilmington, Del.: Michael Glazier, 1988.

Sanders, E. P. *Jesus and Judaism*. Philadelphia: Fortress Press; London: SCM, 1985.

———. "Jesus and the Sinners," *JSNT* 19 (1983): 5–36.

———. *Jewish Law from Jesus to the Mishnah: Five Studies*. Philadelphia: Trinity Press International, 1990.

———. *Judaism: Practice and Belief, 638 b.c.e.–66 c.e.* Philadelphia: Trinity Press International, 1992.

Schmidt, Karl L. and Martin A. Schmidt, "*pachynō, ktl.*" In *TDNT* 5:1022–31.

Schnider, Franz, and Werner Stenger. "Die offene Tür und die unüberschreitbare Kluft," *NTS* 25 (1979): 273–83.

Schniewind, Julius. *Das Evangelium nach Markus*. NTD 1. 5th ed. Göttingen: Vandenhoeck & Ruprecht, 1949.

Schottroff, Luise. "Die befreite Eva." In *Schuld und Macht: Studien zu einer feministischen Befreiungstheologie*, ed. Christine Schaumberger and eadem. Munich: Kaiser, 1988.

———. "Die Befreiung vom Götzendienst der Habgier." In *Wer ist unser Gott?*, ed. eadem and Willy Schottroff. Munich: Kaiser, 1986.

———. *Befreiungserfahrungen: Studien zur Sozialgeschichte des Neuen Testaments*. Munich: Kaiser, 1990. Partial publication in English: *Let the Oppressed Go Free: Feminist Perspectives on the New Testament*, trans. Annemarie S. Kidder. Louisville, Ky.: Westminster John Knox, 1993.

———. "DienerInnen der Heiligen: Der Diakonat der Frauen im Neuen Testament." In *Diakonie—biblische Grundlagen und Orientierungen,* ed. Gerhard K. Schäfer and Theodor Strohm. 2nd ed. Heidelberg: Heidelberger Verlagsanstalt, 1994.

———. "Die Erzählung vom Pharisäer und Zöllner als Beispiel für die theologische Kunst des Überredens." In *Neues Testament und christliche Existenz: Festschrift für Herbert Braun,* ed. eadem and Hans-Dieter Betz. Tübingen: Mohr/Siebeck, 1973.

———. "Feministische Hermeneutik des ersten Briefes an die korinthische Gemeinde." In *Hermeneutik—sozialgeschichtlich,* ed. Erhard S. Gerstenberger and Ulrich Schoenborn. Münster: Lit-Verlag, 1999.

———. "Die Gegenwart in der Apokalyptik der synoptischen Evangelien." In eadem *Befreiungserfahrungen: Studien zur Sozialgeschichte des Neuen Testaments.* Munich: Kaiser, 1990.

———. "Das geschundene Volk und die Arbeiter in der Ernte Gottes nach dem Matthäusevangelium." In *Mitarbeiter der Schöpfung: Bibel und Arbeitswelt,* ed. eadem and Willy Schottroff. Munich: Kaiser, 1983.

———. "Gesetzesfreie Heidenchristentum und die Frauen?" In *Von der Wurzel getragen: Christlich-feministische Exegese in Auseinandersetzung mit Antijudaismus,* ed. Luise Schottroff and Marie-Theres Wacker. Leiden: Brill, 1995.

———. "Gewalt von oben und Gottes Zorn: Evangelium nach Markus 12,1-12." In *Wie Freiheit entsteht: Sozialgeschichtliche Bibelauslegungen,* ed. Claudia Janssen and Beate Wehn. Gütersloh: Kaiser, 1999.

———. "Das Gleichnis vom großen Gastmahl in der Logienquelle," *EvT* 47 (1987): 192–211.

———. "Das Gleichnis vom verlorenen Sohn," *ZThK* 68 (1971): 27–52.

———. "Die Güte Gottes und die Solidarität von Menschen: Das Gleichnis von den Arbeitern im Weinberg." In eadem *Befreiungserfahrungen: Studien zur Sozialgeschichte des Neuen Testaments.* Munich: Kaiser, 1990.

———. *Lydias ungeduldige Schwestern: Feministische Sozialgeschichte des frühen Christentums.* Gütersloh: Kaiser, 1994. English: *Lydia's Impatient Sisters: A Feminist Social History of Early Christianity,* trans. Barbara Rumscheidt and Martin Rumscheidt. Louisville, Ky.: Westminster John Knox, 1995.

———. "Die Schreckensherrschaft der Sünde und die Befreiung durch Christus nach dem Römerbrief des Paulus." In eadem *Befreiungserfahrungen: Studien zur Sozialgeschichte des Neuen Testaments.* Munich: Kaiser, 1990.

———. "Schuldschein," *Neues Bibel Lexikon* 3 (2001): 528.

———. "Verheißung und Erfüllung aus der Sicht einer Theologie nach Auschwitz." In *Religion und Biographie: Festgabe für G. Otto,* ed. Albrecht Grözinger and Henning Luther. Munich: Kaiser, 1987.

———. "Vom Mut, Gott nachzuahmen," *BK* 58 (2003): 82–90.

———. "'We Are Seeds, Not Pebbles': The Parable of the Sower Mk 4:3-8 *parr.*" In *Dialogue Toward Inter-faith Understanding, Yearbook 1984–1985.* Tantur: Ecumenical Institute for Theological Research, 1986.

———. "Wir sind Samen und keine Steinchen: Das Gleichnis vom Sämann (Mk 4:3-8 *parr.*)." In *Bibel und Befreiung: Beiträge zu einer nichtidealistischen Bibellektüre,* ed. Georges Casalis et al. Tübingen Theologischen Fachschaftsinitiativen. Fribourg: Edition Exodus, 1985.

Schottroff, Luise, and Wolfgang Stegemann. *Jesus von Nazareth: Hoffnung der Armen.* 2nd ed. Stuttgart: Kohlhammer, 1981.

———. "Der Sabbat ist für den Menschen da." In *Der Gott der kleinen Leute: Sozialgeschichtliche Bibelauslegungen,* ed. Willy Schottroff and Wolfgang Stegemann. Vol. 2. Munich: 1979.

Schottroff, Luise, and Willy Schottroff. *Die Parteilichkeit Gottes: Biblische Orientierungen auf der Suche nach Frieden und Gerechtigkeit.* Munich: Kaiser, 1984.

Schottroff, Luise, and Marie-Theres Wacker, eds. *Kompendium Feministische Bibelauslegung.* Gütersloh: Kaiser, 1998.

Schottroff, Willy. *Gerechtigkeit lernen: Beiträge zur biblischen Sozialgeschichte,* ed. Frank Crüsemann and Rainer Kessler. Gütersloh: Kaiser, 1999.

———. "Das Gleichnis von den bösen Weingärtnern (Mk 12,1-9 parr.): Ein Beitrag zur Geschichte der Bodenpacht in Palästina," *ZDPV* 112 (1996): 18–48.

Schumacher, Leonhard. *Servus index: Sklavenverhör und Sklavenanzeige im republikanischen und kaiserzeitlichen Rom.* Wiesbaden: Steiner, 1982.

Schürer, Emil. *Geschichte des jüdischen Volkes im Zeitalter Jesu Christi.* 3 vols. New York: Olms, 1970. English: *The History of the Jewish People in the Age of Jesus Christ (175 b.c.–a.d. 135),* trans. T. A. Burkill et al., ed. Geza Vermes and Fergus Millar. 3 vols. Edinburgh: T & T Clark, 1973–1987.

Schüssler Fiorenza, Elisabeth. "The Ethics of Interpretation: Decentering Biblical Scholarship," *JBL* 107 (1988): 3–17.

Seebaß, Horst. "Erwählung I, Altes Testament." *TRE* 10 (1982): 182–89.

Seneca, *De ira.* German: Trans. Manfred Rosebach. Darmstadt: Wissenschaftliche Stenger Buchgesellschaft, 1969.

Shelton, Jo-Ann. *As the Romans Did: A Sourcebook in Roman Social History.* 2nd ed. New York and Oxford: Oxford University Press, 1998.

Shillington, V. George. "Saving Life and Keeping Sabbath (Mt 20:1b-15)." In *Jesus and His Parables,* ed. eadem. Edinburgh: T & T Clark, 1997.

Snodgrass, Klyne. *The Parable of the Wicked Tenants: An Inquiry into Parable Interpretation.* Tübingen: Mohr/Siebeck, 1983.

Soelle, Dorothee. *Mystik und Widerstand.* Hamburg: Hoffmann und Campe, 1998. English: *The Silent Cry: Mysticism and Resistance,* trans. Barbara Rumscheidt and Martin Rumscheidt. Minneapolis: Fortress Press, 2001.

Sonnen, Johannes. "Landwirtschaftliches vom See Genezareth," *Biblica* 8 (1927): 65–87, 188–208, 320–37.

Spranger, Peter P. *Historische Untersuchungen zu den Sklavenfiguren des Plautus und Terenz.* Akademie der Wissenschaften und der Literatur. Abhandlungen der Geistes- und Sozialwissenschaftlichen Klasse, Jahrg. 1960, Nr. 8. Mainz: Akademie der Wissenschaften und der Literatur, 1961.

Stählin, Gustav. "*chēra.*" In *TDNT* 9:440–65.

Stendahl, Krister. *Paul among Jews and Gentiles, and Other Essays.* Philadelphia: Fortress Press, 1976.

Stern, David. "Imitatio Hominis: Anthropomorphism and the Character(s) of God in Rabbinic Literature," *Prooftexts: A Journal of Jewish Literary History* 12 (1992): 151–74.

———. "Jesus' Parables from the Perspective of Rabbinic Literature: The Example of the Wicked Husbandmen." In *Parable and Story in Judaism and Christianity,* ed. Clemens Thoma and Michael Wyschogrod. New York: Paulist, 1989.

———. *Parables in Midrash: Narrative and Exegesis in Rabbinic Literature.* Cambridge, Mass.: Harvard University Press, 1991.

———. "Rhetoric and Midrash: The Case of the *Mashal,*" *Prooftexts: A Journal of Jewish Literary History* 1 (1981): 261–91.

Strack, Hermann L., and Paul Billerbeck. *Kommentar zum Neuen Testament aus Talmud und Midrasch.* 6 vols. Munich: Beck, 1965–69.

Strange, James F. "First Century Galilee from Archaeology and from the Texts." In *Archaeology and the Galilee: Texts and Contexts in the Graeco-Roman and Byzantine Periods,* ed. Douglas R. Edwards and C. Thomas McCollough. Atlanta: Scholars, 1997.

Stuhlmann, Rainer. "Beobachtungen und Überlegungen zu Markus 4:26-29," *NTS* 19 (1972–73): 153–62.

Sugranyes de Franch, Ramon. *Études sur le droit Palestinien à l'époque Evangélique: La contrainte par corps.* Fribourg: Librairie de l'Université, 1946.

Sutter Rehmann, Luzia. *"Geh, frage de Gebärerin . . .": Feministisch-befreiungstheologische Untersuchungen zum Gebärmotiv in der Apokalyptik.* Gütersloh: Kaiser, 1995.

Tamez, Elsa. *The Amnesty of Grace: Justification by Faith from a Latin American Perspective,* trans. Sharon H. Ringe. Nashville: Abingdon, 1993.

Tertullian. *Adversus Marcionem,* ed. and trans. Ernest Evans. Oxford: Oxford University Press, 1972.

Theissen, Gerd. "Der Bauer und die von selbst Frucht bringende Erde: Naïver Synergismus in Mk 4,26-29?" *ZNW* 85 (1994): 167–82.

Theissen, Gerd, and Annette Merz. *Der historische Jesus: Ein Lehrbuch.* 2nd ed. Göttingen: Vandenhoeck & Ruprecht, 1997. English: *The Historical Jesus: A Comprehensive Guide,* trans. John Bowden. Minneapolis: Fortress Press; London: SCM, 1998.

Thierfelder, Helmut. *Unbekannte antike Welt: Eine Darstellung nach Papyrusurkunden.* Gütersloh: Mohn, 1963.

Thoma, Clemens, and Hans-Peter Ernst. *Die Gleichnisse der Rabbinen.* Vol. 3: *Von Isaak bis zum Schilfmeer: BerR 63–100; ShemR 1-22.* New York: Peter Lang, 1996. Vol. 4: *Vom Leid des Mose bis zum Bundesbuch: ShemR 23-30.* New York: Peter Lang, 2000.

Thoma, Clemens, and Simon Lauer. *Die Gleichnisse der Rabbinen.* Vol. 1: *Pesiqta de Rav Kahana.* New York: Peter Lang, 1986. Vol. 2: *Von der Erschaffung der Welt bis zum Tod Abrahams: Bereschit Rabba 1-63.* New York: Peter Lang, 1991.

Tilborg, Sjef van. "An Interpretation [of Lk 12,35-48] from the Ideology of the Text," *Neot* 22 no. 2 (1988): 205–15.

Tolbert, Mary Ann. *Perspectives on the Parables: An Approach to Multiple Interpretations.* Philadelphia: Fortress Press, 1979.

———. *Sowing the Gospel: Mark's World in Literary-Historical Perspective.* Minneapolis: Fortress Press, 1979.

———. "When Resistance Becomes Repression: Mark 13:9-27 and the Poetics of Location." In *Reading from this Place.* Vol. 2: *Social Location and Biblical Interpretation in Global Perspective,* ed. Fernando Segovia and Mary Ann Tolbert. Minneapolis: Fortress Press, 1995.

Townes, Emily M. *In a Blaze of Glory: Womanist Spirituality as Social Witness.* Nashville: Abingdon, 1995.

Ukpong, Justin S. "The Parable of the Shrewd Manager," *Semeia* 73 (1996): 189–210.

Vahrenhorst, Martin. "Gift oder Arznei? Perspektiven für das neutestamentliche Verständnis von Jes 6,9f. im Rahmen der jüdischen Rezeptionsgeschichte," *ZNW* 92 (2002): 145–67.

———. *"Ihr sollt überhaupt nicht schwören": Matthäus im halachischen Diskurs.* Neukirchen: Neukirchener Verlag, 2002.

Ven, Frans van der. *Sozialgeschichte der Arbeit.* Vol. 1. Munich: Deutsche Taschenbuch-Verlag, 1971.

Via, Dan O. *The Parables: Their Literary and Existential Dimension.* Philadelphia: Fortress Press, 1967.

Wartenberg-Potter, Bärbel. "Über die Frage, ob der Verlorene Sohn eine Halbwaise war." In *Für Gerechtigkeit streiten,* ed. Dorothee Sölle. Gütersloh: Kaiser, 1994.

Weder, Hans. *Die Gleichnisse Jesu als Metaphern: Traditions- und redaktionsgeschichtliche Analysen.* FRLANT 120. Göttingen: Vandenhoeck & Ruprecht, 1978.

Wegner, Judith Romney. *Chattel or Person? The Status of Women in the Mishnah.* New York and Oxford: Oxford University Press, 1988.

Weinrich, Harald. *Sprache in Texten.* Stuttgart: Klett, 1976.

Wendebourg, Nicola. *Der Tag des Herrn: Zur Gerichtserwartung im Neuen Testament auf ihrem alttestamentlichen und frühjüdischen Hintergrund.* Neukirchen: Neukirchener Verlag, 2003.

Wengst, Klaus. *Demut: Solidarität der Gedemütigten.* Munich: Kaiser, 1987. English: *Humility: Solidarity of the Humiliated: The Transformation of an Attitude and Its Social Relevance in Graeco-Roman, Old Testament-Jewish, and Early Christian Tradition,* trans. John Bowden. Philadelphia: Fortress Press, 1988.

———. *Das Johannesevangelium.* 2 vols. Stuttgart: Kohlhammer, 2001.

Whiston, William, trans. *The Works of Josephus, Compete and Unabridged.* Peabody, Mass.: Hendrickson, 1987.

White, K. D. "The Parable of the Sower," *JTS* 15 (1964): 300–7.

Wikenhauser, Alfred. "Die Liebeswerke in dem Gerichtsgemälde Mt 25,31-46," *BZ* 20 (1932): 366–77.

Wilckens, Ulrich. "*stolē*" In *TDNT* 7:687–91.

Wilken, Karl-Erich. *Biblisches Erleben im Heiligen Land.* Vol. 1. Lahr-Dinglingen: St. Johannis-Druckerei C. Schweickhardt, 1953.

Willett, John, and Ralph Manheim, eds. "The Foolish Wife." In *Bertolt Brecht: Short Stories 1921–1946.* London and New York: Methuen, 1983, 19–21.

Wright, Benjamin G., III. "*Ebd/doulos*: Terms and Social Status in the Meeting of Hebrew Biblical and Hellenistic Roman Culture." In *Slavery in Text and Interpretation,* ed. Allen Dwight Callahan, Richard A. Horsley, and Abraham Smith. Semeia 83/84. (Atlanta: Society of Biblical Literature, 1998), 83–112.

Wright, Stephen J. *Studies in the Interpretation of Six Gospel Parables.* Carlisle, U.K.: Paternoster, 2000.

Wünsche, August. *Bibliotheca Rabbinica. 13. und 14. Lieferung: Der Midrash Echa Rabbati.* Hildesheim: Olms, 1967.

———. *Bibliotheca Rabbinica: Eine Sammlung alter Midraschim Bd. 1–5.* Hildesheim: Olms, 1967.

———. *Midrasch Tehillim, oder, Haggadische Erklärung der Psalmen, nach der Textausgabe von Salomon Buber zum ersten Male ins Deutsche übersetzt.* 2 vols. Hildesheim: Olms, 1967.

Yee, Gale, ed. *Judges and Method: New Approaches in Biblical Studies.* Minneapolis: Fortress Press, 1995.

Yonge, C. D., trans. *The Works of Philo.* Peabody, Mass.: Hendrickson, 1993.

Young, Brad H. *The Parables: Jewish Tradition and Christian Interpretation.* Peabody, Mass.: Hendrickson, 1998.

Ziegler, Ignaz. *Die Königsgleichnisse des Midrasch beleuchtet durch die römische Kaiserzeit.* Breslau: Schottländer, 1903.

Ziesler, J. A. "Luke and the Pharisees," *NTS* 25 (1979): 146–57.

Zohary, Michael, and Naomi Feinbrunn-Dothan. *Flora Palaestina.* Vol. 1. Jerusalem: Israel Academy of Sciences and Humanities, 1966.

List of Parables Discussed

Index of Ancient Sources

Index of Subjects and Names

Dalman, Gustaf, 72
De la Torre, Miguel A., 1, 94
Debout, Jacques, 239n9
Deissmann, Adolf, 141
Derrett, J. Duncan M., 245n67
"The Dishonoured Master"
  (Kloppenborg), 162
Dodd, C. H., 63, 92–93
Donahue, John, 75, 76, 77
Doorkeeper, parable of (Mark 13:28-37),
  124–28, 130
Dualism in parable theories, 90–98
"Die dumme Frau" ("The Foolish Wife")
  (Brecht), 150–51

Ebach, Jürgen, 83, 238n2
Ecclesiological interpretative tradition:
  defining, 11; and presupposition of
  Christian superiority, 81–82
Eleazar ben Pedat, Rabbi, 64
Eschatological interpretations,
  explanation of, 11–12
Esler, Philip Francis, 229n4

Fig tree, parable of (Mark 13:28-37),
  124–28, 130
Fiorenza, Elisabeth Schüssler, 94
Flusser, David, 59, 94–95, 100–101
Freire, Paulo, 20
"A Fresh Analysis of the Parable of the
  Wicked Husbandmen in the Light of
  Jewish-Catholic Dialogue" (Milavec),
  25

Gebara, Ivone, 120–21
Genre of parable discourse, 108–9
Gerhardsson, Birger, 68, 71, 75–76, 77
Glancy, Jennifer A., 174–75
God's forgiveness and the world of
  finance (Matthew 18:23-35), 196–202;
  eschatological interpretation, 200–
  203; social-historical analysis, 197–99;

translation, 196–97
Goodman, Martin, 166–67
Gospel for the Poor, 86–89
Gospel of Thomas, 107, 226n8
Gottwald, Norman K., 88
Grain: *see* Hoarding grain
Great feast/king's banquet (politics with
  carrot and stick) (Matthew 22:1-
  14), 38–48, 52, 53; ecclesiological
  interpretation of John Chrysostom,
  45–46; eschatological interpretation,
  46–48; social-historical analysis,
  39–45; translation, 38
Great feast/king's banquet (the snubbed
  host) (Luke 14:12-24), 49–56;
  ecclesiological interpretation, 53–55;
  eschatological interpretation, 55–56;
  and radical social politics, 50–53;
  social-historical analysis, 50–53;
  translation, 49
Great Messianic feast of rejoicing, or, the
  partying neighbor women (Luke 15),
  138–56. See also Lost drachma (Luke
  15:8-10); Lost Sheep (Luke 15:3-7);
  Lost son (the father and two difficult
  sons) (Luke 15:11-32)
Green, Joel B., 235n1
Grotius, Hugo, 59

Harnisch, Wolfgang, 92
Harrington, Daniel, 75, 76, 77
Hearing and doing the Torah (the
  "parable theory") (Mark 4:1-20),
  66–78, 129–30; the disciples' hearing
  and understanding, 69; ecclesiological
  interpretation, 74–77; eschatological
  interpretation, 77–78; failed hearing,
  69–72; the parable imagery of sowing
  and yield, 72–73; social-historical
  analysis, 67–74; successful hearing of
  the Word, 68–69; translation, 66–67
Hermeneutical assumptions, 81–89. *See*